D1260099

SLAVOPHILES AND COMMISSARS

Slavophiles and Commissars

Enemies of Democracy in Modern Russia

Judith Devlin
Lecturer in Modern History
University College, Dublin

 First published in Great Britain 1999 by
MACMILLAN PRESS LTD
Houndmills, Basingstoke, Hampshire RG21 6XS and London
Companies and representatives throughout the world

A catalogue record for this book is available from the British Library.

ISBN 0–333–69933–5

 First published in the United States of America 1999 by
ST. MARTIN'S PRESS, INC.,
Scholarly and Reference Division,
175 Fifth Avenue, New York, N.Y. 10010

ISBN 0–312–22200–9

Library of Congress Cataloging-in-Publication Data
Devlin, Judith, 1952–
Slavophiles and commissars : enemies of democracy in modern Russia
/ Judith Devlin.
p.   cm.
Includes bibliographical references and index.
ISBN 0–312–22200–9 (cloth)
1. Russia (Federation)—Politics and government—1991–
2. Nationalism—Russia (Federation)   3. Authoritarianism—Russia
(Federation)   4. Russia (Federation)—Intellectual life—1991–
I. Title.
DK510.763.D486   1999
320.947'09'049—dc21   98–50836
                                                        CIP

This book is printed on paper suitable for recycling and made from fully managed and sustained forest sources.

10   9   8   7   6   5   4   3   2   1
08   07   06   05   04   03   02   01   00   99

Printed and bound in Great Britain by
Antony Rowe Ltd, Chippenham, Wiltshire

To my mother

Contents

Acknowledgements

This work owes much to the assistance received from many quarters. My colleagues in University College Dublin, especially Tadhg O hAnnracháin, Eamon O'Flaherty, Hugh Gough and Peter Butterfield, enabled me to observe the Presidential elections in Irkutsk at first hand, for which heartfelt thanks. I am grateful also to the University for helping to fund my research.

The staff of several libraries in Moscow, London and Dublin gave me much invaluable assistance. In particular, I would like to thank Ms Mairin Cassidy and her colleagues in the library of University College Dublin; the librarians of the State Public Historical Library in Moscow, the Russian State Library and the INION Library; the staff of the library of the School of Slavonic Studies in London; the librarian and staff of Trinity College Dublin.

I am grateful to many Russian friends and experts who kindly and generously gave their time to discussing Russian politics with me and offering advice and guidance. I would particularly like to thank Andrei Mironov and Tanya Vargashkina in Moscow. Successive members of the Irish Embassy in Moscow have given me invaluable practical aid and generous hospitality: my thanks are particularly due to Brian Earls, Tom and Kiki Russell. Many friends in Dublin also assisted my researches, especially Deirdre MacMahon, Michael Sanfey, Anna Murphy, Carla King, John Murray, Aidan Kirwan and Valeria Heuberger in Vienna. Thanks are also due to those who read earlier drafts of this book, especially Professor Stephen White. I am grateful also to Professor R.J. Hill for encouragement and assistance. Finally, the work would not have been written without the assistance of my mother, who dealt with all practical matters while it was on the go.

List of Abbreviations and Conventions

Publications

AiF	*Argumenty i fakty*
IHT	*International Herald Tribune*
Lit. Gaz.	*Literaturnaya gazeta*
MN	*Moscow News*
NG	*Nezavisimaya gazeta*
NYRB	*New York Review of Books*
RG	*Rossiiskaya gazeta*
RM	*Russkaya mysl'*
SK	*Sovetskaya kul'tura*
SR	*Sovetskaya Rossiya*

Conventions

"	= hard sign
'	= soft sign, except where followed by **e**, where it is rendered by **ie**
ky	= style adopted to transliterate surnames such as Pribylovsky Soft Russian **i** is rendered only after **ki** as in sovetskii
ks	= x

Glossary of Parties and Groups

Agrarian Party: Party of former CPSU members and kolkhoz directors founded in February 1993 to protect the interests of the agro-industry nomenklatura. Usually aligned with the KPRF but on occasion ready to collaborate with Yeltsin (to whose camp several of its leaders defected).

All-Union Communist Party of Bolsheviks: Party of unrepentant neo-Stalinists founded in November 1991 and led by Nina Andreeva. Its opposition to the new regime was so extreme as to render it politically irrelevant.

All-World Russian Assembly: Congress of nationalist and Orthodox forces organised by General Alexander Sterligov in May 1993.

Black Hundreds: officially encouraged, pre-revolutionary popular bands of violent, anti-revolutionary, ultra-nationalist anti-Semites.

Brotherhood of St Sergius of Radonezh: A vocal caucus, of extreme nationalist and conservative orientation, within the Orthodox Church. Member of the similarly inspired Union of Orthodox Brotherhoods, founded in 1990.

Christian Democratic Movement of Russia (RKhDD): Founded in April 1990, the political wing of this religiously inspired, fractious organisation moved, under the leadership of Viktor Aksyuchits, to more extreme nationalist positions after 1991, ultimately embracing monarchism. Disappeared from view after 1993.

Christian Democratic Union of Russia (CDU): Liberal Christian group founded in August 1989 by former dissident, Alexander Ogorodnikov.

Civic Union: Caucus, founded in 1993, uniting parties of the centre right and providing a platform for figures like Alexander Rutskoi and Alexander Volsky.

Committee for the Restoration of Christ the Saviour: Nationalist, religious conservation group, broadly opposed to Gorbachev's reforms. Their cause was ultimately adopted by Yuri Luzhkov, mayor of Moscow, who was largely responsible for the rebuilding of the cathedral in the mid-1990s.

Committee for the Saving of the Neva–Ladoga–Onega: Nationalist, anti-reform conservation group, founded in April 1989.

Communist Party of the Russian Federation: Founded in June 1990, as the KP RSFSR, in an attempt by conservatives to prise control of the Communist Party away from Gorbachev, was banned by Yeltsin after the August 1991 coup. Reformed as the KPRF in February 1993 under the leadership of Gennady Zyuganov, following a judgement largely in its favour by the Constitutional Court. A coalition of nationalists, neo-Stalinists and conservatives, the party jettisoned its Marxist heritage in favour of a nationalist socialist programme and winning power at the polls.

Communist Party of the Soviet Union (CPSU): The ruling party between 1917 and 1991. Led by Gorbachev between 1985 and 1991, when it was dissolved by Boris Yeltsin.

Communists for the USSR: Viktor Anpilov's neo-Stalinist election bloc in 1995.

Congress of Civic and Patriotic Forces: Nationalist meeting organised in February 1992 by V. Aksyuchits and others in the hope of founding a nationalist opposition caucus to Yeltsin.

Congress of Russian Communities (KRO): Nationalist organisation, courting the Russian diaspora, founded in 1993–94. Briefly attracted attention in 1995, when it provided a political base for the conservative apparatchiks Yuri Skokov and Alexander Lebed.

Constitutional Democratic Party of Popular Freedom Democratic Russia (Kadets): A party in name only, synonymous with its leader, Mikhail Astafiev. It was initially a liberal democratic group when founded in May 1990, then joined the opposition to Yeltsin in 1992 and associated with conservative nationalist positions.

Democratic Russia: Umbrella organisation for democratic groups and proto-parties founded in October 1990.

Derzhava: Short-lived movement founded to provide a political base for Alexander Rutskoi on his release from prison in February 1994. Proclaimed religious, authoritarian nationalism.

Experimental Creative Centre: Officially funded group of self-styled thinkers and researchers which, in 1990 and 1991 under the leadership of Sergei Kurginyan, attempted to provide ideological underpinning for the restoration of an authoritarian collectivist regime, under ostensibly nationalist credentials.

Fellowship of Russian Artists: Group of nationalist writers and intellectuals, founded in 1988, committed to the conservation of the Soviet system.

Interfronts: Officially encouraged organisations uniting Russians in the Union republics at the end of the 1980s and early 1990s, opposed to republican nationalism and supporting the maintenance of the Soviet Union.

Kadets – see Constitutional Democratic Party of Popular Freedom.

KPRF – see Communist Party.

Labouring Moscow: A neo-Stalinist caucus, founded in November 1991 by Viktor Anpilov and others to oppose every aspect of the reform. Its mainly elderly supporters were active in demonstrations throughout 1992 and 1993, after which it was banned.

Labouring Russia: An attempt to replicate Labouring Moscow at national level. Founded in October 1992.

Liberal Democratic Party of Russia (LDPR): Shadowy party led by Vladimir Zhirinovsky since 1990 and committed by him to ultra-nationalist, imperialist positions. A leading party in the fifth and sixth Dumas.

Memorial: Anti-Stalinist, democratic forum founded in 1988. Initially substantial popular interest declined after 1991. Continues to function as human rights organisation.

Moscow Tribune: Forum for leading Moscow academics and cultural figures in favour of democracy, founded in 1989.

Nashi: Paper organisation invented in November 1991 by neo-fascist journalist Alexander Nevzorov and pro-Soviet Viktor Alksnis, intended as a semi-military arm of authoritarian imperialists.

National Bolshevik Party: Founded in 1993 and led by the neo-fascist writer Eduard Limonov and largely the product of his imagination.

National Republican Party of Russia: Racist, authoritarian nationalist party led by neo-fascist Nikolai Lysenko and founded in 1990.

National Salvation Front: Founded in October 1992 as major opposition forum to Yeltsin and his reforms. Embraced most nationalist leaders and groups. Banned in October 1993.

OFT – see United Workers' Front.

Officers' Union: Nationalist, anti-reform group in the army, founded by Stanislav Terekhov in 1991.

Officers for the Revival of the Fatherland: Nationalist, anti-reform caucus in the army, founded by General Alexander Sterligov in December 1991.

Orthodox All-Russian Monarchical Order-Union (PRAMOS): Miniscule monarchist party founded in 1990. Slightly less extreme than its rivals.

Otechestvo: Nationalist socialist cultural lobby founded in 1989, favouring retention of the Soviet system.

Our Home is Russia (NDR): Official election machine (rather than popular party) of Prime Minister Viktor Chernomyrdin in 1995.

Pamyat': Neo-fascist, anti-Semitic group led by Dmitri Vasiliev from 1985, which spawned many similarly named and inspired, extreme nationalist groups. Active in the late 1980s, it was succeeded by neo-fascist parties, such as Barkashov's Russian National Unity and Vasiliev's less visible Russian Party of National Unity.

Patriotic Bloc: Coalition of communist and nationalist candidates in the 1990 elections.

Popular Patriotic Bloc: Coalition of communists and nationalists in whose name Gennady Zyuganov ran as a candidate for the Russian Presidency in 1996.

Power to the People: Coalition of communists, under former Prime Minister Nikolai Ryzhkov, and nationalists, under Sergei Baburin, in the 1995 elections.

PRES (Party of Russian Unity and Agreement): Moderate, pro-reform election machine and proto-party of Sergei Shakhrai and other former Yeltsin collaborators, founded in October 1993.

Public Committee for Saving the Volga: Nationalist conservation group founded in January 1989, committed against its will by its leader, the writer Vassily Belov, to anti-reform positions in 1990.

RKhDD – see Christian Democratic Movement of Russia.

ROS – see Russian All-People's Union.

Rossiya: Nationalist-Communist deputies' election club and faction in Russian parliament, founded in 1990.

Russia's Choice (then, Russia's Democratic Choice): 1993 election bloc and then pro-reform party of Prime Minister Yegor Gaidar, founded in Autumn 1993 and June 1994.

Russian All-Peoples' Movement: Cossack, Greater Russian election bloc in 1995 elections.

Russian All-Peoples' Union (ROS): Pro-Soviet, later Greater Russian nationalist caucus founded in late 1991 and led by Sergei Baburin. Most supporters were former communists, including many Russian parliamentary deputies.

Russian Communist Workers' Party: Viktor Anpilov's ultra-Stalinist party, founded in November 1991.

Russian Cultural Centre: Cultural caucus founded in 1988 by those apparently intended to present the acceptable face of *Pamyat'* and who hoped to undercut Vasiliev.

Russian National Assembly: Still-born nationalist grouping founded by Aksyuchits and Astafiev in February 1992 to oppose Yeltsin.

Russian National Council (RNS): Ultra-nationalist, racist caucus founded by General Alexander Sterligov in February 1992 to oppose the reforms. Much in view in 1992 and 1993, thanks to the prominence of its leader (although probably enjoying insignificant membership), it was banned after October 1993.

Russian National Unity (*Yedinstvo*): Neo-fascist party led by Alexander Barkashov and founded in 1990. Prominent in the disturbances in October 1993 and banned thereafter (although in practice it continued to exist).

Russian Party: Racist, ultra-nationalist proto-party, founded in 1990 and led initially by Viktor Korchagin and after March 1993 by Viktor Miloserdov. Collective member of Sterligov's Russian National Council.

Russian Party of Communists: A successor to the CPSU founded in December 1991 by Anatoly Kryuchkov.

Russian Unity: Anti-Yeltsin grouping of communist and nationalist deputies in the Russian parliament in 1992–93, formally aligned with the National Salvation Front.

Slavic Assembly: Umbrella group of miniscule, ultra-nationalist, racist parties, active in the early 1990s.

Sobriety (Union for the Struggle for Popular Sobriety): Extreme nationalist offshoot of officious anti-alcoholism organisation, founded in December 1988.

Socialist Workers' Party: A successor party to the CPSU founded in October 1991. Led by, *inter alia*, Roy Medvedev, it envisaged a 'return to Leninist norms'. Overtaken by KPRF.

Society for the Preservation of Historical Monuments: Founded in 1965, largely officious and ineffectual all-Union organisation.

Soyuz: Pro-Soviet lobby founded in February 1990 and led by Colonel Viktor Alksnis.

Union for the Spiritual Renewal of the Fatherland: Cultural political organisation, supporting a revamped Soviet System infused by Orthodoxy and founded in March 1989.

Union of Artists: Official, Party-controlled body, offering emoluments and privileges to conformists and obstructing the work of non-conformists.

Union of Christian Regeneration: Authoritarian nationalist and monarchist proto-party founded by Viktor Osipov in 1988.

Union of Communists: Moderately conservative successor party to the CPSU founded by A. Prigarin in 1991. Briefly active before the revival of the KPRF. Soon overshadowed by larger communist parties.

Union of Cossack Forces of Russia: Monarchist Cossack organisation, enjoying considerable support, founded in July 1991.

Union of Orthodox Brotherhoods: Founded in 1990, it rapidly adopted ultra-nationalist, fundamentalist positions, militating against reform in the Church.

Union of Patriots: General Alexander Sterligov's ultra-nationalist election bloc in 1995. Not a popular organisation.

Union of the Russian People: Pre-revolutionary, authoritarian nationalist and racist party. An attempt was made to revive it in August 1991.

Union of Writers: Founded by Stalin in 1932 to control Soviet writers.

United Council of Russia: Founded in September 1989 by the OFT, *Otechestvo*, the Fellowship of Russian Artists and similar groups to unite the nationalist and communist opposition to reform. Led by Eduard Volodin, it was one of several such, largely unsuccessful fora.

United Opposition: Nationalist and communist lobby founded in 1992 to oppose Yeltsin. The forerunner of the National Salvation Front.

United Workers' Front (OFT): Populist, neo-Stalinist caucus founded by Party conservatives in 1989 to mobilise the anti-reform vote among the workers. Failure to achieve this led to its evaporation in 1990.

Yabloko: moderate, liberal, democratic 1993 election bloc and then party, led by Grigory Yavlinsky.

Yedinenie (**Unity**): Largely moribund caucus of conservative nationalist cultural figures founded in 1989.

Introduction

One of the most striking features of modern Russian political life is the spread of nationalist ideology. Supposedly eradicated in the Soviet Union by Marxism, it re-emerged with virulent force under Gorbachev, in reaction to his liberal policies. Most dramatically, it took the form of the xenophobic, if marginal, street politics embodied by Dmitri Vasiliev's *Pamyat'* but, in what Julien Benda famously called, in 1927, *la trahison des clercs*, it was also expressed by well-known intellectuals opposed to liberalisation, which they saw as the latest betrayal of national tradition.[1] Many leading writers and intellectuals, such as Valentin Rasputin and Igor Shafarevich, lent their moral authority to criticisms of the reforms, questioning the value of such civic rights as freedom of speech and representative goverment, while apparently endorsing anti-Semitism and theocratic authoritarianism. The dissemination of nationalist, collectivist and authoritarian ideas, and the weight which attaches to them by virtue of their spokesmen's status, seem to compromise Russia's future as a peaceful and stable society, in which the individual's freedoms and rights are assured.

This threat is magnified by the context – of growing crime, widespread corruption and poverty, economic dislocation, imperial withdrawal and state paralysis – in which these ideas have been elaborated. The growth of nationalism in Russia coincided with a profound social, political and economic crisis. The power of the State and its capacity to protect its citizens' well-being disintegrated between 1986 and 1996. With the collapse of the Soviet Union, 25 million Russians found themselves stranded abroad, in new states where their well-being and security were frequently threatened. Within Russia, industrial production collapsed, living standards fell, with rising crime, declining birth-rates and life-expectancy all pointing to an acute social crisis. By the end of 1993, 35 per cent of the population was estimated to be living below the poverty line. The mortality rate rose: the average life expectancy of Soviet men fell from 65 in 1986 to 57.3 in 1994; in 1992, for the first time since the Second World War, the death-rate was higher than the birth-rate. An inadequately funded health service was unable to prevent epidemics of the diseases of poverty, tuberculosis, typhoid and diphtheria.[2] This inevitably generated disaffection with government policy and provided the opposition with a potentially receptive constituency. Indeed, analysis of successive election results indicated that nationalists and nationalist socialists attracted most of their support from those on whom the reforms inflicted most suffering – the old, the poorly educated, unskilled workers in the provinces and countryside and employees in vulnerable sectors of industry. It was not a propitious environment for the development of a vigorous democracy.

But the economic and social crisis does not account for the often authoritarian, collectivist and xenophobic orientation of Russian nationalism. While liberal nationalism had its exponents, they were neither numerous nor influential. Most nationalists were conservative or radical opponents of reform and liberalisation. The political complexion of modern Russian nationalism was determined not only by the contemporary context but also by its historical legacy, which furnished anti-reform politicians with an alternative ideology to replace Soviet socialism and, they hoped, win public support for their positions. Far from representing an original attempt to respond to Russia's contemporary crisis, modern Russian nationalism often involved little more than the resurrection of ideas first enunciated a century and a half ago. Its vision was backward- rather than forward-looking, a form of nostalgia and fantasy rather than a realistic political programme.

Historically, Russian nationalism has its roots in Romantic political and social theory and in the mid-nineteenth century debate about reform and modernisation, known as the Slavophile controversy. The Slavophile controversy divided the intelligentsia into two camps: those who believed the answer to the problem of reform and modernisation to lie in emulation of the West and the adoption of its legal, political and economic norms, and the nationalists, who rejected the West in favour of autocratic, collectivist tradition.[3] This division of opinion among the intelligentsia and the political class has remained a constant in Russian history ever since and has re-emerged whenever the question of modernisation has been on the agenda.[4] With the Pan-Slav thinkers of the mid-nineteenth century, Russian nationalism came to be associated with authoritarianism and expansionism and its anti-Western bias was accentuated – especially after the 1905 revolution, when court circles saw Great Russian (or expansionist, State-centred) nationalism as a bulwark against democracy, reform and foreign influence.[5] The fundamental lineaments of Russian national-ism (its authoritarianism, imperial pretensions, anti-Western bias and anti-Semitism) were thus drawn in the later nineteenth and early twentieth centuries.

Russian nationalism was subsequently incorporated, with appro-priate adaptations, into the ideology of high Stalinism[6] and re-emerged, transformed, at the end of the 1960s both in the establishment and among the intelligentsia.[7] One school of thought saw Soviet socialism as distilling the collectivist, patriotic, authoritar-ian traditions of the Russian state and nation.[8] Another form of Russian nationalism emerged during the Thaw: associated with the so-called village writers, this tendency implicitly criticised Soviet com-munism's social engineering and its disastrous effects on Russia's farmers, countryside and environment, on traditional morality and culture. These writers argued, by implication, for the need for national and moral renewal – looking, in some cases, to Orthodoxy for inspira-tion. Solzhenitsyn had a close affinity with these writers, some of whom fell foul of the authorities, although many more retained their positions and privileges in the establishment.

Nationalism, in the last years of the Soviet regime, was thus a hybrid, embracing both communists and their critics, who, whatever their differences in relation to the Soviet system, were broadly at one in their preference for collectivism and in the importance they attached to a strong Russian state, capable of holding the empire together and playing a major role in international affairs. Russian nationalism's re-emergence, during *glasnost'*, was thus not fortuitous, but its subsequent resilience and the strength of its challenge to democracy were far from inevitable.

The first part of this book charts the intellectuals' contribution to the development of authoritarian nationalism and examines the main trends of nationalist thought, on which politicians of the 'irre-concilable opposition' were able to draw in the post-Soviet period. Authoritarian nationalism was exhumed by writers and intellectuals, who attempted to popularise their ideas and clothe them with an aura of intellectual respectability and relevance. The intellectuals thus played an important role in forging a new, or apparently new, political rhetoric, whose interest lay, initially, not in the support it garnered (for this was as yet minimal) but in its character and the fact that it was developed not by marginal groups but by well-educated and well-connected members of the cultural elite. Many essentially disreputable ideas – including apologia for anti-Semitism and author-itarianism – were popularised and found an echo in the street politics of neo-fascist groups. With the eclipse of communism and the Soviet system and the rehabilitation of the Orthodox church, religiously inspired nationalism, sometimes embracing xenophobia and author-itarianism, began to be articulated, although it stimulated little public interest. The 'Greater Russian Idea' (which suggested that the Russians' historical mission necessitated their absorption of smaller neighbouring peoples and their organisation in a powerful, autocratic State) while initially eschewed by most Russians, if enthusiastically propounded by a minority of intellectuals, became one of the *leitmotivs* of post-Soviet politics.

If intellectuals played a key role in elaborating these ideas, their public significance owed more to the interest they elicited among the new generation of politicians in the post-Soviet period. The second part of the book examines the political impact of authoritarian nationalism, from early futile attempts to organise a mass movement inspired by it, to the August 1991 coup, the development of the oppo-sition to Yeltsin and the rise, after 1993, of Vladimir Zhirinovsky and of Gennady Zyuganov's communists. It ends with the failure of the opposition to capture the Presidency in 1996. This study attempts to elucidate why nationalism, contrary to the expectations of some ana-lysts, assumed an authoritarian rather than liberal reformist charac-ter.[9] It examines whether nationalism is central to an understanding of the public mood and the interplay of contemporary Russian politics or whether it is a temporary and marginal phenomenon, owing more to circumstance and the cynicism of its exponents than to genuine popular enthusiasm.

Part I: Ideas

1 The Intelligentsia and the Nationalist Revival

Russian nationalists, when they first emerged openly onto the political stage in late 1986 and early 1987, following the partial lifting of restrictions on public debate, with few exceptions proclaimed their conservatism and opposition to reform. At this stage of *perestroika*, it was not yet clear that the reform wing of the Party was in full command of policy. Despite the pretence at unanimity, the CPSU leadership was in fact deeply divided about the nature of the reforms and the battle between the conservatives and the reformers was not decided until Summer 1988, when the struggle entered a new stage. In this fight for power, both wings of the leadership attempted to influence public opinion and enlisted the support of writers and artists to do so.

Many of the leading representatives of the intelligentsia in Moscow and Leningrad supported the reforms (as they had under Khrushchev a generation earlier), partly because they were among the chief beneficiaries of the growing liberalisation. In mid-1986, Gorbachev had appealed to them to aid him, which they did in their polemical journalism, their plays, films and novels. Alone among the readily identifiable constituencies in Soviet public opinion, the liberal wing of the intelligentsia supported Gorbachev and his innovations. *Glasnost'*, which gave them their head, thus furnished the reform leadership a valuable political weapon in its fight against the conservatives and much more influence over public opinion than endless official propaganda would have achieved. A large body of opinion within the intelligentsia, however, opposed these developments: not only were they hostile to changes which entailed their loss of status, readership and power (control of key institutions and publications) but in principle they also rejected the introduction of reforms inspired by Western philosophy and norms. Just as the liberal intelligentsia rallied around Gorbachev and Yakovlev, most of the nationalist intelligentsia allied themselves tacitly with the Party conservatives.

Despite the relative liberalisation tentatively introduced by *glasnost'*, it was not initially possible for even privileged Soviet citizens – working outside the framework of formal Party politics – to intervene openly in the discussion and formulation of Party policy. Instead, writers discussed the merits of the latest books, films and fashions: a coded debate took place, much as it had done at the end of the 1960s and start of the 1970s (when neo-Stalinist nationalists had tangled with Alexander Yakovlev in the official press and Alexander Solzhenitsyn had debated the same issues with Andrei Sakharov in *samizdat*). The controversies within the intelligentsia, in 1987 and even thereafter, were therefore not merely concerned with the arts and culture: in reality, both camps were preoccupied with high politics and Party policy. The question at the heart of the debate was whether or not to reform the Soviet system: whether to keep the country closed and isolated or to open it up to the West and foreign cultural influences; whether to liberalise the arts, reform the political and economic system along Western lines and reject the Stalinist legacy or to defend the Russian traditions and values supposedly embodied by the system that Stalin had created.

A) THE WEST

A flavour of these debates is afforded by nationalist critics' comments on the West.[1] Belief in the unique health and vitality of Russia and of the degradation of the West survived until the 1980s.[2] It flourished among both neo-Slavophiles and neo-Stalinists – being particularly encouraged among the latter by the official ideology's emphasis on the titanic struggle between socialism (embodied by Russia) and capitalism (incarnated by America). 'I, in any event', claimed the poet Stanislav Kunaev, 'cannot agree that it is possible, when reflecting on the USA – which in today's world personifies the cult of violence and terror – to speak of it as a country "intended for love".' America had always been aggressive and had liquidated the American Indians – unlike Russia which had respected the native populations of Siberia. Compassion was a Russian national characteristic.[3] Neo-Stalinist nationalists insisted on this view of the West as a rapacious pseudo-culture. The critic Seleznev, it was reported with approval in the Slavophile literary journal, *Nash sovremennik*, argued against détente with the West. In his view the 'aggression of anti-culture, of intellectual and moral disarmament, of spiritual colonialism' were widespread. This was a pernicious development: 'imperialism is a cosmopolitan phenomenon'. It was necessary to oppose the idea of détente with those of 'patriotism and national character [*narodnost'*]'.[4]

The overtones of the anti-Semitic conspiracy theories, so deeply ingrained in the neo-Stalinist camp, were already implicit in this argument: not only was Russia pitted against the forces of capitalism and colonial exploitation, but it was also confronted with a deliberate attempt to undermine her. Russia and the West were not only incompatible but also diametrically opposed on moral grounds.

Western imports – ideological, economic and cultural – were rejected by these nationalists. Particular venom was reserved for Western culture, which enjoyed an enormous vogue in the later 1980s, as controls on jazz, rock music and foreign culture were lifted. Punk rock, the novelist Yuri Bondarev suggested, had been introduced into Russia to subvert national morals:

> Who brought this music to us? The radio? TV? Our Komsomol publications? Western American voices? Everyone who amuses himself with this music should himself understand at some time [...] who formed it, in whose name, and what it leads to, what its sense is.[5]

These dark forebodings were fully shared by Alexander Doronin, who found himself fearing for 'the destiny of our youth and thus, the destiny of the country', when he listened to the bourgeois mass-culture broadcast by the contemporary mass media. People should understand that:

> [...] Rock is not just music – it is the religion of evil, which has great destructive power. It is a narcotic and the road to drug addiction. *Metallisty* and punk rockers are also an experiment in collective violence [...].[6]

Western mass culture, according to the novelist Valentin Rasputin, was vulgar, trivial and lacking in spirituality. Its popularisation should be a matter of great concern:

> Comrades, for us [...] the broad attack of mass culture is not an indifferent thing. If we go on looking on it passively [...] we will be [...] cornered and scattered. Our forces are confronted by attacking forces – we are a company opposed by a division which is recruiting, you must remember, among the young. What dubious means of freedom these are – far from being democracy, it is anarchy, the debauch of democracy.[7]

The tendency to see Western mass culture as an aggressive force undermining Russian culture and youth fitted easily with the neo-Stalinism propounded by the film-maker Sergei Bondarchuk, according to which the West was the ideological and political enemy:

> The mass culture of the West can be called a cheque, buying and suborning everything [...] Its doors often remain [...] closed to truth and decency. Man is overwhelmed by worldwide advertisements, which create the idea of false idols, mass culture as a respite before the end of the world American-style (violence, cruelty, obscenity) [...].[8]

These writers' hostility to the West belonged to a long Russian tradition of offended incomprehension and rejection of European values. The usual reaction was to compare the vulgarity of the West with the ascetic nobility of Russia. The writer and critic Anatoly Lanshchikov contended that the provincial city of Ryazan (famed in modern Russia for its food shortages and as the home of Solzhenitsyn, before his emigration) was culturally equal, or superior, to the cities of Holland and Belgium.[9]

One of the principal reasons adduced by the nationalists for opposing *perestroika*, was that it attempted to impose alien norms on Russia. Mikhail Lobanov objected that:

> Being foisted on our country with its sick economy are new theories with the temptation of Americanism, with the mechanical copying of foreign experience, with destructive experiments. Again a revolution. But we must remember that a revolution is a disease, a crisis of faith and of Statehood.[10]

The nationalists pointed to all the other voluntarist attempts to wrest Russia into the modern world, starting with Peter the Great, suggesting that they had brought nothing but evil. Peter's experiment with Russia had been unjustified, according to Lanshchikov: his cutting of the nobles' beards had been a fundamental assault on their dignity, which symbolised his whole approach to Russia. Nonetheless, there were many who thought his methods and aims acceptable, who believed that the 'window on Europe' justified mass punishments, the transformation of peasants into slaves, and the deprivation of the Russian people of their capital. *Perestroika* resembled this earlier misguided attempt to uproot the country, in forcing it into the embrace of, and turning it into a colony of the West – rather than strengthening its independence.[11] Supporters of *perestroika* kept drawing attention to Western experience, although 'left radicalism' had few followers in the West, according to the literary critic, Vadim Kozhinov.[12]

These strictures applied not just to the general orientation of *perestroika*, but extended also to *glasnost'*. The critic Alexander Kazintsev warned:

> [...] It's one thing to criticise one public institution or department or other, it is another thing to criticise the national organism. Here, a particular sense of responsibility is required – for criticism can have both a creative and a destructive principle.[13]

The village writer Valentin Rasputin appeared to agree. Speaking after the Nineteenth Party Conference, in July 1988, on Irkutsk television, he approved Yuri Bondarev's criticisms of the unpredictable and uncontrolled evolution of *perestroika* and also criticised growing freedom of speech: '[...] Now, it seems to me [...] people have started to talk too much [...] To express [one's opinion], publicly and widely, it is necessary for that opinion to be correct [...]'.[14] The writer Vassily Belov compared the press to a 'fallen woman' walking the boulevards and got particularly agitated about a Vologda newspaper's having printed material about sex education. Russian radio, he suggested, was not staffed by Russians (implying that it was in the hands of those omnipresent agents of conspiracy). As for Yegor Yakovlev, the editor of the liberal paper *Moscow News*, Belov preferred 'to keep quiet about those in whose power he is but it is clear [...] but not to everyone, and that's the whole problem and the danger of unscrupulous papers.'[15] This fantasy (about worldwide Jewish anti-Russian conspiracy) had an extraordinary and malevolent hold on the imagination of the nationalist intelligentsia – distorting their understanding of reality and robbing their observations of all authority. Whenever the truth was unpalatable they took refuge in myth – old and new. Brezhnev's economic record was defended.[16] The integrity of leading proponents of *perestroika* and the value of *perestroika* itself were questioned.[17]

These views did not go unchallenged and the resulting polemics not only recalled the conflicts of the past century but even seemed to renew them, largely unchanged. The historian and son of the poet Akhmatova, Lev Gumilev held that the Mongol yoke was an advantage for Russia because it saved her from German dominance and enabled the Russian people to retain their national identity, unsullied by contact with Europe. The historian Natan Eidelman took issue with this theory, arguing instead – in a form of historical polemic long vanished elsewhere – that the Mongol invasion had cut Russia off from the rest of Europe and resulted in the impoverishment and humiliation of the country, inhibiting the development both of political freedom and of economic and technical progress.[18] The liberal intelligentsia to which Eidelman belonged was anxious to reintegrate Russia into Europe, seeing this as the only way of overcoming the political and cultural legacy of the tragic past. The Nobel-prize winning physicist and leading dissident, Andrei Sakharov, had already indicated that he found this renewal of the Slavophile controversy mildly absurd:

> The very classification of ideas as Western or Russian is incomprehensible to me. In my view, a scientific and rational approach to social and natural phenomena is only compatible with a classification of ideas and concepts as true or false [...] I object to the notion that our country should be sealed off from the supposedly corrupting influence of the West [...][19]

With this stance, his one-time companion in dissidence, the mathematician Igor Shafarevich, entirely disagreed. Russia needed to develop independently. He expressed the 'hope that our country will develop organically, on the basis of its 1,000 year history [...] We need for a start to learn to look at least from the point of view of several centuries of our history, to recognise today's life as an organic continuation of it'. Only in this perspective could Russia's problems be successfully addressed.[20] Dialogue with Europe should not involve the sacrifice of Russian independence, singularity or character, according to the critic Lanshchikov:

> Yes, Europe is our common home, but with what and as whom will we appear there? As a supplier of raw materials and a mass consumer of consumer goods or as a partner with an equal claim to dignity? Cultural integration is good, if, of course, it does not recall cultural interventionism.[21]

(Interventionism here referred to foreign troop deployment in Russia against the Bolshevik regime during the Civil War). In short, integration and contact with Europe were of very questionable benefit to Russia.

Russian nationalists were to become even more outspoken in their hostility to the West – rivalling in this respect the nineteenth-century poet Tyutchev:

> 'The modern Western world is a world that left the Church of Christ many centuries ago. Papism, anti-Christian humanism, the anti-clerical reformation, the godless enlightenment, all kinds of

revolution (political, technical, moral) – these are steps on one ladder, leading to the depths of hell. [...] This world loathes Orthodoxy and persecutes it: openly, to the point of bloodshed, revealing its anti-Christian essence [...]', according to one extreme nationalist.[22]

The West's perfidy extended naturally to ideology. Universal values did not exist, according to the neo-fascist publicist Alexander Dugin: the ideology which claimed to be based on them simply masked the expansionist aims of Western culture. The last two centuries had been marked by the opposition of two geopolitical and geocultural centres: Eurasia (or Russia) and America. The collapse of Russia was to be ascribed not to its weakness or to any drawbacks in its earlier organisation or ethos, but to the treachery of groups in Russia, controlled by foreign interests.[23] This belief in a foreign (usually Jewish) conspiracy was more and more common under *perestroika* – as freedom of expression increased and as the explosion of old myths left Russians asking yet another of their perennial questions: *kto vinovat?* – who is to blame?

B) DEMOCRACY AND CAPITALISM

If the West was alien and hostile to Russia, it followed that its political and economic models were as inapplicable to Russia as its culture was deplorable.[24]

This view was most succinctly stated by the writer Alexander Prokhanov, when he observed:

> There is a view [...] that *perestroyka* is supposedly required by the USSR's strategic lagging behind the civilisation of the West [...] Both its meaning and its task are to catch up with the West [...] This view of a 'catching-up *perestroyka*' forces us to copy the West's models, be they scientific apparatuses, rock groups, methods of conducting interviews in the press or administrative and scientific models. Such a copying deprives us of a sovereign path and gives birth to an inferiority complex [...][25]

According to the economist, Mikhail Antonov:

> Our people [...] is an imperial people [*narod gosudarstvennik*]. It created a great power more than a 1000 years ago [...] No matter how much the people's conditions of life changed, its character,

psychological disposition and 'super-idea', comprehended not by the brain but by the soul, remained the same. Therefore, plans to establish democracy along Western lines, a law-based State in the Western sense and other absurd constructions have no future in our country.[26]

This point of view was shared by Alexander Prokhanov and the historian, Apollon Kuz'min.[27] The Russians were a fundamentally state-building people – striving both for national unity and sharing an unparallelled openness of character that made them uniquely suited to their imperial role. This open-hearted generosity had even resulted in their suffering, rather than gaining from their empire.[28] Right-wing nationalists, who typically exhibited xenophobia and were obsessed with Russia's singularity, loved to dwell on the Russians' supposedly outgoing national character. This, of course, did not mean that they believed Russia should extend this openness to or emulate the West in any way. Far from it.

Perhaps the most famous (or notorious) statement of this view was made by Igor Shafarevich in his article 'Russophobia', originally written in the early 1980s but first published in 1989. According to Shafarevich, a number of émigré writers – who were at one with the liberal intelligentsia of Moscow – were bent on undermining the Russian people's self-esteem. Their works attacked Russian history and culture and argued that the only way forward for Russia was to break the links tying it to the past and to substitute for its tragic legacy of despotism, Western liberal democracy. According to them, in Shafarevich's summary:

> Russians are a nation of slaves, who have always bowed down before cruelty and cringed before strong rule, hating everything foreign and hostile to culture and Russia itself is an eternal breeding ground of despotism and totalitarianism, dangerous to the rest of the world [...].

Hence, Russia was confronted with the choice of either democracy or totalitarianism.[29] From this view, Shafarevich dissented. Not only was their interpretation of history anachronistic and unprofessional, he argued, but it was also motivated by a malevolent goal – that of the destruction of the Russian people's moral fibre and self-confidence. This, Shafarevich suggested, should come as no surprise to those who knew Russia, for the disaffected intellectuals, who had always preached revolution and emulation of the West to Russia with such disastrous results, were mainly composed of Jews, whose hostility to the interests of the Slavic people hardly needed explanation.[30] (*Nash sovremennik* later published previously expunged parts of the article, which elaborated on this theme, for the benefit of those unfamiliar with the intricacies of this conspiracy theory).[31] This explained the fuss made by liberals over human rights and particularly those of ethnic minorities (principally, Jews, but also Crimean Tatars and others), political prisoners (a mere 1 per cent of the total, Shafarevich assured us), instead of concentrating on the rights of the majority – the Russian *narod*.[32]

It was almost superfluous to explain that remedies proposed from such a quarter were unsuitable for Russia. Democracy, Shafarevich remarked, was in any event a dubious system. Irrespective of its inherent shortcomings, it was fraught with all sorts of attendant dangers and inconveniences: democracy was always introduced after a social cataclysm and political upheaval. Was it really necessary to inflict this on contemporary Russia? Founded on unlimited popular sovereignty, in which majority rule entailed the oppression of minorities, democracy, in the course of its 200-year history, had failed to create a free society. '[...] In Western society, social freedoms exist through inertia not as a consequence of the principles on which society is founded'. Russia's liberal critics recommended democracy as an alternative to communism – but was democracy capable of overcoming communism? 'Western democracy is constantly giving ground to its antagonist [...] The time is long past when Western democracies were a dynamic force.'

New countries rejected the Western model, as did more and more people in the West itself. Democracy was 'not a long-lasting form. Two hundred years is the limit of its life. [...] The multiparty Western system is a disappearing social device'. Its benefits were considerable but its time was done.[33] In any event, Shafarevich asked, if democracy were as alien to the Russian spirit and tradition as liberals and émigrés suggested, why should Russia opt for democracy as opposed to some form of authoritarian rule?[34] The imposition of democracy on Russia amounted to the spiritual occupation of Russia by Western intellectuals and a 'cosmopolitan' (Jewish) layer of managers in Soviet society.[35]

The idea that the Russian temperament was somehow incompatible with liberal democracy and Western-style law was not new. Dostoevsky had enthused about Russian brotherhood being founded not on law but on love[36] and Konstantin Aksakov, in the 1850s, had believed that the Russians needed an authoritarian monarchy (but not a State) to find true freedom.[37] The writers associated with the neo-Stalinist journal, *Molodaya gvardiya*, in the late 1960s had also insisted on Russia's rejection of Western individualism, capitalism and parliamentary democracy.[38]

Throughout the 1970s and 1980s, Russian nationalists continued to reject democracy and capitalism, as being foreign to the Russian soul. Russia, it was argued, was not suited to capitalism or parliamentary democracy because these were fundamentally individualistic enterprises, whereas the Russian was, at heart, a collectivist. The Russian was uniquely disposed towards socialism – an inclination reinforced by his asceticism and dislike of vulgar consumerism, according to the former religious dissident, Vladimir Osipov:

> The Russian nation, educated by Orthodoxy, was for centuries close in outlook to 'socialism' [...] We still do not know the Russian peasant commune well enough. The land was God's and was redistributed as justice dictated at gatherings of the commune. The commune assumed the care of widows and orphans [...] It would be bad if we were now to move away from even the spirit of comradeship and communality [*sobornost*'], making egoism and individual gain our idols.

The democrats, he warned, made matters worse by undermining fundamental values like patriotism.[39] The writer and editor Stanislav Kunaev also held socialism to be deeply rooted in Russian culture: 'Russia [...] was ready to adopt socialism, by virtue of its traditional, collectivist way of life and thought.'[40]

Vadim Kozhinov agreed – but believed that a new socialist formula had to be found in Russia: not the old Bolshevik internationalism but a socialism rooted in the country's Orthodox heritage and rural traditions and which strove to maintain Russia's greatness.[41] Apollon Kuz'min saw real patriotism as necessarily socialist.[42] Capitalism was a temptation which lured Russia into sacrificing its highest spiritual values in return for the promise of a higher standard of living.[43] It was exploitative, involved living at the expense of others; socialism was fundamentally altruistic. According to the writer Lanshchikov, the capitalist world would never grant equal rights to other countries. The abolition of socialism would result in chaos.[44]

One of the most sustained attacks, in the 1980s, on the Westerners and their model for reform of Russia was mounted by the economist,

Mikhail Antonov. He criticised the Soviet vice-premier, Leonid Abalkin, for suggesting that the West provided an example which Russia should copy. If capitalism was introduced into Russia, the country would be turned into a colony of the West. In any event, the West harboured malevolent intentions towards Russia: it wanted to extract maximum profit from its relations with it; it wanted to use Russia as a site for its ecologically most dangerous and dirty enterprises; it hoped to weaken the USSR as far as possible and turn Russia into a buyer of Western industrial goods and food and a provider of raw materials. Hence, the integration of the Russian economy into that of the rest of the world was not merely undesirable but was part of a grand, malign scheme, to weaken Russia. The Party leadership should declare on whose side they were: with the people (*narod*) or with bureaucratic thieves and the mafia (that is, those who supported capitalism). If they were on the side of the people they should introduce a programme of national salvation. If, on the other hand, they preferred the 'capitalist, compradorist line of our leading scholarly communists, then sooner or later the people will adopt its own leader [*vozhd'*][45] who will have a proper understanding of national interests'.[46]

Antonov was well aware of the resonances of the term *vozhd'*:

'In our time, when the ideas of democracy and the state of law are so popular', he commented, 'the word *vozhd'* is not respected and is assimilated with the cult of personality [that is, with Stalin], but this is wrong. The cult of personality develops when the place of the *vozhd'* is occupied by a person who does not understand the genuine interests of the people. Our peoples, especially the Russian, cannot live without a Tsar at its head. It is impossible to imagine Dmitri Donskoi, for example, referring the question of whether or not to do battle with Mamai to the consideration of a parliament, with its party struggles and ambition, with its public eloquence and behind-the-scenes intrigues of lobbyists. Those who support democracy and the state of law more often than not forget to add the epithet 'socialist' [...] Democracy (that is, bourgeois democracy) and the state of law are a mafia dream [...] The definition of democracy as the domination of an organised minority over the disorganised majority is well known.

Democracy, capitalism and the law-based state were equally odious, a plan to enable the dishonest exploitation of the people:

Our people did not accomplish three revolutions, bear the brunt of a world and a civil war, survive the burdens of collectivisation and industrialisation, in order to end up under the heel of the West and a small group of native compradors obedient to the West.

What Russia needed was to find its own way forward:

Not barracks socialism and not capitalism, not convergence, but its own peculiar [*samobytny*] path of development can save our country and show the world a way out of the blind alleys of modern culture.[47]

Antonov's diatribe bore all the hallmarks of classical neo-Stalinist nationalism: the sharp rejection of liberalism, parliamentary democracy and capitalism; the profession of faith in Russia's unique identity and mission; the alleged correspondence between Russian national character, socialism and authoritarianism.

Not surprisingly, it was not unusual in these circles to find approving references to Stalin, as a 'great, historical, contradictory personality',[48] exculpating him from involvement in the repressions of Soviet rule (which, it was suggested, were really to be understood as a Jewish plot).[49] Many of these views found a sympathetic hearing in the CPSU, especially in the Russian Communist Party.[50] The links between the Party and the conservative intelligentsia were to last until the coup and beyond, yet the appeal of socialist ideology declined, while interest in alternative ideologies grew among the right-wing intelligentsia.

C) EMPIRE

As the appeal of Soviet socialism diminished, that of imperialism grew. It could be argued that the idea of a strong, centralised Russian state underlay Soviet rule almost from its inception and that the Soviet state, as it developed under Stalin, assumed an imperial character.[51] The imperialism, or Greater Russian nationalism, implicit in late Stalinism enhanced the prestige of Soviet power. However, as the integrity of the USSR began to be threatened by minority nationalism in the late 1980s, a school of Russian imperialists emerged whose loyalty to the Party was conditional on the CPSU's capacity to hold the state together and guarantee its international prestige and power.

Early exemplars of this trend were the writer Alexander Prokhanov and the army colonel Viktor Alksnis and his *Soyuz* group in the Soviet parliament as were the Interfronts established in the USSR republics to frustrate their moves towards autonomy.[52] The leading theoretician of modern Soviet Russian imperialism (or National-Bolshevism) was Alexander Prokhanov, a writer of novels celebrating the army, former military research scientist and leader of the anti-reform intelligentsia. Early in 1990, Prokhanov offered two much discussed analyses of the country's crisis, which suggested that the best hope for Russia was the emergence of a regime in which the army, bolstered by nationalist ideology, would play the leading role. Prokhanov saw current events as a repetition of the fall of the Tsarist regime: the tragedy in both cases was the same – the collapse of central authority. This process had started with an attack on socialist ideology, which held the State together; for Prokhanov, the main interest of socialism lay not in its egalitarian message but in this unifying role. As the economy was undermined, the Party was shown to be incapable of holding the country together. The centrifugal forces at work in society were strengthened by their attack on Russia and the Russians. The outcome of these developments would be a civil war, unless steps were taken to arrest the logic of events. The solution Prokhanov proposed represented, he claimed, a third course between Stalinist *diktat* and death: the restoration of a strong Russian national state.[53]

In a later article, published in *Nash sovremennik*, Prokhanov elaborated on this theme. The fault for the collapse of Soviet power could be ascribed to the liberal intelligentsia:

> Today, the Soviet Union is weak as never before [...]. The fault for the collapse [...] lies with the liberals, unthinkingly repeating the experiment of destroying centralism [...] Liberal thought, nourished on a foreign culture and political science, despised the genetic experience of the country and people and is realising an irresponsible experiment.

The army should take power. The CPSU was disappearing and divided: only the army could take over from it. It should act decisively: 'The army should cease democratising itself and finally start to put itself on a war-like footing [*voenizirovat'*]'. The tanks now being moved out of Eastern Europe should be deployed on the country's new borders, as a token of intent. Finally, it was necessary to find a new ideology.[54] As an author of the Appeal to the People, Prokhanov was to show little hesitation in supporting the principle of a coup to oust the reformers and restore the centralised Soviet state.

Prokhanov was devoted not to an ideology (communist or other) but to the aim of preserving or restoring the Russian state.[55] He frankly admitted, after the coup, that he was ready to use any means to achieve this goal:

> What is important is that the state should be preserved. Moreover, it does not matter, essentially, what forces lead to the establishment of this state. Let it even be fascism, for if it is only possible to build a great Russian state at the price of fascism, I would opt for that.[56]

His readiness to endorse fascism is not surprising, for the only ideology which Prokhanov consistently criticised was that of Western liberal democracy.[57] In the post-Soviet period, Prokhanov was to be one of the most consistent and articulate exponents of the authoritarian Greater Russian state.

Among Prokhanov's early allies were deputies in the Soviet parliament who, on 14 February 1990, established the *Soyuz* (Union) group, to defend Soviet unity and power. Led by the colonels, Viktor Alksnis and Nikolai Petrushenko, and dedicated to the maintenance of the Soviet Union, *Soyuz* quickly gained support and by December 1990, at the time of its first congress, had 561 registered members, making it the second largest group in the Congress (after the CPSU faction, with 730 members). By then, the pro-reform Inter-Regional Group of Deputies counted 229 deputies.[58] Its main goal was the retention of the USSR.[59] Its programme, with its emphasis on the central role of the armed forces, state-controlled modernisation and rejection of the democratic transformation of the Soviet Union was clearly authoritarian.[60] Its leaders were thus vocal critics of Gorbachev and the democrats. When, in April 1991, it emerged that Gorbachev and Yeltsin had agreed on the radical transformation of the Soviet Union into a democratic federal state, *Soyuz* leaders called for a state of emergency to preserve the Union. At the group's second congress, in April 1991, Yuri Blokhin proposed suspending the activity of all political parties, banning those that advocated separatism, ending press freedom and outlawing strikes, meetings and demonstrations. Should Gorbachev be reluctant to adopt these measures, the Soviet parliament should assume responsibility for enforcing them.[61] Not to be outdone, Alksnis called for a 'public salvation committee' which 'should save the Union as a state'. Civil war and bloodshed were the alternative.

Alksnis, a Latvian whose father had been executed by Stalin in 1938, claimed that he wanted only 'state centrism', a state that would end the useless babble of political debate and impose order. He spoke for the army, which, he affirmed, 'wants a single state, which is neither capitalist nor socialist. It wants no dogmas.'[62] Alksnis was disingenuous in claiming to be non-ideological. An ideology was indeed implicit in his viewpoint and this was essentially authoritarian, in that he wished to preserve the state constructed by Stalin, despite the wishes of many of its citizens. A form of imperialism, or Greater Russian nationalism, underpinned his ideal of the multinational, centralised and authoritarian Soviet state. Alksnis and his colleagues attempted to organise public support for these positions, announcing the formation of a wider Unionist movement, in Spring 1991.[63] These efforts foundered, when the August coup failed, and, the following Autumn, *Soyuz* was disbanded, although its ideas lived on.

After the failure of the August coup and the break-up of the Soviet Union the following December, the Greater Russian idea (the idea of a centralised, authoritarian, multinational state subordinate to Moscow) appealed to opponents of reform more than ever. It was, however, difficult to justify in the prevailing climate of democratic nationalism and anti-communism. Some neo-imperialists felt that it was no longer opportune to call for the revival of the USSR in its previous form. A new ideology was needed and, as usual, history was raided to provide one. The doctrine which was exhumed originated in émigré circles. In the 1920s, a number of distinguished Russian scholars (including the historian Vernadsky), reflecting on the collapse of their country into revolution and brutal civil war, came to the conclusion that this was the inevitable consequence of trying to foist on Russia mores and institutions alien to her. Like the Slavophiles, they believed that the Petrine reform of the early eighteenth century had been a fatal error. With the Revolution, they argued, the essential Russia had reaffirmed itself, sweeping away the artifices of Western civilisation which Tsarism had introduced. Russia would now recover her true identity, which was neither of the East nor West, but a unique synthetic Slav–Turkic Eurasian civilisation, whose geographic, linguistic, socio-political and spiritual originality they attempted to demonstrate. The Latin–Teutonic West was in decline, they suggested, while Eurasia's youth and vitality could be seen in her all-conquering destructiveness and barbarity.[64]

Vernadsky and his associates were cultivated scions of the aristocracy and upper bourgeoisie, who had little real sympathy for the

Revolution. The spectacle of former Party stalwarts raiding this arsenal of White émigrés to sustain their calls for the restoration of the Soviet order is not without irony. A less unwitting victim of intellectual exploitation was Lev Nikolaevich Gumilev, the son of the executed monarchist poet, Nikolai Gumilev, and the poet, Anna Akhmatova. On his release from half a lifetime of concentration camp and war, Gumilev buried himself in the study of history and geography, in search of an explanation of universal history. He suggested that the rise and fall of civilisations might be attributed to the genesis of several 'superethnos' (or super-nations), which, when infused with quasi-physical energy [*passionarnost'*] suddenly emerged from obscurity to shape history and draw lesser nations into their political and cultural sphere. The 'superethnos' developed and died like any other biological organism. The Teutonic–Latin 'superethnos' had long been in decline, whereas the Greater Russian 'superethnos' (which embraced Slavs, Ugrics, Alans and Turks) was half a millennium younger and its time was still to come.[65] Gumilev felt little sympathy for the West, past or present. He rejoiced that Russia had long been cut off from its debilitating influence: the Mongols, rather than oppressing her and impeding her development, had saved Russia from colonisation by the aggressive, Catholic West.[66] At the end of his life, as Soviet Russia tentatively liberalised, he made clear his opposition to reform. Contacts with the West were not desirable, he opined: 'We do not need any contacts with the Latins, as they are a deceitful, hypocritical [...] people and, furthermore, enemies not friends of Russia.'[67]

The reason Eurasianism and Gumilev's version of it were adopted by the neo-imperialists is clear. Eurasianism suggested that Russia embraced Muslims and other nationalities and that its path of development differed from that of the West. If Russia was indeed a distinct, synthetic civilisation, it should reject Western norms, find inspiration in its own traditions and assert its right to exist (and embrace its neighbours). Eurasianism was just the doctrine that supporters of the erstwhile Soviet Union needed to justify their claims and, in 1992, it became popular.[68] Cultural figures such as Prokhanov and the film-maker, Nikita Mikhalkov preached it. Mikhalkov insisted: 'We had and have and – as I think – will have our own Way, the Eurasian Way [...] Russia, which is not a national but a state formation, has become the East–West (Eurasia)'.[69]

Nationalist journals now included theoretical articles explaining the relevance of Eurasianism to contemporary Russia. The Soviet Union was the heir of Tsarist Russia, which had expressed the geopolitical and geohistorical Eurasian essence of the country, argued Shamil Sultanov. Eurasia was culturally and spiritually antithetical to the West:

> [...] Western culture has finally moved into its final phase of development – the phase of the transient global consumer society. This civilisation [...] cannot last long. [...] Therefore, either this decadent, hypocritical and essentially atheistic Western civilisation will lead to a global apocalypse or it will give way to a different, alternative path of development, based on an unconditional limitation of energy and material consumption, principally different relations with spiritual and sacral creation, the return of the archetypal traditions of humanity. But a clash between these two tendencies is inevitable.[70]

Similarly, Vadim Shtep argued that Eurasianism would enable Russia to fight off expansionist Atlanticism and the influence of those who had sold their souls to the diabolical West.[71]

A more influential exponent of Eurasianism was, for a time, Sergei Baburin, an ambitious Siberian academic, lawyer and parliamentary deputy. Russia, according to Baburin, was 'a special kind of civilisation between West and East': by virtue of her mentality, her culture and her economy, therefore, it was 'impossible' for Russia 'simply to copy Western models'.[72] The Russian idea, as elaborated by Baburin, stressed the imperial vocation of the Russians. Russians were a 'superethnos':

> The Russians are not only an ethnic group, but also a superethnic group, creating a 'milieu for cooperation' between many peoples and ethnic groups, which partly merge into it. [...] The Russians are trying to consolidate themselves [...] both as a nation proper and as a superethnic formation (an 'imperial people').[73]

Russian imperialism was, for Baburin, a condition of the existence of the Russian state:

> The multinational composition of Russia is its fundamental basis and its universal-historical *raison d'être*. [...] The Russian idea [...] is the negation of monoethnic statehood. It is the idea of a spiritually united, multinational (polyethnic) empire (great power), the idea of the multinational (polyethnic) Russian people.[74]

These theories conveniently implied a hierarchy of rights, with those of the imperial nation taking precedence over those of its less significant neighbours. In practical terms, this meant glueing as much as possible of the former Soviet Union back together again, under the aegis of Russia.

The modish dalliance with Eurasianism was to be eclipsed by Vladimir Zhirinovsky's more dramatic and crude imperialism and the appeal of charismatic generals, Alexander Rutskoi and Alexander Lebed, to Greater Russian nationalism. However, the Greater Russian idea, in one form or another, was to become a *leitmotiv* of politics, in the wake of the dissolution of the Soviet Union.

D) THE PEOPLE (*NAROD*)

Nationalist writers insisted on the greatness of the *narod*, or people, and indulged, from the early 1980s, in a vogue for a sort of a neo-Hegelian celebration of the Russian people's historical role. 'The peasant's *izba* (hut) has always saved Russia', the writer Belov contended. 'If we go under it won't be at all because of the Pershings.' It would be because the Russian people had been undermined by voluntarist and conspiratorial attacks on their culture and way of life.[75] The critic Chalmaev had, a generation earlier, suggested that the people 'always acted as the "salvation" of the nobility and of Russia from physical and spiritual degeneracy [...] The people are not a "support", not a caryatid, but the chief and only hero of the historical process.' Stanislav Kunaev also celebrated the Russian's military valour, suggesting that liberty was subordinate as a value to national greatness.[76]

How, in the light of this once great role, could the Russian nation's contemporary travails be explained? The chief instrument for attacking the people had, in the view of one school of nationalist thought, been the Bolsheviks' policies and in particular collectivisation. The novelist Vladimir Soloukhin attacked collectivisation for its destruction of the peasant way of life, his traditions and economic interests. He denounced the inhumanity of the deportations and the abandoning of people in the taiga without food and recalled his own family feeding the skeletons who survived the journey, in his childhood.[77] The tragedy of the peasantry (to which writers like Mozhaev and Rasputin had pointed before the truth about collectivisation had been admitted), had been caused – according to Zuyev – by the triumphalist, cosmopolitan outlook of communist technocrats.[78] Another critic blamed the communist utopians who had run the government in the 1920s and 1930s and who were inspired by the Western futurists.[79]

This view – favoured also by Solzhenitsyn – simply rejected the Revolution and all its works, as an illegitimate experiment bearing 'some of the characteristics of a foreign invasion'.[80] This was a step towards blaming the people's past woes on a Jewish–Masonic conspiracy.[81] It was hardly surprising that the peasantry – with their world shattered by revolution and a fanatical dictatorship – had now sunk into a state of torpor, misery and decline.

The spiritual and physical degradation of the people was of constant concern to conservative nationalists.[82] The anti-alcohol campaign (of which Yegor Ligachev was believed to be the principal proponent in the Politburo)[83] was a cause they took up with particular vigour. Academician Fedor Uglov, who led the Union for the Struggle for Popular Sobriety, commented:

> We must understand that our people (*narod*) and our future are in danger. Today, the fight for sobriety must be engaged in by everyone who loves his Motherland.

Alcohol reduced the quality and productivity of labour, led to crime and accidents, undermined State planning and damaged the Fatherland both materially and morally.[84] 'The growth in the use of alcohol has a deleterious effect on the intellectual level of the people, posing a real threat of degradation.' Not only were the moral and intellectual qualities of the whole people threatened, so too was the country's defence capacity – as a consequence of this degradation.[85] Not content with discerning the dangers of alcoholism for the individual, or even the society at large, right-wing nationalists were convinced that sinister forces were at work. In the view of Vladimir Osipov, alcoholism existed in Russia because 'the mafia needs slaves [...] The Russophobes want to undermine definitively the genetic stock of the Russian people' – an aim also served by the spread of 'porno-business'.[86] The failure of the anti-alcohol campaign was no accident, according to Uglov: '[...] The same forces were at work here, as those which for decades directed their entire propaganda effort, their trade work, industry, mass media to impelling people towards drunkenness and alcoholism.' Their work was 'hidden' but 'very effective'.[87] No matter how guarded in his phraseology, Uglov's meaning was clear for a Russian reader: these evil forces were the 'cosmopolitan' ranks of a world-wide Jewish conspiracy. Elsewhere, his anti-Semitism was less veiled.[88]

It was believed that the Russian people and its culture were under threat: it was a question of 'saving' rather than restoring Russian culture – a process, which had to start with the moral resurrection of the Russian people.[89] According to Alexander Kazintsev, the very sense of the difference between good and evil had been under attack, since the start of the 1980s.[90] This attack on the people's traditional morality and spiritual values was hardly fortuitous: if invaders destroyed the consecrated places of a country, people understood that the enemy was doing this and that his actions were evil. But in contemporary Russia, the destruction of cultural and religious monuments was viewed with an indifference which threatened the people with spiritual annihilation.[91] Shafarevich also saw the present and future in pessimistic, not to say apocalyptic, terms:

> The Russian people and all humanity are now in a frightful crisis, which has, perhaps, no precedent in history. Everything is under threat – the forests and rivers, the soil and waters, the moral values and physical strength of the people.

There was only one hope and that was to return to tradition and the people: '[...] Salvation depends on closeness to tradition, on the ability to feel the courage of the people, to feel its history.'[92] These views, largely shared by the former dissident and writer Leonid Borodin,[93] are partly explicable by the context of the constant upheavals and tragedies through which Russia has passed in this century and which, having impoverished the country and its people, led to an almost unprecedented assault on its culture and society.

But while loud in their lamentations over recent Russian history and its effects on the Russian people, criticism of the country's past by the liberal intelligentsia was rejected as little better than treachery. Igor Shafarevich invented a term for the liberals' rejection of Russia's authoritarian traditions and their Western orientation: russophobia. Nationalist writers attacked *Aprel'*, the liberal faction within the Writers' Union, for its supposedly anti-Russian interpretation of national history:

> Russia is 'a thousand-year-old slave', [...] 'what can a thousand-year-old slave give to the world?' – these are slanderous catchcalls about Russia and the Russian people [...] Russophobia in the mass media of the USSR today has reached and surpassed foreign, anti-Russian propaganda from overseas.[94]

Russophobia was no innocuous mistake, in the eyes of Shafarevich and others. 'Russophobia is inspired from without and from within' and its effects were deliberately destructive.[95] While anti-Semites like

Kuz'min saw Russophobia as the ideological arm of the anti-Slav, Jewish conspiracy, the theory of Russophobia had initially gained currency and fed on neo-Stalinist hostility to the West. The critic Yuri Seleznev had stated this position as early as 1985:

> Our ideological opponents understand as well as we the importance of the problem of the Russian people as the unifying, cementing force in the Soviet State. This is why anti-Sovietism more and more clearly takes the form of open Russophobia. Russophobia is nothing more than the strategy of the imperialist 'first strike' on the moral centre of our power.[96]

Hence, Russophobia was a theme initially exploited by both neo-Stalinists and dissident nationalists to attack liberal critics of the Soviet regime.

It was argued that the long-suffering Russian people had been sacrificed to the extravagant theories and claims of an intellectual class, largely indifferent to their fate.[97] The intelligentsia, according to the right-wing television journalist, Alexander Nevzorov, had its own caste structure and consciousness and its own religion, consisting in the veneration of freedom and democracy. Anyone disagreeing with these views was condemned as mad or fascist in outlook. But the problems which they raised constantly in the press and media – which they controlled – had nothing to do with the problems of the people (*narod*). Hence, their influence was unjustified and their role irrelevant.[98]

E) ANTI-SEMITISM

One of the chief sources of controversy between the Westernising and the conservative nationalist intelligentsia was anti-Semitism. Anti-Semitism was widespread among the nationalist intelligentsia and was to be more openly expressed as *glasnost'* developed. One of the reasons anti-Semitism existed in Russia was that far from any effort having been made to eradicate it, through re-education and information, it enjoyed some patronage within official circles.[99] While Tsarist policies of active discrimination were largely suspended in the 1920s, Jews continued to suffer from popular prejudice[100] and from government oppression (this time, as capitalists and 'bourgeois'). Not, however, until the 1940s was anti-Semitism adopted as an active State policy: in the post-war period, under Zhdanov, Stalin's cultural commissar, anti-Semitism was disguised as national resistance to the 'cosmopolitan' enemy and culminated in the 'doctors' plot' of 1952 in which several leading Jewish doctors and writers were arrested on the charge of trying to poison the country's leadership. Only Stalin's death averted a second bloodbath, akin to that of 1937. The wave of anti-Semitism of the late 1940s and early 1950s was important because it engendered a hybrid form of anti-Semitism that fed off earlier atavisms. The 1930s had assiduously inculcated in the population the myth (and fear) of the 'enemy of the people' – the hidden opponent of the revolution, who was trying to undermine the people's revolutionary achievements and whom every honest citizen was honour-bound to unmask. The War built on this image, by appearing to confirm the validity of the regime's xenophobic and paranoic propaganda: Hitler's attack showed how perfidious the outside world really was. This impression was all the stronger in that the regime devoted almost no attention to the Holocaust or to any of the issues it raised. Furthermore, it minimised the contribution of other countries to the victory in the Great Patriotic War, as the Second World War was called, thus distorting the popular understanding of what had really happened and what it meant. Stalinism thus built up a siege mentality and the last ideological construct of Stalinism, anti-Semitic nationalism, exploited and reinforced it.

A final twist was given to Russian anti-Semitism by the Arab–Israeli conflict. The Soviet Union had allied itself, for strategic reasons, with the Arab countries, notably Egypt and Syria, in the 1960s and it attempted to construct the appearance of popular support at home for its foreign policy, largely for propaganda purposes. As a result, anti-Zionism emerged and enjoyed a degree of official encouragement. From the mid-1960s on, a series of anti-Semitic and anti-Zionist books were published under academic imprints.[101] These were followed up by a number of militarist and anti-Semitic novels – Valentin Pikul' being the leading exponent of the genre. A final factor which encouraged the growth of anti-Semitism was the official reaction to the demand for the right to emigrate. As the regime reverted to more repressive policies in the early 1970s and as hope for change and liberalisation declined, so the campaign for the right to emigrate developed. Discriminatory policies against Jews were again practised in education, culture and other spheres and this fuelled the pressure to emigrate. However, as this was seen as an admission that the Soviet Union was not the paradise it claimed to be, the State refused to grant its citizens passports and the problem became a major human rights issue. The fact that it was raised in international fora and by the international press to criticise the Soviet Union was then adduced by the regime as proof that those who wished to emigrate were disloyal. This was also to become a familiar theme in the writings of the nationalist intelligentsia.[102]

Thus, when we come to examining modern anti-Semitism in Russia, we should remember that the myths on which it reposes, far from having been exposed, had been encouraged and even inculcated by decades of propaganda. Many leading nationalist writers grew up in an atmosphere in which they were urged to look for the enemy within, the 'enemy of the people', who was subverting the State and betraying the country to its foreign enemies. Germany had been forced to confront the truth, in its zero hour, but Russia never fully came to terms with Stalinism – much less with its psychological mechanisms. Nor did Russia digest the experience of the Second World War and the genocide of the Jews. Russian nationalists' reaction to de-Stalinisation and the collapse of its empire was thus influenced by their early experience and outlook and by the former regime's unscrupulous ideology.

When *perestroika* started, anti-Semitism was a form of neo-Stalinism and was integrated into its anti-Western ideology. The writer Kuz'min argued against the strand of official communism which emphasised universal values and internationalism:

> [...] The meaning of 'international' cannot be distinguished from 'cosmopolitan'. And what is more, the abstract concept of the 'universal' is the ideology of the cosmopolitan bourgeoisie.

Hence, the struggle against the international bourgeoisie preached by communism, was identical with the fight against the 'cosmopolitan' (that is, Jewish) bourgeoisie. Jewish capitalists pursued their goals through a conspiratorial organisation, Masonry.

> [...] The basic dialectical contradiction of the modern world is the contradiction between work and capital [...] The real masonic organisation incarnates the principles of the corporative bourgeois state, where each gets his share of what has been stolen from the working population in accordance with his place in the secret or open hierarchy.[103]

Thus Soviet Russia's campaign against capitalism was also necessarily a campaign against the Jewish people.

As *perestroika* developed, however, and fewer people continued to believe or proclaim their belief in the righteous struggle against capitalism and the West, anti-Semitism too began to change. Like anti-Western and anti-reform sentiment, it became increasingly strident in the late 1980s. There were a number of reasons for this – among them, resentment of Western influence, fears about the loss of the empire and the uncertainty and disorientation caused by the assault on Stalinist ideology, in which many had long blindly believed. The instinctive reaction to the revelations about the economic and social failures of the communist system and about the crimes committed under Stalin was to look for a scapegoat. A theory which rapidly gained currency was that which suggested that the Russian revolution and the policies pursued under Lenin and Stalin were all part of a Jewish plot. 'There is no need to guess about the role of the masons in the February revolution', Kuz'min affirmed. '[...] It is now well known that only one Minister of the Provisional Government was not a mason.'[104] What this masonic presence might mean was explained by Kozhinov. 'The idea of the complete denationalisation of Russia, of its culture and language, by no means occupied the last place in the political programme of the Trotskyite [...] bloc,' Kozhinov assured his readers in November 1986. (Trotskyites were taken to mean Jews, because Trotsky was a Jew). The modernism of the 1920s, its attacks on the traditional in art and culture were part of a conspiracy against Russia and its peasantry. The fact that many young people today failed to understand this meant that they were also unable to grasp what was happening around them. 'It was also essential to know and understand past tragedies, because they have still not been fully overcome and because it is necessary to prevent their repetition.'[105]

Within a few years, the caution which had prevented Kozhinov from saying exactly what he meant was no longer necessary. In what was supposed to be a review of the peasant poets of the 1920s and 1930s, the editor of *Nash sovremennik* Stanislav Kunaev tried to suggest that the fate of the Russian 'national' peasantry during collectivisation was engineered by Jewish Bolsheviks. Why then should anyone feel pity for them, when they were destroyed in 1937?[106] A much-toted pretext for failing to support Alexander Yakovlev's efforts in rehabilitating those killed during the Terror and his general condemnation of Stalinism was the argument that this was a one-sided campaign – which ignored the sufferings of the people, especially during collectivisation, and confined itself to elements within the Party leadership.[107] '[...] Now those who conducted the genocide of the Russian people, and other peoples too, are trying to pass themselves off as victims,' commented Valentin Pikul', one of the principal exponents of this line of reasoning. Besides, the leadership itself was a dubious force. *Nash sovremennik* printed a list of people with Jewish-sounding names who had held high office in the 1920s and 1930s. It was, the journal suggested, like a telephone directory. Nowadays, however, there was not a single Jewish name in the Foreign Ministry or other high echelons of the bureaucracy. Was this proof of discrimination against Jews? No, it was suspicious: could it really be true that there were no Jews in the higher administration? Obviously not, he suggested, they were there, hidden. As for Gorbachev, he was their conscious or unconscious agent: 'If one is to believe M.S. Gorbachev when he says that he has returned to the Leninist path, then he must also bring Jews back into the Kremlin [...]'.[108]

From this to believing in a fully fledged conspiracy was but a short step. 'Russia has always had many enemies', the writer Pikul' observed.[109] Chief among these were the forces of Jewish masonry:

> The masons' main aim is the conquest of the whole world. Most masonic symbols and rituals are taken from Judaism. The masons' arguments about freedom, equality, fraternity are verbal trumpery and are intended to mask the real aims [...] The denial of love of the Motherland, of historical memory, the destruction of the family, of national and patriotic feelings are one of the modern masons' principal tasks,' Pikul' explained, summarizing the views of neo-Stalinist anti-Semites.[110]

He had written a book exposing how these 'secret forces' had undermined the Russian monarchy. Entitled *Unclean Forces*, it had been published in an abridged form in *Nash sovremennik* in 1979 – thereby unleashing a furore and provoking sharp attacks from such critics as Valentin Oskotsky, who accused Pikul' (hardly unfairly!) of anti-Semitism. Pikul' claimed that Central Committee Secretary Zimyanin had telephoned him, on the publication of his work on Rasputin, to say that he had placed 'us all in a very difficult position' – which, if true, suggests that Pikul' enjoyed sympathy in high quarters, even if it could not be openly expressed. Pikul' became an almost total recluse, believing his life to be at risk (and enjoying the sympathy of many on the right as a result).[111] His morbid fantasies continued to enjoy some popular appeal, however. An unexpurgated version of *Unclean Forces* appeared in a provincial literary magazine in 1989,[112] while it was on sale all over Moscow in the Spring of 1992.

In this context, therefore, it comes as no surprise to find another writer extolling the merits of the *Protocols of the Elders of Zion*. This officially inspired Tsarist forgery, which purported to present a plan for a Jewish take-over of the world (and which was openly on sale in Moscow from 1990 on)[113] was studied by Stanislav Kunaev, who found it illuminating:

> This is a book of iron instruction and recommendations about the creation of a mechanism of power over the people; a book about how to govern the people, how to 'divide and rule', [...] how to complete State negotiations and to use mass revolutionary movements for the aims of the caste [...] It was written by anonymous evil demons [...].

It deserved a place in the library beside Macchiavelli, Nietzsche, Trotsky, Pol Pot and Hobbes. The only way of dealing with the 'Hebrew element' was to bring it out into the open and make Jews adapt to other nationalities. This was all the more necessary in that the existence of a Jewish plot had been exposed by writers like Begun and Romanenko, who had studied the evidence afforded by the Zionist movement.[114] (Romanenko was a prominent figure in the neo-fascist movement in Leningrad, while Begun – who enjoyed an academic position in the Belorussian Academy of Sciences – was embroiled in controversies in the late 1980s on account of his virulent anti-Semitism. Both were linked with *Pamyat*').[115]

In short, in the view of these writers and their supporters, a war of sorts was being conducted. The critic Kazintsev claimed to have found a book, in which Trotsky, Sverdlov, Martov were celebrated as heroes of Israeli history. Why did they deserve this accolade? Because, in the words of Kazintsev's alleged source, '"they directly or indirectly tried to annihilate our greatest enemies – Orthodox goys"'.[116] The reality of this source is not of immediate concern to us here; what is of interest is that such a text could be deemed worthy of attention – or considered as proof of a political plot to undermine Russia. A writers' conference in Leningrad University in 1987 indicated that these views were by no means the preserve of a small number of isolated writers. A note from the floor was sent up to the panel observing: 'In my opinion, some ministries and departments are directed by our enemies from over the ocean.' Mikhail Lemeshev, an economist who published in right-wing nationalist journals, responded that he 'did not have the right to deny that economic war is being conducted' and that the 'weakening of our economic potential is the aim of our enemies'.[117] At the same meeting, a theatre critic and neo-fascist activist Mark Lyubomudrov, alleged that 'Russophobes' were running the theatre world in the hope of 'annihilating Russian talent'. This campaign had been underway for many years – several notable writers and critics had died in its cause:

> Vampilov, of course, did not die. He perished, like an intelligence officer in combat. In that [...] battle, the critic Shukshin, the poet Rubtsov, the artist Vasiliev [...], the critic Seleznev perished [...] Vampilov died at the very start of the Third World War, which we are continuing to wage today.[118]

This was by no means exceptional rhetoric or an isolated example of extreme anti-Semitism.

The Russian Writers' Union (to which most of the writers we have been considering belonged) was notorious for its anti-Semitism in the late 1980s. Its proceedings became increasingly strident – provoking deep divisions in the Writers' Union and in particular within its Moscow branch. The Plenum of the Managing Board of the Russian Writers' Union, held in November 1989, was particularly vitriolic. Consider the intervention of the critic Tatyana Glushkova (who rose to prominence chiefly through her participation in the polemical battles of the late 1980s). The current debates in literary circles were: 'an argument between Zionism, the worst form of universal fascism, and humanity'. Glushkova represented humanity: her opponents, such as the writers Pristavkin and Yevtushenko, were to be understood to represent fascism. 'How many Russian writers, the true sons of the Russian land [...] are to groan under the heel of the oppressor, of usurpers?' They were suffering like Palestinian children. The assembled intellectuals should help their brothers, for 'Russian blood [...] is not just water [*voditsa*]'. She went on to defend an anti-Semitic speech made by another writer, the previous day and, addressing the editor Anatoly Ananiev, declared: 'You will not wipe clean with all your black blood the poet's righteous blood.'[119] This was a reference to Anatoly Ananiev's supposed treachery in publishing in the journal *Oktyabr'* Sinyavsky's *Walk with Pushkin*, which was interpreted by the right as a Jewish attack on Russia's greatest poet. At the end of these extraordinary proceedings, Yuri Bondarev, Chairman of the Russian Writers' Union, who had co-presided at the meeting, responded to criticisms with the comment: 'Where are the proofs of this same anti-Semitism?'[120]

It is hardly surprising, in the light of these incendiary exhortations by those who claimed to be among the country's educated elite, that more simple folk were ready to move from theory to action. In

Krasnodar, a Union of Russian Nationalists, founded on 18 January 1992, called for the re-formation of the Black Hundreds, to defend home, country and family from the enemy (the *nedrug*).[121] This proposal to re-establish the pre-revolutionary bands responsible for the pogroms had its antecedents – notably in the proto-fascist movement, *Pamyat'* which developed with *perestroika* and with which leading nationalist writers were to flirt in the late 1980s – thereby provoking the bitter criticisms of their liberal counterparts. These views did not go uncontested, however, with the papers *Sovetskaya kul'tura* and *Izvestiya* challenging manifestations of anti-Semitism in the courts (no doubt with Alexander Yakovlev's encouragement).[122]

F) OPPOSITION TO *PERESTROIKA*

Given these antagonisms, it was perhaps predictable that the nationalists' hostility to reform should be voiced unambiguously. Conservative nationalists' open opposition to *perestroika* was first expressed in March 1987 at a meeting of the secretariat of the board of the RSFSR Writers' Union, when its First Secretary, Sergei Mikhalkov, aligned himself with the conservative Politburo member, Ligachev, remarking: 'Behind the slogans "Long live *glasnost'*!" and "Long live *perestroyka*!" there are concealed ... speculators, mediocrities and very shady people.' Yuri Bondarev agreed, comparing the situation with that which prevailed in

> July 1941 [...] when the progressive forces, showing unorganised resistance, retreated before the battering onslaught of civilised barbarians ... If this retreat should continue and the time of Stalingrad not come, then it will end with our national values and everything which represents the spiritual pride of the people being toppled into the abyss.

Ligachev responded positively, endorsing these warnings in July 1987.[123] For the next three years, sharp battles were to be fought, ostensibly about culture but essentially about State policy and the power of the conservative and nationalist establishment within the regime.[124]

At the outset, the nationalists' opposition to *perestroika* was expressed principally in their attacks on the literary works, in which the earliest denunciations of Stalinism and the old order were voiced.[125] Apart from their ideological objections to the content of these novels, developments in the literary press and the Writers'

Union posed a serious challenge to their interests. As the nationalists held key positions in both the Soviet and the Russian Writers' Union – in effect, having almost total control of the latter and exercising decisive influence in the former – liberals had moved towards secession. The first step in this direction was taken with the establishment, on 10 March 1989, of *Aprel'*, a committee of 'Writers in Support of Perestroika' headed by Anatoly Pristavkin.[126] Liberal writers initially wanted not to split the Union but to effect a democratic reform of its structures and turn its activities away from political control towards the protection of writers' civic and professional rights; to this end, they proposed new democratic rules for the Union.[127] At its inaugural meeting, Pristavkin declared that they did not want an independent union but legislation to protect writers from censorship and arbitrariness.[128] Within weeks of its creation, *Aprel'* drew about 350 writers to its ranks – including many of the most distinguished (Adamovich, Rybakov, Iskander, Tolstaya, Voznesensky, Yevtushenko and Okudzhava) – a figure which rose to around 600 the following year.[129] Before long, *Aprel'* was involved in most liberal and democratic fora – including Memorial, Moscow Tribune and subsequently Democratic Russia.[130]

Not surprisingly, their conservative opponents felt threatened by these developments – Yuri Bondarev even referring to the activities of *Aprel's* committee as a 'tank attack'.[131] One of the sharpest of these criticisms, which resumed most of the right-wingers' reservations about *Aprel'*, was published in *Den'* in July 1991. It claimed:

> [...] It is you and your co-believers, who fill up the parliaments, offices, ministries, editorial offices and who, under the appearance of renewal during the five years of destruction of the USSR, annihilated the institutions of power, killed the economy, science and culture, impelled the people towards misery, fratricide and mass emigration [...][132]

The bitterness with which *Aprel'*'s foundation was greeted was beyond doubt. Speaking at the Russian Writers' Union Plenum in November 1989, Valentin Rasputin believed that the Union should split because of the incompatibility of the two groups: 'It is a question of a different attitude to the people, to culture, to morality; we cannot go on together.'[133] In Tatyana Glushkova's view, the formation of *Aprel'* was a provocation. Its supporters' speeches were even worse than their writings: she had been appalled, at a meeting, to see them foaming at the mouth, saying abominations about Russia and the Russians.[134]

The scandal which erupted over the attempt by a neo-fascist group (Konstantin Smirnov-Ostashvili's *Pamyat'*) to break up an *Aprel'* meeting at the Central House of Writers on 10 January 1990,[135] added to the bitterness of the exchanges between the two camps in the literary world. *Aprel'* responded by adopting a declaration which condemned some members of the Russian Writers' Union for their active complicity with *Pamyat'* and their ideological support for racism and anti-Semitism. Rejecting anti-Semitism, chauvinism and imperialism, *Aprel'* observed that these attitudes strengthened the hand of those who wanted to impose a form of dictatorship on Russia. 'We are for democratic pluralism, but not for the abdication to fascism. There is no other name for the propaganda of hatred of other peoples.' They demanded that the government take immediate measures against the wave of anti-Semitism in the country.[136]

Condemned in these sharp terms, it is not surprising that the conservatives struck back[137] with an open letter to the Supreme Soviet and the Central Committee, describing *Aprel'*'s denunciations of the 18 January incident as 'a provocation':

> In recent years under the banner of proclaimed 'democratisation', the building of a 'state of law', under the slogans of the fight against fascism and racism, the forces of social destabilisation have been let loose; on the extreme edges of ideological *perestroika*, the successors of open racism have advanced.

They used the press to promote their noxious aims:

> The representatives of the native population of the country are being poisoned en masse, persecuted and defamed, in a manner unprecedented in history and are in essence being declared 'beyond the law' [...]
>
> The outcasts of current 'revolutionary *perestroika*' are, in the first place, the Russian people.[138]

By now unabashed in their hostility to *perestroika*, the nationalist opposition was also reluctant to condemn *Pamyat'*: it was a small, a necessarily unrepresentative group, they suggested, whose size had been exaggerated. Its nationalism was no more extreme than that of other nationalities, with which the liberals professed sympathy.[139] It was this equivocation – indeed, their apparent sympathy – with the rise of fascism that sealed the division between the right and the left in cultural politics.

CONCLUSION

On the nation, its destiny and its relations with the West, Russian nationalists – neo-Stalinists and dissident Orthodox alike – held views influenced both by nineteenth-century Slavophile thought and, more fundamentally, by the ideology and paranoid atmosphere of Stalinism on the other. The neo-Stalinists, as *perestroika* developed, were impelled towards a form of authoritarianism based less on communist ideology than on romanticized accounts of history and religion. Former dissident nationalists, such as Shafarevich and Osipov, were also broadly inclined towards authoritarianism and they found themselves drawing closer to former neo-Stalinist nationalists like Kuz'min and Kunaev in the late 1980s. They were united in their support for the strong state, military might, the primacy of Russian ethnic interests and in their hostility to the West, liberal political reform and capitalism (all of which were seen as alien to Russia's traditions).[140] These attitudes inevitably led them into conflict with the liberal intelligentsia. While some of the nationalists' concerns were understandable – even arguably valid (on the evils of collectivisation, on pollution, on conservation of the historic heritage, on the spiritual consequences of several decades of hypocrisy, terror and isolation), their treatment of these themes suffered from their partiality, insularity and even xenophobia. As the country emerged from decades of tyranny, their ideas threatened to replace one variety of obscurantism with another, particularly as a new generation of politicians cast around in the ruin of Soviet socialism for new ideas with which to justify old policies.

2 Neo-Fascism

The nationalism espoused by the anti-reform intelligentsia in the late 1980s was essentially conservative: the restoration of the Brezhnevite order was at the heart of its platform. Only with the demise of the Soviet system in late 1991 did this orientation change and the intellectuals adopt more radical positions, demanding the overthrow of the Yeltsin regime. Initially, something approaching a return to the old order was hoped for, but, increasingly, a new nationalist dispensation was envisaged. This evolution towards the radical right was foreshadowed by the nationalist intelligentsia's ambivalent attitude towards *Pamyat'* in the late 1980s. The emergence of this group, and others like it, which were widely seen as neo-fascist, indicated that the intelligentsia were not alone in their authoritarian and xenophobic nationalism and that their ideas were capable of exercising wider appeal.

In the early 1990s, the proliferation of neo-fascist groups preaching xenophobic, authoritarian nationalism was seen as an alarming indication of a society in crisis, vulnerable to political extremism. Particularly after the 1993 elections, democratic opinion in the capitals was increasingly concerned with this threat, of which Zhirinovsky was the most dramatic manifestation.[1] Were these groups really a significant force in the political life of Russia or were they the inevitable product of economic and political upheaval, destined to remain marginal and isolated, indicative only of social malaise?

Is it appropriate to speak of such a phenomenon as fascism in modern Russia? Historians have notoriously failed to agree on the meaning of the term 'fascist' but most have concurred that some characteristics are common to the fascist movements that were born of the inter-war social and political crisis: these include the goal of a renewed, nationalist authoritarian state, expansionist and culturally radical in vocation, militaristic and charismatic in political style and inspired by hostility to liberalism, communism and traditional conservatism.[2] The possession of some or all of these features has enabled historians to categorise some movements as fascist. Stanley Payne has distinguished between the conservative authoritarian right, occasionally popular, and traditional in outlook, from the radical right (which,

34

while often ideologically akin to fascism, lacked its wider support and relied on traditional elites such as the army) and fascism proper, which was distinguished above all by its obsession with cultural and spiritual revolution and its innovative political style.[3] Adopting this classification, Gennady Zyuganov and his followers in the KPRF might be seen as playing a role analogous to that of the conservative right in inter-war Europe while neo-fascists, in modern Russia, would appear to be a marginal force, despite their kinship with radicals, such as Zhirinovsky, and their debt to both traditionalists and radicals in the intelligentsia.

Nonetheless, the similarities between many contemporary Russian nationalists and their fascist predecessors are striking. Modern Russian nationalism, like classic European fascism, has criticised capitalism, Marxism, democracy, individualism and weak state institutions and has been aggressively chauvinistic and xenophobic.[4] If the ideology of modern Russian nationalism is in many ways indebted to inter-war fascism, the debt has not generally been acknowledged. However, some groups and figures have consciously emulated these forerunners and proclaimed fascism as a model to be copied. Not content with offering variations on the theme of the evils of capitalism, democracy and foreigners (especially those from the Caucasus and Jews) they have also tried to distinguish themselves by their political style (affecting the uniforms, rallies, embryonic youth movements and leadership cults characteristic of classical fascism). It is the combination of an aggressively nationalistic ideology, and often explicit admiration for the pioneers of fascism, with a distinctive, political style which will be considered here as defining neo-fascism in modern Russia.[5]

A) THE SOVIET PERIOD

a) *Pamyat'*

Of the early neo-fascist groups which emerged in Russia between 1986 and 1987, Dmitri Vasiliev's *Pamyat'* gained most notoriety. Its origins lay in cultural clubs sponsored by the All-Union Society for the Preservation of Monuments and with the unofficial commemoration of the fourteenth-century battle of Kulikovo field (in which the Russians had defeated the Mongols). Initially formed in 1980, as the 'Society of Booklovers' of the Aviation Industry Ministry, it adopted the name *Pamyat'* (memory) in 1982. Until 1985, the society confined itself to organising cultural evenings to celebrate the Russian national heritage as reflected in architecture, art, poetry and history.[6] Dmitri Vasiliev, formerly a secretary to the nationalist painter Ilya Glazunov, began to attend *Pamyat'*'s meetings in 1984 and by, the end of 1985, the society, now led by Yelena Bekhterova, had become avowedly anti-Semitic. On 4 October 1985, *Pamyat'* organised an evening devoted to Moscow's cultural heritage. Vasiliev spoke, claiming that Moscow's architectural legacy had been deliberately ruined in the 1930s by Lazar Kaganovich (Stalin's associate and Politburo member) and the head of administration for architecture and construction in Moscow: these personages, it was explained, were Jews, who were acting under instructions to destroy the Russian capital.[7] Shortly afterwards, Bekhterova was attacked in the street, as a result of which she was left an invalid. Although those responsible were caught, rumours attributing the incident to Zionists were widely accredited and furnished Vasiliev with a pretext for regaling a *Pamyat'* meeting with a reading of the text of the *Protocols of the Elders of Zion* in December 1985 and claiming that Zionists were plotting to take over the world by the year 2000. After this, Vasiliev effectively took control of the society, turning it into a political rather than a cultural movement.[8]

Pamyat' first came to wider public attention on 6 May 1987, when about four hundred *Pamyat'* supporters demonstrated in Red Square to protest against the proposed victory monument at Poklonnoe Gore.[9] The demonstrators also demanded official recognition and a meeting with Gorbachev and Yeltsin to discuss their concerns.[10] Surprisingly, *Pamyat'*'s leaders were not arrested: on the contrary, Yeltsin met them and, according to his own account, urged them to continue their cultural and conservation work and remove their extremists.[11] This was not an aberration, for Yeltsin reportedly called for dialogue with *Pamyat'* in the context of reviving Russia's spiritual traditions in his 1990 election manifesto.[12]

In fact, little was known about *Pamyat'* or its 'extremists' at this point and it was only after the meeting with Yeltsin that articles in the Russian press began to discuss the movement and criticise its anti-Semitism.[13] *Pamyat'*'s publications contained numerous denunciations of the 'dark forces' and 'enemies' supposedly hidden in the Party and working to destroy the Russian nation, forces which *Pamyat'* soon identified with the liberals, Alexander Yakovlev and Vitaly Korotich. According to *Pamyat'*, these elements represented Trotskyism (the

Jewish plot): since 1917, they had mounted a sustained attack on the Russian people – their culture, economy, ecology and even their existence (with the Terror, their promotion of alcohol and, latterly, the Chernobyl explosion, which they had organised, and their control of the mass media).[14] Criticisms of *Pamyat'* in the liberal press might be ascribed to 'Ziono-Masonic circles devoted to the cult of Satan.'[15] These comments were not as purely fantastic as we might imagine: they were directed at Politburo member Alexander Yakovlev and indicate the kind of venom liberals had to withstand and which they tolerated in Gorbachev's new dispensation.

Between 1986 and 1988, *Pamyat'* continued to campaign on the need to defend Russia and Russian culture from the Jewish 'threat' – organising, early in 1986, several evenings devoted to this theme, culminating in an address to the Russian people:

> We recognize A REAL ENEMY AND HIS SECRET PLANS! But what is he like, this enemy? How can we tell his animal-like face, which is often hidden behind the mask of loyalty and good will? [...] THE ENEMY IS HE, who creates a commotion about anti-Semitism, slavophilism, chauvinism, as soon as it is a question of national culture, history, traditions and customs of the people! [...] THE ENEMY IS HE, who denies the presence of ZIONISM AND MASONRY in our country [...][16]

When the journalist Yelena Losoto attended a *Pamyat'* meeting in 1987, she found all these themes reiterated. Not only was holy Moscow, the Third Rome, destroyed by Zionists, but the media were controlled by 'cosmopolitans'; rock music groups were deemed satanic; science and the economy were being destroyed by 'the enemy'; Masonic-Zionist networks were everywhere. In the light of all these threats, it is not surprising that the audience was called to arms to defend themselves.[17]

Anti-Semitism was the dominant element in *Pamyat'*'s programme but other themes also emerged, although they hardly amounted to a utopian or revolutionary vision of the future. In common with most modern Russian nationalists, *Pamyat'* supporters were essentially backward-looking, although the past to which they aspired was largely idealised and imagined. Their hostility to the modern world was reflected in slogans such as: 'Down with giant cities! The modern city is madness!' Instead, they suggested, Russia should return to the pastoral lifestyle of old: private farming should be encouraged, freedom of conscience guaranteed and the rights of the Orthodox church restored, the Russian language and folk culture renewed.[18] The modern world was decadent and its evident decay was not accidental. The decline of the nation was due to both spiritual neglect and the machinations of the enemy. The rejection of the past and its values, the inculcation of alcoholism, abortion, debased foreign culture, the decline of the family all contributed to the crisis of contemporary Russia.[19]

However, *Pamyat'* offered some proposals for remedying the situation. Vasiliev increasingly emphasized the importance of Orthodoxy for the spiritual renewal of Russia. Russia, he explained in 1989, had made the fatal mistake of replacing spirituality with technocratic progress. As a result, 'we turned a State of Morality, Spirituality, Discipline and Order into embittered, undisciplined, unspiritual and to some extent immoral people'. This was one of the main reasons for the decline of the nation. Now, 'without faith in God, without Orthodoxy [...] it will be impossible to unite the nation'. An important role in the spiritual education of the nation could be played by a national morality guard, which could mount the strictest check on 'the aping of the worst examples [...] of bourgeois so-called culture'. 'Pornographic freedom and all-permissiveness are not freedom of the spirit', commented Vasiliev. 'It is a devilish cabbale'. It was essential to counteract these influences by emphasizing patriotism, national heroism and history and preventing the export of 'evil pop-culture, which flows to us from the backwoods of the West'.[20]

As political freedom grew and the power and prestige of the Party declined, Vasiliev felt able to reject communism *in toto*.[21] However, this did not imply enthusiasm for the West either. From the start, *Pamyat'*'s leaders had voiced their hostility to the West and its culture and, by the end of the 1980s and start of the 1990s, this extended to its political and social organisation.[22] By then, Vasiliev favoured a *zemskii sobor* (the Muscovite era Assembly of the Land) to endorse a return to monarchism, which would help to restore a single, strong Russian state.

Vasiliev's fears about the enemy 'over the ocean' and within were voiced frequently at public meetings in the later 1980s[23] and were apparently applauded enthusiastically by audiences of several hundred people.[24] *Pamyat'* was able to reach out to a wider audience, by means of cassette recordings, which were dispatched to sympathisers who lived elsewhere.[25] It seems clear that their message was well received in some quarters: journalists who criticised *Pamyat'*'s anti-Semitism received a large post, often sympathetic to Vasiliev.[26] The organisation attracted a great deal of attention and by the end of 1987 claimed the support of around 20 000 followers in Moscow. Leningrad *Pamyat'* claimed to enjoy the support of 10 000 sympathisers.[27] Its followers liked to appear in the streets sporting black shirts and boots. By 1990, however, the KGB claimed that *Pamyat'* had only 1000 members throughout Russia.[28]

In 1986–87, *Pamyat'* groups, or bodies with a similar programme, were founded in Leningrad and several Siberian cities.[29] The phenomenon of Russian neo-fascism was, therefore, not confined to Moscow. According to leaders of Leningrad *Pamyat'*, Zionism was the main reason for the collapse of the economy and for cultural and social decadence. The essential aim was to ensure that Russia be governed by Russians and thereafter that the land be given back to the peasantry. Its manifesto explained the movement's *raison d'être* in the following terms:

The national patriotic front *Pamyat'* is a general movement, which has as its aim the rebirth of the Russian as well as of the related Ukrainian and Belorussian peoples while fully respecting other nations. It was born spontaneously, in response to the exceptional humiliation, spiritual and physical annihilation, to which these peoples were subjected in our century. During it, our country lost 60 million people, of whom a large proportion were of Slavic descent. Our ancient culture was [...] mercilessly trampled upon; in the RSFSR [...] 40 per cent of all architectural monuments perished; many talented writers and artists disappeared into the camps; for decades, our history was suppressed [...] We became a people without roots. Everywhere interest in how our ancestors lived is dying, because trivial mass culture, brought to us from the West or created here by a denationalized intelligentsia, has been violently and maliciously inculcated in our empty souls and minds [...] We became a poor people, a people who cannot live without foreign bread, meat and butter. Right before our eyes, we are being transformed into a technically backward power, on a level with India or Brazil. The frightful degeneration and extinction of the Russian people has begun [...] If we do not die out from the declining birthrate, then the polluted water, air and soil will kill us [...] Having made a revolution and won victory in a most cruel war, the Russian people today feels deceived and insulted and in astonishment is asking when and why the bright future disappeared over the horizon.[30]

This manifesto not only reveals the disillusionment and humiliation upon which the new fascism fed but also the similarity of inspiration between at least some neo-fascists and elements in the nationalist intelligentsia. Many of the same concerns were voiced: the decadence of the Russian people, the declining birth-rate, the effects of pollution and mass culture; hostility to the westernising intelligentsia and the West; resentment of Russia's loss of international status and power; fear of becoming an economic colony; and partly critical attitude to the Soviet past – in particular to Stalin's destruction of the country's architectural and cultural legacy. The ideological solidarity between this branch of the fascist movement and the intellectuals writing in *Nash sovremennik* is evident.

However, the neo-fascist movement was neither homogeneous nor united.[31] On the contrary, it was much given to disputation and division. Vasiliev's *Pamyat'* ultimately broke into at least seven groups – distinguished from each other principally by their relation to communism. From the start, Leningrad *Pamyat'* had two wings – pro- and anti-communist. By the late 1980s the prestige of communism had generally declined among the neo-fascists, for whom monarchism and other forms of religious and national authoritarianism became more important.[32] The first split in the Moscow organisation arose when, in mid-1987, Igor Sychev and his followers left Vasiliev, initially professing a form of national socialism. Igor Sychev, a member of the Union of Artists, and Tamara Ponomareva (of the Writers' Union) headed a *Pamyat'* movement which called for:

SOCIALISM NOT FOR THE SAKE OF THE STATE SYSTEM, BUT SOCIALISM FOR THE SAKE OF THE PEOPLE *[narod]*. TO NATIONAL SOCIALISM FROM STATE SOCIALISM THROUGH NATIONAL REBIRTH!

They demanded separate cultural, academic and political institutions for Russia, proportional representation of Soviet nationalities in political and public institutions (thus ensuring Russian dominance therein) and an end to russophobia (criticism of xenophobic nationalism in the liberal press).[33] They also expressed their hostility to economic and cultural liberalisation.[34] Sychev stressed the importance of 'de-Zionisation', subscribed to the theory that the Revolution had gone off the rails because 'non-native' people had seized key positions of

State and had proceeded to destroy the Russian people, through direct oppression and cultural warfare (including inculcation of alcoholism).[35] Sychev's *Pamyat'* was intended to be a respectable version of the movement, but its links with the Party establishment became weaker as Sychev moved towards monarchism.

Another *Pamyat'* leader in Moscow was Konstantin Smirnov-Ostashvili, who originally supported Sychev but founded his own *Pamyat'* organisation in Autumn 1989 to concentrate on anti-Semitic propaganda.[36] In Autumn 1989, Nikolai Filimonov was expelled for alleged financial dishonesty: as a result, Filimonov and his supporters founded a rival organisation, also called *Pamyat'*; maintaining close links with the Society for the Preservation of Historic Monuments, this group also supported monarchism, by late 1989.[37] In 1990 Filimonov's group split – with the emerging rump identifying with Stalin and Hitler in their fight against Zionism. Valery Yemelyanov led a pagan branch of *Pamyat'* that considered Christianity a form of Zionism. In Moscow, the National Bolshevik wing of *Pamyat'* was led by the Popov brothers from 1987 on.[38] None of these groups had more than a handful of members but their political and social impact was considerable – partly because of the attention paid to them in the press and partly because of the support they enjoyed among sections of the intelligentsia and the Party.[39]

b) Nationalist Intelligentsia and *Pamyat'*

Pamyat' owed an intellectual debt to the authoritarian nationalist intelligentsia.[40] The ascription of the Bolshevik revolution and then Terror to a Judaeo-Masonic conspiracy, the designation of alcoholism as part of a campaign against the Russian people, the hostility to the liberal mass-media were not confined to *Pamyat'* and marginal circles of unbalanced fanatics. It was shared by some members of the Writers' Union and might also be encountered in the pages of official literary journals, such as *Nash sovremennik*. Some *Pamyat'* leaders went further than deriving their ideas and declaring their sympathy for the nationalist intelligentsia and their journals: they attempted to organise support for them. One of *Pamyat'*'s leaders, Konstantin Smirnov-Ostashvili (the leader of the attack on the *Aprel'* liberal writers' club meeting in the Central Writers' House in January 1990) founded the 'Club of the Friends of the Journal *Nash sovremennik*' in February 1989. Later this Club extended its support to *Molodaya gvardiya*,[41] which published Novosibirsk *Pamyat'*'s programme in July 1990.[42]

If leaders of various *Pamyat'* groups professed admiration for right-wing writers, they, on occasion, reciprocated, much to the indignation of their liberal critics. The journalist Losoto's famous article in *Komsomolskaya pravda*, on 22 May 1987, which opened the campaign of criticism of *Pamyat'*, induced the nationalist critic Vadim Kozhinov to criticise Losoto herself and to suggest that *Pamyat'* was not as bad as she suggested. Losoto's attacks on *Pamyat'* amounted, he implied, to an attack – from a Trotskyite perspective – on the Russian people (whose cause *Pamyat'* claimed to represent). She tried to justify the destruction of historic monuments: she failed to admit that the ruin of Russian culture was part of a plan implemented, from 1927 on, by 'those for whom Tyutchev was "organically alien"'. Her suggestion that the blowing up of the Cathedral of Christ the Saviour was to be deplored on aesthetic or religious grounds was ridiculous: the significance of the building was military, it symbolised 'above all a popular victory and not "the Tsar and God"'. *Pamyat'*, it was true, did not attract him: it included too many demagogues – but deformations were always to be expected in the discussion of any complex problem and excesses were inevitable at the start of any movement. *Pamyat'* had many worthwhile cultural and historic aims and should not simply be dismissed. '[...] Is her article not a far more dangerous "deformation" of *glasnost'*, than even the most dubious cries of *Pamyat'*'s orators?' he asked in conclusion.[43]

Apollon Kuz'min joined in this castigation of Losoto (and of Yuri Afanasiev, who had also criticised *Pamyat'*):

> [...] Such serious charges – of chauvinism, fascism, anti-Semitism, which both authors whine about, must be proved. In fact, how is the unbiased reader to know why Zionist readers' letters are anti-Semitic forgeries and anti-Semitic ones [...] are without fail by *Pamyat'*? The reader does not understand these arguments because for many decades fascism's and anti-Semitism's predatory grin has been seen most clearly in the Lebanon, on the West Bank of the Jordan, in the Gaza Sector, where the genocide of the great Semitic Arabic peoples is hidden by the ideals of the slave-holding epoch [*sic*].

Losoto, Afanasiev and others who attacked *Pamyat'* were really engaged in attacking the Russian people: 'In all these and similar publications, it is a question of [...] the people's historic memory. It is against precisely this which the fight is really being waged.' The origins of these attitudes lay in the 1920s: the idea was to cut the people off from their past so that they could more easily be manipulated. The consequences of this policy – the destruction of monuments, people, culture and traditions – could not simply be blamed on the command administrative system: someone manipulated and inspired this system. The implication, not explicitly stated by Kuz'min, seems to have been that Jews and Masons were again responsible. Kuz'min went on to defend Vasiliev (and *Pamyat'*) from his critics, suggesting that they were championing the cause of the Russian people.[44]

Most writers who expressed a degree of support and sympathy for *Pamyat'* did so because of their interest in the long-suffering Russian people and in the preservation of Russian cultural monuments and of the countryside. Few were repelled either by its anti-Semitism or authoritarianism, which, as we have seen, were in fact shared by many nationalist writers. When Valentin Rasputin intervened in the debate, in July 1987,[45] to express a measure of support for *Pamyat'*, he compromised his reputation. Unlike Kuz'min and Kozhinov, Rasputin was respected as a writer and his remarks caused an instant furore. Having insisted on the importance of historical memory, Rasputin went on to extol the virtues of the informal conservation movement. Rasputin was one of the early champions of the cause of conservation in Russia and thus had a natural interest in its development as an independent public movement. He seems, however, to have believed that *Pamyat'* was no more than a respectable cultural, conservation lobby. Listing all the signs of decay in Soviet society, he asked, was it at all surprising that people wondered who was guilty and that they came to extreme conclusions. *Pamyat'*, he said, had not been allowed to answer the charges made against it in the press. The real reason they were assimilated with the Black Hundreds was because the extreme left wanted to heap the blame for current problems on them. The people who had betrayed Russia needed to find a scapegoat, so as to save their caste interests. *Pamyat'* was a convenient victim of their machinations. What was happening now resembled the events of the 1920s: 'patriots' and 'memory' were now terms of insult and it was forbidden to recall or celebrate the Russian past, which was condemned as primitive. The reason that he devoted so much attention to *Pamyat'*, Rasputin explained, was because he feared that criticisms addressed to it would undermine the rest of the conservation movement also.[46] It is clear that Rasputin sympathised with *Pamyat'*'s professed concern for Russia, its culture and people and that he believed it to be more worthwhile than its critics, whose self-interest and dishonesty he denounced. His harsh condemnation of *Pamyat"*s critics – which echoed, though in rather more measured tones, those of Kuz'min and Kozhinov – included no word of censure for *Pamyat"*s anti-Semitism.

Alexander Kazintsev was closer to Kuz'min in his clear obsession with anti-Semitism. Discussing criticisms of *Nash sovremennik* writers and of *Pamyat'* for anti-Semitism, he insisted that russophobia really existed – for example, among *refusniks* and abroad (in the historian Richard Pipes) – and that he and his companions had every right to discuss it. The journalists Losoto and Petrov (the latter a scourge of the right from *Sovetskaya kul'tura*) were attempting to destabilise Russia – and not content with rhetoric, had already passed to action.[47] The editor of *Nash sovremennik*, Stanislav Kunaev, agreed. Russophobia was a real force in society. 'The *Pamyat'* society exists [...] because the anti-Zionist committee headed by [...] people of exclusively Jewish extraction completely fails to function'. The OGPU, Party leadership and Gulag had not been run by Russians. Now Vasiliev had been threatened by the KGB – it was clear that the old pattern was being repeated: '[...] Only the Russian movement is threatened with repression.'[48]

Stanislav Kunaev expressed his views at greater length in an interview published in March 1989. All Soviet history had represented an attack on the Russian people, its culture and traditions:

> [...] After all this, the emergence of the society *Pamyat'* is a natural, legitimate reaction of the national organism, a reaction to the russophobia (fear of everything Russian and hatred of it) which is deeply rooted in our society.[...] *Pamyat'*, having developed in the middle of the 1970s, was the first to raise the most important questions of our time: it fought against the river diversion project, when it was forbidden to speak of this in the press; it fought against the policy of making drunkards of the people, when during the years of stagnation this was an official economic policy; it fought for the conservation of Russian cultural monuments. I relate to the *Pamyat'* society as does Valentin Rasputin. I understand the pain of these people on account of Russia, of its current position, of all the ruin and humiliation it has suffered.

Pamyat' supporters had some deficiencies: little erudition, inability to debate convincingly, a preference for meetings rather than educational work, poor organisation. 'But these are the shortcomings of any currently active, young informal movement.' *Pamyat'* was now fighting to save the Volga. Was this bad? No – what was bad was *Pamyat'*'s lack of access to the media and to the organs of power: only Russia lacked a Central Committee and other agencies to represent its interests.

> I think the isolation of *Pamyat'* and its persecution by the press is a consequence of *Pamyat'*'s touching directly on the Russian–Jewish problem. But it [this problem] really exists. Does *Pamyat'* consider *Nash sovremennik* as being on its side? I do not know. I am not acquainted with the society's leaders. But if it is so, let them read on.[49]

Kunaev summarised the position of most writers who were ready to indicate their support for *Pamyat'*: the movement deserved to be praised for its defence of the Russian people and Russian culture; if it was anti-Semitic, there was no reason to be ashamed – on the contrary, *Pamyat'* was exposing a truth, which its critics were anxious to hide.

Many prominent members of the nationalist intelligentsia pledged their support – or qualified support – for *Pamyat'*. Some were careful about how they framed their comments. The painter Ilya Glazunov explained his position on *Pamyat'* cautiously:

> [...] I have always been and remain a Russian man, a Soviet citizen, a patriot, an internationalist. I have no contact with *Pamyat'*. There are many good people among *Pamyat'*'s members – patriots of the country, of the Soviet people. I regret to think that as well as these healthy forces in our society there are sometimes adventurers and chauvinists [...] I am in favour of patriotism, for real service of the cause of conservation of national monuments [...] We must emphasise what is positive.[50]

This amounted to the kind of carefully worded approval pledged by Rasputin. The Siberian writer Viktor Astafiev was, typically, less guarded in his response but he seems to have been unclear about political developments within *Pamyat'* in Moscow and Leningrad. In August 1987, he commented that he knew little about *Pamyat'* but those whom he knew to be involved in the movement in Irkutsk were learned, decent and respectable people. The press deprived the movement of the right to explain its position; free speech was being denied. Its good work on culture, ecology, forest conservation and folklore was all ignored. The Party wanted to suppress the movement 'and if you want to know my position in this storm, if it breaks out, then I will be on *Pamyat'*'s side [...] I will be for truth and for the people!'.[51]

Viktor Aksyuchits, the Moscow-based leader of the Christian Democratic movement, who could have been in no doubt about *Pamyat'*'s character, tended to agree:

> I am pleased that in *Pamyat'* many of our topical problems have been openly raised for the first time. I think that in certain circles of the capital's intelligentsia very exaggerated ideas exist about the dangers posed by the *Pamyat'* society.[52]

Members of the Russian Writers' Union, who drafted an open letter of complaint about their liberal critics, agreed that the dangers posed by *Pamyat'* were exaggerated: these calls were used to try to hide the real dangers posed to Russia by Zionism.[53] There is evidence to suggest that the wing of the literary establishment which opposed *perestroika* generally sympathised with *Pamyat'*. Vasiliev managed to address a nationalist writers' meeting in Leningrad in 1987, when his condemnations of democracy and *perestroika* were applauded.[54] Support for *Pamyat'* was even expressed in an extremely anti-Semitic intervention at the November 1989 Plenum of the Russian Writers' Union.[55] These attitudes were sharply condemned by intellectuals of a more liberal inclination. Academician Dmitri Likhachev, suggesting that the opponents of *perestroika* did not really belong to the intelligentsia, commented that too few writers had taken a position against *Pamyat'* and pointed out that silence could have dangerous consequences. Fedor Burlatsky, Gavriil Popov, Natalya Ivanova were among those who condemned the nationalist intelligentsia's indulgence for *Pamyat'*.[56] The sympathy extended to *Pamyat'* by some writers pointed to a flawed political culture. But *Pamyat'* did not succeed in attracting broad popular support. It was weakened by scandal and rivalry and its early popularity proved short-lived. Instead, in the post-Soviet period, it was overtaken by other neo-fascist groups, whose leaders had in many cases been introduced to extremist politics by Vasiliev. Until the fall of the Soviet regime, *Pamyat'* seemed as unrepresentative of the political climate as neo-fascist groups elsewhere. This situation was to change, however, with the deepening economic and social crisis after 1991, when neo-fascist groups proliferated and when ideas on which they drew began to infiltrate mainstream politics, influencing the language of the political elite.

B. The Post-Soviet Period

The political and economic crisis after 1991 clearly furnished a propitious climate for the development of neo-fascist movements. After the violence associated with the Parliament's resistance to Yeltsin's decision to disband it and Zhirinovsky's success at the polls in December 1993, commentators were especially agitated by the threat of fascism.[57] Such was the perceived danger that the President issued a decree on 23 March 1995 to improve attempts to prosecute and eradicate neo-fascist and extremist groups. The ineffectual character of the decree prompted some analysts to speculate that it was inspired more by the desire to win the forthcoming Duma and Presidential elections than by any real concern about fascism.[58] In early Spring and Summer 1995, the Duma held hearings on the fascist threat at the suggestion of Russia's Democratic Choice. However, given the propensity of nationalists to refer to democrats as fascists (and vice versa), the proceedings were rendered ineffective and confusing, with two contradictory draft laws being introduced, one sponsored by moderate communists and democrats against fascist propaganda (in the normal sense) and another proposed by Zhirinovsky's LDPR and national communists against fascist (in the sense of liberal democratic) activity. Ultimately, neither these, nor an anti-fascist law proposed by Moscow City Council were adopted.[59] Existing legislation was clearly inadequate in preventing neo-fascists from publicising their activities and ideas, but to what extent this was due to the nature of the laws rather than the law-enforcing agencies and their attitudes is difficult to determine.[60] Arguably, it was not the disaffected extremists of neo-fascism who undermined Russian democracy but the shortcomings of the political elite, which paid lip-service to democracy while doing little to strengthen it institutionally or socially by their policies or practices.[61]

a) Russian National Unity

Of the many neo-fascist groups which emerged in the early 1990s, Russian National Unity (RNU) was among the most notorious.[62] It was founded in 1990 by Alexander Barkashov, a former member of *Pamyat'* and bodyguard of Dmitri Vasiliev.[63] Barkashov sought inspiration in *Mein Kampf* and claimed that he and his supporters were 'national-socialists'.[64] The ideology to which the RNU subscribed was inspired, above all, by racism and xenophobia. Twentieth-century Russian history could be explained only in this light, Barkashov suggested. The 1917 revolution, whose genocidal consequences for the Russian people were indisputable, had been engineered by Western imperialists bent on the exploitation of the manpower and resources of the rest of the world. The only barrier in the way of these rapacious capitalists in their search for world domination was collectivist

Russian autocracy, the political antithesis of the Western world. Hence, it had been necessary to destroy the Russian empire by fomenting revolution. The agents of revolution, were of course, Jewish intriguers bent on the subjugation of the Russian people.[65]

Perestroika was only the latest stage in this process: it had been initiated when foreign exploiters had decided to cast off the mask of communism and move on to the direct and accelerated pillage of Russia.[66] Similarly, the collapse of the Soviet state was not an accident but had been deliberately provoked. Now, the Russian people were to be further weakened by the promotion of democracy, political pluralism and separatism. They could resist this attack only by uniting on the basis of race and blood:

> Russia's enemies are making every effort to destroy the national unity of the Russian people once and for all, through different political parties, the artificial sharpening of social conflicts, alien religions and sectarian teachings [...] We must form a national movement not on political, social or religious bases but on the basis of common origins – blood kinship and commonality of national character – spiritual kinship.[67]

Barkashov vented his particular ire on the USA and Jews. The USA was populated by morally dubious misfits and inferior races. This international mish-mash naturally engendered a State both decadent and aggressive:

> This international rabble, spiced with a pretty quantity of negroes, brought from Africa, became the basic element in the so-called 'great American nation', which built the State of the USA and constructed a new Babylon [...] Today, the USA rules over the West and wants to rule over the whole world [...]. Vampirish, parasitical 'Western civilisation', principally the USA, is the foreign-policy manifestation of those forces hostile to the Russian People.

The USA itself, and especially its arms industry, was ruled by the Jewish bourgeoisie and, hence, the West and America represented a familiar enemy. Naturally, the RNU could not compromise with these forces.

> Our strategic line in relation to the USA and 'Western civilisation' has been splendidly expressed in a popular song of the 1930s, written [...] on just this theme: '[...] We'll plunge a knife into the vampire's throat and the world will become good again!'[68]

Despite Barkashov's references to Hitler, he was clearly indebted also to the anti-Western and anti-Semitic campaigns of later Stalinism and to the paranoid and aggressive political culture it encouraged, with its emphasis on hidden internal enemies and militarism.

Not surprisingly, Barkashov rejected democracy and liberalism. Democracy was a fraud: in reality, political parties were controlled by those who financed them (inevitably, these were identified with Russia's Jewish enemies). Democracy was: 'a nonsensical idea. Never and nowhere had it really been put into practice (for in reality power can only be in the hands of an elite).' It had been adopted 'by Zionists and masons to debase nations and seize world domination'.[69] Liberalism involved sacrificing the State and nation to the individual, with ultimately pernicious effects.[70] Instead, Barkashov favoured an authoritarian government, which would act in the interests of all social groups but would not permit the nation to be weakened and divided by political parties.[71] Dissent and difference would not be tolerated: hence, russophobia (criticism of nationalist policies) would be punishable by law, only Russian national religions would be tolerated. Although private property would be permitted and private farming encouraged, socialist policies would be pursued to promote national unity: workers would be guaranteed minimum wages and rights, social security would be paid, the State would own natural resources, which could not be traded or sold off. Given the importance of national regeneration, strict laws would be implemented to protect the nation's genetic stock: intermarriage with elements which would damage the purity of the genetic stock would not be permitted, eugenics were to be encouraged, a higher birth-rate, maternity and family values were to be promoted.[72] Central Asians and Caucasians would be allowed to live in their historic lands but the RNU would introduce strict birth-control laws 'to cut their numbers down to a minimum'. Jews would not be allowed to emigrate to Europe and Israel lest this strengthen the hand of Zionists.[73] Barkashov did not go into details about his plans for Russia's Jewish population – although he indicated that they would be deprived of civil rights – but his professed admiration for Hitler and propensity to deny the reality of the Holocaust was indicative of his intentions.[74]

As his prescription for the new Russia could not be implemented immediately, Barkashov proposed action to hasten the RNU's advent to power. He argued for the need for a new young elite, prescribed the formation of RNU units throughout the country, devoted to propaganda and military and sports training of cadres.[75] RNU was strictly organised, with a military unit at its heart. Only 'racially clean' elements were allowed to join.[76] What mattered, according to Barkashov, was to come to power, whether peacefully or by force.[77]

Barkashov meant what he said. He claimed to have supported the 1991 coup and the RNU took an active part in opposition politics, joining for a time both Sterligov's Russian National Council and the National Salvation Front, although it believed both organisations to be devoted to outdated political ideas.[78] It sent volunteers to fight in Abkhazia, Pridnestrovie (the breakaway Russian enclave in Moldova) and Serbia against enemies of the Orthodox Slavs.[79] What galvanised public attention, however, was the RNU's participation in the White House's resistance to President Yeltsin's attempt to disband it. From 21 September 1993, Barkashov furnished a unit of over 100 armed guards to defend the parliament and it took an active part in the subsequent fighting in Moscow. As a result of this, the movement was banned and Barkashov arrested, until he was amnestied by the Duma in February 1994.[80] He admitted that the RNU was motivated more by hatred of Yeltsin and his 'pro-Zionist, pro-American dictatorship' and his hope of seizing power in the chaos than by any great love for Khasbulatov, Rutskoi or parliamentary government.[81]

Despite these credentials, the RNU was free to engage in propaganda and demonstrations the following year.[82] Claiming a network of 350 regional groups, the RNU's membership and organisation seemed impressive and it was reckoned by some experts to be the most substantial of the neo-fascist parties. However, estimates of its membership varied wildly: from about 2000 nationwide in 1994 to 25 000 in 1996.[83] It was able to produce a newspaper, with an estimated print-run of 150 000 copies.[84] However, the RNU was weakened by a number of factors. Firstly, Barkashov's poor relations and frequent disputes with potential allies and his refusal to participate in elections isolated and marginalised the party. When a representative of the party stood, exceptionally, for election to the parliament in Autumn, he won only 5.9 per cent of the vote.[85] Secondly, the RNU's overtly racist ideology and militancy damaged its political ambitions. Others were able to exploit the same well of discontent, without incurring the same degree of odium.

b) Neo-fascist luminaries

Barkashov was not an isolated figure on the windswept fringes of Russian political life. His cult of leadership, youth, aggressive athleticism and authoritarianism was shared by other neo-fascists. In Irkutsk, Anton Romanov, a city council deputy and karate instructor, had many evident affinities with Barkashov (which did not prevent him declaring his allegiance to Nikolai Ryzhkov's Power to the People movement and officially supporting Zyuganov in the June 1996 Presidential elections.) Banners hung on his run-down headquarters, proclaiming 'Youth! Beauty! Strength! the Motherland!' Within, scrawny adolescents wrestled beneath numerous photographs of the tubby leader in karate tunic brandishing swords on mountaintops and in deserts. Romanov was reluctant to discuss his views with foreigners, which was partly explained by his belief that the West had undermined the Russian state in order to exploit its wealth and people and that Yeltsin was manipulated by hidden forces who wanted to destroy Russia. Hence, he thought, the military, patriotic education of the young was important. The need to restore Russia as a Great Power, with a large army, was axiomatic. This could only be achieved under a strong leader. None had as yet come to the fore in contemporary Russia: since the demise of Stalin (under whose portrait Romanov sat), Russia had lacked great leaders. Khrushchev and his successors had been incompetent or even treacherous. Zyuganov was only a slight improvement on them and was worthy of support in the 1996 presidential elections only because he alone had a chance of stopping Yeltsin's re-election. Stalin's time had been an age of great leaders – even in the West. Only a renewal of this heroic period could save Russia now.[86] His club's cult of youth, physical fitness and military prowess was an accurate barometer of Romanov's political disposition, which did not prevent him enjoying some popularity in Irkutsk as a part-time educator and local politician.

A neo-fascist who enjoyed national notoriety was the writer Eduard Limonov. Exiled to Paris in the 1970s, Limonov returned to Russia after the fall of the Soviet regime, accepting the post of KGB chief in June 1992 in Zhirinovsky's putative shadow cabinet (a post from which he later resigned on the grounds of Zhirinovsky's alleged Jewish origins). What initially attracted him to Zhirinovsky was his commitment to the restoration of a powerful Russian state.[87] Limonov was bitterly critical of the West. It was a decadent civilisation, devoted to consumption and materialism. It had produced nothing of cultural note for over a generation.[88] Nor was it merely innocuous:

One must understand that human rights are a new form of aggression of Western imperialism [...] It is demanded of us that we – the

Arabs, Russians, Chinese – [...] renounce our own political and
social traditions, [...] we are being forced to adopt capitalism (it is
the same thing as democracy) [...].[89]

The West, he later explained, had, with its many invasions, shown that
it was Russia's enemy. *Perestroika* and democracy had been foisted on
Russia as a means of debasing and destroying Russia.

Instead, Russia should turn east and seek allies in Asia and Islam.
The only remedy was to strive for national regeneration by rebuilding
a powerful Russian state, within the natural boundaries of its civilisation (which Limonov saw as largely coterminous with the Tsarist
empire) and on the basis of Russia's collectivist traditions. A national-
socialist revolution was necessary, Limonov declared, when he
founded his National-Bolshevik party in 1993:

> Only by means of a NATIONAL REVOLUTION can the Russian
> people preserve its territorial, economic, national and cultural
> unity. The three basic principles of the NATIONAL REVOLU-
> TION are: a national Russian policy, [...] a national economy for
> the benefit of all elements in the population, new national
> leaders.[90]

Limonov saw himself in this light and made no secret of his cult of
heroism, self-sacrifice, violence and physical fitness. He professed his
admiration for Mishima (and his body, a 'superb knot of muscles') and
Gabriele d'Annunzio. Russian 'greats' were all victims, whereas he
loved heroes, youth, violence. Luckier than Mishima, he had fought in
Yugoslavia (and regretted being unable to equip the Serbs with
nuclear weapons) and Pridnestrovie and dreamed of a violent death:
'One should die in battle, in a shoot-out, during an uprising.'[91] In all of
his attitudes, Limonov was an unequivocal fascist. For all his desire 'to
find a gang', as he put it, he remained an eccentric figure on the
fringes of Russian politics, interesting as a barometer of intellectual
fashion, on the right, rather than as a political actor.

Another intellectual who flirted with fascist ideas was Alexander
Dugin, one of the leading apologists of the 'conservative revolution'
in post-Soviet Russia. Dugin was indebted to Lev Gumilev for his
Eurasianism, with which he concocted his half-pagan, half-Orthodox
theories for the political and moral regeneration of Russia. Another
source of inspiration was inter-war fascism and national-socialism, to
which he devoted long appreciative articles for the benefit of neo-
phytes in his openly pro-fascist magazine, *Elementy*.[92] To unite the

opposition, Dugin proposed a common ideal of a 'powerful and supranational continental empire', which would restore natural justice to the Russians, fight against russophobia and be a super-power.[93] Eurasia, as Dugin defined it, was not confined to the former Soviet Union but stretched – as the cover of the first issue of *Elementy* made clear – from Vladivostok to Dublin (with a capital located in Moscow, now renamed the Third Rome).[94] To achieve this goal, a revolution against the modern world was required, including the rejection of Western democracy (as the individualistic, atomised, rationalistic West was at odds with the communitarian, metaphysical East).[95] Dugin proposed an authoritarian state, dominated by a heroic elite and inhabited by an aggressive, self-sacrificing nation, interested not in material well-being but in expansion into Eurasia and beyond, and, which, through its triumphs, would become a 'superethnos', a form of 'Godmanhood', 'children of the sun', super-men. Russians would be the core ethnos of the 'new, eschatological nation' (from which Jews would be banned). The new society would be anti-capitalist and socialist.[96] This delirious combination of Gumilev, Soloviev, Nietzsche and theorists of fascism, contemporary and historical, might normally have been expected to confine Dugin to, at the least, disreputable obscurity but, instead, he was a regular contributor to the opposition press, where he was presented as an authoritative intellectual.

One of the best-known apologists of neo-fascism was the Leningrad broadcaster, Alexander Nevzorov. Initially and mistakenly seen as a hero of *perestroika*, on account of his sharp exposés of crime on Leningrad television, Nevzorov aligned himself unequivocally with the enemies of democracy in January 1991 and remained a consistent critic of reform thereafter. He affirmed that the democrats had brought Russia to her knees, imposing alien values on her, destroying the state and impoverishing her people.[97] Despite standing for election to the Duma in 1993 and taking his seat, he made no secret of his contempt for the parliament and for parliaments in general.[98] Not only were such Western imports as democracy and freedom deplorable but so too was economic liberalisation, especially privatisa-tion. However, Nevzorov was not, and, he claimed, never had been a communist – despite his avowed admiration for the NKVD and its successors. He had allied himself with the communists because ulti-mately they had preserved Russia's unique identity and heritage, espe-cially in the essential matter of statehood: 'We had a Russian empire [...] This empire was called [...] the USSR [...] They [the communists] were capable of maintaining the Russian empire.' Russia was not coterminous with the contemporary Russian state: 'For me, Russia is the Motherland without borders or customs' barriers.'[99]

What Russia needed was authoritarian rule. Her future was bound to be 'one hundred per cent authoritarian'.

> Inflation and economic misery – these are things that can be stopped only by order based on power, only by command, only by dinning into people's heads and hearts the fear which is essential for state-building [...] The Russian was never free in the sense that the sexual member could be shown on television, porn-ads published in the papers and [...] one could spit in the face of one's own nation [...] The state can only be authoritarian, it can exist only by preserving the fear which has to be. After that, order can be imposed quite easily.[100]

Monarchism was impractical in modern Russia: authoritarian Presidential rule was a more realistic alternative.[101]

It was one of Nevzorov's constant laments that despite all the talent he could discern (the ex-KGB General Sterligov, Zhirinovsky, the writer Alexander Prokhanov) no-one of sufficient stature had emerged to fill this role. One of the few figures whom he praised consistently and with whom he did not fall out was the neo-fascist Alexander Barkashov. He was a man of action, not afraid of blood – unlike the incompetent leaders of the 1991 coup.[102] The coup had failed, above all, for want of heroes, despite all its supporters who were ready to die for the Motherland:

> The weakness of the GKChP was evident. It was evident that the coup leaders were possessed by a petty intellectual fear of blood, as though history has ever been made with anything else. He who is afraid of blood does not make history.[103]

Hence, Nevzorov praised all those who were ready to use force in Tbilisi, the Baltics, in October 1993 (and even the loathed President Yeltsin in the war in Chechnya).[104] His love of 'strong' leadership led him to hang a portrait of Stalin in his office in the Duma and to deny the extent of his oppression and the numerous victims of the Gulag.[105]

True to his belief that Russia required action by a heroic minority, he and Viktor Alksnis formed, in November 1991, the largely symbolic organisation *Nashi*, to fight for the restoration of a Greater Russia.[106] He claimed that he wanted to: 'prepare cadres capable of cleansing and restoring Russia [...] We need to create a people's guard' composed of 'people who are outstanding and strong'.[107] All that was needed to take power was two thousand people.[108] Not only did Nevzorov not find his small group of heroes, however: he failed to distinguish himself in the disturbances of 1991 and 1993 and contented himself with filming the war in Chechnya (to celebrate the army's actions there). Given these views, his election to the Duma in 1993 pointed both to the alienation of public opinion in St Petersburg and the parlous state of Russian political culture. Nor was he the only neo-fascist to be elected to the parliament. Nikolai Lysenko, the leader of the neo-fascist National Republican Party of Russia was elected for Saratov in 1993.

c) National Republican Party of Russia

The National Republicans, with between 10 000 and 14 000 members and branches in several cities in European Russia, were one of the more successful neo-fascist groups in 1994 and 1995.[109] Like Barkashov, Lysenko had been an active member of *Pamyat'* (in Leningrad) in the late 1980s, before founding the National Republicans in April 1990.[110] Originally hopeful of restoring an Orthodox monarchy, by 1991, Lysenko rejected both pre-revolutionary tradition and Soviet socialism in favour of a 'third way', a new Russian State ideology that would neither be of the East or the West:

> We are against international communism and against cosmopolitan Western democratism. We are for an original path of development for the Fatherland.[111]

Talk of the 'third way' was then fashionable in nationalist and right-wing Party circles and Lysenko appears to have been influenced by the national-communist Sergei Kurginyan:

> 'We propose to all the peoples of Russia,' he wrote,' and above all, to the Russian people to start the fight for construction of a new great Empire – an Empire of technological and intellectual supremacy over the whole world.'

This was the only way Russia could avoid the slavery intended for it by 'transnational capital'. 'New thinking' was 'a diversion by the West, especially the USA, against Russia'. Pacifism was dangerous and illusory: in reality, a war for the technocratic leadership of the world was being fought; refusal to acknowledge this could lead only to 'a form of genocide' and 'consumer degeneration'.[112]

Lysenko, an ambitious politician, generally hid his anti-Semitism and the party's programme denounced chauvinism,[113] although racism informed the Party's positions. Lysenko was strongly anti-Turkic, advocating policies restricting the civil rights of Russia's Muslim and Caucasian populations. He accused Turkey of harbouring plans to establish a pan-Turkic empire, with the aid of Russia's Turkic and Muslim population, to enslave Russians and take over traditional Russian territories and Russia itself.[114] The party programme advocated excluding the Central Asian republics and the Caucasus from the new Russian state, while suggesting that Russia should occupy these areas militarily and exact tribute from them (to pay for the 'economic genocide' perpetrated on the Russian people by the 'southern mafia').[115] The party manifesto spoke of the need for 'a programme of sanitising the nation's genetic stock' and for a policy of 'de-internationalisation' of education and culture.[116] Despite Lysenko's subsequent attempts to present himself in a more respectable light,[117] he and his party were committed to unambiguously racist and xenophobic policies at home and abroad.

In the short term, Lysenko believed, a government of national unity should be formed to end political and economic chaos and assert Russia's status as a great power within her natural boundaries.[118] The government Lysenko envisaged was to be authoritarian. While the party programme promised to guarantee freedom of speech and religious belief, it was not ready to extend these rights to those who practised russophobia or professed alien religions, emphasising that an Orthodox revival would be encouraged by the State. Despite calling for popular sovereignty, the Republicans wanted to ban political parties and movements funded or supported, openly or covertly, from abroad and to disband all elected bodies from provincial level down. The programme promised equality before the law in one place, while demanding discrimination against Muslims and favouring Russians elsewhere.[119]

The party's democratic postures were thus misleading. Its economic policies (which combined support for 'national' private enterprise and farming with state ownership of land, natural resources and the arms industry, central planning and state control of banking, foreign trade and guaranteed social welfare)[120] were heavily indebted to Soviet socialism, although Lysenko professed more admiration for German national socialism.[121] The party both rejected Western democratic, liberal and economic practice in favour of exclusive nationalism.

With these positions, it is not surprising to find the National Republicans in alliance with authoritarian nationalists and socialists in the National Salvation Front and General Sterligov's Russian National Council.[122] Despite many shared positions, these alliances were relatively short-lived, less on account of fundamental divergences of principle than of personal rivalry.[123] Apart form its youth organisation (which dispatched volunteers to South Ossetia and Pridnestrovie, before being banned by the State prosecutor in February 1993),[124] the party was less militant than Barkashov's Russian National Unity. Lysenko held back from open involvement in the disturbances of October 1993, which subsequently enabled him to run, successfully, for parliament (a position he failed to retain, despite strenuous efforts, in the more normal conditions of 1995, when the opposition vote was fragmented).[125] The loss of parliamentary representation relegated the party to the irrelevant fringes of Russian politics. This marginality was attributable not so much to the extremism of their ideas (Zyuganov was scarcely more moderate, apart from his more veiled racism), as to changed circumstances, with the emergence after 1993 of an increasingly well-organised and institutionalised opposition in the shape, above all, of the Russian communist party (the KPRF).

CONCLUSION

Neo-fascist parties and groups were symptomatic of the crisis which followed the collapse of Soviet power. They were not, however, isolated warts on an otherwise healthy body politic, as their rhetoric and ideology initially enjoyed the support of a significant element in the cultural establishment, in the twilight of the Soviet regime, and had much in common with the mainstream opposition to Yeltsin, as it developed in the mid-1990s. What distinguished the neo-fascists was their militancy, their explicit racism and avowed admiration for and imitation of earlier fascists (something their larger rivals were careful to avoid). Despite the attention paid to them in the press, therefore, the neo-fascists were increasingly overshadowed by mainstream politicians. After 1993, an institutionalised opposition to Yeltsin emerged, based on political parties (principally the LDPR and the KPRF) and factional representation in the Duma, with a popular mandate for ideas that were not remote from those advanced by the neo-fascists: the restoration of a strong Russian State, the defence of Russians, the resurrection of traditional values, and the rejection of the West, its liberal capitalism, democratic traditions and cultural influence. The neo-fascists' thunder was stolen by the official opposition by 1995 and 1996.

While this did not stop the neo-fascists' activity, their popular support, measured by membership of their parties and opinion polls, was always limited. The extent to which their attitudes were shared by the Russian public is a matter of controversy. Some writers have argued that racial prejudice and intolerance of minorities is widespread among Russians.[126] Brym and Degtarev, analysing a poll taken in Moscow in October 1992, believed anti-Semitism to be common, although Jews were not as disliked as Gypsies, Azeris, Chechens and other peoples from the Caucasus. 13.6 per cent of respondents believed in a global Zionist plot against Russia.[127] Other scholars contested the view that anti-Semitism was common, pointing to findings that indicated that the overwhelming majority of Russians rejected such attitudes.[128] However, these data from 1992 also revealed that surprisingly large minorities endorsed racist myths or felt unable to condemn them. It was hardly reassuring that 13.3 per cent of Russians believed that Jews should be punished for crucifying Christ (down from 17 per cent in a poll taken the previous Spring) while 34 per cent did not know whether they agreed or disagreed with this proposition. 9.3 per cent believed that it would be better if all Jews left Russia, while a significant group were unable to reject this proposition. In another poll of early 1992, if only 9 per cent believed to an extent in a Zionist conspiracy, while 26 per cent did not, 65 per cent could not decide.[129] Such views fed off myths printed in what had hitherto been the mainstream press: both *Molodaya gvardiya* and *Pravda* published articles on alleged ritual murders by Jews.[130] Furthermore, there is some evidence to suggest that racism, while a marginal phenomenon in the late 1980s, grew after 1991, when successive polls indicated that increasing numbers of Russians admitted to or harboured hostility to other ethnic groups.[131] Attitudes to race (and to political authority) which were characteristic of the neo-fascists seem, therefore, to have been held by a small but growing number of Russians in the early 1990s. In addition, if only small minorities endorsed extreme racist positions, a much larger group hesitated to reject or condemn such ideas. This significant body of confused or indifferent opinion was potentially open to persuasion by extremists.

However, these potential sympathisers did not identify with the neo-fascists. A poll of May 1990 put support for *Pamyat'* at 1–2 per cent of the RSFSR population, with 6 per cent support in the cities and none in the countryside, where it was virtually unknown.[132]

Although *Pamyat'* was one of the best known neo-fascist groups, successive polls indicated that it enjoyed very little support. According to a poll of December 1992, only 2 per cent of respondents gave Vasiliev and 5 per cent *Pamyat'* a positive rating (as against 43 per cent for the Vice-President, Alexander Rutskoi); 15 per cent reacted negatively to Vasiliev and 31 per cent negatively to *Pamyat'*, while the 'don't knows' were by far the largest category. Few parties or leaders scored well in this poll, which pointed to the public's profound political disenchantment.[133] The membership of successive neo-fascist groups was, as we have seen, insignificant. Although Lysenko's National Republicans managed to win a seat in the Duma in 1993, they were not to repeat this success in 1995, and they remained a marginal force. Russia's neo-fascists, and analogous groups such as General Sterligov's Union of Patriots and Vladimir Miloserdov's Russian Party,[134] rather than joining forces, competed against each other, running separately in the 1995 elections, where their scores were derisory. Lysenko's Republicans won 0.48 per cent of the vote; the mainly Cossack Russian All-Peoples' Movement won 0.12 per cent; Barkashov's RNU ran two candidates, who won 2.46 and 0.6 per cent of the vote; Eduard Limonov won 1.84 per cent in Moscow; Alexander Dugin 0.87 per cent in St Petersburg. The Russian Party, with its programme of saving Russia from the Yiddish–Masonic plot, by reviving the 'Russian Idea' of *sobornost'* – conciliarity or collectivism – and rejecting Western parliamentarianism, ran several candidates in single-seat constituencies, winning between 5.6 and 0.6 per cent of the vote. General Sterligov, whose authoritarian and Orthodox monarchism distinguished him (as it did the Cossacks) from purer neo-fascists, was unable to collect enough signatures to enable his Union of Patriots to participate in the list voting, but he himself won 8.61 per cent of the vote, running against the former communist and Speaker of the Duma, Ivan Rybkin. Overall, the neo-fascists and minor groups with analogous views were estimated to have won approximately one million votes in December 1995.[135]

Thus only a tiny percentage of the total electorate supported parties or candidates with overtly fascist sympathies. If formal neo-fascism remained on the margins of political life, too disputatious and contemptuous of democratic institutions to take advantage of the opportunities they offered, the evidence of the elections both in 1993 and 1995 was ambiguous. While few self-declared fascists were elected to parliament, parties whose views were in many respects similar (such as Vladimir Zhirinovsky's Liberal Democratic Party) were well-represented there. Asked to respond directly to fascism, most Russians reacted negatively, but confronted with ideas about race and political authority characteristic of fascism, the results were inconsistent and ambivalent. Most Russians feared the rise of fascism but they were often unclear in identifying this threat: most equated it with Nazism, often failing to recognise its modern and homegrown incarnations. A poll of mid-1995 suggested that most Russians feared but could not define fascism.[136] The significance of the growth of fascism lay, therefore, neither in its place in disorientated public consciousness, nor in its clear political influence or appeal, which were negligible, but in the fact that it was not an isolated phenomenon. As fascism spread among disaffected youth and intellectuals, kindred ideas became common among the elites in post-Soviet Russia: its formal supporters may have been few, but the attitudes and ideas (such as authoritarianism and racism) on which it drew were surprisingly well-represented not only in cultural and academic circles but increasingly in the Russian parliament, and were more prevalent in public opinion than support for or membership of the neo-fascist parties would suggest.[137] Russia's neo-fascist parties may not have been poised to take power, on account of their poor organisation and lack of mass support, but they were not alone in voicing authoritarian and xenophobic nationalism and their values reflected those prevalent in post-Soviet cultural and political life.

3 Russian Orthodoxy and Nationalism

The temptations of extremism were not countered by the revival of institutionalised religion. Historically, Orthodoxy played an important role in forming and preserving Russian national consciousness: it embodied Russian culture during the Mongol domination and, from the Middle Ages until the twentieth century, Orthodoxy was fundamental to the Russian's sense of identity and statehood.[1] In the light of this heritage, it might have been expected to play an influential and beneficial role in inspiring the new Russian nationalism, which emerged with the decline of Soviet power. However, it failed to do so and the reasons for this are to be found in the history of its relations with the state and society and the problems it faced in the post-Soviet period. These resulted in religion's having a weak moral influence: instead, attempts were made to capture the authority of Orthodoxy and harness it to narrow political ends.

Traditionally subservient to the state since the time of Peter, the Church was unprepared to resist the onslaught of the Soviet authorities, which initially tried to destroy it and then, especially during the War, to exploit its residual popularity. As a result, the Church emerged from Soviet rule partly discredited (for its collaboration with the regime) and weakened both by the secular impulses of modernisation and by a long history of oppression. Its moral authority was uncertain, its capacity for independent action limited. The challenges of the post-Soviet period (which included allegations of KGB infiltration, competition from foreign 'tele-evangelists' and the Orthodox Church Abroad, and the establishment of autocephalous churches, independent of the Moscow patriarchate, in some of the former republics of the Soviet Union)[2] impeded its development as an autonomous and authoritative voice in public life. It was thus not well placed to resist attempts to exploit it politically.

These attempts were characteristic above all of authoritarian nationalists, who, after the demise of Soviet communism, sought a new ideology to justify the rejection of the West and hoped to find it in Orthodoxy. As, in the pre-revolutionary period, the Church had been a pillar of Tsarist rule and had been enthusiastically embraced by enemies of modernisation and democracy (such as Leontiev and Pobedonostsev), they found a rich vein of conservative, religiously inspired nationalism to mine. Liberal nationalists had less to fall back on. Never a staunch advocate of liberty and democracy, the Church was confronted by a vocal community committed to conservative nationalism. The hierarchy, traditionally subservient to the state, lacked the confidence to redefine the Church's role and reassert its authority and independence. Even had the Patriarch wished to repudiate the Church's reactionary traditions and supporters, its weakness, in the post-Soviet period, would have prevented him from doing so.[3]

A. LIBERAL NATIONALISTS

The Church was nonetheless able to point to a number of outstanding liberals in its ranks. The chief democrat in the Church was undoubtedly Father Gleb Yakunin, a former political prisoner who, in 1990, became a leader of Democratic Russia and a deputy in the Russian parliament. Unlike other former dissidents, such as Vyacheslav Polosin and Dmitri Dudko, Yakunin did not change his views or retreat into xenophobic nationalism. His condemnation of the Church's links with the Soviet regime and attempts to extirpate this legacy led him into conflict with the hierarchy, both in the Soviet and in the post-Soviet periods.[4] Yakunin's religious belief led him not towards nationalism but to radical democracy.

Another outstanding liberal in the Church was Father Alexander Men', who, unlike Yakunin, was principally preoccupied with problems of spirituality and religious renewal rather than politics. Like Yakunin, he believed the Church to be dominated by conservatives, opposed to reform and Westernisation. Anti-Semitism and even support for fascism were common, in his view, although these attitudes were more pronounced among the lower clergy than the hierarchy.[5] Father Men' condemned these attitudes and the bigotry and xenophobia they entailed as incompatible with Christianity.[6] Similarly, he criticised the Church's long association with autocratic and authoritarian rule. He deplored the Church's subordination to the state and its consequently weak traditions of evangelism and charitable work, believing that the authentic voice of spirituality had been marginalised in the eighteenth and nineteenth centuries. This situation had left the

Church unable to resist the pressures which the Bolshevik regime exerted on it.[7] Alexander Men' was unequivocal in his denunciation of Stalinism, which he saw as being a moral as well as a political evil. Rather than authoritarian rule, the Church needed a liberal regime, where freedom of conscience and the separation of church and state were guaranteed.[8] Thus, while praising the Church's role in preserving national culture and identity in the past, Men' did not identify with the ultra-nationalist wing of the Church. He believed in the universal relevance of the values he preached and his position was thus at odds with exclusive nationalism: 'One wants to believe in the victory of reason, freedom, humanity, even if this victory will never be complete in this world.'[9] In October 1990, not long after expressing this hope, this courageous and gifted priest was murdered by unknown assailants.[10]

If Father Men' was concerned with a religious revival of universal significance, the historian Dmitri Likhachev was preoccupied with a cultural revival which would give substance and depth to the democratic reform. For Likhachev, Orthodoxy was a fundamental and original element in Russian culture: it had helped to unify and defend Russia in the past; however, this had led to dependence on the state, many of whose faults the Church ultimately inherited. Nonetheless, Orthodoxy should not be identified with autocracy: its future, like that of all society, lay in freedom, the separation of church and state, which would enable it to recover its authentic voice just as it would promote cultural renewal. For Likhachev, Orthodox Christianity preached universal values, which were incompatible with chauvinism.[11] While celebrating Russia's cultural achievements and playing a leading role in defending Russian culture both as a scholar and as a campaigner for cultural and ecological conservation, Likhachev was no narrow nationalist. He insisted that national cultures are the product not of a single ethnic group but of communication and interaction between diverse nationalities. The society he hoped to see emerge from the reforms was to be both morally renewed and pluralistic.[12] He believed that a multicultural, multinational society was fundamental to Russian identity and a *sine qua non* of a vibrant civilisation.[13] Aggressive and chauvinistic nationalism was, in his view, a sign of weakness. Opposing Greater Russian nationalism, he insisted on the importance of cultural diversity and of the individual: it was the strength and stability of its traditions, not armed might, that made a nation great.[14] Likhachev's liberal nationalism was not characteristic of the intelligentsia in the early stages of *perestroika*, when liberals and reformers evinced little interest in Russian nationalism. Nor did Likhachev attempt to exert wider public influence through political activity.

For a figure whose nationalism was not only liberal and Orthodox in inspiration but also politically organised, we must turn to Alexander Ogorodnikov.[15] Ogorodnikov, a religious dissident, had been released from prison in the amnesty of 1987 and, on 4–7 August 1989, he and sympathisers from the scattered informal circles of democratic Christians founded the Christian Democratic Union of Russia.[16] The Union described itself as 'a political party, uniting Christians of various confessions, who have as their goal the spiritual and economic renaissance of Russia and the creation on its territory of a democratic, law-based state on the principles of Christian democracy'. It was concerned above all with legal reforms that would guarantee civil rights and political pluralism.[17] The Union's main political demands included the introduction of a multi-party, parliamentary system of government and a market economy; and the right to national self-determination.[18]

The Union's principles, which Ogorodnikov drafted, stressed the priority of the individual and his rights over those of the State and, in this, Ogorodnikov distinguished himself from most Russian nationalists, who were ready to subordinate the individual to the collective. Although the Union was specifically religious in inspiration, it saw itself as embracing a wide range of concerns (ecological, philosophical, religious, educational and charitable).[19] Its nationalism was not xenophobic but based on tolerance and on a vision of Russia as part of the world community:

> The CDU of Russia sees the future of Russia in terms of the rebirth of Christian spiritual culture and morals [...] the democratic values of world civilisation – a parliamentary system, a market economy, free labour and a well funded social programme. [...] The CDU of Russia sees the future Russia as an important and indivisible part of world Christian civilisation.[20]

This openness to the rest of the world and to universal values distinguished the CDU from most other religious-nationalist groupings. It was reflected most clearly in its stance on the national question. Unlike most other parties, the CDU believed that the respect of human rights held the key to the problems posed by ethnic conflict in the USSR. The USSR should be transformed into a confederation of independent states. The integrity of Russia itself should be maintained, but its centralised structures should be replaced by federal ones.[21] Hence, Ogorodnikov's Christian Democrats preached a liberal, enlightened nationalism, based on the respect of human and national rights.

The CDU did not, however, succeed in setting the tone for religious and nationalist politics in the new era. Estimates of its membership vary between a few dozen people, to three or five thousand.[22] Its development was hindered by its fractiousness and naiveté – perhaps by its roots in that element of dissident culture which accounted for its liberal idealism.[23] In the post-Soviet period, the party was active in trying to promote political harmony but made little impression on the public, with Ogorodnikov failing to get elected to the 1993 Duma and the party and its allies unable to participate in the 1993 and 1995 elections for lack of organisation and support.[24] Its moderation meant that the CDU was overshadowed by more strident rivals, like Aksyuchits' party, more attuned to the political conflicts of the post-Soviet era.

B. NEO-SLAVOPHILES

Liberal religious nationalism was perhaps too innovatory to be successful in post-Soviet Russia and it was outflanked by the radicalism of both government liberals and the nationalist opposition. More influential was the attempt to revive Slavophile tradition with its romantic revolt against modernity. The neo-Slavophiles stressed the Orthodox character of the Russian people, which supposedly alienated them from Western political and economic norms. Instead of Westernisation, the neo-Slavophiles advocated a return to tradition: like their mentors, they did not reject democracy and liberalism out of hand but cultivated instead a supposedly national religious interpretation of these concepts, which ultimately traduced them. The leading exponents of this approach were Alexander Solzhenitsyn and Viktor Aksyuchits. Both men were ambivalent in their commitment to democracy and unenthusiastic about contemporary Western culture, especially in the forms in which it was transmitted to Russia. Instead they drew inspiration from a romanticized picture of pre-revolutionary Russia, which stressed the importance of Orthodoxy for national prosperity and power. The neo-Slavophiles were characterised by their evolution away from relative liberalism, in the hopeful days of 1990, to relative intolerance and revanchism by 1993.

a) Solzhenitsyn

The most famous neo-Slavophile in modern Russia was the Nobel-prize-winning writer and former dissident, Alexander Solzhenitsyn. Long a critic of communism, Solzhenitsyn was originally inclined to ascribe the crisis of contemporary Russia to the ills of communist rule:

> For 70 years, in laboured pursuit of a purblind and malignant Marxist-Leninist utopia, we have lost a full one-third of our population – lives yielded up to the executioner or squandered in the ineptly, almost suicidally waged 'Patriotic War'. We have forfeited an earlier abundance, destroyed the peasant class [...][25]

When he finally returned to Russia in Spring 1994, after 20 years in exile, however, he was equally scathing about Russia's new rulers and the effects of the reforms, referring to the post-Soviet period as the 'Great Russian Catastrophe' and comparing it with the seventeenth-century Time of Troubles and 1917:

> The Catastrophe entails above all – our dying out. [...] Catastrophe also in the stratification of the Russians as if into two separate nations: the immense provincial-village heartland and an entirely disparate minority in the capital, alien to it in thought and Westernised in culture. Catastrophe in today's amorphous state of Russian national consciousness. The Russian question at the end of the twentieth century stands unequivocal: shall our people *be* or *not be*? [...] If we persist in this way, who knows if in another century the time may come to cross the word 'Russian' out of the dictionary?[26]

This apocalyptic tone notwithstanding, Solzhenitsyn's affinities with the nineteenth-century Slavophiles were obvious in his romanticization of rural Russia (where the true virtues of the nation and hope for the future lay, he assured audiences) and his hostility to Westernisation.[27]

Not only was Solzhenitsyn appalled by Western popular culture and its penetration of Russia,[28] he had clear reservations about the importation of Western economic and political norms too. Capitalism and socialism were equally repugnant without 'God's breath' and self-imposed moral limitations. In his address to the Duma in 1994, and elsewhere, Solzhenitsyn bitterly criticised the economic reforms, asserting that they had robbed the people, impoverished the State, enriching only a small corrupt minority who were indifferent to the fate of the *narod*. The introduction of capitalism and the emphasis on profit (or 'booty', as Solzhenitsyn called it) was morally debilitating, just as it had been in the past, when Alexander II had emancipated the serfs. The democratic reforms were a sham: power was in the hands not of the people but of a cynical and remote minority in Moscow, he contended, not entirely unreasonably; the elections were a fraud, most voters were not registered or, if they were, they were too intimidated to vote independently.[29]

In the 1970s, Solzhenitsyn had made his reservations in principle about parliamentary democracy and political pluralism clear, arguing that they were morally divisive and indicative of the West's political and spiritual crisis. Authoritarian rule could be as conducive to human well-being as democracy; the Soviet system was terrible not because it was authoritarian but because it refused to allow moral freedom, requiring citizens to surrender to a lie.[30] With the end of Soviet rule, Solzhenitsyn amended his views only partially. Contemporary democrats had repeated Peter the Great's mistaken attempt to impose Western political norms in Russia, without regard for her cultural identity and circumstances:

> [...] In seventy-year-old totalitarian soil, what democracy can sprout overnight? [...] Only in caustic mockery can we term our system of government since 1991 as democratic; that is, as rule by the people.[31]

Russia should seek its own new form of government: it could not simply copy the West.[32]

However, Solzhenitsyn was unlike most nationalists in his readiness to envisage some form of democracy for Russia. He believed that a strong, authoritarian State would have to be retained while Russia developed new political structures and reorientated itself spiritually and culturally.

> [...] We happen to have ended up on the side with a tradition of strong central authority, it behoves us not to make rash moves towards chaos. For 1917 has taught us, anarchy is the ultimate peril. Unless one craves revolution, a State must possess qualities of continuity and stability.

As a result, Solzhenitsyn had approved of Gorbachev's introduction of a strong presidency.[33] While questioning the merits of universal suffrage and direct elections,[34] Solzhenitsyn stressed the importance of revivifying Russia by means of political and economic reforms at local level, while maintaining a strong, central authority. Democracy should initially be introduced to the village and county. This would obviate the dangers of the manipulation and suborning of the new system by the unscrupulous and the ambitious. Gradually, this local democracy could be built on, finally embracing the whole country. Solzhenitsyn believed that the *zemstva* – the agencies of local self-government in the later nineteenth century – provided a model which, suitably amended, might be emulated by modern Russia.[35]

Solzhenitsyn's notion of liberty, however, was not consonant with that of the modern liberal – either in Russia or in the West. His approach to politics was that of a moralist – and in this, he is distinctly reminiscent of his intractable nineteenth-century predecessors, Tolstoy and Dostoevsky. In particular, he shared Dostoevsky's (and the Slavophiles') tendency to reject the legalistic spirit of the West. The Russians – according to Kireevsky and Konstantin Aksakov – were united in a community of feeling with their fellow countrymen and the Tsar: their political institutions and liberty were founded not on a narrow legal definition of their rights but on spirituality.[36] Solzhenitsyn inclined towards this approach:

> The structure of the State is secondary to the spirit of human relations. Given human integrity, any honest system is acceptable, but given human rancour and selfishness, even the widest-ranging of democracies would become unbearable.[37]

That constitutions and laws are needed precisely because man is incorrigible and that laws may be judged good insofar as they minimise the effects of his rapacity seems not to have been entirely appreciated.

> No constitutions, laws or elections will by themselves assure equilibrium in society. [...] A stable society is achieved not by balancing opposing forces but by conscious self limitation: by the principle that we are always duty-bound to defer to the sense of moral justice.[38]

At heart, for all his concern for Russia's well-being, Solzhenitsyn was incapable of dealing with the real problems of political reform, because politics were repugnant to him:

> Politics must not swallow up all of a people's spiritual and creative energies. Beyond upholding its rights, mankind must defend its soul, freeing it for reflection and feeling.[39]

This was the iconoclastic language not of the political reformer but of the writer and moralist.

Nonetheless, his concern with liberty (even if his definition of it owed more to religious than to political and legal conceptions) distinguished Solzhenitsyn from most other right-wing nationalists. In 1990, he did not support the imperialism advocated by many nationalists, arguing that those republics which wished to declare their independence from Moscow should be free to do so. The essential Russian State he believed to consist of Russia, Belorussia and the Ukraine, as well as the areas of Kazakhstan populated mainly by Russians. This area he saw as the historic heartland of Russia. He pointed to the centrality of the early medieval kingdom of Kiev to Russian historical development, adducing this, not without reason, as evidence of the cultural unity between Russia and the Ukraine. Far from being strengthened by its empire, he believed, Russia was impoverished by its many fractious dependencies. It was to the country's advantage to grant the rebellious republics their independence.[40] By 1994, however, he had changed if not his central thesis at least the tone in which it was expressed. The collapse of the Soviet state he took to be a disaster, a 'colossal historical defeat' for Russia, which had stranded 25 million Russians in new artificial states, which deprived them of their cultural and political rights. He castigated Yeltsin for accepting the internal borders of the Soviet Union and abandoning those Russians left outside them. He argued vigorously for the recovery of the Ukraine, Belorussia and Kazakhstan, sharply criticizing the leaders of these new countries.[41] Why, he asked, should the Russians be the only people not to have the right of self-determination, the right to demand reunification?[42]

His writings in the mid-nineties revealed Solzhenitsyn as a conservative, Greater Russian nationalist.[43] His political instincts may be gauged from his judgements on Russia's past rulers: his praise of the authoritarian Nicholas I and Alexander III (for concentrating on 'the inner health of the nation') is eloquent, especially as Alexander was associated with the policy of Russification, which deprived the Empire's national minorities of cultural, religious and political rights.[44] Solzhenitsyn himself appeared insensitive to the rights of other nationalities.[45] While rejecting a racist or ethnic definition of nationality and insisting on cultural kinship as the defining criterion, he rejected the pluralistic view of culture proposed by Dmitri Likhachev. While the Russian state could be multiethnic [*rossiiskii*], its culture could only be national [*russkii*]; international and multiethnic [*rossiiskii*] culture were meaningless terms, he insisted.[46]

For Solzhenitsyn, the key to recovery was a moral and national renewal. While there were some practical measures that could be taken, what mattered above all was morality:

> It is not true that the economy decides everything. Morality is the decisive factor and it can be established not on unlimited enrichment but on self-limitation and self-denial.[47]

Solzhenitsyn had preached the renunciation of the consumer economy and the ideal of technological progress with all the zeal of a prophet for twenty years.[48] The modern world was essentially uncongenial to the ascetic Solzhenitsyn. Materialism had overwhelmed and diminished man:

> [...] From [...] technocratic Progress, from oceans of superficial information and cheap spectacles, the human soul does not grow, but instead grows more shallow and spiritual life is only reduced. [...] We have lost something pure, elevated and fragile.[49]

In this context, Solzhenitsyn was critical of the assaults on the Orthodox church (including the competition of foreign sects, the climate of capitalist materialism). An Orthodox Christian himself, he nonetheless evinced little enthusiasm for the institution of the Church in Russia, believing that it too needed to be renewed.[50] The religious morality that underpinned his political convictions appeared to owe as much to nineteenth-century philosophy as to the contemporary Church and, by the mid-1990s, it at times seemed that Solzhenitsyn believed his moral authority to be greater than that of the Patriarch and that it was his role, as much as the Patriarch's, to call Russians to repentance and moral and spiritual rebirth.

The liberality of his anathema did little to endear him to the new Russia, despite the initial interest with which his views had been greeted, when he had finally been able to express them again in Russia in 1990,[51] and despite the courtesies extended to him on his return in 1994 (which included a meeting with the President in November 1994 and an address to the Duma the previous October).[52] He broadcast his opinions in a regular television programme, provoking more sarcasm and hilarity than enthusiasm.[53] For many young Russians, Solzhenitsyn had simply waited too long to return: he had missed his moment. Furthermore, Solzhenitsyn was too much of an iconoclast to be ready or able to cooperate with other nationalist critics of Yeltsin. Ultimately, politics mattered less to him than morals.

b) Russian Christian Democratic Movement (RKhDD)

If Viktor Aksyuchits, unlike Solzhenitsyn, was an active and ambitious politician, his views on the need for moral and spiritual renewal and on the collapse of the Russian state were close to those of Solzhenitsyn, of whom he claimed to be a follower.[54] Born in Belorussia, Aksyuchits had received a specialised military education, served in the armed forces and joined the CPSU, before turning to philosophy and discovering Russia's religious thinkers of the nineteenth century, an interest which resulted in his being expelled from university. He contributed to *samizdat* publications, before helping Father Gleb Yakunin to found and then lead the Russian Christian Democratic Movement (RKhDD) on 8–9 April 1990.[55] Among those involved were the former dissident, Gleb Anishchenko, the newly elected deputy Father Vyacheslav Polosin, the human rights' activist Valery Senderov and the monarchist writer Vladimir Karpets.[56] Fundamental to the new movement were the ideals of Orthodoxy: however, there was no agreement on the practical implications of these ideals, which were open to both liberal and nationalistic interpretations. While some members of the Party placed the individual and his prerogatives (above all, the demand for civil liberties, the separation of church and state) at the centre of their demands, others were to cherish Orthodoxy for its role in inspiriting the Russian nation in its millennial struggle to establish the Russian state. The programme adopted in 1990 revealed these tensions.

The movement stressed the importance of moral renewal on the basis of Orthodoxy:[57]

> The bidding of Christianity has been transmitted to us by the Russian Church. And therefore our return to the Father's house is above all a return to Russian Orthodoxy.[58]

They also saw 'enlightened patriotism' as one of the pillars of reform, defining this in terms of a Christian duty – even of a mission:

> Patriotism is love of the Motherland, discovered by free spiritual self-determination and this feeling is justified before the face of God, as it appears in the course of humble service in fulfilling the Creator's intentions about my [*sic*] people and my Motherland.

The nation which failed to implement God's plan for it would perish. Defence of the nation and Motherland was a sacred duty:

We receive the Motherland through God and from God and thus it is for us sacred and we must defend it from desecration.[59]

The Motherland had a divinely ordained, though as yet unspecified mission to accomplish and a glorious future awaited it.[60]

This hotch-potch of Hegelian and Slavophile ideas recalled the intolerant nationalism of the previous century. Its obscurantism was fraught with implications of authoritarianism and cultural conflict. If the Motherland were sacred, then it was a religious duty – not a mere civic duty – to defend it. Yet this holy essence remained undefined, nor was it clear who might define it: the Church? politicians? leaders of the Christian Democratic Movement? Neither was it obvious when and on what grounds the nation might be deemed to be under threat: would secession of territories from the State, criticism of its religion or culture constitute such a threat? What measures might be invoked to protect the Motherland? If it came to violent conflict, were the defenders of the Motherland to be deemed to be engaged in a holy war? The Movement's declaration on patriotism, with its sense of exclusive righteousness, was at odds with the idealistic liberalism of other parts of its programme.

Anti-Communism was originally another fundamental tenet of the movement.[61] However, unlike the Movement's religious nationalism, its anti-communism tended towards political liberalism, translating into an initial political programme which stressed human rights, civic freedoms and political and economic pluralism.[62] It wanted the State to restore churches and monasteries and pay damages to the Church; and it demanded the introduction of legislation to defend the Church's rights and the separation of Church and State.

The movement was divided on inter-ethnic relations, with one group emphasizing the importance of tolerance, mutual respect and cultural and political freedoms, while another was more concerned with the integrity of the Russian State and the resuscitation of the Orthodox Church and Russian culture. On the one hand, the RKhDD demanded autonomy and equal cultural rights for all nationalities and called for an end to the USSR's 'imperial' structures. However, it warned:

[...] The process of separation should not degenerate into a senseless or irresponsible break-up of the country [...] Secession should be accomplished only by means of a plebiscite of the whole population of the territory in question.

The Russian State should also elaborate a policy to defend the interests of Russian minorities in breakaway territories.[63]

The tension between libertarian and conservative nationalist tendencies did not develop immediately, however. The RKhDD was encouraged by the fact that 12 supporters had been elected to the Russian parliament in March 1990, although its membership and the readership of its paper remained small.[64] The party became a noted, if reluctant member of the Democratic Russia movement and its deputies (who included Aksyuchits, Yakunin and Polosin) voted with the democratic faction in the parliament, while one of its deputies, Father Vyacheslav Polosin, was chosen to head the parliamentary commission on freedom of conscience and was instrumental in the adoption of the first law guaranteeing this in Russia, in Autumn 1990.

Gradually, however, authoritarian nationalism became the predominant trend in the party. The renegotiation of the Union Treaty, launched following the 17 March 1991 referendum and the Novo-Ogarevo agreement, meant that political parties had to decide whether to support the centralised state, in the form of a renewed USSR, or to opt instead for a looser federation of independent states. Aksyuchits pronounced in favour of a strong centralised state.[65] The emphasis on strong State institutions, territorial integrity and Russian national grandeur impelled the Christian Democratic Movement towards the right – a tendency which accelerated sharply after the August putsch, with the collapse of the old Union structures and the growth of centrifugal pressures within the Russian Federation itself, threatening the territorial integrity of the republic and further diminishing the strength and prestige of Russia. The Christian Democrats under Aksyuchits began to move towards the national communist opposition in Spring 1992.[66] This evolution resulted in the gradual alienation of some of the Christian Democrats' leading figures, which in turn increased Aksyuchits's power.[67]

Asked to defend his association with authoritarian and anti-democratic forces, Aksyuchits claimed that his co-operation with the neo-Stalinists under Viktor Anpilov was 'normal'. 'Today the Communists represent the opposition which the ruling regime has deprived of the freedom of speech and the press'. These prohibitions applied also, he suggested, to the Christian Democrats. 'I would be glad to serve the President if he faithfully served the Motherland', Aksyuchits explained, but the President and his supporters were 'engaged in the pursuit of an anti-State and anti-national policy. As an honest person I cannot be loyal to it.' Hence, he and the new Communist forces were justified in attempting to topple the government. The Congress of Peoples' Deputies should force the President's resignation and 'form an emergency body for running the country' until all disputed issues had been decided. The methods that the 'emergency body' would implement would 'of course [...] be tough'. It would declare an 'economic emergency'. 'All attempts at revising borders will be cut short [...] With the republics that have left Russia, there will be a need to go over to world prices in trade and abolish borders and customs posts.'[68] This authoritarian, imperial policy – with its salvation committee, imposed harmony and deferred elections – differed little from that of the putschists the previous year.

This new orientation was confirmed in the new party programme and declaration adopted in June 1992. The situation in Russia was declared to be a 'national catastrophe', which jeopardised the survival of Russia 'as a great and original great Power'. Only a return to the millennial traditions of Russian statehood, founded on a national-religious revival and the rediscovery of the communal (*sobornaya*) Russian idea could save the country.[69] The first and most important task was to restore a single Russian state, by uniting under its auspices the Slav states of the former Union, areas in the newly independent states mainly inhabited by Russians and other territories which felt themselves 'drawn' to Russia.[70] The defence of the Russian diaspora should become one of the key elements of foreign policy.[71] Aksyuchits reiterated these demands, partly because he saw the state as the means whereby the nation's culture and existence were preserved and developed.[72]

Although Aksyuchits claimed that his party represented centrist, traditional conservatism[73] and although he refrained from joining the National Salvation Front, his rhetoric, from 1992 on, was indistinguishable from that of the national-communist opposition. He depicted Yeltsin and his government as traitors, who had delivered the country and nation up to the exploitation of rapacious foreigners and who, by their liberal economic and cultural policies, were deliberately hastening the collapse of the state and the eradication of national traditions. Western norms could not be translated to Russia, without regard for her history and culture.[74] In practice, too, Aksyuchits was a sharp opponent of the President, supporting the parliament and staying in the White House, during the Autumn 1993 crisis.[75]

Despite the professions of support for civic liberties in the Party's programme, Aksyuchits's commitment to liberal democratic ideals was as short-lived as his support for the democratic movement. By 1993, he had declared himself a monarchist, although he espoused the idea of a national dictatorship as a more realistic short-term solution to the problem of governing Russia. The parliament, he argued, should adopt a temporary dictatorship to establish a strong unitary Russia and end the expansion of the West at Russia's expense.[76] The fact that the revised party programme envisaged establishing the Orthodox church as the State religion and obliging the media to inculcate patriotic values[77] confirm that Aksyuchits had left liberalism far behind.

This nostalgic nationalism did not win the party enough support to participate in the 1993 elections and it lost its parliamentary base. This provoked a crisis, with the Moscow branch leaving to join the Russian National-Right Centre, an alliance of Orthodox nationalists supporting the restoration of the pre-revolutionary Russian empire and the revival of Orthodoxy as the cornerstone of a national-state revival.[78] This group exploited Orthodoxy for aggressive nationalist ends: as the former dissident Zoya Krakhmal'nikova observed, they valued it as a national, state-building religion, in which the nation, state and motherland took the place of God.[79] Increasingly, former communists found these positions congenial and many were alleged to sympathise with the party.[80] The RKhDD's confessional, patriotic view of the state had little in common with West European Christian democracy.[81]

C. FUNDAMENTALISTS AND MONARCHISTS

The neo-Slavophiles moved away from the relative liberalism of their initial positions as the Russian crisis deepened. Others were more consistent in their opposition to Westernisation. These were Orthodox fundamentalists and monarchists, who tended to cling to a Manichean view of the world: the conflict, they believed, was no longer between communism and capitalism but between Orthodox-Slav civilisation and the Latin-Germanic world of Western Christendom. In short, these theorists of renewal looked back to the nineteenth century, although to Leontiev and Danilevsky rather than Marx and Engels.

They suggested that Russian character and tradition, as formed by Orthodoxy, favoured a form of authoritarian rule that enhanced state power, national well-being and justice and eschewed the divisive liberalism and parliamentarianism of the West and its empty, formalistic legalism. Some idealised the Tsarist social and state order and sought to revive the theocratic official nationalism on which the late nineteenth-century monarchy had been based. By the mid-1990s, monarchists and Orthodox nationalists were to find themselves sharing the Tsarist apologia for autocratic rule with the communist leader, Gennady Zyuganov.

With the celebration of the Millennium of the Baptism of Rus', in 1988, nationalist writers felt emboldened to express their interest in Orthodoxy and pre-revolutionary national tradition. This tendency was accelerated by the collapse of the CPSU's authority and, by 1990, several writers and intellectuals proclaimed their religious beliefs, eschewing their socialist past, while some declared their sympathy for monarchism. Yuri Naguibin and Mikhail Antonov announced their conversion to Orthodoxy. Igor Shafarevich was able to preach the need for Orthodox renewal openly. A number of public movements were founded, in which Orthodoxy played an important role (for example, the Committee for the Restoration of the Cathedral of Christ the Saviour).[82] Mikhail Antonov was elected to lead the Union for the Spiritual Renewal of the Fatherland, an organisation which attempted to popularise a religiously inspired nationalism capable of resisting the West's egotistical and spiritually bankrupt civilisation. He considered *perestroika* an attempt by the West to take over and exploit Russia. Only by turning to the cultural heritage of Byzantium could Russia recover: neither politics nor economics but moral and spiritual renewal held the key to her regeneration.[83]

This period coincided with a renewal of interest in monarchism. Several small monarchist groups were founded in the Spring and Summer of 1990. It was not uncharacteristic of the mood of the moment that, at the end of the 1980s, Dmitri Vasiliev renounced socialism and became an apologist for authoritarian monarchism instead. In Summer 1990, there was a vogue for Tsarist memorabilia – photographs of Nicholas II and his family, royal genealogies, badges – for demonstrations to mark the death of the Tsar and his family and to honour their memory, and for articles and books about them, which for the first time became readily available. However, this does not mean that the Russian voter envisaged monarchism as a viable political alternative: it corresponded more to the sympathetic interest in and curiosity about the country's past, whose true history had been for so long distorted, and to the interest in the Silver Age (the period of rapid political, economic and cultural development between 1890 and 1914.)

Monarchism remained the domain of a small number of authoritarian nationalists, even in the ideological confusion that followed the collapse of communism's prestige. One of the first monarchists to declare his sympathies openly was the writer, Vladimir Karpets, who at the Plenum of the Russian Writers' Union in November 1989, intervened to express the hope that the regime founded in 1917 would draw to a close and suggested that Russian patriots should unite around the saints consecrated by Orthodoxy. 'Let us be faithful to our Motherland and our murdered Sovereign,' he declared, referring several times to the Tsar's family and the need to honour them.[84] This speech caused a furore – as references to the monarchy and the assassination of the Tsar and his family had hitherto not been tolerated.[85]

The monarchist groups which were founded in 1990 were united in their opposition to Western influence, democracy and capitalism: instead, they supported the revival of Orthodoxy and the restoration of the monarchy. They were, however, divided in their sympathies. One branch of monarchism was legitimist, calling for the return of the Grand Duke Vladimir Kirillovich, while the other supported a constitutional monarchy, based on the October 1905 Manifesto and called for a *zemskii sobor* (the Muscovite Assembly of the Land) to elect the tsar. One group sympathised with the reactionary wing of the Russian Orthodox church, while the other was critical of the Church's record of collaboration with the Soviet regime and supported the claims of the Church Abroad.[86]

The more moderate of these groups was the Orthodox All-Russian Monarchical Order-Union (PRAMOS), founded on 16–19 May 1990, following a two-year campaign to have the royal family's remains reburied and a monument erected at the site of their execution in Yekaterinburg. Calling for the restoration of a Russian Orthodox monarchy, PRAMOS also demanded laws and measures to establish religious liberty, promote religious education and missionary activity and favoured extending the jurisdiction of the far from liberal, but uncompromised in relation to Bolshevism, Church Abroad. PRAMOS's liberalism was not ideological but circumstantial, for it envisaged a hierarchical society and a theocratic state.[87] Only opposition to communism and comparison with rival monarchists made PRAMOS look liberal. Like other monarchist groups, its formal support was microscopic but its followers swelled the ranks of opposition demonstrations in the post-Soviet period.[88]

PRAMOS's chief rival was Vladimir Osipov's Union of Christian Regeneration. In the late 1980s, on his release from prison where he had been held as a religious dissident, Osipov launched himself back into religious-nationalist agitation.[89] He edited, for a time, the monarchist, nationalist paper *Russkii vestnik* (the Russian Messenger). After disagreements with his colleagues, Osipov went on to found the Union of Christian Regeneration on 27–28 April 1990. It was committed to the restoration of the Tsarist empire (excluding only Finland and Poland) under the autocratic monarchy of Grand Duke Vladimir Kirillovich. Its 1990 manifesto professed a Manichean worldview, suggesting that history was shaped by the struggle between the spirit of evil and God. The Tsar had been ritually murdered by the forces of evil, which remained active in contemporary Russia, attacking Russian Orthodox culture, the God-bearing Russian people and the Great Russian state, in the hope of establishing the universal reign of Anti-Christ.[90] Russia would not recover unless her people repented, turned to God and his representative on earth, the Tsar:

> We support neither 'socialism' nor 'capitalism', that is we choose neither totalitarianism nor democracy. We will not take an alien but our own way – we support an Orthodox Russia. We have had enough of foreign ideas and slogans. Russia needs not ideology but faith, not politics but spirituality, not democracy but conciliarism [*sobornost'*], not a union of republics but a great power [...][91]

Osipov managed to attract sympathisers and supporters. A monarchist conference that he helped to organise in Moscow on 21–23 September 1990 was attended by almost four hundred delegates. It distinguished itself not only by the vehemence of its opposition to all things Western or reformist (democracy, press freedom, ecumenism) but also by its anti-Semitism. Judaism was identified as a 'savage cult' whose leader was the devil; the Jewish-Masonic mafia was responsible for the murder of the Tsar and for Russia's current travails. References to the Black Hundreds and the Union of the Russian People were enthusiastically applauded.[92]

Osipov and his Union subsequently allied themselves with a number of branches of *Pamyat'* (Smirnov-Ostashvili, Kulakov) and other extreme groups that professed Orthodoxy.[93] This association did not prevent him from appearing in the pages of *Nash sovremennik* in 1990 and 1991, alongside his old companion in dissidence Igor Shafarevich.

He also took part in the foundation, in January 1991, of the anti-Semitic *Slavyanskii sobor* (Slavic Assembly) which united several proto-fascist and extreme nationalist groups and which he later left because of his disagreement with its pagan wing.[94] However, far from being isolated on the lunatic fringes of politics (where he was indeed active),[95] Osipov was associated with many of the principal fora of opposition to Yeltsin and his government.

Theocratic monarchism was characteristic also of the Cossacks, who were a colourful presence at patriotic gatherings.[96] The Cossacks were descended from the rebellious and independent frontiersmen of southern Russia, and prided themselves on their traditions of freedom, military prowess and loyal service to the later tsars and the Orthodox Church. The Cossack revival, which dated from Spring 1990, had been originally conducted under the auspices of communism: many of the *atamans* of the early regional Cossack groups came from the CPSU and security forces. Their first body, which attempted to unite Cossacks throughout the state (the Union of Cossacks) soon split, however, into White and Red factions, with pro-Yeltsin anti-communists establishing the Union of Cossack Forces of Russia.[97] Initially, Cossacks hoped to remedy injustices perpetrated under the Soviet regime and demanded rehabilitation (Cossacks had fought against the Bolsheviks and Soviet forces in the Civil and Second World Wars), the restitution of confiscated property and regional autonomy. Throughout 1990–92, they were preoccupied with problems of organisation and cultural renewal, attracting a large following, estimated at 700 000 supporters and 150 000 members in 1992.[98] Increasingly, however, their romantic historicism led them to favour the nationalist and Orthodox positions with which they were traditionally associated, a tendency which was accentuated by the inter-ethnic conflicts in the North Caucasus, where Cossacks were attacked by Chechens.[99] Local Cossacks began to argue for military action to maintain the unity of the Russian state and offered their services to the Russian authorities, which, at first cautiously and then, as the Chechen crisis deepened, more assiduously began to court them. By the mid-1990s, Cossack leaders supported the revival of a strong, unified, Orthodox, Russian state, which would restore order within its borders, if necessary by military means, and made clear their hostility to liberals such as Yegor Gaidar and the human rights' activist, Yelena Bonner.[100] The Cossacks were among the largest and the most influential of the monarchist groups, by virtue of their history and strategic significance.

Most monarchist groups, though, were marginal and politically insignificant. However, they were symptomatic of Russia's political malaise: their xenophobic rhetoric was reflected in the language of high politics and reinforced a moral climate which tolerated irresponsibility and even venom. The reasons for this were manifold: not until 1995 did the President contemplate any serious action to prevent the activities of neo-fascists. Freedom of speech was exploited by right-wingers to spread misconceptions and myths. Furthermore, several established journals, men of letters and even priests, instead of denouncing anti-Semitism and xenophobia, appeared to entertain these ideas themselves, encouraged chauvinistic organisations and patronised apologists for such myths, such as Alexander Dugin.

For writers like Valentin Rasputin, Orthodoxy was an essential component of Russian national identity. According to Rasputin, the origins of Russia as a culture and nation were to be found in the baptism of Rus'. Orthodoxy had formed the Russian national character. Whereas the West was materialistic, practical, formalistic and superficial, Orthodox Russia was distinguished by the depth and idealism of her spirituality. The Russians' religious character insulated them against the tide of European revolutions, which in the nineteenth century had renounced personal amendment in favour of reforming the external world. Russians preferred inner to external freedom, their own organic democratism to Western democracy, the justice of God to that of man-made laws.[101] The harmony of Russian Orthodox civilisation had been shattered by the intelligentsia which had deliberately attempted to undermine Russian spirituality by introducing the people to the temptations of materialism. Even though persecuted, the Church had played an important role in the twentieth century, defending the Russian people from external attack, encouraging patriotism, inspiring great art.[102] It followed, according to Rasputin, that Orthodoxy could be a powerful element in extirpating the evil effects of the current reforms, whose aim was to destroy the state and deliver Russia and its people to Western exploitation. Russia should cease trying to copy the West, for the West was bent on the destruction of Russia and its political and social institutions were incompatible with Russian tradition. The country could be saved only by the revival of the Russian idea, of national consciousness, of which Orthodoxy (and no other religion) was an essential element.[103] A critic of Westernisation under *perestroika*, who had endorsed the principle of the August 1991 coup by signing the Appeal to the People, Rasputin consistently supported the irreconcilable opposition after the fall of Soviet power.[104]

Several writers and artists shared Rasputin's outlook. Chief among them was Ilya Glazunov, whose kitsch canvasses provoked controversy and popular enthusiasm in the 1970s and 1980s by their inclusion of references to Orthodoxy and national history.[105] By 1987, Glazunov was ready to profess the nationalist vocation of this art: its function was to stimulate a rebirth of national traditions and consciousness, he claimed.[106] An ardent enemy of modernism (which he once condemned as 'Satan's revolt against God'), Glazunov suggested that 'the artist is the high priest and custodian of the spirituality and traditions of his nation's centuries'-old culture'. All art was therefore religious and national.[107] Equally, religion and spirituality (including that of the ancient Aryans) were fundamental to the Russian culture he wanted to revive. Not for nothing did *Pamyat'* leader Dmitri Vasiliev spend several years working as Glazunov's secretary. Like Vasiliev, Glazunov's nationalism was to lead him to monarchism. In an article published in 1991, Glazunov called for a constitutional monarchy and extolled the Tsar as a ruler anointed by God to bring unity and stability to the country.[108] Glazunov's later pronouncements confirmed that his sympathies lay with pre-revolutionary Tsarism and its pillars of Orthodoxy and Greater Russian nationalism.

More extreme were the views of the economist and publicist Mikhail Lemeshev, a frequent contributor to *Nash sovremennik*. He rejected the intellectual and political legacy of the Enlightenment and French Revolution, seeing it as a fatal renunciation of God (God had let his displeasure be known by sending Chernobyl as a warning to errant humanity). Not only Russia but the entire world was on the brink of social and ecological disaster. If Russia suffered particularly badly, this was because its international enemies, led by Zionism, were intent on undermining the Russian state and nation and undermining its wealth. To realise their plans, they had infected Russia with the evils of capitalism, democracy and liberalism. Orthodoxy and democracy were incompatible.[109] Russia should draw on her own traditions, returning to Orthodoxy and reconstructing herself as a unitary great power:

> What is the way to the salvation and regeneration of Russia? There is only one way – a national return to Orthodox belief, to our historical world outlook. Only in this way can the great organising triad of Russian life – 'Orthodoxy – Autocracy – Nationality' – be recovered.[110]

Lemeshev was not a simple nostalgic conservative (although his economic prescriptions reveal his desire to return to the Soviet past), as his anti-Semitism and belief in the exclusive virtues of the Russian genetic code show.[111] Like other well-known writers and controversialists in the intelligentsia, he lent respectability to ideas of no intellectual standing.[112]

These views, reminiscent of the excesses of nineteenth- and early twentieth-century Russian nationalism, were representative of the flight into nostalgic obscurantism which characterised a significant section of the Russian intelligentsia. While monarchism as a realistic political alternative enjoyed little support among the public (a poll in 1994 finding 9 per cent in favour of a tsarist restoration), a not wholly dissimilar authoritarian and collectivist nationalism was espoused by a considerable section of the intelligentsia, as the 1996 elections showed, when an academic caucus of socialist and patriotic scholars was formed to back Zyuganov's patriotic bloc.[113] Papers, bulletins and books, depicting the West as the incarnation of evil, democracy and the rule of law as unnecessary and even maleficent and enlarging on the benefits of authoritarian rule were common in Moscow and St Petersburg after 1991. Partly the result of propaganda, isolation, censorship and half-truths, the spread of these views reflected the growing alienation caused by the prolonged and deep social and economic crisis, which hit the previously relatively cossetted intelligentsia particularly hard. But these ideas were contagious, as the proliferation of (albeit microscopic) parties[114] and as their incorporation into the rhetoric of as significant a party as Zyuganov's communists indicated.

One of the most notorious foci of xenophobic nationalism within the Church was the Union of Orthodox Brotherhoods, which was founded under the auspices of the Holy Synod in October 1990 to encourage charitable and educational work and revive parish life.[115] The Brotherhoods soon became popular: by the following May, the Union claimed that 70 brotherhoods were affiliated to it, of which the most active and influential were the Brotherhood of Saint Sergius of Radonezh at Zagorsk and Osipov's Union of Christian Regeneration.[116] The Brotherhoods, far from furnishing an example of philanthropic piety however, soon became involved in nationalist politics, opposing reform and liberalisation and defending the Great Russian state. They appealed to Ukrainians not to vote for separation from Russia in November 1991.[117] However, the first real source of controversy was provided by the Brotherhoods' third congress, in June 1992, where, in the presence of the Metropolitan Ioann of St Petersburg, the chief topic of discussion was the problem of ritual murders: those of Tsar Nicholas II and his family, murdered by 'Yids'; of Andrei Yushchinsky, the victim, according to the Brotherhoods, of a ritual murder by the Jew Beilis; and of Serbs in the former Yugoslavia. Demanding an end to the alleged ritual murders of the latter, the meeting discussed the desirability of canonising the former. Another source of indignation was ecumenism, in particular the Patriarch's cautious attempts to improve relations with other confessions. His innocuous overtures to a meeting of Jewish rabbis in New York (where he called for rapprochement between the Jewish and Orthodox communities and acknowledged the Christian debt to Jewish tradition) were greeted as a betrayal of both Orthodoxy and the Russian nation. The Patriarch's speech, it was suggested, could be explained only by the presence of treacherous Masons within the hierarchy.[118] Although the proceedings caused some moderates to break away from the Union, the Patriarch did not condemn them and the Brotherhoods continued to agitate for their xenophobic brand of Orthodoxy, undisturbed by authoritative criticism.

The Brotherhoods favoured the theocratic monarchism advocated by Osipov and their patron, the Metropolitan of St Petersburg. Politically, they were therefore aligned with the critics of democracy. They opposed contacts with the West and the outside world, believing ecumenism to give the Vatican and other foreign sects the opportunity of subverting the Orthodox Church. Ecclesiastical reform they greeted with even more venom than political and social change, accusing those who wanted to renew the liturgy or introduce any innovations of attempting to destroy the Church from within. In addition, the Brotherhoods were infamous for their anti-Semitism. One of their leaders, Father Kirill Sakharov, expressed these sentiments, in an interview in 1992. He opposed ecumenism, suggesting that instead Orthodoxy needed to be defended from the attacks of expansionist Catholicism, Protestant sects and 'Satanic' cults. Above all, he was hostile to Judaism: the Brotherhoods had been indignant about the Patriarch's speech in New York not because they were anti-Semitic, he affirmed, but because of their concern for Orthodoxy. It was not the Jewish people but 'Talmudic Judaism' that they condemned. How could they not be outraged when the Kremlin, which, with its saints and cathedrals was the physical and spiritual centre of Orthodoxy, was used to celebrate Chanukkah: of course the Brotherhood condemned such incidents in strong terms. Apparently, Kirill believed that such gestures posed a threat to the Church's existence and were part of a plot to undermine it. It was doubtless to counteract the supposed influence of Masonic double-agents within the hierarchy that the Brotherhoods called for strict church discipline and intense scrutiny of promotions to the episcopate.[119] Such attitudes were not excep-tional,[120] as a series of open letters to the Patriarch condemning ecu-menism and Church reform as heresy and treason confirm.[121] The Brotherhoods' xenophobic orientation was confirmed by their fourth congress, in February 1993, which passed a resolution affirming that Tsar Nicholas II had been the victim of a ritual murder by Jews, demanded the restoration of Ivan the Terrible's secret police to stamp out Judaism in the Church and called for Ivan's canonisation for fighting against 'Judaic heresy'.[122]

The deepening political and economic crisis made it difficult for the Patriarch to hold the balance between reformers and fundamentalists in the Church. His attempts to match the social and political liberal-isation of the early 1990s with cautious liberalisation in the Church provoked extreme opposition, which can be gauged from an open letter to the Patriarch published by leaders of the Brotherhoods from the Petersburg area, in February 1993. This protested against the Patriarch's ecumenical policies in characteristically apocalyptic terms, calling for unity and retrenchment against the enemy: 'In the present cruel time of troubles we can jointly resist Satanic attempts to annihi-late Holy Russia only by uniting around our iconic saints, having revived in our souls holy zeal "for God's sake".' Certain forces, the authors observed, seemed to be using the Patriarch's name in their interests, which were far from coinciding with those of Russia and the Church. Examples included the Patriarch's speech in New York and his call for unity with Jewish believers. This had almost provoked a schism. Was the Patriarch not aware of the bitterness and suffering wrought by the heresy of 'Yidophiles' [*zhidostvuyushchie*] on Russia? His speech was a scandal. Another outrage was the ban imposed on the Metropolitan of St Petersburg, which prevented him from publish-ing in official church publications, when Ioann was only a patriotic defender of the Church and Russia.[123]

The growing influence of fundamentalists in the Church was noted with concern by devout laymen. Dmitri Pospielovsky observed that nineteenth-century monarchist and anti-semitic works were being reprinted in 'huge quantities' by the Brotherhoods. In many seminar-ies, students absorbed the prevalent atmosphere of xenophobia and paranoia, believing in the existence of Judaeo-Masonic plots and the imminent apocalypse.[124] Another source of pressure on the Church hierarchy was the competition offered by the very right-wing Russian

Orthodox Church Abroad (ROCOR), which attracted clerics and con-gregations who resisted ecclesiastical discipline. One of the reasons why Church right-wingers, and their leading representative, the Metropolitan of St Petersburg, were not condemned by the Patriarch, it has been suggested, was the possibility that they might defect to the Church Abroad.[125] The Church Abroad in the inter-war years was notorious for its links with fascism and, in the contemporary period, this affinity reasserted itself when the Church established sympathetic contact with *Pamyat'*.[126] In fact, its positions in some respects resem-bled those of fundamentalists within the Russian Orthodox Church: both were akin to the spirit of the pre-revolutionary Black Hundreds.

Extreme nationalists within the Church were active not only in resisting reform but also on the wilder fringes of politics, where they associated with the irreconcilable opposition to Yeltsin, sometimes embroiling the Patriarch in their affairs.[127] The Patriarch, presumably on the basis of inadequate briefing, attended the All-World Russian Assembly, organised by the ultra-nationalist ex-KGB General Alexander Sterligov, which was held at the Danilov monastery in Moscow in May 1993. This argued for the reconstitution of the USSR, rejected the Presidency (in favour of the soviet system) and affirmed that Western political ideas, such as the separation of powers, were unsuitable for Russia. The meeting also offered a definition of Russian identity that owed more to the powerful nineteenth-century reactionary Konstantin Pobedonostsev than to modern experience: Ukrainians, Belorussians and Orthodox believers should, it was sug-gested, all be counted as Russian.[128] These views were characteristic not of the Patriarch but of Ioann, the Metropolitan of St Petersburg and Ladoga.

While the Patriarch attempted to ignore the political uses to which Orthodoxy was sometimes put, Ioann, the Metropolitan of St Petersburg and Ladoga,[129] was a notorious and voluble supporter of nascent Black Hundredism. In June 1993, he published an apologia for anti-Semitism, defending the authenticity of the *Protocols of the Elders of Zion*. These outlined, he affirmed, a plan of world domina-tion, based on the subversion of the Russian throne, nation and Orthodoxy by means of 'the poison of liberalism', constitutionalism, the press and money. The US aided this project.

[...] Against Russia, against the Russian people , a dirty war [...] is being waged. According to the plan of its devilish instigators, our land and people are destined for destruction and this is because of its faithfulness to its historical calling and its religious dedication [...][130]

Ioann opposed democracy, civil liberties and capitalism both in principle and in their application to Russia, where they had led, he claimed, to the collapse of Russia as a great power. According to Ioann, this was not an accident but part of a plan. The point of democracy, he believed, was to undermine strong, traditional societies, ruin their spiritual and religious bases, destroy the national state and give power to a transnational corporation, which was none other than the international capitalist, cosmopolitan elite, which sought world domination, principally through crushing Russia.[131] The very concepts of democracy, liberty and equality were flawed and fraudulent: they reflected neither the natural not the true moral order. Nowhere did democracy lead to popular rule; the direct vote was 'amoral and destructive'. As for 'the thesis about human rights', it amounted only to 'the absolutisation of the individual', which, while appropriate to the West was alien to Russia and led to 'the inevitable degradation of public morality and morals', the destruction of the nation, class enmity and war. The legal guarantee of human rights was a 'fatal error' and the whole edifice of formal law was 'equally fatal for the spiritual health of the person and for the basis of state civilisation'. Like Alexander III's arch-conservative Procurator of the Holy Synod, Pobedonostsev, Ioann believed that the traditional Russian approach, which emphasised inner freedom, and the law of 'love, peace and tolerance' were more conducive to the well-being of State and society.[132] 'Democratic civilisation', he affirmed, 'encourages the cult of violence and depravity, tolerance of evil and the perversion of human nature'. The nation would lose its identity, the State its power and integrity, where it was introduced.[133] Instead of these evils, Ioann proposed a return to a theocratic autocracy, in which the Tsar ruled to glorify God:

> Such a high power, one and indivisible [...] independent of the caprices of the crowd, linked with the people not through paper casuistic scholastic legality but through the living daily experience of collective [*sobornoe*] unity [...] freely and voluntarily limits itself in its intentions and acts by God's commandments and the truths of His Law.[134]

Nor did the Metropolitan confine himself to theory. He proposed action too. One of his pastoral letters (which affirmed the restoration of Russian State power [*derzhavnost'*] and theocratic absolutism to be the main moral responsibility of patriotic Russians) was adopted by General Sterligov as the programme of his Russian National Council. This was understandable as Ioann urged Russians to reject the ideological chimeras of the reformers, including the rights of man, the consumer society and the right of national self-determination. It was time to recognise that power was founded not on law, the people, a party or an elite but on religious and national ideals: only he who embodied these ideals had the right to rule. The ideal state was national, religious, hierarchical and authoritarian.[135]

This anti-semitic cleric blessed other extreme nationalist gatherings and gave interviews to neo-fascist journals like *Elementy* (in one of which he alleged that ecumenism led to murder and that the West was trying to undermine the Russian state, army and church).[136] The failure of the Holy Synod to condemn his views suggested, as one Orthodox believer commented, that some members of the hierarchy sympathised with him.[137] He was certainly not alone, as the activities of the Union of Orthodox Brotherhoods indicated.[138] One of the most highly placed and visible bishops of the Church, Ioann lent his moral authority and that of the Church to disreputable causes and ideals and undoubtedly helped to legitimise and popularise them.

The Patriarch found himself giving ground on many issues to the right-wingers. An attempt to silence Ioann elicited public protests, while condemnations of anti-Semitism were undermined by the support anti-Semites received from other hierarchs and influential figures, such as Father Vyacheslav Polosin, whose work in the parliament now tended to inhibit rather than defend religious freedom.[139] In response to xenophobic opinion in the Church, repeated attempts were made in the parliament from 1993 on to control the activities of 'non-traditional' religions in Russia, culminating in the introduction, in Autumn 1997, with the President's ultimate approval, of an essentially unconstitutional law, which effectively banned Catholic and Protestant churches from operating in Russia.[140] By then, the Patriarch had retreated from the liberal positions he had occupied at the start of the 1990s, emphasising instead consolidation and retrenchment. The rebuilding of the Church of Christ the Saviour in the centre of Moscow (a campaign dear to the hearts of Orthodox nationalists) was significant not only as a symbol of the political elite's new ideological orientation, but, as the Holy Synod had contributed large sums to the project, pointed to the growing influence of nationalists within the Church.[141]

CONCLUSION

The Church was, therefore, not entirely successful in its (not very strenuous) attempts to escape the embrace of the State, politicians and reactionary nationalists, in the late 1980s and early 1990s. The association of Orthodoxy with proto-fascist or extreme nationalist groups and with the smaller, but obscurantist monarchist groups which emerged in 1990 did little to enhance the Church's authority.[142] Nor did the growing interest in Orthodoxy of erstwhile National Bolsheviks and luminaries of authoritarian nationalism in the intelligentsia improve its standing. In some cases, this interest was genuine. More worrying for the Church, however, was the attempt by authoritarian nationalists to capture the prestige of Orthodoxy for their own purposes, as the authority of communism declined. It seems unlikely that this was related to a serious or sincere interest in religion. Even the anti-communist, democratic wing of the religious renewal of the late 1980s, as exemplified by Aksyuchits, began to move towards more and more conservative and even extreme nationalism, leaving the Church hierarchy after the coup isolated in its attempts to restore its authority by moving towards more liberal positions (for example on ecumenism).

The post-communist vogue for mysticism entailed not only a return to conventional spirituality but also manifested itself in eccentric and dubious ways. Various forms of paganism were popular in proto-fascist circles,[143] while among the nationalist intelligentsia, there was a fashion, in the late 1980s, for a kind of new pantheism. The critic Lanshchikov envisaged the advent of 'an entirely new kind of man', more in tune with nature. Positivism would be replaced with a new 'world-sensibility'; the change in store for humanity was comparable to the replacement of antique paganism with Christianity.[144] Alexander Prokhanov at one point professed to believe that: 'It is essential to re-create the traditional type of individual [...] This meek type of gardener, forester is the archetypal harmoniser' of human relations.[145] Shafarevich, like Solzhenitsyn, believed in returning to a simpler form of life, in which the relations between man and nature would be restored to their previous state, pollution would end, the country and nation would be saved from physical annihilation.[146] While Shafarevich and Solzhenitsyn stressed the importance of Orthodoxy, the ecological theme – justly a cause of concern among the nationalists – occasionally led to extravagant theories which had little to do with conservation or moral renewal, for which the right clamoured so insistently.

In this atmosphere, rationality was sacrificed to the thrills of hitherto forbidden fantasies, which many must at heart have known to be false. The affinities between extreme nationalism and pseudo-mysticism, which assumed alarming proportions after 1990,[147] were demonstrated when the television hypnotist and healer, Anatoly Kashpirovsky, was elected to the Duma on the LDPR ticket, in December 1993. Neither position could withstand critical analysis, hence both preferred to refer to 'unknown forces' (beneficent or evil) and hidden or spiritual energy (of 'the national soul', the healer) to explain and justify their contentions.

Unfortunately for the Church, Orthodoxy was exploited in a similar vein by politicians, agitators and even churchmen, who were either cynically indifferent to religion or chose to interpret it to reinforce their political and racial prejudices. In all this, the voice of the Church, at best uncertain and faint in the Soviet period, tended all too often to be drowned out, while religion became a fad or was incorporated into and subordinated to an authoritarian nationalist ideology. The late 1980s and early 1990s were marked by the rise, primarily in cultural circles, of an authoritarian nationalism, hostile to the West and its influence, and favouring a return to a traditional national order, identified initially with the Soviet and increasingly with the Tsarist past. Despite this traditionalism, exponents of nationalism were increasingly wedded to a political radicalism associated with calls for the violent overthrow of the Yeltsin regime. Was this a largely insignificant fashion or did the nationalism espoused by intellectual and cultural figures influence late Soviet and post-Soviet politics and, if so, what impact did it have?

Part II: Politics

4 The Genesis of the August Coup, 1989–91

The first steps in the passage from cultural and ideological polemics to political organisation were prompted by the rise of the democratic movement in 1989. Early attempts to rally anti-reform opinion in a Russian nationalist movement failed. By late 1988, it was clear that the reformist intelligentsia enjoyed far more popular support than the nationalists. Readership of the main liberal journals and papers had grown dramatically, while the circulation of nationalist organs had stagnated or declined.[1] The first independent civic organisations were almost all democratic in orientation and the most popular and authoritative of them, Memorial, was committed to anti-Stalinist and liberal-democratic ideals. The liberals' popularity was confirmed in March 1989, when for the first time in Soviet history, partially democratic elections were held to a new legislature, the Congress of People's Deputies. Many famous members of the democratic intelligentsia were elected to the new parliament, despite the fierce opposition of the Party hardliners. Moscow sent a particularly large number of reform-minded intellectuals to the Congress, as did the Academy of Sciences. Despite the bias of the authorities against the democrats, the nationalist intelligentsia was relatively thin on the ground, while the Party *apparat* and its high officials suffered a humiliating and unexpected defeat: the electorate, instead of voting obediently for the Party chiefs, plucked up the courage to reject some of them.[2] This was the nationalists' and conservatives' first serious reversal of fortune. Their opposition to reform was reinforced by the growing threats to the integrity of the Soviet Union, the loss of Eastern Europe, the erosion of central authority and the rapid spread of Western influence and political and economic ideas after 1989.

A. THE QUEST FOR POPULAR SUPPORT

Initially, the nationalists and Party conservatives tried to recover from the setback of the Spring 1989 elections. A first move was the foundation in Leningrad by Party hardliners of the United Workers' Front (*OFTL*) in June 1989, professing a brand of populist Stalinism. Calculated to appeal to the unskilled manual workers of the Soviet Union's decrepit industries, whose interests were threatened by rationalisation, the Front proclaimed aggressive egalitarianism, demanding an end to market reforms and more power for manual workers, especially over the new parliamentary structures and the mass media. Founded during the Summer and Autumn of 1989,[3] ostensibly as a popular proletarian movement, both its constitution and its subsequent role in the foundation of the Russian Communist Party confirm that it had close links with the Party conservatives[4] and was intended to mobilise public opinion against reform. It was hoped to do this by building on popular resentment of corruption, deprivation and poverty. Hitherto, these ills had been laid at the door of the Brezhnevite and conservative *apparat* – initially by Gorbachev and his team, but increasingly, and with disastrous effects for the Party's authority, by the newly emerging democratic movement. Now the conservatives thought they could turn the tables on their opponents – pointing to rising crime rates, inflation, shortages and declining living standards and the dishonesty of those involved in co-operative businesses – which were the only palpable results to date of the economic reforms launched by *perestroika*.

The text which launched the movement was a declaration, purportedly issued by a number of Leningrad workers, denouncing the growth of crime, inflation, instability and corruption and demanding that workers take matters into their own hands and 'act together with healthy forces in the Party and State in the general struggle for the interests of the people, for the Motherland'.[5] The worker should be paramount in society, according to a resolution adopted at the Front's first Conference, a week later on 13 June:

> The worker should be the master of the country. Society's entire economic political and spiritual life should be subordinated to his interests.[6]

The documents adopted the following month by the USSR organisation differed hardly at all from these earlier declarations, but placed greater emphasis on the danger of the 'collapse of the USSR and the restoration of bourgeois republics'.[7] The Russian Workers' Front, founded in September 1989, also subscribed to this platform.[8]

The Leningrad Workers' Front programme played not only on people's fears but also on their hopes. Its demands included an increase in workers' real wages, unspecified measures against inflation, the extension of holidays to include a minimum month-long break, improved maternity leave, an increase in pensions and wages in line with minimum pay levels, the provision of free medicine for all; flats to be gurarranteed to every family. Its calls for measures to combat speculation and corruption were also intended to feed on popular discontent with the high prices and the poor quality of goods sold in co-operative shops. Nonetheless, the *apparatchiki* who helped to inspire this programme could not entirely overcome their old instincts: an end to night work was demanded – except in 'continuous work' factories. The programme also called for the reinforcement of workforce discipline, the struggle against 'all-permissiveness', irresponsibility, 'parasitism' (as failure to work in an approved job as elective unemployment was called) and non-labour incomes.[9] These demands revealed the Front's officious inspiration.

In the cultural sphere, the OFTL programme was distinctly illiberal: Houses of Culture, theatres and concert halls were to be taken away from the control of the intelligentsia and given over instead to the workers who should also control the mass media. *Glasnost'* should apply only to the investigation of social inequalities (for example, those between white- and blue-collar workers). It should seek to inculcate a correct appreciation of the 'contradictions' of the past', fight against the falsification of history, especially excessive stress on the role of the individual in history (that is, the suggestion that the individual Stalin should be called to account for the excesses carried out under his rule). Education should have nationalist, class and military-patriotic bias. In a gesture to potential supporters in the patriotic camp, the Front demanded a campaign against 'unspiritual' mass culture (which was usually seen as evidence of the pernicious influence of Western capitalism, intent on undermining the moral fibre of Soviet youth). Efforts should be made to encourage the rebirth of Russia in the political, cultural and economic spheres: the restoration and conservation of historic monuments should be supported, as should the demand for the creation of a Russian Academy of Sciences.[10] The Front's programme was thus largely neo-Stalinist.[11]

Throughout 1990 and 1991 the Front continued to whip up the fears of what Russians still called the 'lumpenproletariat'[12] and to criticise Gorbachev.[13] However, its popularity was limited: a poll of September 1989 put support for the OFTL at 350 000 (as opposed to the democratic Leningrad Popular Front's one million). In the 1990 elections to Leningrad City Council, in which it campaigned on a neo-Stalinist programme, calling for a return to the planned economy and workers' rule, it won only ten out of 400 seats. Nationally, the Patriotic Bloc, to which it belonged, failed to win a single seat to the Russian Parliament.[14] The OFT's hostility to democracy became more pronounced, as its inability to attract popular support was revealed. One of its young leaders in Moscow, Igor Malyarov, inveighed against the new 'bourgeois Presidency' and reaffirmed the OFT's opposition to parliamentary democracy.[15] But its leadership became increasingly involved in inner-Party politics, neglecting the futile task of developing a popular neo-Stalinist movement.[16] The circumstances which might have permitted the OFT to become a popular force did not yet exist. The Party still remained at the helm and it was enough for it to be seen to be associated with, or behind a movement, to discredit it, while people still hoped that economic reform might improve their lives. According to Boris Kagarlitsky, the OFT was a mass movement only in the Baltics and Moldavia, where the Russian minority was under threat.[17] As Vera Tolz observed, the spontaneous workers' movement which started with the Kuzbass strikes of mid-1989, far from showing sympathy for the OFT, inclined instead towards the democrats.[18] In the absence of popular support, the OFT lapsed into obscurity in late 1990 and 1991, discouraging the Party's neo-Stalinists and persuading them of the difficulty of winning power with popular support.

The nationalist intelligentsia also tried to mobilise public opinion against the reforms in a number of cultural clubs and patriotic fronts. The Russian Cultural Centre, founded in late 1988 and headed by Tamara Ponomareva (a poet and member of the USSR Writers' Union) was one of the first of these groups. Its roots dated back to the late 1970s, she explained, to a cultural society concerned with the 'renaissance of the country's monuments, ecological problems and the development of Russian art'. They had helped to restore monasteries and monuments and held musical and literary evenings. It seems that the Cultural Centre's origins were indistinguishable from those of *Pamyat'*.[19] Ponomareva herself had been involved with *Pamyat'* in the early 1980s, when it was a nationalist cultural organisation, and subsequently became a leader of the sculptor Igor Sychev's branch of *Pamyat'*, apparently on the prompting of the Moscow Party Committee, which was anxious to restrain some of its wilder antics.[20] These contacts suggest that elements in the Party and intelligentsia were – despite the reigning internationalist revolutionary ideology – far closer to what was classically identified as the extreme right, rather than the extreme left of the political spectrum. The affinities between Party hardliners and conservative Russian nationalism were also suggested by the Centre's political orientation, as explained by Ponomareva. The Russian Centre intended to '[assist] the State and public organisations' in cultural policy and to strengthen inter-ethnic friendship. By 1989, the promotion of good inter-ethnic relations meant, in conservative Russian circles, not liberal pluralism but the maintenance of the unreformed Soviet Union and opposition to minority nationalism and the demands of the republics for more rights and freedoms.

Paradoxically, the tendency to deny the prerogatives of other nations went hand in hand with increasingly strident insistence on the rights of Russians. The Russian Centre's demand for the creation of a separate Russian Academy of Sciences, of a Russian theatre which would stage plays about the history and life of the people (*narod*) was typical of this attitude.[21] It also reflected a widely held view, within this milieu, that the people who had suffered most from the Soviet system were the Russians themselves: their culture, 'ethnos' and prosperity had been sacrificed initially to the Bolshevik utopia and later to the cause of worldwide revolution and the minorities in the Union. The balance between the resource-starved Russian provinces and the subsidized ethnic minorities and republics had, conservative nationalists believed, to be redressed. The answer was to be found not in a simple redistribution of resources but in the strengthening – cultural, economic and political – of the Russians' place within the Union. This viewpoint seemed to look back to the Tsarist empire with regret. In practical terms, this was an authoritarian programme in that it implied conserving an unpopular order and asserting Russian hegemony over other nations.

The similarly inspired Fellowship of Russian Artists was founded in later 1988 to 'preserve the union of the peoples of Russia' and assist the cultural and economic renewal of Russia.[22] It hoped to found cultural centres throughout Russia to promote greater awareness of issues such as 'the army and the people', inter-ethnic relations and the environment and hoped to foster the recovery of traditional mores and values :

[...] When we are asked what we support, which party or group, for what ideals we live, we answer soberly and quietly – our ideals are historic: Faith, the Nation (*narod*), the Fatherland. Our Party is Russia.[23]

The Fellowship extolled national unity and strength at the expense of liberty and democracy:

> Thank God that the nation and not the 'public' always and in the first place decide the historic destiny of Russia [...] The great nation, which is not ashamed to call itself Russian, binds with fraternal feelings all State servants, who care for the future of the Fatherland [...], created the army and navy – the military union of defenders of its peace and interests. The nation is not talkative or eloquent, for from experience, it knows that politicians' words mean absolutely nothing without its support [...] It stays silent until such time as its existence and State unity are threatened [...].[24]

What mattered, therefore, was the integrity of the State and its pillars, the armed forces and the nation. Democracy and public debate, it suggested, were self-indulgent, meaningless and even dangerous exercises. The Fellowship enjoyed the support of many cultural luminaries but had only about five hundred members in Moscow: hence, despite the activism of its leaders who represented the organisation in several anti-reform Fronts in 1989 and 1990, the Fellowship did not play an influential independent public or political role.[25] Its failure to attract a significant popular following relegated it to the margins of public life and it served mainly as a barometer of opinion among the nationalist intelligentsia.

Part of the problem was the proliferation and competition of similar clubs, such as *Yedinenie* (Unity), a society of nationalist writers founded on 14–15 June 1989 at the behest of the novelists Yuri Bondarev (who was also President of the Russian Writers' Union) and Valentin Sorokin. Like other cultural groups of nationalist inspiration, it was imperialist in outlook, having as its declared aim the strengthening of 'fraternity' between the peoples of Greater Russia, the protection of Russian minorities in the Union republics and the improvement of the image and ethos of the army. In addition, the club hoped to assist the renaissance of the Russian national spirit and culture. Yuri Bondarev was elected its president. *Yedinenie* clearly hoped to become the cultural counterpart of the Interfronts, which mobilised ethnic Russians' resistance to secessionist movements in the Baltics and Moldova and whose foundation, in mid-1988 and 1989, was encouraged by Party hardliners.[26] *Yedinenie* attracted little attention, however, until 19 August 1991, when its Presidium welcomed the attempted coup in the warmest of terms: 'We support and approve it with our whole hearts, soul and being.'[27]

A feature of the early years of nationalist organisation were the new ecological-cultural associations, which were also often led by well-known writers and cultural figures. Neo-Slavophile nationalists, such as Valentin Rasputin, had long been involved in the conservation movement, leading campaigns to prevent the diversion of the Siberian rivers (which had a successful outcome) and to preserve the unique ecology of Lake Baikal, which was threatened by ill-conceived economic development.[28] The disastrous impact of Soviet planning and industrial development on the environment, public health and the long-term well-being and prosperity of large areas of the country only began to be acknowledged by the authorities in the mid- to late 1980s and it provoked widespread public concern. Neo-Slavophiles believed that this admission substantiated their criticisms of the Bolshevik attack on Russian tradition and its pursuit of modernisation regardless of the cost and they were encouraged by the popular support for conservation. One of the main new conservation groups, with which the nationalist intelligentsia became involved, was the Public Committee for Saving the Volga. Founded on 27 January 1989, it was chaired by the village writer Vasily Belov. Belov ensured that it supported the nationalist cause throughout 1989 and controversially in the 1990 elections. The association, which had profited from the wave of interest in 'green' issues in the late 1980s, lapsed into obscurity in the second half of 1990, as ecological questions were overshadowed by economic and constitutional problems.[29] The Committee for Saving the Neva– Ladoga–Onega, established in April 1989 to campaign against pollution of the lakes and rivers around Leningrad, was unambiguous in its hostility to reform. Its chairman, the theatre critic and member of the *Nash sovremennik* editorial board, Mark Lyubomudrov, was famous for his anti-Semitism while his deputy was the film director Yuri Riverov, notorious for his association with *Pamyat'* and *Otechestvo*. The Committee fielded 56 candidates in the 1990 elections to Leningrad City Council, of whom only one was elected.[30] Conservative and authoritarian nationalists found that even ecology could not win them significant public support.

An organisation which eschewed the neo-Slavophiles' implicit and explicit criticisms of the authorities was *Otechestvo* (Fatherland). At least five organisations of the same name were founded in Russia between 1986 and March 1989, of which the Moscow branch was the most significant and orthodox.[31] In Moscow, *Otechestvo* was founded not, as in Leningrad, by marginal extremists but by writers working on the literary journals *Molodaya gvardiya, Nash sovremennik* and *Moskva* on 24 March 1989 and the nationalist intelligentsia played a leading role in it.[32] Its first conference was held in Moscow on 20 May 1989 and Apollon Kuz'min, a historian and regular contributor to *Nash sovremennik*, was elected chairman, with Alexander Rutskoi, the Afghan war hero who subsequently became Russian Vice-President, as his deputy.[33]

Otechestvo emphasised the importance of socialism, especially 'scientific socialism and the methodology of Marxism-Leninism'. It was also committed to the maintenance of the Soviet Union, as a socialist supranational state. Consequently, it stressed its desire to 'to encourage [...] friendship between the peoples of the USSR' and demanded the strengthening of central rule in the interests of stability. The rights of minority nationalities were overlooked while those of Russia were emphasised, as Russian nationalists claimed that Russians had hitherto been discriminated against by the State, which had failed to give Russia separate cultural institutions. As Kuz'min put it: 'Russian colonialism is distinguished from British colonialism. If in England the mother country lived at the expense of the colonies, in Russia, the colonies lived at the expense of the mother country.'[34] The organisation's sympathy for the army and empire (and the support it claimed to enjoy among some officers) was reflected in a resolution condemning the media's negative attitude to the 'military-patriotic education of the young generation, its discrediting of the Soviet army, its contempt for the services of war veterans and serving Soviet soldiers and officers, military internationalists [...]'.[35]

Otechestvo represented one of the earliest and most consistent attempts of pro-communist nationalists in the intelligentsia to organise a popular nationalist socialist movement. Kuz'min summed up what the movement was meant to represent:

> *Otechestvo* means realistic living conditions for everyone [...] *Otechestvo* means a territorial community [*obshchnost'*] and [...] we will strengthen its integrity [...] We will work for the cleansing of our environment [...] We will work to ensure that people are aware of their historical heritage, traditions, national memory [...] *Otechestvo* means a certain social-economic order, whose destruction would entail great sacrifices and would yield no beneficial results [...] *Otechestvo* means a certain conception of social justice [...] *Otechestvo* means a certain social-political system. We intend to assist in its perfection.

There was no question of destroying the social and political system the people had created.[36] This programme, with its emphasis on social justice, army and empire, and cultural heritage, was meant to appeal to the Russian working class, the military, those with relatives in the republics or employed in the military-defence sector of the economy (a constituency estimated at about 40 million). However, *Otechestvo* failed to appeal to public opinion: it had only an estimated three hundred active members in 1989, and of the 132 candidates it fielded in the 1990 elections to Moscow City Council, only nine were elected (chief among them was Viktor Anpilov).[37] After this poor showing, *Otechestvo* faded from view.[38]

The Union for the Spiritual Renewal of the Fatherland also attempted to galvanise support for national, socialist and imperialist resistance to reform. Founded in Moscow on 16–17 March 1989,[39] it was led by the economist Mikhail Antonov. It pledged itself to Soviet socialism and denounced the tentative reforms of the economic system as an attempt to undermine the independence of the USSR and turn it into a colony of the West, while calling for Orthodox renewal. It demanded a government of 'patriotic forces' to defend the Russian nation, strengthen the Soviet army and repel Western influence.[40] Although Antonov converted to Orthodoxy in August 1990, the Union continued to support the CPSU, opposing the CPSU's renunciation of its 'leading role' (its political monopoly).[41] Apparently unaware of voters' antipathy to the Party, the Union's leaders appeared to believe that Soviet socialism remained potentially popular and all that was required was to give it a nationalist gloss.

Nationalists made several abortive efforts, between 1989 and 1991, to copy Democratic Russia by uniting the disparate nationalist and socialist organisations that opposed reform. Led by writers and artists, with discreet support from right-wingers in the Party and security forces, it was hoped that the resulting front would emulate the popular fronts in the Baltics and rally wider public support for the conservative agenda. The project failed, as the nationalist socialism that the conservatives propounded found no resonance in public opinion, as the fate of the 'patriotic', anti-reform bloc in the Spring 1990 elections demonstrated.[42] The patriots' election manifesto attacked the reformers' economic and cultural liberalism for undermining the living standards of the Russian people and encouraging crime, alcoholism, the decline of family life and the mass-media's attacks on the army and security forces. The manifesto warned:

THE FATHERLAND IS IN PERIL! [...] Will Russia preserve her political and economic independence, her cultural identity [...]?[43]

The cultural figures and Party hardliners in the bloc wanted to preserve the sovereignty and integrity of the Soviet Union, which was threatened by the rise of minority nationalism. The reforms were seen as undermining the status of ethnic Russians outside the Russian Federation, hence the bloc demanded protection for the Russian minorities in the Republics, such as the Baltic States, whose resurgent nationalism threatened traditional Russian hegemony. Russia should cease subsidising the rebellious nationalities; its resources should be concentrated on itself; Russian institutions should be created – as in the other republics – and Russians should no longer be submerged in all-Union institutions (whether in the media or academe).[44]

The Patriotic Bloc performed poorly in the 1990 elections at both national and local level. Of the hundreds of candidates it fielded nationwide, not one was successful. None of its 61 candidates in the capital were elected in the first round: despite their fame, neither Stanislav Kunaev (with 13.7 per cent of the vote in the first round) nor Ilya Glazunov (with 12.12 per cent) survived the second ballot. By contrast, the democrats won 57 out of 61 seats in Moscow (with Party candidates accounting for most of the balance).[45] In the elections to the Moscow City Soviet, the bloc's support was also disappointing, with 2.2 per cent of the overall vote in the first round and 2.9 per cent in the second round (although they scored 12 per cent and 41.9 per cent respectively in one constituency). Their poor showing has been ascribed to the generality and irrelevance of their programme and their poor organisation.[46] Opinion polls confirmed that the nationalists (as opposed to the *gosudarstvenniki* or imperialists) attracted little support in Moscow at this time.[47]

This failure to appeal to the public disabused conservatives of their ability to manipulate the State's new democratic institutions and propelled them towards open support for a coup and authoritarian rule. The most immediate consequence of these failures was that the Party hardliners returned their attention to the levers of power (the Party and the State) and renewed their efforts to capture them. A first step in this direction was taken with the creation, in June 1990, of the Russian Communist Party. Yet the Russian Communist Party, founded at their insistence despite the wishes of the reformers, was to justify neither the hopes of the Initiative Movement nor the fears of the Party centrists and reformers. Despite Gorbachev's move to the right in Winter 1990–91, the conservatives were disappointed both by their failure to control the new party effectively and by their limited influence on society. While some neo-Stalinists called for a return to orthodoxy, other Party conservatives considered a nationalist reform-ulation of their position. In this, they found willing allies in the intelligentsia.

B) THE IDEOLOGY OF THE 'THIRD WAY'

Authoritarian nationalists and communists devoted the first months of 1991 to devising a new nationalist socialist ideology around which an anti-reform front or 'third force' could be rallied and which would legitimate their attacks on the liberal reformers and democrats. They drew heart from Gorbachev's move to the right in Autumn 1990 and the dismissal of his more liberal advisors and colleagues. An early sign of the nationalists' recovery from the defeats of 1989 and 1990 was the foundation of two new right-wing papers at the end of 1990 and early in 1991. The Leningrad broadcaster, Alexander Nevzorov,[48] started his paper *Narodnaya pravda* and the USSR Writers' Union entrusted Alexander Prokhanov with *Den'* (Day), which was to become the paper of the 'spiritual opposition' to Yeltsin in the 1990s.

Eduard Volodin, a correspondent of *Sovetskaya Rossiya* and leader of the United Council of Russia was to the forefront in proposing a tactical alliance between the nationalist intelligentsia and the hardlin-ers in the Russian Communist Party. In February 1991, he published a long apologia for National-Bolshevism in *Den'*, in which he suggested that the post-1917 regime had twice saved Russia from foreign domi-nation, initially during the Civil War and then in the Second World War, when the people rallied to socialism to preserve the nation and State. National-Bolshevism thus was 'an historically progressive phe-nomenon and fulfilled the task of saving the Fatherland'. It was rele-vant now too, when 'Russia is on the brink of a State catastrophe' as 'a consequence of the rush to Western-style democracy. It is again a question of the very existence of the country and the people.' An alliance between the Russian Communist Party and nationalist intelli-gentsia would have similarly salutary effects for Russia in her present troubles, Volodin argued. The Communist Party would have to rally to the right-wing nationalists for it was in a different position:

> Distanced from power by the creators of *perestroika*, abandoned by its own establishment, headed by the hybrid ranks of democratic radicals, this party is obliged and consciously will rally to 'National-Bolshevism' and this will be its last chance to survive, to retain

political significance in society, and, having thrown off cosmopolitan internationalism, to try to become the party of working men.

The key question for the Party was therefore to decide on its relations with the national patriotic movement 'in order to preserve the nation, in order to save our statehood'.

Volodin suggested that his own objections to the communist regime were rooted in opposition not so much to socialism *per se* as to 'internationalism'. It was not communism and Orthodoxy that were incompatible but 'internationalism' and Orthodoxy. If the CPSU were to rid itself of the cosmopolitan element, then, he implied, there would be nothing to prevent Orthodoxy resuming its role as the 'collective unifier of the Russian people'. Anti-Semitism enabled the authoritarianism of the old regime to be fused with the re-emerging prestige of Orthodoxy and was thereby revived in a new, collectivist nationalism. As Volodin explained, the nation could be protected against its external enemies if National-Bolshevism were revived and updated:

> On the basis of Orthodox spirituality and of historic tradition we are capable of erecting the bastions which will defend Russia from hordes of ideological nomads and political adventurers.[49]

Volodin attempted to give effect to these ideas. Under his guidance, the United Council for Russia took part in a conference organised by the Russian Communist Party on 27 February 1991. As indicated by its decidedly un-Marxist slogan: 'For a great, united Russia!', the Conference attempted to mobilise nationalist communist opinion behind the platform that was to inspire the 1991 coup: the maintenance of military might and the integrity of the USSR. The Conference founded a still-born Patriotic Union, which Volodin was elected to lead. Its rhetoric was more significant than its practical impact, in that it showed how far some Party conservatives were ready to go in exploiting nationalism and even xenophobia. Its address to the Russian people warned:

> Our great power [...] is in mortal danger [...] By the will of thoughtless and short-sighted politicians, we are becoming defenceless, deprived of allies, powerful weaponry and consciousness of the need for defence. We are being prepared for the humiliating lot of the satellite, without our own national policy, aims or historical mores [...] We must without delay renounce individual, group and party dissension and restore strong and powerful rule, capable [...] of defending the [State's] borders, defending its citizens [...] Only a

strong, rational, politically active power is capable of rescuing Russia from tragedy.[50]

The readiness of Russian Communist Party hardliners to jettison socialism in order to defend the Soviet system was underlined by the intervention of the Party's First Secretary, Ivan Polozkov:

> We are ready for any cooperation with all political tendencies, if this will enable the preservation of statehood. Our cooperation is based on the recognition of patriotism as a basis for uniting.[51]

The attendance of monarchists, Muslims, Orthodox believers and priests, 'scientific anti-Zionists', former dissidents like Osipov as well as Party members testified to the Party conservatives' new eclecticism.[52] This disparate gathering was, in turn, ready to greet the Russian Communist Party as the only powerful body animated by the 'greater Russian ideal' and to urge it 'to formulate an ideology of national salvation'.[53] The meeting pointed to the breakdown of the old political culture and the emergence of a new one, based on new alliances and antipathies.

The elaboration of a new theoretical basis for authoritarianism pre-occupied conservative Party members and nationalists throughout 1991. An influential role in this process was played by Sergei Kurginyan's Experimental Creative Centre, which was funded by the governments of both Ryzhkov and Pavlov.[54] Kurginyan, who ran one of Moscow's experimental theatre groups (*Na doskakh*) was thought to maintain contact between official Party circles and authoritarian nationalists in this period. In 1991 the Centre ran the club *Postperestroika* (a title taken from a book of the same name, published by Kurginyan in 1990).

Postperestroika outlined the group's theories on economic reform. Kurginyan and his associates recommended a plan of economic modernisation which involved concentrating resources on a small sector of privileged firms and granting Dickensian powers to employers in this sphere. This plan obviated problems such as privatisation, unemployment and the loss of central control, proposing instead a new version of 'acceleration' (*uskorenie*), the concept with which *perestroika* had begun. The new plan would enable the USSR to achieve technical progress and, hence, 'spiritual leadership', without sacrificing the essentials of the command economy.[55] Kurginyan was the *bête noire* of the democrats.[56] He was close to the Pavlov government, whose incompetent economic policies he attempted to justify in March 1991.

Confirming Pavlov's attempt, the previous month, to blame Western security services for the USSR's financial problems, Kurginyan asserted that financial wars were no illusion. Russian democrats who believed that the West would help contemporary Russia were mistaken: vast sums were not required to undermine the rouble and provoke hyperinflation, such as Russia was experiencing.[57]

An indication of the Centre's political orientation was provided by Vladimir Ovchinsky,[58] in an analysis of the democratic movement in February 1991. The Centre had researched the rise of the informal movement in the USSR, particularly in the Baltics, he claimed, and had concluded that the development of national tension was provoked consciously as part of a global policy of destabilising the State. The national movements of the ethnic minorities were connected with leaders of the black economy, secret services of foreign countries, foreign embassies and such (presumably dubious) organisations as the UN and the European Parliament. Hence, the development of these movements in the USSR fitted into the West's plans to destabilise its enemy and to break it up into as many small units as possible. There was only one answer for Russia, according to Ovchinsky: 'The path of restoration of the State will be painful, requiring the rejection of certain democratic (or rather "pseudo-democratic") conquests.' He proposed the introduction of a state of emergency and wide-ranging measures to restore order, eradicate terrorism, inter-ethnic conflict, economic crime and sabotage.[59] In short, Ovchinsky's analysis amounted to an apologia for the reintroduction of authoritarian rule, the abolition of democratic reforms and the preservation (if necessary by force) of the USSR. Similar analyses by the Centre, calling for the introduction of a state of emergency and 'stabilising' measures, such as those adopted by the 1991 putschists, were submitted to the CPSU and later published.[60] It is not surprising that Pavlov's government was willing to fund a research centre which came to conclusions which coincided so fully with its own instincts.[61]

That Party hardliners looked benignly on Kurginyan and hoped he would furnish them with new ideological clothes in which to present themselves to the public is indicated by the space they gave to his views. Kurginyan made it clear that he was proposing a politically authoritarian, economically modern and culturally traditionalist regime, controlled by great industrial and agrarian corporations but in which the interests of the State were paramount and in which an intellectual elite would enjoy economic and cultural privileges (including relative freedom). The 'post-industrial socialism' which this regime would embrace would be neither Marxist-Leninist nor democratic but a 'third way' between exhausted democracy and the hopeless return to the past, for which many conservatives longed.[62] His combination of modernisation with authoritarian elitism and nationalism was not so much forward-looking, however, as reminiscent of the fascism of the 1930s.

The first of his long theoretical articles appeared in the Moscow party paper at the end of March 1991. In this, Kurginyan suggested that, for historico-cultural reasons, as well as for reasons of State security, the USSR could not follow the Western path of development. The USSR belonged, he argued (without acknowledging the debt to Danilevsky and the Eurasians) to a separate cultural type: an Orthodox–Muslim, Eastern communitarian tradition, at odds with Western individualism. Neither psychologically nor culturally were Russians likely to respond to capitalism. Russia must find its own path of development:

> The Soviet type of culture is a special alloy [...] The culture born of Orthodoxy and Islam excludes the possibility of transition to a classical Western system of stimuli and motivation.[63]

The CPSU's hostility to the West and the political and economic models the West embodied, classically based on the supposed antithesis between socialism and capitalism, was given a hitherto unorthodox twist: it could be justified if not on grounds of ideological incompatibility and class war, then on the basis of cultural diversity and historical antipathy. Instead, he proposed 'innovatory political centrism': the 'third way', neither Western capitalism, consumerism and liberal democracy nor a return to Stalinism or Tsarist theocracy.[64] It would, its author hoped, consolidate all realistic forces around the 'salvation of the country and the State', by committing the USSR to a path of development based on geopolitical realities, the country's 'cultural-historical uniqueness', its traditions and resources, emphasizing the role of the State as the motor of the economy and as a leading player in science, culture and industry. The command system of economic management should in its essentials be retained; the internal security forces should be strengthened in their fight against crime, corruption and attempts to undermine State security. In this way the Soviet Union would develop rapidly as a leading economic power and as a new type of civilisation.[65]

Kurginyan was to develop these ideas in a subsequent article, which was presented as an alternative draft CPSU programme (for adoption at the projected Twenty-ninth Party Congress) and prepared at the behest of the Moscow Party Committee. In this, Kurginyan adopted a position close to that of the National Bolsheviks of the 1920s, emphasising the importance attaching to the survival of the Soviet Union[66] and the mobilising power of nationalism (in its collectivist, Slavophile variant). He started by rejecting Marxism as the ideological basis of the Party:

> Today, it is necessary to acknowledge that Marxism-Leninism in the current situation can be regarded as a fundamental ideal of the past but not as one that can present itself as the essence of a modern understanding of the development of social processes and megatendencies [*sic*].
> In this sense, calls to return to Leninist sources, to a Marxism-Leninism purified of deformities, do not correspond to the urgency of the situation.

The idea of communism as the highest form of social development and the idea of a universal model of human development, without reference to tradition and culture, had to be reconsidered. This did not mean that the Party should be disbanded: on the contrary, since it was the main structure on which society and the State were based, its survival was vital.

Collectivist nationalism would enable the Party's fortunes to recover. Marx had been wrong about the motor of history: nations, not class war, impelled history. The nation should be understood as a cultural-historical entity.[67] Turning from nineteenth-century socialism, the Party ideologue looked to nineteenth-century nationalism for solutions. Happily, this furnished a messianic and eschatological model which fitted neatly into the space vacated by Soviet Marxism, requiring only a minor adaptation of world-view on the part of the faithful. Conveniently, with romantic Slavophilism to draw on, the rejection of Marxism did not entail the rejection of collectivism or a closer approach to the West. Each nation had its own role to play in history, Kurginyan argued. The West and the East were destined to follow different paths of development. Those of the East were just as viable as the Western model, which the Russian left was so anxious to adopt. Russia belonged to the East and could not follow the Western path. East and West were incompatible:

> As the analysis of the multifarious forms of social organisation of Western and Eastern society has shown, despite all their variety,

two types may be distinguished – the individualistic and, in many ways contrasting and opposed to it, the communitarian, communal [*obshchinnoe*] (or communist) [...]

Individualistic societies were characterised by a developed market system, which undermined social cohesion and tradition and resulted in the development of 'atom-individuals', battling against each other for survival. The more developed the industrial economy, the further removed was the individual from nature, the freer he was in relation to the community but the greater his isolation and alienation. Communitarian societies, in which the individual was restrained and sustained by the community, were more harmonious, consoling and organic; they were more creative and avoided the crises to which Western societies were prone.

Postulating two different types of civilisation, Kurginyan was able to reject Western political and economic norms as alien to Russia and the Soviet Union. This approach had the additional advantage of furnishing a justification for the retention of the Soviet empire:

Clarification of the fact that the Russian and other peoples who inhabit the territory of the USSR belong to the Eastern type [of civilisation], the conscious following of this path cannot but enable egoistic centrifugal tendencies to be overcome and these people to be united.

Kurginyan provided Party hardliners with new justification for rejecting reform; instead of appealing to discredited Soviet socialism, they were able to present their support for the command economy as support for traditional Russian collectivism, their insistence on political centralisation and authoritarianism as Russian nationalism. As Kurginyan put it:

Communism is not just an invention, but the historical destiny of the peoples inhabiting our country and as long as our State lives, it will not change this path.

His article ended with an appeal to all those who cared for the country's historic traditions and for the State as a value in itself to unite behind his programme.[68] The attention accorded to him testifies to the Party conservatives' readiness to jettison orthodox Party ideology in favour of earlier Russian nationalist theory. Kurginyan thus represents a clearly discernible tendency among some Party hardliners, in the first half of 1991, to develop a form of nationalist socialism.

Not everyone, however, was convinced of the benefits of alliance – or at least of open alliance – with the Party. Vladimir Bondarenko, Prokhanov's deputy at *Den'*, observed: 'Today, the question asked more and more often in society is: who will become "the third force"?' Certainly not the left intelligentsia, with their detestation of all that was connected with the State, with Great Power status and with Russia's national heroes. Why, Bondarenko asked, were all the attempts so far made by the right nationalists to consolidate so unsuccessful? They had devoted much time and effort to the task of creating a mass following; they had thinkers (Kozhinov, Shafarevich, Antonov), writers and artists (Rasputin, Belov, Astafiev, Glazunov), organisations (*Yedinenie, Otechestvo*, the Union for Spiritual Renewal), 'but we have still not succeeded in crossing the key threshold, in attracting millions of supporters [...] There are many good commanders but without an army. Where is the army? What is preventing people from rallying under the banner of the patriotic movement?' The answer, to Bondarenko, was clear: 'No matter how good the current leaders of the RCP [Russian Communist Party] are, the initials themselves are enough to put people off. We must say goodbye to National-Bolshevism.'

Instead, he contended, the hope for the future lay with the army. 'The army is the only force capable of saving Russia.' The patriotic movement should acquire a power-base – that of the military-industrial complex. 'It is precisely the army which has always thought in terms of state power. The army has always been on the side of the State. Today the army understands more and more the need for patriotic structures. If the Party leadership is destroying the State, the army has no vested interest in that leadership.' However, Bondarenko hastened to assure his readership (he was writing within a month of the August 1991 coup), 'it is not a question of some sort of coup [...] it is not a question of a version of Pinochet or South Korea, although the results have shown that this option is not so bad, no, we are talking of the constitutional option of General de Gaulle and General Eisenhower [...] The army, in current conditions, will move away from Communist ideology and will adopt for its armoury the idea of a *national Russia*.' This would be strengthened by the adoption of Orthodoxy as a State religion. Not only the army would support the new regime, the directors of the space programme, of the country's leading enterprises, entire branches of industry which were capable of competing with their American counterparts should be represented in the Supreme Soviet. 'The outstanding engineer, industrialist, member of the defence establishment, commander has no place in the left-wingers' camp.' It was they who ruled in England and America and who should come to power in Russia.[69]

In essence, the forces which Bondarenko was anxious to marshal under the banner of the nation and Orthodoxy were the same as those which were then drawn up under the flag of communism and which constituted the right-wing of the CPSU. They were also identical with the forces that backed the 1991 coup. Bondarenko's disclaimers about his approval of a coup in which the army would take power were clearly disingenuous, as were his references to de Gaulle and Eisenhower. What he wanted was the seizure of power by the army to restore Russian State power, retain the USSR, halt economic reforms and reverse the transition to the market, possibly retaining some form of parliament for purposes of legitimation.

Bondarenko had reason to believe that his formula might find favour among the army, although the results of the previous month's presidential elections revealed the lack of popular support for these ideas. When General Albert Makashov ran against Yeltsin, on an authoritarian, militaristic ticket, he won only 3.9 per cent of the vote.[70] Nonetheless, *Den'* tried to whip up support for a take-over by the army, at first covering Makashov's campaign sympathetically and then profiling General Igor Rodionov (the commander immediately responsible for the Tbilisi massacre in 1989) and the Defence Minister, Marshal Dmitri Yazov, and conducting long interviews with figures such as the Soyuz leader Viktor Alksnis.[71] Yazov was portrayed as a 'father' figure, alone on a par with the Patriarch Alexei II. In all these articles, the intention was to suggest that anti-democratic forces had numerous potential, heroic leaders – men already tried and tested in the role – and that they were acting in the best intentions. *Glasnost'*, democracy and disarmament were attacked in the sharpest terms:

> [...] All this dirty repulsive stream which is pouring constant abuse onto the army – *Ogonek*, *Vzglyad* [...] *perestroika* academics [...] it isn't simply abuse, but is a well-planned counter-propaganda operation to disarm the opponent's forces. A war is being conducted and our army is being annihilated [...]

General Rodionov commented.[72] Admiral Chernavin and Oleg Baklanov – who took part in the same interview – expressed similar views, supporting the maintenance of the army's political role and military power and rejecting disarmament and the restructuring of the defence industry.[73]

Readers of *Den'* could hardly have been in doubt about the preferences of both the editors and those profiled by them: the generals, defence industry chiefs and certain sections of the Party. An interview with Viktor Alksnis, published in *Den'*, shortly before the coup left no room for doubt on this score. Asked about a closed session of the Supreme Soviet, in which the Defence and Interior Ministers (Yazov and Pugo) and the head of the KGB (Kryuchkov) had all called for a state of emergency,[74] Alksnis confirmed that the reports were true:

> [...] The heads of these government structures, who possess the fullest information, announced: our country is on the brink of death. And if emergency measures are not taken, I emphasise – EMERGENCY MEASURES, then OUR COUNTRY WILL CEASE TO EXIST![75]

Given the convention of the political culture in which people like Prokhanov operated, a clearer signal of forthcoming events could not have been given.

Were Prokhanov and other members of the nationalist intelligentsia involved in the 1991 coup? Their sympathy was not in doubt. According to one theory, the coup was prepared with the assistance of Prokhanov and Kurginyan.[76] If not actively involved in its planning, Prokhanov and Kurginyan were certainly among its leading ideologists and supporters. The gesture most widely seen as a token of the nationalist intelligentsia's support for a coup was the 'Appeal to the People' (*Slovo k narody*) published in *Sovetskaya Rossiya* on 23 July 1991 (and also in *Den'*, 15, 1991) and of which Prokhanov was reputedly the principal author. In the hysterical tones by then habitual in the right-wing press, the Appeal announced that the State and Motherland were dying, falling apart before the authors' eyes. This was the fault of the corrupt leadership of the country, which was being manipulated from abroad. The entire Soviet population, including Buddhists, Vedists and the Orthodox Church, was urged to unite in a 'national-patriotic movement' whose aim was to be 'the salvation of the Fatherland'. Among its immediate aims were to prevent the 'fateful' collapse of the State and economy and the strengthening of Soviet power. The army was accorded particularly warm words:

> We are sure that the fighters of the army and navy, faithful to their sacred duty, will not permit a civil war, the destruction of the Fatherland and will act as the trustworthy guarantor of security and the bulwark of all healthy forces in society.

There was no shortage of talent to prevent the collapse of the USSR and its economic system:

> There are thinkers, spiritual creators who can visualise the national ideal. The Soviet Union is our home and our bulwark, built with great effort by all peoples and nations, which has saved us from contempt and slavery in the dark years of invasion! Russia is one and beloved! – she is calling for help'.[77]

This intemperate address to the army and masses was signed by leaders of the nationalist and National-Bolshevik intelligentsia, by members of the Party *apparat* and right-wing officers: the writers Yuri Bondarev, Alexander Prokhanov, Eduard Volodin and Valentin Rasputin; the sculptor and *Pamyat'* supporter, Vyacheslav Klykov;[78] the singer Lyudmila Zykina; two generals – Boris Gromov and Valentin Varennikov; the *Soyuz* leader, Yuri Blokhin; the Russian Communist Party Central Committee Secretary, Gennady Zyuganov; the embryonic 'red directors' Vasily Starodubtsov (who had founded the 'Peasant Union' to resist the privatisation of agriculture) and Alexander Tizyakov, of the Association of State Enterprises and United Military-Industrial Complex. This was the grand alliance *Den'* had been preaching for months. Some of the more obscure names in this list were to achieve greater fame as members of the Emergency Committee installed by the coup: Varennikov, Starodubtsev and Tizyakov were among its leaders.

The significance of the Appeal did not escape notice: Vladimir Zhirinovsky expressed his support for its proposal, in a long article published in *Sovetskaya Rossiya* at the end of July. The Appeal should act as a tocsin. The State was being destroyed from within.

> The Appeal to the Nation somehow reminds me of a mobilisation call-up. It is bitter to think that not everyone will listen and understand. People [...] do not feel the danger.[79]

The signatories did not intend to delay either and on 5 August announced that they had started work on founding the National-Patriotic Movement, referred to in the famous Appeal. The failure of the coup, however, disrupted these plans.

The sympathy between the Conservative nationalist intelligentsia and Party hardliners, however, was clear for all to see. The welcome extended by some imprudent writers[80] to the coup simply confirmed what was already well known: that most of the nationalist intelligentsia opposed democratic reform, economic and cultural liberalism and were ready to support the right-wing of the Party and State. From flirting with anti-Semitic and marginal proto-fascist movements, in the later 1980s, the conservative nationalist intelligentsia had moved into the political mainstream, as the main apologists and theoreticians of a new form of authoritarianism. Rejecting the influence of the West, they explored forms of nationalist socialism and were ready to emulate examples of dictatorial and military rule furnished by the Third World. There was little reason for them to object in principle to the coup.

C. THE 1991 COUP

The August 1991 coup was the culmination of a series of attempts by Party hardliners to reassert their political control: in late 1990, their capture of key positions in the State had been followed by attempts to suppress the democratic movement in the Baltics and to decapitate it in Russia, by marginalising Yeltsin. When this failed and Gorbachev realigned himself with the democrats, in April 1991, the conservatives began to consider the effective removal of Gorbachev as the only means of preventing the deconstruction of the Soviet system.

At a closed session of the conservative USSR Congress of Peoples' Deputies, in mid-June, conservatives attempted to wrest power from Gorbachev by constitutional means. On 17 June, the Prime Minister Pavlov appeared before the Union Congress demanding extraordinary powers, including the right to declare a state of emergency. The Interior Minister, Boris Pugo, Defence Minister Yazov and KGB chief Kryuchkov spoke in favour of transferring Gorbachev's powers to Pavlov, implying that Gorbachev should go. 'Our Fatherland is on the brink of catastrophe', Kryuchkov warned. Urgent measures were needed to put an end to the destructive process – not more talk about humanism and universal values.[81] Some deputies even called openly for Gorbachev's removal. Gorbachev's intervention on 21 June managed to retrieve the situation. Clearly, the hardliners could not expect to succeed by parliamentary measures alone.

Yeltsin's election to the Russian Presidency on 12 June 1991 and the negotiations on the new Union Treaty, which was to be followed, within six months, by a new constitution and elections to a new Union parliament and Presidency, made the issue urgent. The Union Treaty was finalised at the end of July for signature on 20 August 1991. It vested sovereignty in the new republics, which were to delegate limited authority to the Centre (which would also have sovereign status) on foreign affairs, defence and economic policy. The republics were to supervise the Union's execution of these policies and to retain ultimate control over the budget and taxation. Anticipating this settlement, Yeltsin pressed on with a series of reforms intended to strengthen his fledgling State. Moves to establish an independent security service were renewed with Kryuchkov's reluctant assistance and on 20 July 1991 a decree banning the CPSU from all places of work and institutions of State was passed. It finally seemed as if the old regime's economic, political and ideological stranglehold on the State was about to be broken.

The unreconstructed Union was fundamental to the Soviet power system and its achievements. The centralisation on which it was based grew in importance with the abolition of the Party's political monopoly in March 1990, for it enabled power to be retained and decisions to be taken by a small group of people in Moscow and it alone, it seemed, held the State and the disintegrating economic system together. The centralisation on which it was predicated had enabled the Soviet Union to attain superpower status, by allowing resources to be concentrated on the army and the defence industries and the entire economy to be subordinated to their requirements. Since it guaranteed, and even seemed to justify, their power, it was thus inconceivable that the Party and State's conservatives should allow the Union to be dismantled. It was for this reason that they organised the putsch for the day before the signature of the new Union Treaty on 19 August 1991.

Its organisation was an apparently last-minute affair, agreed at KGB chief Kryuchkov's *dacha* on 18 August 1991.[82] Unable to act with the callous indifference to legal forms that had characterised Soviet interventions in the satellite States, the coup leaders did not seem to realise that, in the more complex world that then existed in Russia, a palace coup was more difficult to engineer than in the time of Khrushchev.[83] It was not enough – nor was it now possible – to summon a well-disciplined Party plenum and instruct it to pronounce judgement. Power was now too widely dispersed to allow a self-appointed group of Party functionaries to seize it with an appearance of legality. Even when the use of force was reluctantly embraced, the coup leaders were unable to contend with politicised and canny generals, such as Grachev, who finally decided not to support them.[84]

The failure of the coup was nonetheless a surprise. Its leaders lost their nerve and had not planned adequately. The only area in which the ground had been carefully prepared was that of ideology. The coincidence between the aims and rhetoric of the coup leaders and of the theorists of the 'third way' were obvious. Despite their disclaimers about their commitment to reform, democracy and private enterprise, the plotters were unambiguously opposed to civic liberties – as their restrictions on freedom of the press and association indicated – and to democracy, which they saw as undermining State power and unity. The democracy and freedom they envisaged did not include the right to dissent, as their comments on the existing democratic movement indicated:

> Using the freedom they have been granted, trampling on the newly grown shoots of democracy, extremist forces have appeared committed to the liquidation of the Soviet Union, the ruin of the State and the seizure of power at any price.[85]

To make their restrictions more palatable, the putschists offered the public a populist socialism of the OFT variety, promising lower prices and hinting at higher wages.[86] They did not appeal to Marxism-Leninism to win support, relying instead on Greater Russian nationalism (imperial pride) and the desire for law and order:

> In a serious, critical hour for the fate of our Fatherland and our peoples, we appeal to you! [...] Our multi-national people has for centuries lived filled with pride for its Motherland [...] Everyone to whom the Motherland is dear, who wants to live and work in peace and confidence, who does not want to see the continuation of bloody interethnic conflict, who sees his Fatherland as independent and prosperous in the future, must make the only correct choice.[87]

In short, if in practice the plotters wanted to restore the Soviet order as it had existed before *perestroika*, they justified their regime with an ideology that was overtly nationalist and authoritarian rather than Marxist.[88] This adjustment was, of course, forced on them by changes wrought in public opinion by *glasnost'*, but it indicates the secondary importance of orthodox communist ideology in the later Soviet regime and the readiness of the conservative Party elite to amend or even jettison key elements of it. The re-emergence of communism in the form of a nationalist, authoritarian and populist socialism in the post-Soviet period was thus prefigured by developments in the Party before the 1991 coup.

The ignominious collapse of the coup in the panic-stricken flight and drunkenness of its leaders had consequences which overshadowed the insignificance of its authors. The State and political system they had sought to preserve were swept away and a new political era began. If its forms were different, however, the political culture of the new age was indebted to that which had preceded it. Nowhere was this more evident than in the rhetoric and aims of the new opposition.

5 The National Salvation Front, 1991–92

The August coup was a fiasco – due both to a failure of nerve and to the depth of Gorbachev's reforms: even the KGB and the army had their reforming wings, which opposed the plotters. However, the democrats' victory in August 1991 was more apparent than real, partly because of the confusion of their strategy and the ambiguities of their political style. Rather than introducing the necessary reforms, reorganising the judiciary and the administration, bringing forward a new constitution, renewing the victors' democratic mandate, or consolidating his power-base by courting the support of his erstwhile allies in the parliament and rewarding their leaders with office and emoluments, as they expected, Yeltsin retreated increasingly into a style of government reminiscent of Soviet high politics: intrigue behind closed doors, rule by a team of close advisors, with a subordinate and sometimes marginalised government.[1]

What changes Yeltsin did decide on were controversial and not endorsed by popular vote: economic shock therapy and the dismantling of the Soviet Union. He put an end to the power struggle of the previous eighteen months by simply abolishing one of the players – the old Soviet Union – and refusing to envisage a reformed Federation. This ensured that there could be no further threat to his power from Gorbachev but was a humiliating shock for most Russians, who could not conceive of a Russian state without the Ukraine and Belorussia or, to a lesser extent, its Caucasian and Central Asian dependencies. The dissolution of the Soviet Union (decided on in a Belorussian forest between Stanislav Shushkevich, Leonid Kravchuk and Yeltsin, without the participation of the other republican leaders – but subsequently endorsed by them in the Belovezha Accords of December 1991 – and without the democratic agreement of the relevant population, except in the Ukraine) was not only psychologically traumatic but also created enormous practical problems, for the army, the economy and for society, in the shape of a large and vulnerable Russian diaspora of 25 millions, who now found themselves to be aliens in foreign states, sometimes deprived of civic rights.[2] The collapse of the Soviet Union also led to Russia's loss of great-power status: her presence at international fora did not disguise her loss of prestige or the fact that, once a rival of the West, Russia was now rather a client state, its foreign policy aligned with that of the West, its economy directed, as it seemed to the public, according to foreign theories and increasingly in need of foreign aid.

Other than this, the chief thrust of the reform was concentrated on monetary and fiscal policies. Liberalising prices, when the giant sectoral monopolies that dominated the Soviet economy had not been dismantled, when the infrastructure and legal basis for a competitive market economy had not been put in place, was, as critics from left and centre observed, likely to lead to inflation, falling demand and living standards. Although acute shortages of consumer goods soon ended, the goods that appeared in the shops were beyond the pocket of many Russians. The government's slow and unsteady course towards structural economic reform was inhibited by the parliamentary opposition, deepening the economic crisis and resulting in a substantial proportion of the Russian population living below the poverty line.[3] The Western-orientated young economists who advocated and implemented this approach were inevitably associated with the collapse of Russian power and the growing poverty and lawlessness of the country. The popular democratic movement collapsed: the cultural intelligentsia retreated to their studies; the crowds were too busy surviving to bother with demonstrations.

The parliament soon found itself at odds with the President. Within six months of the 1991 coup, the dual power which had paralysed the Soviet Union between June 1990 and August 1991 developed again, this time within the Russian Federation, with the President and parliament disputing the right to rule. The parliament had been elected in Spring 1990 in conditions of comparative freedom and democracy (although before the formal introduction of a multi-party system) and its pretensions were not without foundation. The constitution was contradictory: it proclaimed both President and parliament to be the highest authority in the State. Furthermore, the presidency was the parliament's own creation: the parliament, in May 1991, had voted to establish a democratic presidency and had defined the prerogatives of the office, before investing Yeltsin with additional temporary powers in November 1991.[4] Yeltsin, however, was disinclined to attend to the reservations and claims of the parliament and generally made only minimal concessions to the parliament's views.[5] The result was conflict and a constant atmosphere of political crisis, which started in

March–April 1992, when the first clash between President and full parliament took place.

The new regime was, therefore, from the start encumbered by practical and psychological problems. The collapse of the Soviet Union was a blow to the pride and self-confidence of Russians. It left Russia unanchored historically, geographically and culturally. What did it now mean to be Russian? No longer could Russians claim the messianic role ascribed to them by Party ideology for most of the twentieth century. Their modern title to a world role and regional hegemony had been based on the pretensions of Marxism-Leninism: bereft of this justification, Russians were no longer sure what they contributed to international affairs. Their world role was diminished, their regional dominance challenged and even territories which they were accustomed to view as part of Russia or as traditionally belonging to her now broke away. An independent Ukraine struck at the roots of Russian historical identity, given Russians' propensity to see in the rise of Kiev the origins of the Russian state and culture. Now it was no longer clear even where Russia was, where her borders legitimately ran: should Russia include only those lands where ethnic Russians were in a majority and, if so, what about the areas inhabited by the large Russian diaspora now outside Russia, and conversely, those areas within her borders where ethnic minorities predominated? Should language, religion, history or (as increasingly seemed the case, with the possible fragmentation of the Russian Federation and the threatened breakaway of the richer provinces) wealth determine exclusion or inclusion in the new Russian state? Neither language nor religion were satisfactory criteria of identity, given that historically Russia had been an multi-ethnic state. Nor were tradition and history a helpful source of inspiration given the controversial records and legacies of both the Tsarist and Soviet regimes.

Russian nationalists' response to these dilemmas was not uniform. Some were reluctant to renounce the ideology which had made the Soviet Union a unique and formidable power in the twentieth century, believing that Russia could not regain her place in the world or rebuild her statehood unless socialism was reintroduced. Many communists hoped for the restoration of the Soviet state within its old boundaries. Others were more concerned with re-establishing Russian historical identity. For some, this entailed reclaiming Tsarist rather than Soviet tradition: in effect, this meant seeking to restore most of the pre-revolutionary empire (which was, with the exception of Poland and Finland, almost coterminous with the Soviet Union), while seeking moral renewal in Orthodoxy and appealing to such supposedly unifying theories as (Slav) nationality, collectivism or Eurasianism (to accommodate the Muslim minorities). Others saw this option as unrealistic, realising that the longer the post-Soviet order lasted, the more difficult the restoration of the Soviet empire became. Instead, they limited their demands to reunification with Belarus, the Ukraine and sometimes north Kazakhstan (where Russians predominated) and measures to help the Russian diaspora elswhere. Most of these pragmatists and many of the Tsarist traditionalists were ready to envisage some form of mixed economy. All, however, were at one on the need to restore a powerful, at least partially reunited Russian state, capable of challenging the West and incarnating a unique anti-Western culture. Equally, they were united in their strident opposition to Yeltsin and his government's course. For this newly emerging opposition, the primary task in the immediate post-Soviet years was to mount a challenge to Yeltsin's reform course and the Westernisation it entailed, in the name of Russian state power and tradition. The political environment could not have been more propitious for the emergence of a nationalist opposition. At the start of the new era, however, its position seemed to have been fatally weakened by the defeat of the August 1991 coup. The CPSU and Communist Party of the RSFSR were banned by Yeltsin and their property seized in a series of decrees issued in August and November 1991. This threatened to remove a still potentially powerful constituency and the most effective political machine in the country from the political scene and to deprive the nationalist critics of democracy of their most significant ally.

A. THE COMMUNISTS

A number of attempts were made to fill the vacuum on the left with new communist parties, of Leninist or Stalinist orientation, each of which claimed to be the true heir of the Party and its enormous resources. At least six proto-communist parties were founded in November and December 1991, corresponding to the various tendencies that had emerged on the conservative wing of the CPSU since 1989 – from the Leninists and reform communists of Marxist Platform to the OFT and the neo-Stalinists.[6]

At one end of the spectrum was the Socialist Workers' Party, whose leaders included the former dissident, Roy Medvedev, and the former

Central Committee Secretary and the last leader of the Communist Party of the RSFSR, Valentin Kuptsov. Founded on 22 December 1991, it was reformist in orientation, committed both to political pluralism and a mixed economy. It retained close links with the old party nomenklatura, attracted the support of many communist deputies in the Russian parliament in 1992 (including Ivan Rybkin and Mikhail Lapshin) and, by the start of 1993, claimed 100 000 members. Closest to Medvedev's reform Leninism was the Russian Party of Communists, founded on 14–15 December 1991 by members of Marxist Platform and led by Anatoly Kryuchkov. Committed to a more democratic form of Soviet socialism, the RPK was one of the most active of the new parties in promoting communist reunification. A similar position was adopted by Alexei Prigarin's Union of Communists, which was founded in November 1991. These two parties were reckoned to have 2000–3000 members.[7] More uncompromising in its opposition to reform was the Russian Communist Workers' Party, founded on 23–24 November 1991 and led by the fiery former foreign correspondent, Viktor Anpilov, Viktor Tyulkin (of the conservative communist Initiative Movement) and for a time by the colourful General Albert Makashov. Calling for the abolition of the parliamentary system, it demanded the re-creation of the Soviet Union as a workers' state based on the command economy and opposed private property. In a characteristically Stalinist synthesis of nationalism and communism, Anpilov explained:

> Having criminally ruined the USSR, the Belovezha separatists condemned the people to poverty and vegetation under the yoke not only of our 'own' native but also of foreign capital [...] The unity of Russia is an essential condition of her [Russia's] existence. We support one Soviet Union and one Russia as federal states in an unchanged constitution of the USSR and Russia. The nationalisation of land, mineral wealth, equipment [...] is the only possible guarantee of [state] unity.[8]

Anpilov was to make this one of the most successful of the successor parties, claiming a membership which rose from an early 10 000 to 80 000 by late 1993. This was largely due to Anpilov's militancy. Unlike other communist leaders, he devoted little time to theory or to establishing alliances with the rest of the opposition or to communist unity – preferring to denounce those who strayed from the straight path of Stalinism.[9] Finally, Nina Andreeva led the All-Union Communist Party of Bolsheviks, founded on 8–9 November 1991 to uphold Stalinism.[10] These strident parties were well placed to exploit the growing discontent with the direction and impact of reform in the post-communist order.

One of the most effective of the new communist groupings was Anpilov's Labouring Moscow (which in October 1992 helped to form the nationwide front, Labouring Russia), a popular movement opposed to Yeltsin's policies. Throughout 1992 and 1993, Working Moscow organised many demonstrations in the capital, which drew substantial crowds onto the streets to protest against shortages and price-rises. Fiery denunciations of Yeltsin's treachery and the evils of the market, of foreign influence and the dissolution of the USSR were the staple fare of these meetings, which were supported not only by elderly communists but also by Baburin's and Osipov's nationalists.[11] These activities culminated in the disturbances in Moscow in October 1993, in which Anpilov and his supporters took an active role, forcibly lifting the siege of the White House. Subsequently banned and with its leader proscribed, Labouring Moscow remained a symbol of the defiance of the older generation of communists and of their alienation from the new regime.

More important, however, was the decision by a group of hardliners from the RSFSR Communist Party to challenge the legality of Yeltsin's decrees banning both it and the CPSU. Fifty-two democrats in the parliament retaliated with a counter-charge to the effect that the Party had violated the Soviet constitution and international law. The two pleas were taken together. In July 1992, the trial of the CPSU opened in the constitutional court, under the presidency of the much-criticised Valery Zorkin.[12] The trial of the Party, a major political event in which many of the leaders of the old regime starred, lasted six months. On 30 November 1992, the Court issued its judgment: Yeltsin had exceeded his powers in disbanding local branches of the Party and thus his prohibition of the Party as a whole was illegal but he had been justified in banning its ruling bodies. Although this adjudication was intended as a compromise, it coincided with the parliament's decision to release the leaders of the 1991 coup, who had been in prison for over a year and whose trial had been progressing at a snail's pace in tandem with the hearings on the Party. Taken together these moves were seen as a reverse for Yeltsin and his democratic supporters and as a triumph for the communists. They lost no time in taking advantage of the opportunity they now enjoyed to organise the Russian Communist Party anew, based on a network of local Party branches. The second party congress was held on 13–14 February 1993 (the June

1990 congress of the Communist Party of the RSFSR being considered as the first one): many of the August coup leaders attended and they reconstituted the party as the Communist Party of the Russian Federation (the KPRF) under the leadership of Gennady Zyuganov, to oppose Yeltsin's policies and promote the recovery of Russia as a Great Power and nation. The new party, which claimed almost half a million members, was the most formidable political organisation in the country. The question was whether the communists and their nationalist allies could work together effectively. The KPRF's emphasis on patriotism seemed to be designed with this strategic alliance in mind.

B. NATIONALISTS

Stimulated by the collapse of the Soviet state and Russia's loss of great power status, new nationalist groups proliferated. Generally authoritarian and collectivist in vocation, at one in their hostility to the new political and economic order, they attracted many former communists from the conservative wing of the CPSU. One of the first of these nationalist organisations was the Russian All-Peoples' Union (*ROS*), which was founded on 21 September 1991. Its chief preoccupation was with the collapse of Russia as a great power and the crisis of Russian statehood and identity that it entailed.[13] Many of its adherents were former Party members.[14] Sergei Baburin, the young law professor from Siberia who was elected to head ROS, had been a member of the CPSU until its dissolution and now emerged as one of the leaders of the collectivist nationalists.[15] As many communists belonged to the movement, ROS's early policy statements betrayed a strong communist influence.[16] The Western model of economic reform was rejected as alien to Russian tradition. Baburin explained that whereas Western conservatism was based on individual property rights, Russian conservatives believed collectivity and conciliarity (*sobornost'*) to be at the heart of Russian nationhood and statehood.[17]

Initially, ROS was concerned with preventing the collapse of the USSR and then with the preservation of historical Russia, which it defined as the territories of the former USSR and the heartland of the tsarist Empire.[18] Its main aim it declared to be 'the regeneration of Russia, her historical statehood, social-economic power, territorial integrity, culture and customs [...]'[19] Hence, at their first congress in December 1991, delegates advocated a more assertive and independent policy towards minority nationalities and the West.[20] Their nostalgia for the Soviet order and belief that it should have been retained was reflected in their openly expressed sympathy for the August coup leaders.[21] Initially in favour of the restoration of the USSR, they later realised that this was unrealistic.[22]

From its inception, ROS made clear its rejection of Western models of organisation and development. It warned the government against mechanically following foreign examples and 'the by no means disinterested prescriptions of international financial circles'.[23] Not only was foreign advice suspect; it was inappropriate: foreign models were ultimately inapplicable in Russia on philosophical-cultural grounds. According to Nikolai Pavlov, liberal democratic ideas had led to bloodshed, upheaval and civil war: only a strong State power was capable of defending the citizen and guaranteeing security and order.[24] Sergei Baburin was unequivocal in his rejection of Western democracy. While stressing the need for a strong unified State, he appeared to favour democratic principles, but not in the form they took in the West:

> We have an understanding of popular sovereignty which is indeed different from that of Western Europe. And, what is more, from that of Asia. Because Russia was and remains [...] a unique state and a separate civilisation. Neither Western nor Eastern clothes suit us – we have to make our own.[25]

Western forms of democracy were inappropriate in Russia because they were based on capitalism, which was alien to Russia and doomed to fail there. 'A peculiarity of our culture throughout the centuries was its communal [*obshchinnaya*] economy and communal culture'. Hence, 'socialism – or collectivism – are deeply rooted in our [...] history' and private property could not be the basis of democracy in Russia.[26]

ROS' apologists suggested that Russia had to find her own solutions to the problems of political and economic organisation. Russia was part of Europe, it was argued, insofar as it was a great power, but it was also 'a particular world, a particular civilisation, gathering to itself the achievements of other cultures but trying, at the same time, to retain its internal organic wholeness'.[27] According to Baburin:

> The Russian Way [...] involves profound and consistent reforms in an atmosphere of conciliarity [*sobornost'*], of spiritual community [*obshchnost'*], of social-psychological, economic, political-legal

unification of the most diverse layers in Russian society [...] In Russia, individuality was always appreciated, but individualism was not exaggerated.[28]

This was a coded rejection of such Western manifestations of individualism as classical liberal capitalism and democracy.

If the individual was to be sacrificed to State power and cohesion in the political sphere, so on the economy, ROS emphasized the role of the State more than private enterprise. ROS rejected privatisation of land, middle- and large-scale enterprises and called for a slow transition over ten years to a market economy, during which time incomes would be controlled by the state. How the market could emerge in a firmly collectivised, command economy was not explained.[29] There were both practical and ideological reasons for this: firstly, only a State-dominated economy could convert Russia into a superpower that could rival the West in the foreseeable future; of more immediate interest to the new owners of the dilapidated factories and enterprises of the Russian heartland was the continuation of State subsidies, which might enrich them even if they did not benefit their companies. Hence, the mixed economy ROS envisaged was one in which the State played a leading role, ensuring the modernisation of strategically important sectors of the economy and a minimum of social justice.[30] This was the 'third way' advocated by Sergei Kurginyan – a path of development, supposedly peculiar to Russia, that lay between socialism and capitalism.[31] Baburin himself declared his own adherence to a kind of national socialism, proclaiming his conviction that 'the basis of Russia's worldview in the twenty-first century is national-patriotic socialism'.[32]

ROS attracted considerable attention on account of the activities of its leader, who was a prominent figure in all opposition fora. But it disappointed Baburin, who had hoped that all opposition groups would be united under its leadership. In this, he overlooked the fact that many other nationalists and former communists had similar ambitions and that many other newly formed movements aspired to this role.[33] Public support for the movement was minimal. A poll of December 1992 indicated that few people had heard of it (although Baburin was quite well-known) and it had an approval rating of only 3 per cent (as against Baburin's personal rating of 12 per cent).[34] Only 53 people took part in its founding conference in October 1991, although 400 delegates attended its first congress the following December, and 528 delegates were present at the second congress in

February 1993. Its support declined after the defeat of the parliament in October 1993. Membership figures were kept secret, suggesting that ROS was a movement with an active organisation and popular backing in name only. Nonetheless, its support in the Russian parliament until October 1993 reflected the influence of its ideas in the new political class.[35]

The Winter saw the formation of other national-communist groups, hostile to the new regime, such as Stanislav Terekhov's Officers' Union, which called for the overthrow of Yeltsin's government by force and Officers for the Revival of the Fatherland, founded by former KGB General Alexander Sterligov in December 1991.[36] These developments testified to growing discontent in the army, which was suffering acutely from the consequences of withdrawal from Eastern Europe, the disintegration of the USSR and economic reform. Its loss of prestige and resources, the confusion of strategy and the privations suffered by soldiers and officers provoked growing disenchantment with reform, especially among officers, a disillusionment which was reflected in successive opinion polls and in the army's support for Zhirinovsky in 1993. A poll of officers in February 1992 revealed strong opposition to the dissolution of the USSR, with 71 per cent supporting a return to a united state within the borders of the former USSR.[37] A poll in November 1992 indicated that only 19 per cent of servicemen supported the government while 56 per cent opposed its policies. These trends were accentuated in the mid-1990s, as the army's position continued to deteriorate: *Der Spiegel* published a 1994 poll of officers, which found that six in every ten officers opposed Yeltsin as President; only a minority supported the government's policies on privatisation and market reforms, while 62 per cent of generals and colonels believed that authoritarian rule was required to end the current chaos.[38] Confidential polls suggested that support for Zhirinovsky remained high in the army in 1995 (at 15.6 per cent), while by January 1996, 21.5 per cent of servicemen supported Zyuganov and 18.4 per cent Zhirinovsky, with Yeltsin trailing in sixth position with 4.2 per cent support.[39] Yet despite these early efforts to mobilise the army politically, it refrained from throwing its weight behind the emerging opposition. Its high command profited from the new regime, while its lower echelons were profoundly disorganised and demoralised by the reforms.

Deprived of strong institutional support and with public opinion still largely uncommitted, the opposition organised slowly on the margins of political life, with little to restrain its instinctive extremism.

Alexander Sterligov became one of its leading figures. The eccentricity and extremism of his views belied his background at the heart of the Soviet and post-Soviet establishment. After a career in the KGB and counter-intelligence, he worked as an administrator in Nikolai Ryzhkov's government and, in 1991, became *chef de cabinet* of Ivan Silaev's Russian Federation government and then an aide to the newly elected Russian Vice-President Alexander Rutskoi, whom he helped in the defence of the White House in August 1991 and accompanied to Foros on his mission to liberate Gorbachev. He took part in the arrest of KGB chief Kryuchkov and was rewarded with the rank of Major General. Only in December 1991 did he leave Rutskoi (just as the Vice-President's criticisms of Yeltsin's government were beginning to be noted) to organise opposition to Yeltsin in the army and intelligentsia.[40] Involved in several opposition fora and allegedly funded by the RAU corporation (like another Rutskoi aide and future Zyuganov adviser, Alexander Podberezkin), Sterligov was elected leader of the newly founded Russian National Council (*RNS*). The Council was dedicated to the replacement of the Yeltsin government by a government of national salvation and had been established on 15–16 February 1992 on the initiative of a group called the Slavic Assembly which united figures from the wilder fringes of Russian nationalism and neo-fascism.[41] This influence was reflected in the Council's xenophobic rhetoric, which depicted the 1917 revolution and the entire Soviet period as an international plot against the Russian people. Despite the extremism of the Council's orientation, well-known figures (including the writer Valentin Rasputin, the Krasnoyarsk red director Petr Romanov and the communist ex-apparatchik Gennady Zyuganov) supported it.

Despite 20 years as a Party member, Sterligov retained little interest in Marxism-Leninism, declaring the Bolshevik and Marxist heritage to be an alien and dangerous interruption of Russian tradition. The revolution had been orchestrated by Russia's Western and Zionist enemies, he asserted. The West 'had conducted a struggle to liquidate Russia as a whole state, as a powerful element of world geo-politics'. The current crisis was merely a new aspect of this struggle: conducted on behalf of Western capital by a fifth column of democrats, it was intended to ensure 'the ethnic disappearance of the Russians'. Only a rebirth of the Russian soul could resist this 'civilised genocide', whose real perpetrators were international Jewry.[42]

Sterligov presented himself not as a Marxist but as a nationalist:

> I am a Russian nationalist, or more exactly a patriot. The main character trait of a KGB officer was patriotism, love of the Motherland, and not mythical, including communist ideals.[43]

Communism, he believed, had no future: everything positive in communism was to be found also in Orthodoxy. The Orthodoxy Sterligov had in mind was that professed by Metropolitan Ioann of St Petersburg (whose plea for a revival of traditional Russian theocratic autocracy he adopted as the RNS programme) not that of Father Alexander Men', whom he considered a traitor.[44] Russia should return to her national roots, her own millennial form of statehood: this could take the form of a monarchy, but a *zemskii sobor* (the Muscovite Assembly of the Land) should decide the issue. Sterligov's sympathies clearly lay with the autocratic imperialist elements in Russian tradition.[45] He rejected democracy, affirming that democratic institutions had failed Russia. Russia should 'recognise that all forms of Western democracy are alien and unacceptable to us'.[46] Russia should eschew Western models of development not only because they were unsuited to the country but also because the West was hostile to Russia:

> Talk of the necessity of Russia's return to Western civilisation is senseless and illiterate [...] Russia has its own historical mission – to keep the geopolitical balance between the East and the West in the Eurasian space.[47]

He advocated, instead, an authoritarian state: a strong central government (ideally, at present, a government of national salvation with unlimited powers in foreign and domestic policy) and indirect elections on a corporatist basis to a *zemskii sobor*. The Presidency was acceptable in the short term, as long as the incumbent was not Boris Yeltsin.[48]

Russia's destiny lay with other Slav nations, he argued. Essentially, Sterligov and his followers hoped for a restoration of the Soviet Union – even if they came to accept the reunification of the three Slavic peoples (the Ukrainians, the Belorussians and the Russians) as a short-term goal.[49] These imperial ambitions were not incompatible with Russian nationalism, according to Sterligov:

> Russian [*russkii*] does not have a racial or genetic meaning but a cultural-historical one. All who accept and affirm the values of Russia, the uniqueness and originality of Russian [*rossiiskoi*] statehood as a union of many peoples, are Russian.

Hence, the Russian nation and State were potentially multi-ethnic, if not culturally pluralistic.[50] The Council supported these views. From the outset, the movement called for the resignation of the Gaidar government, which it characterised as an 'administration of national treachery' for its policies of impoverishing the people, ruining the economy, dismantling the country's defences and dismembering the State. Instead, Russia should return to the planned economy, while – as in the 1930s, they warned – a state of emergency should be proclaimed to enable effective measures to be taken against economic and political crime.[51] The RNS was committed to the restoration of an authoritarian, preferably monarchical, centralised state, based on an Orthodox national revival and coterminous with the post-war Soviet state.[52]

The Council attracted attention, participating in many opposition demonstrations throughout 1992 and 1993, but it failed to make common cause with other opposition groupings, largely because Sterligov saw them as a threat to his position. In 1993, despite his deteriorating relations with other opposition leaders,[53] Sterligov continued, along with the rest of the opposition, to denounce Yeltsin, paradoxically (but like most other authoritarian groups) supporting the parliament against the President in the battle for power. This alignment was prompted not by love of parliamentary democracy but by hatred of Yeltsin. The tactic misfired, when Yeltsin subdued the parliament and proscribed the Russian National Council and other nationalist organisations in October 1993. Marginal and extreme, the Council was a shadowy organisation, which some observers believed to have been inspired by the KGB or even by members of Yeltsin's entourage.[54] It refused to reveal its membership but affirmed that 417 delegates from 72 organisations attended its founding congress and 1250 delegates its first congress in June 1992. It still claimed 50 branches in Russia after its proscription, although it had largely disappeared from view. Lack of popular support was to inhibit Sterligov's attempts to play a significant part in politics.[55] When he formed an electoral bloc (the Union of Patriots) for the 1995 elections, he was unable to collect enough signatures to present a federal list and, while several candidates ran in single-seat constituencies, none were elected and Sterligov himself mustered only 8.61 per cent of the votes in his Moscow constituency.[56] While ROS had links with hardline parliamentarians, the RNS appeared to have connections with former members of the security services. Like most nationalist organisations, it offered a platform to hardliners and opportunists from the old establishment, rather than functioning (as it had hoped) as an organisation mobilising and expressing public opinion. Like Baburin's ROS, with which it competed, the RNS was interesting principally as an indication of the political instincts of some members of the political and cultural elite rather than as a barometer of public opinion.

Like these former communists, some democrats turned to authoritarian nationalism in 1992. The democratic movement before the coup had been held together by anti-communism rather than by identity of political instincts. Already in 1991, it became clear that some democrats attached far more importance to State power and the retention of Union structures than more radical reformers. After the coup and the collapse of the Soviet Union to which it led, three groups withdrew their qualified support for the radicals. Chief among these were the Christian Democrats, led by Viktor Aksyuchits, and the Kadets, led by Mikhail Astafiev. Although both parties purported to draw inspiration from liberal democratic principles, they became increasingly preoccupied with the survival and defence of the Russian nation state, which, they believed, Yeltsin had undermined. The terms 'liberty' and 'democracy' soon disappeared from their vocabulary to be replaced by those of 'state' and 'nation'.

Mikhail Astafiev's Constitutional Democratic Party – the Party of Popular Freedom, founded in September 1990, was the offshoot of an attempt in 1989–90 to revive the pre-revolutionary liberal-democratic tradition. A tiny proto-party, claiming over 2000 members in 1990 and 5000 in 1993,[57] Astafiev's Kadets defined their general orientation as 'liberal-conservative' but their readiness to sacrifice the individual and his rights to the interests of the State deprived the Party of any real liberal character.[58] They were reticent in their references to human rights and they paid scant attention to the individual. According to their creed, the individual's rights were circumscribed by those of the State and their emphasis was, even at the outset, on the need to preserve State power and institutions rather than the prerogatives of the individual. Instead of referring, like other early democratic parties, to world practice and international law, Astafiev's followers preferred to talk of patriotism and Russia's unique qualities.

Their affinity with the CPSU's nationalist and conservative wing was clear even before the fall of the Soviet regime in the style and the content of their proclaimed policies on the national issue:

In the event of the disintegration of the Union, the KDP (PPF) does not exclude the possibility of a review of the borders of the

Russian Federation, which were arbitrarily drawn to the detriment of Russia's interests, by means of a referendum in regions bordering the current Russian Federation, if over 50 per cent of the population of those regions consists of Russian speakers who identify with Russia.[59]

Hostility to the nationalist aspirations of the Soviet republics permeated this and analogous declarations. This attitude to the collapse of the USSR coupled with the need to prevent the disintegration of the Russian Federation and the multiplication of independent fiefdoms, where Moscow's writ no longer ran, enabled communists and formerly democratic nationalists to draw closer in 1992. Like Aksyuchits's Christian Democrats, the Kadets turned to Greater Russian nationalism, rejecting minority separatism and Western influence and alluding to the value of Orthodoxy and *sobornost'* (the mystical unity of the nation) in holding the state together.[60] Anti-communism became a secondary issue and this enabled former democrats to work with erstwhile communists in the service of the traditional, imperial Russian state.

The first months of 1992 were to see Astafiev's Kadets and Aksyuchits's Christian Democrats associate themselves with ex-communists' increasingly strident demands for an end to Yeltsin's democratic government and the restoration of authoritarian rule, in the interests of Russia. In November 1991, both parties left Democratic Russia and, in February 1992, the centrist faction (*Narodnoe soglasie*) to which they had hitherto belonged. They were by then drawing closer to the national-communists of ROS under Baburin. A month after the introduction of Gaidar's shock therapy, on 8–9 February 1992, these groups organised the Congress of Civic and Patriotic Forces, to establish the Russian National Assembly (*Rossiiskoe natsional'noe sobranie*) as a counterweight to Democratic Russia.[61] Neo-fascist as well as more moderate nationalist and centrist groups attended the Congress as did the usual constellation of nationalists from the cultural world.[62] The Assembly intended to work for 'the re-creation by political means of a single Russian [*rossiiskii*] state in its historical borders'. The treaties dissolving the USSR were denounced as illegal and unconstitutional. The Assembly rejected the new borders of Russia and demanded the return of the Crimea and other areas where Russians constituted a majority of the population or which were traditionally regarded as part of Russia.[63] To this end, it called for the replacement of Yeltsin's government, which had destroyed the State and was now ruining the people and the economy, with a government of national recovery.[64] Far from being a manifestation of moderate nationalism, the assembly warmly applauded several fiery speeches, including one delivered (against the wishes of the organisers) by *Pamyat'* leader Dmitri Vasiliev.[65] This attempt to establish a national-communist front foundered on the rivalry of the participants. But it was significant because it marked the defection of some democrats to the nationalist opposition and the collapse of the united democratic front, which had been in the ascendant for the previous two years. It also indicated how polarised politics in the new order rapidly became: in this, the new regime, far from breaking with previous political patterns, merely continued earlier traditions of sharp conflict and intolerance.

However, the repeated attempts to form a united national-communist front to oppose liberal, Western-oriented reform finally began to meet with success in Spring and Summer 1992. On 10 March 1992, the formation of a 'united opposition' was announced to force a change of policy on the government at the next full session of the parliament, which was due to meet at the start of April. Under the heading: 'Justice. Nationality. Statehood. Patriotism', the signatories warned of the collapse of the State, the Russian Motherland, the loss of national tradition and the threat to the well-being and even existence of the Russian people. To avert this catastrophe, a united opposition was needed to defend 'the unity and integrity of the Fatherland' and demand the rejection of the treaties disbanding the USSR, social justice and state protection for all Russians, including those outside the boundaries of the Russian Federation.[66] Several successor parties to the CPSU, anti-communist and post-communist nationalist groups agreed to cooperate in the united opposition.[67] This attempt to coordinate the opposition's forces succeeded where previous efforts had failed because the groups involved retained their separate identities, organisations and leaders.

The opposition's first practical step was to form a parliamentary bloc – Russian Unity – to which five parliamentary factions adhered.[68] Formed on 6 April 1992, on the eve of the Sixth Congress of People's Deputies, when disenchantment with Yeltsin's government had already set in, Russian Unity was the largest bloc in the Russian parliament, commanding approximately 310 out of 1040 votes in April 1992 and 330 votes in December 1992.[69] Nationalists and communists were thus powerfully represented in the new institutions of democratic Russia. They occupied an increasingly visible place in public life, participating in noisy rallies throughout 1992–93, even if their support appeared to be derived from marginalised and less dynamic sections of the population: pensioners, older unskilled workers, tough unemployed young men. Throughout 1992, the opposition demanded the resignation of the Gaidar government, an end to Yeltsin's special powers and a government responsible to the parliament (rather than one appointed by and answerable to the President). By Autumn, they demanded Yeltsin's resignation, reproaching him with dismembering the country, ruining the economy and sacrificing Russia's interests to her enemies.[70]

As the economy failed to recover, the chorus of opposition from the moderates (led by Arkady Volsky and Nikolai Travkin) and the parliament mounted. The national and communist opposition's confidence grew and they coordinated their extra-parliamentary support and institutional power in the National Salvation Front, which was formed on 24 October 1992. The founding congress was attended by almost two thousand delegates, the leaders of the Russian Unity parliamentary bloc, religious and cultural nationalists, communists and imperialists.[71] From the communists and ROS to the National Republicans, most of the leading opposition forces and groups in Russia were represented in its councils.[72] What enabled these diverse forces to come together? Above all, it was the threat to the State and national integrity posed by Western values and influence, according to one of the Front's leaders, Ilya Konstantinov:

> [...] They are united by one main thing: the categorical rejection of Yeltsin's policy, recognition of the great danger of 'Yeltsinism' as an openly anti-national, anti-popular, anti-State, pro-Western regime. Despite all the differences of their ideological credos, all the members of the Front are nationalists [*pochvenniki*], all reject the Western system of values, the Western path of social development.[73]

Blaming Yeltsin and the democrats for the dissolution of the Soviet Union and collapse of the economy, the Front demanded a reversal of economic and foreign policy: greater attention should be paid instead to the defence of national interests abroad and to living standards at home.[74] The Appeal to the Citizens of Russia which launched the Front accused Yeltsin not merely of incompetence but of deliberate treachery:

> [...] The tragedy that has overtaken the country is the result of a deliberate anti-popular policy of the ruling elite and not of errors or

miscalculations of 'inexperienced' leaders. Treachery cannot be 'corrected'; it must be punished with all the severity of the law.[75]

The Front's programme differed little from that of the 1991 coup leaders: it called for state control of the economy and the imposition of a state of emergency and authoritarian rule to impose order, guarantee social justice and rebuild a strong, unified State.[76] The NSF became the main extra-parliamentary forum for the united opposition. Despite its heterogeneity, it was united on support for a strong Russian state and rejection of Western liberalism and democracy, which were seen as alien to and dangerous for Russia. The economy was also a sensitive issue. Many in the national-communist camp inclined to a collectivist approach to the economy but, increasingly, national and communist leaders were ready to admit a measure of reform and liberalisation. What they insisted on was that this reform should be very gradual and that neither State power and strategic interests (principally, the military-industrial complex) nor general living standards should be sacrificed to it.[77] These views did not amount to a coherent economic policy: its ambiguity was prompted by the need to court different constituencies, both Soviet socialists, non-communist nationalists as well as former communists, who had adapted to and profited from the new economic order.

The disintegration of the USSR was the Front's preferred theme. NSF leaders insisted that the dismemberment of the USSR had been illegal and stressed the need to restore State unity: 'A most important part of the NSF programme is the action taken to re-create a united State, capable of being the heir of the Russian empire and the USSR'.[78] However, the Russian Federation showed signs of fragmenting and this became an additional source of concern to all nationalists and state-builders. 'Decisive action' was needed, the NSF leaders warned, to prevent the country falling apart. While some leaders (such as the communist leader Gennady Zyuganov) were relatively moderate, others, including General Albert Makashov, called for military units to be organised to carry out the orders of the political council of the united opposition, should anarchy make intervention necessary.[79] Speaking at the NSF's first Congress in October 1992, Igor Shafarevich set the tone, warning that Russia's fate was similar to that of Germany after the Second World War: its educational and economic power were under attack. Germany had saved itself by aligning itself with the West – but Russia should never agree to become a docile ally of the West. Alexander Prokhanov reiterated this view in a subsequent interview with Jonathan Steele:

At the hands of their paid agents, the Americans are taking revenge on Russia for its recent greatness and refusal to submit. Our race, character and culture are being wiped out once and for all. They are stifling a temperament and a view of the world which were unique and which, over ten centuries, had carved a place in history through faith, understanding and love.

He too argued against importing democracy into Russia: like Shafarevich and Solzhenitsyn, he saw it as a prelude to revolution, chaos and loss of power.[80]

Yeltsin promptly denounced the Front at a speech at the Foreign Ministry on 27 October 1992 and the following day, he banned it by decree (presenting this as a measure to defend the constitution).[81] The NSF retaliated, as the communists had earlier, by demanding a ruling from the Constitutional Court – thus forcing Yeltsin to lift the ban on 13 January, two days before the Court's ruling, which found his decree unconstitutional.[82] This victory for the right coincided with the overturning of the President's proscription of the Russian communist party and the Parliament's decision to release from jail the August coup leaders. The anti-democratic opposition had recovered from their setback in 1991 and, regrouped and reorganised, were in a position to take advantage of the deepening power struggle between the President and the parliament and move to the offensive.

CONCLUSION

However much decried in the press and despite the attention which their fiery rhetoric drew, support for the radical opposition was still limited. Polls put the communists' and nationalists' combined support at 6.8 to 10.8 per cent of the population, which, although low, was not much lower than that of the democrats (with 9 to 11.9 per cent). The communists' support was relatively consistent at around 6 per cent of the population between January 1992 and June 1993, while that of the nationalists grew from 0.8 per cent to 4.8 per cent. Far more typical than support for either ideological and political camp, however, was ignorance and alienation, with almost a third of those polled unable to indicate a strong preference and between 22 and 39 per cent declaring that they would not vote at all in an election.[83] Stephen White and his colleagues also found ignorance and rejection of all parties far more typical than recognition and support. A poll of December 1992 indicated that 730 respondents identified with no party, while 398 were Yeltsinites, 345 centrists, 286 communists and 118 national patriots. The new nationalist and communist parties and their leaders were not well-known. While Nina Andreeva, Vladimir Zhirinovsky and Alexander Rutskoi (who was then Vice-President and not yet clearly in the nationalist camp) were known by between 30 and 44 per cent of respondents, the parties they led were unfamiliar and inspired little enthusiasm: 68 per cent were unfamiliar with Zhirinovsky's LDPR, 19 per cent were negative and 2 per cent positive about it; 54 per cent did not know of Vasiliev's *Pamyat'*, 15 per cent were hostile to it and 5 per cent approved. Nationalists fared worse than communist parties, according to this study: ROS (with 80 per cent unable to pronounce on it and 3 per cent supportive), the Kadets (74 per cent unfamiliar and 4 per cent supportive) and the Christian Democrats (73 per cent unfamiliar and 5 per cent supportive) all appeared to reflect the preferences of the political and cultural elite rather than to represent the views of the electorate.[84] On the other hand, support for authoritarian and nationalist attitudes was not insignificant among the public, according to polls,[85] so these dismal results may have been due more to the leaders' failure to communicate and build up local organisations and the general distrust of political parties and growing alienation from politics than with hostility to the nationalist and communist parties' message.

Disenchantment with the new regime was growing, but neither the communists nor the nationalists benefited from a transfer of allegiance away from Yeltsin. Instead, public alienation from all forms of politics became pronounced as did the volatility of public opinion, which matched the growing instability in politics. In the absence of a mobilised public opinion, the struggle for power was concentrated within the political elite in the new State institutions and was fought largely without reference to citizens' preferences: in one instance where the population was brought into play, it was not so much consulted as manipulated (in the plebiscite of April 1993).[86] Russian politics was to remain in 1993 as much an internecine struggle within a privileged minority for power and its emoluments as it had been in the Soviet era: the rules of the game had altered, in that the struggle was public, the rhetoric had changed but the vast majority of the citizens of Russia were neither involved in nor felt that they exerted any real influence over political life.

6 The Advent of Vladimir Zhirinovsky

A. POLITICAL CONFLICT 1992–93

By October 1992, Yeltsin was contemplating the introduction of a state of emergency to overcome the increasingly obdurate opposition of the parliament to his rule.[1] Throughout the next calendar year, from October 1992 to October 1993, Yeltsin and the parliament disputed the right to control the government: a series of constitutional crises followed, in December 1992 and March–April 1993, in which the Parliament consistently tried to deprive Yeltsin of his powers and to make the government answerable to it, to which Yeltsin responded by threatening to prorogue it and call a constitutional referendum. As the parliamentary leaders felt their power and political careers to be increasingly threatened, they became more extreme in their rhetoric and actions.

Many deputies who had initially supported Yeltsin, were dismayed by the social consequences of the economic reform. Instability in the 'near abroad', the difficulties of the Russian diaspora, the loss of the Union, the state of the army were also serious and genuine concerns. Opposition to Yeltsin grew rapidly in the parliament, at the end of 1992, especially when, complaining of a creeping coup and pronouncing the parliament impossible to work with, Yeltsin threatened, on 10 December 1992, to appeal over its head to the electorate to decide the issue of who ruled Russia.[2] Yeltsin's challenge to the parliament in December 1992 served to alienate former supporters and many centrist deputies moved to the right. Whereas the centre had commanded an estimated 370 votes in April 1992, in December, it voted with the Russian Unity faction, confronting Yeltsin with a solid bloc of about 630 opponents in the full parliament – a bloc that subsequent events only consolidated.[3]

In March 1993, the constitutional crisis deepened when the parliament stripped Yeltsin of his special powers. Yeltsin retaliated, appearing on television on 20 March to announce that he was introducing a period of 'special administration' in advance of a constitutional referendum to be held the following month. This decision was pronounced unconstitutional: in the event, when the decree was published, Yeltsin's advisers omitted any reference to a 'special' form of administration. However, by threatening to override the parliament, Yeltsin destroyed the last vestiges of the political centre: the impetuous Vice-President Rutskoi finally broke with Yeltsin, while previously undecided deputies now backed the Speaker of the Parliament, Khasbulatov, and the opposition. The hardliners fell short of the two-thirds majority needed to impeach the President by only 72 votes. This failure forced the parliament to compromise and agree to a referendum on 25 April 1993, which endorsed the President's power and his government's policies rather than the parliament.[4]

Khasbulatov, began in a series of meetings and speeches to court the hardline opposition.[5] Also moving closer to the radical opposition during Spring and Summer 1993 was another of Yeltsin's offended ex-collaborators, the Vice-President Alexander Rutskoi. He exemplified a new kind of Russian politician, eschewing the mandatory blandness cultivated by the apparatchik in favour of a vigorous personal style, which exploited his military background (as an Afghan war hero) and emphasised his overriding commitment to Russia and its traditions. Initially inconsistently, he took up ideas hitherto confined to the nationalist intelligentsia and the more marginal extremes in political life using them to reinforce his bid for power. Rutskoi was at best ambiguous in his commitment to liberal and democratic modernisation. He attracted diverse supporters and advisers, some of whom were impressed by his incarnation as a democrat while others were determined to place him at the head of the emerging conservative and nationalist opposition to Yeltsin. Rutskoi oscillated between these two groups but his instincts seemed closer to Greater Russian nationalism than to liberalism and it was to the *derzhavnik* side of the political debate that he finally and definitively rallied.

Rutskoi came to prominence as Yeltsin's Vice-President between 1991 and 1993 and latterly as a leader of parliamentary resistance to Yeltsin's policies. A decorated airforce colonel, he made his first excursion into politics in Spring 1989, when he was elected deputy leader of *Otechestvo*,[6] and stood for election to the Congress of Peoples' Deputies in Moscow in 1989 on a programme reputedly written by members of *Nash sovremennik*'s board.[7] Certainly, its tenor was consistent with the line taken by the journal, expressing antipathy to the West and to the reforms:

ENOUGH of transforming our country into a raw materials adjunct and colony of the West! SHAME on those who [...] trade in their native land, handing the nation over to the cabbale of foreign capital.

The country should avoid copying the bourgeois democratic model which gave power only to the wealthy.[8] Rutskoi's interviews at the time reflect his hostility to the political and economic reforms,[9] and when he was elected to the Russian parliament in Spring 1990, it was on a conservative CPSU ticket. He criticised the reforms for undermining Soviet power insisting on the importance of maintaining the unity of the USSR.[10] His 22-year membership of the CPSU left a deep imprint on Rutskoi's political outlook. His break with the Party came reluctantly: he remained a member of the Party until expelled in August 1991.[11]

His political views were changing, however, as he was exposed to the atmosphere of frantic political debate in Moscow at the turn of the decade. When he aligned himself with Yeltsin in March 1991, at a key moment of the power struggle between the neo-Stalinists and the democrats, he justified his rebellion against the Party hardliners in terms of popular and national sovereignty. But although the principles which he invoked were fundamental to democratic theory, their application to the Soviet Union had consequences Rutskoi did not foresee. In his speech to the Russian parliament in March 1991, he both supported Russian republican sovereignty and opposed 'the collapse of the Union, [...] the impotence and chaos in the country'. Similarly, he declared in favour of both 'the power of the Soviets in a democratic sovereign republic' and of 'the institution of real popular sovereignty through presidential rule'.[12] Rutskoi clearly did not appreciate the tensions and even contradictions inherent in this position. He had voted for Russian republican sovereignty in 1990. However, the demand for separate Russian political institutions, originally expressed by Rutskoi's erstwhile friends in *Nash sovremennik*, was adopted by the Russian democrats principally for tactical reasons in the quest for power and legitimacy. The impact of this strategy on the Union was not apparent to all its supporters at the time – as Rutskoi later admitted.[13] Clearly, in March 1991, Rutskoi misread the mood in other republics of the USSR and did not appreciate that the demand for national sovereignty was not compatible with the preservation of the Union.

By the end of the year, any ambiguity about these problems had been dispelled. Ignored by Yeltsin and his entourage, disappointed in his expectations of the democratic victory of August 1991, which he had helped to achieve, Rutskoi reverted to nationalist positions, criticising Yeltsin's foreign and economic policies.[14] By January 1992, prompted by members of his entourage with links with the security services, he began to make overtures to the developing nationalist opposition. He published three articles signalling his opposition to the break-up of the USSR and the dismantling of its economic system.[15] Essentially, he advocated turning away from Western liberal political and economic models, reasserting strong state control of key sectors of the economy and re-establishing the Greater Russian state, appealing to nationalism and tradition.[16] He criticised the intellectuals of the democratic movement for having undermined the Russian-Eurasian state,[17] replacing it with the powerless and unstable Commonwealth of Independent States, and Gaidar for pursuing a policy of 'economic genocide'.[18] This political collapse was, he asserted, accompanied by a paralysing spiritual decay and vacuum, which was filled by forces alien and hostile to Russia.[19]

Instead, Russians should 'keep in view the problem of preserving Russian [*rossiiskaya*] statehood, and [...] restoring a single democratic state on the territory of a wider Eurasian space'. The fact that such a state could not be re-established democratically, Rutskoi preferred to ignore. Democracy had to be adapted to Russian statehood and tradition: it could not develop overnight. In the interim, a strong power was needed to regulate the political and economic situation, under the supervision of democratically elected institutions. Democracy did not mean unlimited individualism.[20] As a token of his own decisiveness, Rutskoi called for a state of 'economic emergency' to enable the state recover control of key sectors of the economy, to prevent the ruin of a great power and people.[21]

Russians had a number of duties, he told Aksyuchits's Congress of Civic and Patriotic Forces in February 1992, chief of which were the restoration of Russia's true identity and the rebirth of faith and morals. At issue was 'the future of our great power' and even its physical survival. Russia did not need democratic experiments and genocidal policies of the kind proposed by Gaidar's government. Now that the USSR had been destroyed, Russian statehood was under threat. But Russia was not an artificial construct but a living organism, a 'spiritual, linguistic and cultural whole'. It was the product of centuries and could not simply be dismembered. The key to Russia's survival and the 'unity of the peoples inhabiting this vast Eurasian continent' should therefore be sought in Russia's unique historical experience:

> We are not the West's pupils or teacher. [...] We have a task ahead of us: to create an original all-Russian spiritual culture – from the Russian heart, Russian contemplation in Russian freedom, discovering the essence of Russia. And RUSSIA should be a word uniting us all. This is the sense of the Russian idea.[22]

In fact, this 'new' idea was an old one (elaborated by the émigré Ivan Ilyin, to whose political thought Rutskoi was introduced by the film director, Nikita Mikhalkov). Rather than enthusing his audience (which covered the entire range of anti-communist nationalism, including supporters of Vasiliev's *Pamyat'*), Rutskoi was greeted with derision and some hostility: they were unimpressed by his unwillingness to translate his criticisms of Yeltsin's government into resignation from the post of Vice-President.[23] Rutskoi thus lost the opportunity of leading the emerging opposition, which he had clearly tried to court. His appearance at a forum, which included *Pamyat'* whose opposition to the government was manifest, caused an immediate furore and fatally compromised him with Yeltsin. The latter was too shrewd to dismiss him, however, burdening him instead with the marginal and intractable problem of agricultural reform.

Throughout the summer, Rutskoi continued to criticise the government's policies and to preach the need for the restoration of the powerful and unitary Russian State. His greatest wish was that 'Russia should get up from its knees, become a great power.'[24] In his interventions on Ossetia, Pridnestrovie and the Crimea, Rutskoi showed that he meant what he said about maintaining Russian state unity, restricting local autonomies and strengthening Russian influence.[25] This tactic not only alienated minority nationalities, it also lost him the support of Russia's provincial barons, whose power grew as that of Moscow declined.[26] By late Autumn, this approach had failed to change the balance of power in Yeltsin's circle and by December, Rutskoi had moved back to a more confrontational approach, siding with the Parliament against the government. By March 1993, still formally Vice-President, Rutskoi moved into outright opposition to the President, calling for the resignation of the government, which he accused of widespread corruption, an end to reform, a new constitution and the *de facto* re-creation of the USSR (through the exercise of economic pressure).[27]

As relations between President and Parliament and Vice-President deteriorated, Civic Union collapsed: no political centre-ground was left.[28] Unanchored in any political base, Rutskoi began to drift closer to the ultra-nationalist National Salvation Front.[29] Ultimately, Yeltsin dismissed him from his post as Vice-President in September 1993. The final confrontation between Yeltsin and Rutskoi, in Autumn 1993, was the dramatic culmination of a conflict that had lasted almost two years. By the time he found himself besieged in the Parliament, in October 1993, Rutskoi's position was diametrically opposed to that which he had adopted during the previous siege, in August 1991: he pledged himself to releasing the leaders of the 1991 coup and imprisoning Yeltsin and the government. He assured Alexander Prokhanov:

> [...] We are fighting not only for the fate of Russia, we are fighting for the fate of the Soviet Union! As soon as we achieve victory here in Moscow, we will restore again our great power, which has served as a guarantee of the defence and development for many brother nations![30]

Rutskoi had returned to his spiritual roots in *Otechestvo*.

The polarisation and intensification of the political conflict was just what extremists like Alexander Prokhanov wanted and they attempted to encourage it, while allying themselves with Yeltsin's opponents. By Summer 1993, the wider opposition to Yeltsin began to coalesce.[31] At its second congress, on 24–25 July 1993, the National Salvation Front, despite splits,[32] rallied behind the Parliament. It called for power to be handed over to the soviets (an old Bolshevik slogan, now adopted by Khasbulatov), for the formation of a government of national salvation, responsible to Parliament, and the abolition of the Presidency.[33] The congress called for action:

> Only the people can decide their fate: either they lose their motherland and become enslaved or they turn their back on the decaying regime and bring order into their own house.[34]

The time for hesitation had passed:

> We have no choice: either we go over to the attack and replace the criminal regime, or we will be repressed and will lose the Motherland [...] The NSF as the avant-garde of the liberation movement should in the shortest possible time regroup its forces and go over to the strategy of permanent offensive.[35]

Several delegates demanded the violent overthrow of the regime. Ilya Konstantinov declared: 'Either we go over to decisive action and sweep away the criminal regime or we lose Russia.'[36]

The radicals appeared to believe that Russia was 'on the eve of a national-liberation revolution'. Prokhanov called for 'self-defence' units, trained in hand-to-hand fighting to be formed in consultation with the army and Interior Ministry.[37] Towards the end of August, the NSF's leaders reiterated their support for Khasbulatov and participated in wider pro-parliamentary fora which he organised.[38] By contrast, Gennady Zyuganov's Communist Party was more cautious in its opposition to Yeltsin and took care to distance itself from the fiercer demagogues in the NSF.

B. THE OCTOBER CRISIS

The culmination of the conflict between the President and the Parliament was the October 1993 crisis, when Yeltsin finally dissolved the Parliament. While both the parliamentary leaders and Yeltsin had been engaged in a bitter battle for power, neither side had hitherto strayed irrevocably into unconstitutionality or unequivocally espoused violence as a solution to the crisis. In suspending the parliament, on 21 September, assuming emergency powers and calling for elections to a new legislature and a constitutional referendum on 12 December 1993, Yeltsin acted illegally and provocatively, but his action was the logical outcome of his entire approach in the previous two years and was the result of the collision course on which both parties were set. The Parliament was left with little room for manoeuvre. But it too reacted hastily and intemperately: on 22 September, with the support of the Constitutional Court, it deposed Yeltsin for violating the constitution and appointed Rutskoi as acting President. Several extremists joined the parliamentarians in the White House: on 23 September, a number of these, headed by Stanislav Terekhov, led an inept assault on CIS military headquarters killing two civilians and prompting Yeltsin effectively to lay siege to the White House.

For the next fortnight, the Parliament was surrounded by Interior Ministry (MVD) troops: Yeltsin offered inducements and threats to persuade the Parliament to accept his decree, but an albeit diminishing corps of deputies continued to resist. By the night of 28–29 September, only 200 deputies remained in the Parliament.[39] When the Moscow Patriarchate attempted to mediate, at the start of October, neither the Parliament nor Yeltsin showed any real readiness to compromise.[40] Yeltsin had received the backing of the security forces (principally the Security Ministry – comprising most of the branches of the ex-KGB – and the Interior Ministry) at the start of the crisis and had little inducement to back down.[41] The parliamentary leaders believed they enjoyed wider support in the provinces than was in fact the case.[42]

This situation suited the irreconcilable opposition, who, by supporting the Parliament, were able to pose as defenders of legality and constitutionality in a series of alarming appeals.[43] Terekhov – arrested for the attack of CIS HQ – was only one of the extremists who rallied to the defence of the Parliament: Alexander Barkashov, of the neo-fascist group Russian National Unity, and Viktor Anpilov, the populist neo-Stalinist leader of Labouring Moscow, were also present in the parliament building. These figures were coordinated by National Salvation Front leader, General Albert Makashov, who had run against Yeltsin in 1991 on a national communist ticket (garnering 3.9 per cent of the vote).[44] The presence in the building of these unelected extremists, who were not fully controlled by Khasbulatov and Rutskoi, undoubtedly contributed to the bloody dénouement of the crisis.

When a crowd of Anpilov's supporters broke through the MVD cordon, on 3 October, lifting the siege of the Parliament, the extremists were anxious to attack. Rutskoi and Khasbulatov, who by then had been carried away by the momentum of events and the crowd's triumphant mood, appeared on the White House balcony and urged the crowd to attack the nearby Mayor's office and, thence, the television station, Ostankino, in the north of the city. A fierce gun-battle ensued, in which Makashov, Anpilov, Barkashov and Konstantinov took part.[45] It was this attack which finally enabled Yeltsin to persuade the reluctant army (which in October 1992 and March 1993 had refused to get involved in the political crisis) to commit itself to the Presidency and to put an end to the disturbances in Moscow by bombarding the Parliament the following day (4 October).[46] After this, Yeltsin banned most nationalist and communist groupings and publications, despite the fact that most communist parties (except Anpilov's) had been relatively measured in their backing of the parliament or, like Andreeva's party, uninvolved in the crisis.[47]

The prominent role played by extremists in the crisis enabled Yeltsin to describe the Parliament's resistance to his decree disbanding it as a communist–fascist coup. However, it is not clear that

Khasbulatov and most parliamentarians wholeheartedly endorsed the National Salvation Front's agenda or desired the adoption of violent tactics to resolve the crisis until they lost their heads on 3 October.[48] It may be more accurate to suggest that the siege of the White House enabled the extremists to play a more dramatic and influential role than their popularity justified. Firstly, their popular support – as measured in polls and elections until December 1993 – was consistently low. In the 1991 presidential elections, candidates whose platforms corresponded most closely with the NSF platform also performed poorly (with Makashov scoring 3.9 per cent and Zhirinovsky 8.1 per cent of the vote).[49] On the first anniversary of the 1991 coup, although support for the democrats had dropped from 62 per cent to 42 per cent, approval of the putschists remained insignificant, rising from 4 per cent to only 7 per cent.[50] In a poll of April–May 1993, only 3 per cent supported the National Salvation Front. None of the nationalist or communist leaders figured among the political leaders in whom the sceptical public expressed most confidence in mid-October 1993.[51]

Secondly, the irreconcilable opposition's political ideas (rejection of Western liberal democracy, collectivist nationalism, imperialism) were not central to the political struggle in 1992–93. Although Khasbulatov drew closer to the radical opposition in Spring and Summer 1993, it would be a mistake to see the Russian Parliament and its leadership as unequivocally espousing the revanchist views of the NSF.[52] The largest parliamentary faction, Russian Unity, although ostensibly committed to the NSF's programme, was a coalition of groups with different interests at heart and different, sometimes rival leaders: it included relatively pragmatic figures, who could be tempted by the emoluments of office, as well as ideologues like Konstantinov. The parliamentary opposition to Yeltsin was focused not on the anti-democratic imperialism of the NSF but on the desire to establish the Parliament's as opposed to presidential rule. Power rather than ideology was at the root of Khasbulatov's defection from the democratic camp. The interpretation of the crisis which sees it as having pitched an embattled democratic President against supporters of authoritarian collectivism and neo-fascists is oversimplified. Both Parliament and President enjoyed a (however imperfect) democratic mandate, yet although both sides claimed to act in the name of democracy, neither were exemplars of democratic practice.[53] The radicals' part in the 1993 events was more coincidental than central to the political crisis of 1993. The real issue was a battle for power between pragmatic rather than ideologically engaged elites. This was to change after the

December 1993 Duma elections, which transformed extreme nationalists and national communists into the official opposition and
ensconced them in the new Parliament.

C. 1993 ELECTIONS

After the October bombardment of the parliament, Yeltsin and his
allies in the democratic camp had apparently vanquished the parliamentary opposition with the dissolution of the Parliament, the calling
of elections to the Federal Assembly[54] and a vote on a new constitution heavily weighted towards the President. The democrats, however
compromised by their support for Yeltsin, appeared to enjoy public
support,[55] while both the centre[56] and nationalists were in disarray,
their freedom to organise and publish having been curtailed or even
suspended. For the nationalists and communist opposition, the
October crisis had serious consequences: all their major publications
and organisations – including the NSF, Russian Unity, the Russian
National Council, the Officers' Union and the KPRF – were proscribed. Although the ban on the communist party was lifted, it
seemed that Yeltsin's nationalist critics had been discredited and
fatally weakened by the fiasco at the White House.[57] How, therefore,
did they manage to recover?

The democrats' hubris contributed to their defeat. They enjoyed
practical as well as tactical advantages – privileged access to the
media, transport, government flights. It was assumed they would win –
so much so that they treated the elections as a testing ground for the
presidential elections, running against each other.[58] The election
results came as a traumatic shock to most analysts and politicians.
Contrary to expectation, the anti-regime parties won a higher percentage of the vote (with 43.3 per cent of the party-list preferences) than
the democratically oriented parties (Russia's Choice, PRES,
Yabloko), which scored 30.1 per cent. Of the anti-Yeltsin forces,
Vladimir Zhirinovsky's Liberal Democratic Party of Russia topped the
poll, with 22.9 per cent of the party-list vote, well ahead of Gaidar's
Russia's Choice (with 15.51 per cent). To make matters worse,
Zyuganov's communists (the KPRF) came third, with 12.4 per cent of
the vote, followed by their allies, the Agrarians, with 7.99 per cent.
Only a recovery by Russia's Choice and a weak performance by the
LDPR in the single-seat constituencies, where the KPRF and
Agrarian vote held up, retrieved the situation to some extent, as half

the seats in the lower house of the Parliament were directly elected by constituencies (and half by proportional representation from the national party lists). Nonetheless, the LDPR was the second largest party in the Parliament (with 64 seats) behind Russia's Choice (with 66 seats), with the KPRF in third place (48 seats) and the Agrarians fourth (with 33 seats).[59] Many notorious nationalists were elected to the Duma, including the imperialist television journalist, Alexander Nevzorov; the nationalist writer and former émigré, Eduard Limonov; the chairman of the Stalin society, Omar Begov; the leader of the neo-fascist National Republican Party, Nikolai Lysenko.[60] Doubts were cast on the accuracy of the results of the elections to the Duma and on the legality of the vote on the constitution, but they were not ultimately challenged.[61] The situation was not as disastrous as it seemed, however, as, according to the new constitution which had just been adopted, power was concentrated in the President's hands. The new Duma had almost no control over the nomination of the government and virtually none over foreign policy or the budget, and its decisions could be overridden by the more moderate Upper House, the Federal Council. Nonetheless, Zhirinovsky's apparent victory confounded everyone. Where had he come from?

D. THE ZHIRINOVSKY PHENOMENON

Ideologically, Zhirinovsky derived from the world of Russian authoritarian nationalism, where he was a relatively obscure figure, overshadowed by far better known thinkers and agitators. He was, as he liked to emphasize, a man of the people, living in a modest two-room flat in a pleasant if unfashionable suburb of Moscow.[62] In this, he was unlike the stars of the new elite, many of whom had occupied relatively privileged positions in the academic, political or administrative structures of the old regime. Zhirinovsky, by contrast, came from Alma Ata in Kazakhstan, where he grew up in a crowded communal flat with his widowed mother. Much has been made (principally by him) of the deprivations of his childhood. Being a poor Russian in what he felt to be a backward and alien, if subject, country, where the national minorities (in reality, the local majority) often competed successfully with Russians for scarce resources, opportunities and privileges, seems to have turned him into a racist, deeply hostile to the Turkish and other ethnic minorities of the Muslim east and south.[63]

It is therefore strange that Zhirinovsky should have chosen to study Turkish when he left school and even stranger that a nobody from Central Asia should have had the opportunity to study in an elite specialist academy in Moscow, from which the KGB and other strategic security, economic and political institutions recruited. The presumption must be that Zhirinovsky was talent-spotted by the authorities – as other elements in his biography also suggest.[64] However, his promising career in the Soviet overseas trade network was cut short by indiscretion;[65] throughout the declining years of the Soviet regime, Zhirinovsky's unpredictable and unconventional temperament frustrated his ambitions – leading to sackings, preventing promotion and acceptance of his application for Party membership. He was a misfit, too prone to state his views and discuss politics, at a time when bland conformity was required.[66]

He took to the waters of political pluralism with relish when it became possible in 1987, helping to found the Liberal Democratic Party in December 1989 and March 1990. The party's original programme was indeed liberal: it called for a law-based state, political pluralism, a mixed economy – including the right to private property – and legally enshrined human rights.[67] This was a line which Zhirinovsky, who wrested control of the party from its liberal co-founder by October 1990, soon amended. He claimed that the party did 'not want to generate anti-communist hysteria or abolish the Communist Party' nor did it 'support the call "Down with the KGB"'. By December 1990, Zhirinovsky and the Liberal Democratic Party demanded the formation of a government of national salvation. He and his party helped to establish a 'centrist' bloc of largely fictional parties, which was received at the highest political level (*inter alia* by Anatoly Lukyanov and KGB Chairman Kryuchkov) and called for a military crackdown in the Baltics and Russia at the start of 1991, the closing of the Russian and Baltic parliaments, the banning of political parties and the introduction of Presidential rule by decree.[68] In Moscow, in 1990, there were widespread rumours about the party's links with the KGB. These were raised with Zhirinovsky in an interview in *Moscow News*, which noted the extraordinary publicity accorded to the party by *Pravda*, which published an article about its formation on its front page, while the activities of other informal groups were consigned to obscurity. Zhirinovsky denied the connection and journalists who tried to investigate the issue were threatened.[69] After the 1991 coup, documents from the Central Committee Archive were discovered, which purported to establish that Zhirinovsky had indeed cooperated with the CPSU and Russian Communist Party and had been funded by them.[70]

Thus, by 1991, Zhirinovsky's liberal posture had been abandoned in favour of the imperial nationalism, which he made the centrepiece of his campaign for the Russian presidency that year. He stressed the need to re-establish a strong, centralised Russian state to withstand the threat posed by democratisation and the growing nationalism of the ethnic minorities.

> We must all become citizens of Russia. But by Russia, I understand the whole territory of our state, from the Baltics to the Pacific and from Kishinev to Kamchatka.[71]

He exploited the theme of Great Russia and the need to defend it with all the more ardour because he guessed that many Russians felt humiliated by the Soviet Union's declining power, cohesion and prosperity. He discovered a key element of his constituency: army officers, the Russian diaspora in the republics and relatively poor provincials:

> Russians today are the most insulted, disgraced and abused nation [in the USSR] [...] For me, the Russian question is the central one. I will defend Russia and the Russian language over the whole territory of the USSR.[72]

The idea that Russia had been deprived of her rightful place in the world and should be restored to it was a balm to those injured spirits. This and the allied theme – that Russians had sacrificed themselves for other nationalities throughout the Soviet period and that these ungrateful people had turned on their benefactors – were a constant refrain in Zhirinovsky's rhetoric after 1991 and especially in the 1993 campaign. Here was the authentic voice of the poor colonist, the miserable scion of the ruling nation who nursed resentment against all around him – whether in Algeria, South Africa or Kazakhstan.

Rather than acknowledging the pressure for change, Zhirinovsky recommended putting the clock back, if necessary by force. Economic pressure should be put on the republics to force them to return to the embrace of Mother Russia:

> As for the ex-Soviet states, Russia supported and fed them under the communists ... Stop helping them and they won't last a month. Why should we inflict suffering on ourselves? Let others suffer.[73]

Abolition of the republics' sovereignty, autonomy, economic and political rights and their subordination to Moscow became the basis of his political campaigns both in 1991 and 1993.[74] He also emphasised the importance of reorientating foreign policy: it should concentrate not on East–West relations but on the North–South axis, as Russia needed to expand through Turkey, Iran and Afghanistan down to the warm waters of the Mediterranean and the Indian Ocean.[75]

Zhirinovsky sometimes envisaged this goal in terms of international cooperation in a new age of imperialism, with the USA, Europe and Russia sharing the world between them.[76] More characteristic, however, were sharp denunciations of the West as an enemy, which conspired with its fifth column of democrats to reduce Russia to slavery and exploit her resources: 'What does the West do for us? Westerners come here to buy cheap resources, to conquer our markets, to pay us slave wages.' Russia had to cleanse herself of 'this contagion'. The decline of Soviet power had been engineered artificially as part of a 'plan to destroy Russia', carried out by Russia's rivals, who dreamt of annihilating her powerful economy and armed forces.[77] The secret war against Russia was led by America, which had come with talk of liberalisation and democracy, brandishing hamburgers and pornography.

> In the twentieth century, three wars were conducted against Russia and the third and last (*perestroika*) was the cleverest and quietest. Everything is very cleverly camouflaged under beautiful correct slogans: 'democracy, law, justice, human rights'. But as a result the country has been crushed, the state has collapsed, the economy been destroyed [...].[78]

An act of genocide was being perpetrated:

> The nation needs to be saved today [...] Otherwise, in the next century, there will be an end to the Russian nation. It will die, like Byzantium [...] Each year, there are fewer of us [...] In twenty to thirty years [...] we will cease to exist as a nation.[79]

Zhirinovsky's xenophobia outstripped that of most of his main political rivals. All Russia's problems started in the south with the ethnic minorities of the Causacus, he claimed, generally recommending their expulsion from the Russian body politic and restrictions on their right to trade in Russian cities.[80] His call for a crackdown on crime and corruption was a very popular theme for voters not overwhelmingly repelled by the openly racist terms in which it was often cast.[81] Jews too, with their former control of the Bolshevik party and now of the media and the democratic movement, were suspect. 'Not for anything will I permit Russia to be governed by anyone who does not recognise himself to be one hundred per cent Russian', Zhirinovsky promised.[82]

Zhirinovsky's apocalyptic and xenophobic vision was propounded alongside declarations of allegiance to human rights and the rule of law. The party programme (even in its later versions) promised to guarantee equality before the law and a law-based state (although Zhirinovsky commonly called for discrimination against minorities). It supported political pluralism, envisaging elections to a legislature and a democratically elected presidency.[86] However, the government Zhirinovsky envisaged was one in which all executive power was concentrated in the President's hands, with the parliament in a subordinate role. Only a powerful President could put an end to crime and corruption.[87] When pressed on his attitude to democracy, Zhirinovsky suggested that Western democracy was alien to Russian tradition and that Russia needed to find a 'third way':

> Democracy and capitalism are not enough to enable us to resolve all our problems, we must seek new ways. Classical Western democracy at the very least perplexes me [...] I reject the Western model: it is unjust and directly contradicts Russian reality.[88]

His penchant for authoritarianism was reflected in his occasionally favourable references to Stalin and Hitler (although, predictably, he was not consistent in his praise for either leader).[89] Rather than repeating their formulae, he preferred – doubtless aware of the need to avoid the odium of too close an association with these paragons – to insist on the need for an original model of state and social organisation for Russia. By 1995, he had found it in a Russian variant of national socialism: 'National socialism has nothing in common with Hitlerism [...] The philosophy of national socialism is the philosophy of the ordinary man [...]'.[90] This was his target audience: the man whose modest expectations had been disappointed by governments past and present. To satisfy him, Zhirinovsky proposed adequate pensions and social security payments, full employment, an end to privatisation, which had made the few rich at the expense of the many, law and order and a strong State, with a powerful army.[91]

His aggressive nationalism, his exploitation of feelings of humiliation, his xenophobia, his economic formulae prompted many observers to see him as a fascist.[92] But Zhirinovsky eschewed typical aspects of fascism – failing to develop militarised party structures, abstaining from participation in attempts to seize power by force – and professing (however misleadingly) a commitment to democracy and the rule of law. Jonathan Steele has suggested that Zhirinovsky should be seen as a populist.[93] He was an adept political communicator, capable of performing on television, entertaining rather than boring the electorate. Not only his message but his way of conveying it (his empathy, his humour and his style) were important in attracting attention and support.[94] He adopted a resolutely up-to-date appearance and manner, realising that the beards, Cossack uniforms and peasant garb affected by some nationalists were off-putting to the young and the modern. A propos of this, he observed: 'Many years ago, I understood that dreary "bearded" nationalism puts people off. Russian nationalism must be modern, intellectual, aggressive, fashionable, if you like.'[95]

He showed that he knew how to campaign and, in this, he had few rivals. His use of language was lively, humorous and colourful, his images memorable, if only because they were so irreverent and unabashedly vulgar.[96] He spoke the same language as many ordinary Russians. He knew that he would not carry the sophisticated urban vote and his populist campaign was not intended to woo the intelligentsia. He adapted his message to suit his audience, empathising with, rather than patronising, his audience:[97]

> I represent the middle stratum which earns 200 roubles and lives in a two-room apartment. I am just like you and I understand that these awful prices in the commercial and cooperative stores are beyond our pockets ... Women of Russia ... I know things have been hard for you ... I share all of your anxieties: the eternal queues, the shortages ... You must be provided for.[98]

These skills enabled him to win support, especially among young men in the army and state factories and in decrepit provincial towns.[99] In his repudiation of Soviet and Tsarist tradition, his populism and modernity of political style, Zhirinovsky belonged to the radical rather than the conservative or neo-fascist right.

This approach won Zhirinovsky 6.2 million votes (8 per cent) in the 1991 Presidential elections, placing him third behind Yeltsin (with 59.7 per cent) and the former Prime Minister, Nikolai Ryzhkov (with 17.6 per cent).[83] However, this performance did not prepare analysts for Zhirinovsky's success (with 22.9 per cent of the vote) in the 1993 elections. He was an obscure figure in the nationalist camp, isolated within it and confined to the extreme margins of political life. His party seemed, like most parties at the time, more imaginary than real and it had not been represented in the Parliament before 1993.

Furthermore, Zhirinovsky was unwilling to cooperate with potential allies, despite sharing many of their concerns. He was drawn neither to the neo-Stalinist nor to the neo-Slavophile collectivists: his economic thought, though implausible and often contradictory, embraced private enterprise, although by 1993, he called for a halt to the dismantling of the state sector and the conversion of the military-industrial complex.[84] Politically, he was astute enough to see that power could be won through the ballot box as well as by force and that he could govern with ostensibly democratic institutions. For this reason he warmly welcomed Yeltsin's draft constitution in Autumn 1993, as it gave sweeping powers to the Presidency.[85] Crucially, despite having supported the August 1991 coup, he did not ally himself with Yeltsin's opponents in Autumn 1993. This ensured that he, almost alone in the nationalist camp, was free to campaign for the anti-Yeltsin vote in the 1993 elections.

E. CONCLUSION

Was the vote for the LDPR and the communists in 1993 a ringing endorsement of authoritarian nationalism and imperialism or a protest vote; an aberration or the start of a long-term retreat from democracy? The question is perhaps misconceived in that it pre-supposes that Russians were voting under normal conditions and were fully aware of the choice they faced and its implications. It overlooks a number of exceptional factors. Firstly, a fully democratic political culture and system had not yet been created in Russia. Russia's political pluralism did not correspond to a developed multi-party system and the degree of pluralism that prevailed in the country varied in accordance with geography and social conditions. Few of Russia's political parties were cohesive, well-organised or even present throughout the state. Many were little more than extended political clubs or recently formed electoral blocs. Their programmes were often woolly and irrelevant. The chief exceptions to this rule in Autumn 1993 was the KPRF which had an extensive network, party discipline and a relatively professional organisation.[100] The democrats, after an initial euphoric phase of party building in 1990, paid inadequate attention to the mundane task of building an infrastructure of popular support and failed to establish a broad democratic party. Not until the elections were imminent did they again try to establish a mass party: this attempt was undermined as three competing parties emerged, mainly composed of rival politicians, their allies and clients, more akin to the old CPSU clans than to popular political parties and distinguished more by their personal rivalries than by deep divergences of orientation and political preference.[101]

The electorate was largely unfamiliar with the political leaders and still more with the programmes of the parties they led. A poll of 30 October 1993 found that over 50 per cent of voters were unfamiliar with the programme of the party they intended to vote for. Another poll showed that 75 per cent could not identify the parties led by Volsky, Travkin or Zyuganov.[102] The banning of several opposition papers contributed to this problem. Journalists were criticised for offering little independent or critical comment on the participants and for bias towards Russia's Choice.[103] The absence of effective organisation and adequate information thus inhibited the interplay of forces presupposed by democracy and probably distorted the vote.

The depth of the political and economic crisis also made this a difficult election for the democrats to fight. They were inevitably associated in the public mind with the problems under which the country was labouring – falling living standards, rising crime and corruption, growing insecurity. The political elite of post-communist Russia was undifferentiated in the popular mind: but a general image of ambition, fractiousness and corruption had been created by the endless crises and scandals of the previous two years. The metropolitan elite, from which many of Russia's new leaders had emerged, were widely resented, especially in the provinces. Not for nothing were the leading democratic politicians known as the new *nomenklatura*. This image, compounded by the failure to communicate and build up a network of support in the country was unhelpful in attracting votes. Thus support for Yeltsin did not necessarily imply enthusiasm for his more obscure democratic collaborators.

Conversely, given the personalisation of politics in post-communist Russia, a vote against the democrats did not necessarily mean a vote against democracy *per se*. The democrats' poor score has been seen as registering protest against specific figures and policies, rather than a positive endorsement of the alternative ideology. The electorate's tardiness in deciding for whom to vote[104] is suggestive of the irrelevance of the ideological debate, the general terms of which were well-known, and the relative importance of the personality and power of the candidates. The pattern of voting supports the thesis that the vote was personalised rather than ideologically inspired. In the nationwide voting on the party lists, Zhirinovsky outstripped the democrats:[105] but he was better known, thanks to his effective and colourful television performances. In the single-seat constituencies, where individual candidates were pitted against each other, democrats, communists and above all independents performed well, overshadowing Zhirinovsky.

Finally, it has been observed that the LDPR's performance has been overstated. In fact, no one party won the elections: independent, non-aligned candidates won more seats than any party. The LDPR was not represented at all in the Federation Council. One journalist noted that diametrically opposed conclusions might have been drawn about Russia's political profile, had one of the two voting systems actually used been adopted to the exclusion of the other. Had the results been determined solely by direct voting in the constituencies (where the LDPR won five seats as against Russia's Choice's 30, the KPRF's 16 and the independents' 141 seats) Russia would have seemed tolerably democratic in instinct. With a fully proportional voting on national party lists, the LDPR would have been by far the largest party and Russia would have appeared to be semi-fascist in its political preferences.[106] It may thus be a mistake to interpret the results of the 1993 elections in terms of ideological, programmatic party politics. Patronage, personality and protest were probably more important than ideology in determining how the electorate voted in 1993. The elections suggested that voters were volatile and disaffected, rather than wedded to authoritarianism and collectivism. However, the real significance of the elections was overshadowed by the LDPR's apparent triumph. The political prestige of right and left wing nationalism was greatly enhanced: its leaders were established in the new parliament and enjoyed the authority of a popular mandate; the nationalists and communists had come in from the cold, appearing in the guise of the official, institutional opposition. Popular disenchantment had given opportunists and politicians preaching authoritarian nationalism a chance to ensconce themselves at the heart of the new political system.

7 Zyuganov's Communists and Nationalism, 1993–95

How did Zhirinovsky's aggressively nationalist LDPR and Zyuganov's revived communists, the KPRF, use the opportunity afforded by their electoral gains? Did they succeed in establishing their authority and strengthening their power base in Russian society and institutions? Those who saw the 1993 election results purely as a protest vote were dismayed when the parties were not tamed by their victories. The LDPR retained a significant constituency in the December 1995 Duma elections, while Zyuganov's communists, at least in their official rhetoric, became increasingly committed to a form of socialist nationalism, which seemed to preclude the possibility of their becoming a social-democratic party.

A) THE LDPR

The 1993 elections suggested that the re-emerging KPRF had most to fear not from the democrats, who were associated with Gaidar's unpopular economic policies and with the collapse of the Soviet state, but from rivals on the nationalist wing of the political spectrum. The press devoted much alarmed attention to the tiny neo-fascist parties. The most threatening of these tendencies was represented by Zhirinovsky, who appeared to have demonstrated their popular appeal. However, his strength was more illusory than it seemed. Most analysts concluded that his support was unstable and that his parliamentary power was not an accurate reflection of his following in the country.[1] Even the real size of his party was disputed: it claimed 80 000–83 000 members in April 1993 but only 40 000 the following October, while elsewhere membership was estimated at 100 000.[2] Opinions about its strength in the regions differed, with some writers believing it to be numerous and well-organised, while others pointed to the absence of successful candidates in the constituencies as evidence of its weakness in the provinces.[3] Similar confusion reigned about its finances: funding was thought to have come from foreign sympathisers (including Jean-Marie Le Pen and Erich Honecker) and the black market (the LDPR allegedly benefited from a Russian money-laundering operation in Holland). Zhirinovsky insisted that the party's income derived from membership dues and voluntary contributions, but offered no proof of this. However, he appeared to have prosperous patrons: his close associates (his deputy, Alexander Vengerovsky, and his running-mate in 1991, Andrei Zavidiya) included some newly wealthy businessmen, who claimed to have funded him between 1991 and 1994.[4] The LDPR was widely believed to have had KGB backing, which may have been the source of the party's initial income.[5] The impression given by the party's finances and organisation was that the party was not so much a real political organisation, based on regional networks, as a proto-party, organised around a dynamic personality and useful to some business circles.[6]

That the party was largely a one-man show was suggested both by Zhirinovsky's attitude to it and by the divisions which beset it after 1993. Zhirinovsky was anxious to maintain his hegemony over the party, feeling that his colleagues might be emboldened to challenge him in the light of their electoral mandate. He not only ensured that he monopolised media attention (for example, by congratulating the amnestied parliamentary leaders on their release from prison, in February 1994) but, more significantly, he sought to institutionalise his power. At the LDPR's fifth congress, on 2–3 April 1994, the party rules were changed to allow Zhirinovsky to be confirmed as leader until the year 2004. The party's voting rights were restricted, with the congress electing only the leader (a function it had *de facto* abdicated for a decade) and the governing councils of the party being appointed henceforth by Zhirinovsky alone. Congresses were no longer to be held annually but every three years.[7] Zhirinovsky also struggled unsuccessfully to strengthen party discipline in the Duma, where the LDPR constituted the second largest bloc of party deputies.[8]

Zhirinovsky's tactics proved divisive, especially within the parliamentary party. Only 35 deputies in the 64-strong LDPR fraction were members of the party; others had simply stood for election on the party ticket, but were resistant to following Zhirinovsky's lead at all times.[9] By April 1994, five deputies had left the fraction, criticising the leader's policies and behaviour and many more soon followed them.[10] The party's performance in the Duma was ineffective, partly due to poor discipline. Alexei Zavidiya believed that up to half the members of the fraction were closer to the communists and a quarter more to

Russia's Choice than they were to Zhirinovsky – an assessment with which the communist Viktor Zorkaltsev broadly agreed.[11] Zhirinovsky's tendency to quarrel with his deputies and the party's lack of internal cohesion undermined his ability to build on his electoral success and construct a powerful organisation.

The party was also bedevilled by the inconsistency of Zhirinovsky's criticisms of the government. Although he made populist noises about the need for increased social security payments, and about the evils of private property in land and economic reform, which he denounced as a corrupt and criminal programme of theft, he voted for the 1994 and 1995 budgets.[12] His support of centralisation and a strong executive, which had prompted him to support Yeltsin's draft constitution in 1993, led him to endorse the war in Chechnya in Winter 1994. However, after an abortive attempt to draw closer to Yeltsin in January 1995, he resorted to criticising the conduct of the war, especially after the Budennovsk hostage crisis in June 1995, when he supported no confidence votes in the government.[13] This approach contrived to alienate both supporters and enemies of the President, without winning Zhirinovsky new admirers or endowing him with new-found respectability. It confirmed his image as an unpredictable maverick. In defending himself, Zhirinovsky observed, not without reason, that he had not moved to the President's side, but that the President had adopted the LDPR's position on Russian statehood.[14]

Zhirinovsky's failure to consolidate his electoral successes was due not only to his dictatorial and erratic temperament and the weaknesses of his party's shadowy organisation: his electorate was volatile. He appears to have benefited from a protest vote in 1993 and this was hard to consolidate. Unlike the communists who commanded the loyalty of elderly and unskilled voters, Zhirinovsky's support was not determined solely by obvious sociological factors. True, he appealed to army officers, especially in 1993 (when up to 40 per cent of the military voted for him in some areas), which was understandable in the light of the crisis of funding and loss of social prestige the army suffered after 1991 and the overwhelmingly nationalist and imperialist opinions of the senior officer corps.[15] However, his supporters were not predominantly old, poor and ill-educated: many were skilled young men, albeit often employed in vulnerable state factories or the bureaucracy in the provinces. Party members and deputies were surprisingly well-educated.[16] Unlike the elderly, indoctrinated communists, Zhirinovsky's supporters expressed no strong loyalty to the LDPR.[17]

True, LDPR voters tended to prefer authoritarian to freely elected governments, to be more xenophobic and intolerant of minorities than other electors and to be less inclined to blame communists than the current government for Russia's difficulties, but not all Zhirinovsky's ideas were shared by his supporters. His calls for increased expenditure on arms and nuclear weapons, for the armed defence of Russian nationals abroad and his warnings about a foreign threat to Russia appear to have been greeted with some scepticism.[18] These findings suggested that Zhirinovsky's vote might swing to other parties exploiting some of the same ideas and the LDPR was confronted with a comparatively well-organised rival in the KPRF. Furthermore, Zhirinovsky was in no position to deliver results for his supporters, as he pointed out in his defence of his parliamentary record before the 1995 elections.[19] By 1995, polls indicated that the public overwhelmingly distrusted Zhirinovsky (63 per cent trusting him not at all in March, while 3 per cent trusted him totally) with only 7 per cent believing, in January 1995, that the LDPR represented the interests of people like them, a level of voter identification confirmed by polls taken the previous year.[20] Zhirinovsky was thus expected to lose votes in the 1995 Duma elections, when the KPRF supplanted it as the leading anti-reform party.

B) THE RISE OF THE KPRF

In late 1991, few observers would have predicted the communists' recovery and their re-emergence in the mid-1990s as one of the main foci of opposition to Yeltsin. Both as an organisation and as an ideology, communism was exceptionally discredited in the aftermath of the coup. How was their recovery to be explained? Was the communists' rapid recovery not a sign of a political culture compromised by its penchant for authoritarianism? While communist parties in other East European countries retrieved some of the ground they had lost quite quickly, this was at least partly explained and excused by their transformation into social-democratic parties, which renounced authoritarian rule. By contrast, the KPRF remained ambiguous and inconsistent not only about the market economy but also about the political traditions of liberalism. Its pronouncements on democracy and history, its espousal of collectivist nationalism gave little encouragement to those who looked for signs of its conversion to democratic and liberal norms. However, the party exploited the opportunities provided by political pluralism and liberalism to build up its support. Did this point to a real change of heart rather than to its traditional pragmatism in pursuit of power? Were Zyuganov and his associates ready to jettison the legacy of Lenin in favour of democracy?

What sort of party had re-emerged onto the political stage? Anatoly Lukyanov insisted that the KPRF was 'the same Marxist-Leninist party' as before the collapse of the Soviet Union.[21] This suggested, misleadingly, that the CPSU and the KP RSFSR had been united parties, rather than coalitions embracing social-democrats, nationalist neo-Stalinists and orthodox Marxist-Leninists. The KPRF was also a coalition of different trends: modernisers, nationalists and putative Marxist-Leninists. While the modernisers, who were based in the Duma, were not Western-style social democrats, they were the most inclined to adapt to circumstances and embrace elements of democracy and the market economy. Led in 1993–96 by Zyuganov's deputy, Valentin Kuptsov, the Speaker of the 1995 Duma Gennady Seleznev and the chairman of the Duma committee on economic affairs (and ex-head of Gosplan) Yuri Maslyukov, they were, however, ready to accept the nationalist line advanced by Zyuganov and his supporters in their pursuit of power. The orthodox communists (who included Anatoly Lukyanov and Generals Makashov and Varennikov) inclined more to Stalinism than to the reform 'Leninism' of figures such as Roy Medvedev, using their influence at the end of 1994 to have the draft party programme amended to include many positive references to the Stalinist legacy, although thereafter they lost ground to Zyuganov. Their views were not reflected in the Party's campaign platforms in 1995 and 1996 and they blamed Zyuganov's failure in the Presidential elections on this.[22]

Although the party leaders voiced different preferences about the direction to take, they compromised on the programme and tactics in the hope of winning power.[23] Late in 1993, Zyuganov persuaded most of his colleagues that power could be won more readily through the ballot-box than wrested by force from Yeltsin. As he put it, he had become 'flexible' following Lenin's example, preferring to work within the system to establish a patriotic government of national unity and transform the regime legally.[24] Hence, in December 1993, the KPRF decided, unlike its rivals on the left of the political spectrum, to participate in the elections to the new parliamentary assembly, the Duma. The results vindicated this decision: with 48 seats and 12.4 per cent of the vote, the KPRF became the third largest party in the Duma.[25] With the LDPR, the KPRF was thus one of the chief beneficiaries of the elections. Consigned to the political wilderness in November 1991, the party was now ensconced in one of the main political institutions of the new regime and enjoyed a popular mandate.

For this revisionist approach to be successful in the long term, the KPRF had to refurbish its image as an electable, responsible party and develop an effective party machine. Its work in the Duma helped the party to achieve both these aims.[26] However, the party had a difficult legacy to overcome in consolidating and extending its support: communism's prestige had been greatly eroded in the twilight of the Soviet era and neither the failed August coup nor the obstreperous opposition of communist sympathisers in the Russian parliament thereafter added to its attractions for most Russians. Ideological renewal was essential. However, in the climate of 1992 and 1993 and given the desertion of most reformers in the CPSU to the democratic camp in 1990 and 1991, few party members were inclined to seek answers in the arsenal of Western or liberal ideas. Apart from this temperamental inclination to reject Western reforms, there was, after 1993, a more important reason why the party leadership embraced Greater Russian nationalism. Zhirinovsky's success at the polls suggested that revanchist nationalism had struck a chord with the Russian people and the KPRF's leaders were reluctant to abandon so potentially numerous a constituency to this unpredictable rival on their right. Led by Zyuganov, they were persuaded that the KPRF should try to extend its appeal beyond its natural constituency to the nationalist vote, which had supported Zhirinovsky and which included critics of communism. Hence, the party's election manifestoes contained only enough allusions to classical Soviet socialism to keep the Party's neo-Stalinists on board, while dwelling at length on 'patriotic' themes. Throughout 1994 and 1995, this line was maintained, despite criticism from the left. If the party's adoption of nationalism was pragmatic rather than principled, it was nonetheless significant for it helped to introduce a mystical, collectivist doctrine to mainstream political debate: the ideas espoused by a once controversial group of intellectuals were now propounded by Russia's two leading parties, the LDPR and the KPRF.

a) Ideology

Hence, ideologically, the revived KPRF strayed far from the pastures of orthodox Marxism and Leninism, appealing to traditional Russian nationalism at least as much if not more than to classical socialism in its programme documents and election manifestoes. The party leader, Gennady Zyuganov, went to some lengths to portray himself as a greater Russian nationalist in his theoretical writings.

At the second party congress, in February 1993, when the party was allowed to resume its political activities, many communist activists hoped to re-establish the old CPSU on Marxist-Leninist lines, reuniting the several splinter parties that had been founded after the collapse of the Soviet system. Another wing of the movement hoped to establish a reformed, social-democratic party. However, there was no agreement on what constituted ideological orthodoxy: Stalinists, reformists and Leninists were not only at odds among themselves but also dissented from the predominant nationalist line propounded by Zyuganov.[27] However, if the Congress failed to reunite all the strands of post-Soviet communism, it nonetheless constructed the largest political organisation in the country, claiming 500 000 members,[28] and committed it to a clearly nationalist socialist line.

The reformist elements smuggled into the KP RSFSR's early declarations in 1990 by the democratic wing of the party[29] were largely absent in the programme declaration adopted by the congress; instead it set the revanchist tone that was to be characteristic of the party, announcing that 'the Fatherland was in danger' and faced imminent collapse, due to the treachery of *perestroika* liberals and Yeltsin's democratic government. The Russian economy, its army, power and influence in world affairs, the well-being of its people had all been compromised by the reforms. It was still possible to prevent total collapse, 'to restore national dignity, the people's well-being, respect for the Motherland', but only 'through popular sovereignty and socialism, the consolidation of all fully democratic and patriotic forces, united by the idea of saving the Fatherland'.[30] The coalition envisaged was not, therefore, animated exclusively by socialism, but by concern for the Russian state and nation. Socialism was necessary because it alone could guarantee the survival and prosperity of the Russian state:

> The KPRF [...] will fight stubbornly for Russia's return to the path of socialist development. Departure from this path led to the collapse of the Union and has threatened Russian state sovereignty. The KPRF considers that only socialism corresponds to the interests of Russia and the absolute majority of its population.[31]

The values to which the party adhered were not those of classical Marxism but a nationalistic reformulation of them.

Hence, the KPRF dosed its largely rhetorical internationalism with caveats about patriotism and national tradition, including among its principles 'patriotism and internationalism, brotherhood of the peoples and respect for national traditions'.[32] What internationalism meant was clarified further on in the document: like 'brotherhood of the peoples', it amounted to little more than the reincorporation of the newly independent nations of the CIS into the Greater Russian state, a revived Soviet Union:

> Communists call for the complete integration of the independent states, formed in the territory of the former USSR, into an economic, scientific and conservationist whole [*yedinstvo*], for a single foreign policy.

They warned that the Russian diaspora in 'the so-called Near Abroad' would not be neglected.[33] True, they suggested that these aims would be achieved by agreement, but neglected to specify how reunification could be effected in the absence of this.[34]

True to the legacy of Soviet socialism, the KPRF rejected Yeltsin's economic reforms, opposed privatisation of industry and farming and the operation of market forces, calling instead for centralised state direction of the economy, state control of prices and foreign trade and collective rather than private property. In a gesture to public opinion, they demanded measures to promote social equality, including social security guarantees, free health, education, subsidised housing and index-linked pensions and benefits.[35] The party clearly hoped to exploit the economic and social crisis and appeal to an unskilled workforce, threatened by economic rationalisation and reform to garner support.[36]

The inspiration for this collectivism appeared to lie as much in hostility to the West and its culture as in enthusiasm for Marxism. The party showed little sympathy for democratic principles of government. While demanding human rights and freedoms, as a matter of necessity, it failed to endorse democracy as it is generally understood, calling instead for 'socialist democracy, workers' power in the form of Soviets'.[37] The rejection of conventional democracy and capitalism was underpinned by hostility to foreign cultural influences and to America, in particular. The party opposed 'the total commercialisation and Americanisation of the cultural sphere'.[38] Foreign involvement in Russia could be malign:

> We are categorically opposed to the plunder of national wealth by home and foreign capitalist operators, to the transformation of Russia into a raw-materials' appendage of other countries.[39]

To counteract nefarious foreign influences, the KPRF abandoned classical Marxism's aggressive atheism. On the contrary, Russian communists now declared their support for the:

> progressive patriotic work of distinguished representatives of the Russian Orthodox church [...] who actively call for the spiritual rebirth of Russia and the defence of her [territorial] integrity.[40]

Hence, the party which emerged from the period of proscription preached not classical Marxism but a form of socialist nationalism, which was indebted to trends in the Party that pre-dated the fall of the Soviet regime. Its economic populism was influenced by the neo-Stalinism of the United Workers' Front, its nationalism to the Party's flirtation with National-Bolshevism in Spring 1991. This ideological eclecticism repelled the more orthodox new socialist parties, several of which decided against uniting with the KPRF.[41] On the other hand, it gained the party allies in the nationalist camp and reinforced the growing opposition to Yeltsin. The KPRF declared its readiness to become 'the party of those who want to regenerate the Fatherland'.[42]

It has been suggested that the KPRF's flirtation with nationalism was of little significance and that the Party subsequently moved back to more orthodox Marxist positions.[43] However, the programme adopted at the Party's third congress on 22 January 1995 did not represent a significant departure from its earlier declarations: rather it developed and elaborated on themes already present in its earlier document.

The clearest example of this is the defence of the CPSU's history and record, where the neo-Stalinists' influence was clear. Whereas in 1993, the Party's destiny had been deemed 'great and tragic' and its victories acknowledged to have been achieved at the cost of the occasional 'deformation' of socialist principles, by 1995, any hint of apology was absent from the programme. Any problems encountered in the past (a less than fully effective industrial sector, an incomplete revolution in economic management) were overshadowed by the achievements of the Revolution: the people had gained political and economic power, were given new social and cultural opportunities, the country had been industrialised at heroic speed and, thanks to this, the Great Patriotic War had been won. Inevitably, this was achieved at a cost: the initiative of the working classes was inhibited – but, the programme implied, was this not a price worth paying for the survival of Russia and its revolutionary society? Of course, the Party had been obliged to struggle not only against foreign imperialists but also against internal enemies, petit-bourgeois careerists, even within the ranks of the Party itself – in the shape first of Trotskyites and later of those calling for Russia's 'return to world civilisation' (that is, the Party reformers in the late 1980s). Only if one understood this internal struggle could one explain the Terror. The real problems in the Soviet path of development had come not with Stalin (who had equipped and saved the socialist Motherland) but with his incompetent and perfidious heirs, such as Khrushchev. With the exception of Andropov (the former KGB chief and Party leader who, the programme claimed, gave Russians democratic elections, freedom of speech and political association), the Soviet Union's leaders degenerated further, ultimately into open treachery. These renegades put the press (under *glasnost'*) into the hands of 'slanderers and haters of our country', who, 'using the methods of psychological warfare' blackened the Soviet and Russian historical record, opened the way to black capital and 'anti-national' (*anti-narodnye*) forces who tried to undermine Soviet power and the unity of the State. Gorbachev and Yakovlev, Shevardnadze and Yeltsin were thus 'personally responsible' for betraying the Party, ignoring national interests and destroying the Fatherland.[44] Happily, the corrupt element had now been expelled from the ranks of the communist faithful and the KPRF represented all that was healthy and constructive in Soviet history.[45]

The glorious heritage of the Soviet past to which the KPRF laid claim was that of Stalinism. Stalin's rule had been creative and beneficial: under him, the Soviet Union had flourished, its external and internal enemies had been crushed (so much for those who had reservations about policies which covered the country with concentration camps), the State had been held together and ordinary people had benefited from great material and cultural progress. Decadence had set in with reformers like Khrushchev and Gorbachev; the closer the Soviet Union had drawn to the West, the worse it had been for Russia.

As in 1993, the KPRF argued that socialism was essential for Russia's survival as a nation and a great power. However, it was primarily in terms of Russian greatness and tradition, rather than in the eschatological terms of inevitability and justice favoured by Marx, that the case for retaining socialism was argued. In the past under Lenin and Stalin, socialism had saved Russia.[46] In the modern world, riven by the clash of two great forces, socialism and capitalism, a similar choice faced Russia:

History is again posing the people of our Motherland the same choice as in 1917 and 1941: either a great power and socialism, or the further dissolution of the country and its definitive transformation into a colony. *One can boldly assert that in essence the 'Russian idea' is a deeply socialist idea.*[47]

This was an argument first put forward in the 1920s by nationalist intellectuals (former Whites) forced into emigration by their active opposition to the Bolshevik regime.[48] It is ironic to note the neo-Stalinists of contemporary Russia adopting arguments first advanced by former Whites, whose chief preoccupation was the power and integrity of the Russian empire.

This ideological debt to earlier Russian nationalism was evident throughout the programme. The first section insisted at some length on socialism's dynamism and historical significance: it would continue to dispute with the exploitative and exhausted capitalism of the developed world the right to shape the destinies and future development of mankind.[49] The programme then examined Russia's historical role as the embodiment of socialism and progress. Soviet Russia had been in the vanguard of humanity for much of the twentieth century. This was no accident: collectivism (concern for the well-being of the community and State), idealistic spirituality (as opposed to the grubby consumerism and materialism of the West) and messianism were at the heart of Russian tradition and were common to both imperial and Soviet Russia, enabling the latter to build on the inheritance and achievements of the Tsars:

The complex intertwining of geopolitical, national and economic circumstances made Russia into the bearer of cultural and moral traditions, whose basic values are communitarianism [*obshchinnost'*], conciliarism [*sobornost'*], patriotism, the closest mutual ties between the individual, society and State power [*derzhavnost'*]; striving to realise the highest ideals of truth, goodness and justice (spirituality) [*dukhovnost'*]; equal rights and equal value of all citizens without reference to their national, religious or other differences (nationality) [*narodnost'*].[50]

The internationalism of the last provision should deceive no-one – especially in the context of a document that everywhere emphasised the value and importance of the Russian State, Russian culture and tradition: the nationality the writers had in mind was the state-based, composite all-Russian nationality (*rossiiskii* rather than *russkii*), which subsumed minority nationalities within the Russian cultural and political sphere.

In fact, this plea for Russia's socialist spiritual heritage was a bowdlerised version of the nineteenth-century theory of official nationality, which the Imperial Russian State claimed to embody. In the 1830s, Nicholas I's Education Minister Uvarov proposed a state theory based on the three principles of 'autocracy, Orthodoxy and nationality' (*samoderzhavie, pravoslavie* and *narodnost'*). The KPRF simply took over the idea of nationality (*narodnost'*) and adapted those of Orthodoxy and autocracy in the light of Romantic nationalist social theory and later Imperial practice. 'Autocracy' (*samoderzhavie*) was amended to the related idea of 'supreme power or sovereignty' (*derzhavnost'*), the promotion of State strength and unity rather than of liberalism and democracy, and a line successfully pursued by Stalin, as the Party had earlier observed, and by the Tsars. 'Orthodoxy' became 'spirituality' and was implied also by the references to conciliarism (*sobornost'*), a concept first elaborated by Uvarov's contemporary A.S. Khomiakov and placed by him at the heart of renewed Orthodox theology and Slavophile political and social theory. *Obshchinnost'* or communitarianism too was a concept first developed by religiously inspired Romantic nationalists in the mid-nineteenth century: the harmony and unity of Russia's communal way of life, according to these theorists, distinguished it from the West and meant that Western political and economic practices were alien to Russia. These ideas were taken up and adapted both by Russia's conservatives and her revolutionaries later in the century and were revived by contemporary Russian communists because they furnished an apparently new justification for rejecting reform and returning to the past.

Hence, Russia's modern communists no longer attempted to justify socialism in terms of historical development as conceived by Marx but were in fact closer, and even ideologically indebted, to Marx's Russian nationalist and religious opponents. Their vocabulary and ideas were derived less from classical Marxism than from nineteenth-century apologists for Russian autocracy and Russian Orthodox nationalism. For the new communists, socialism and capitalism continued their titanic struggle but the contest between these great socio-economic systems was realised in terms of the clash of civilisations and cultures, rather than in terms of debate or conflict between universally valid ideologies. This understanding of history was closer to theories of the conflict between the religious East and materialist

West, of vibrant Eurasia and decadent Europe first launched by nineteenth-century reactionaries like the poet Fyodor Tyutchev, Ivan Aksakov and Nikolai Danilevsky and elaborated in the 1920s by émigré scholars than to Marx's historical materialism and dialectic.[51] It was to provide the rationale for the Party's anti-Western foreign and economic policies.[52]

The essence of the Party's programme was to look back to the Soviet Union, whose essential features – economic, social, political and international – the Party hoped to recover. This meant to reverse, over time, Yeltsin's economic policies and return to State control of the economy;[53] to end the pro-Western orientation of foreign and defence policy and the independence of the 'near abroad'. The 'dissemination of Westernism and Americanism, historical vandalism, the cult of profit force and depravity, egoism and individualism', the disparagement of Russian and Soviet history and of Lenin were to be replaced with 'respect for the traditions of communitarianism (*obshchinnost'*) and collectivism, for Russian language and culture'.[54]

Not only was capitalism rejected, but the Party's statements about that other Western import, democracy, were ambiguous. The Party insisted on the importance of:

> Popular sovereignty, meaning the constitutional power of the working majority, united through the Soviets and other forms of democratic self-government of the people.

In the late 1980s, the call for more power for the workers was adopted by Party hardliners and opponents of democracy in the belief that an electoral system weighted in favour of the unskilled working class and a return to voting at the workplace was more open to control by the Party hierarchy. That a similar intention informed this demand is suggested by calls elsewhere in the programme for a new constitution, for the re-creation of the Soviets (which were undemocratic), for new electoral laws maximising representation of workers in the organs of power. As the country returned to the old order, the Party looked forward to a system which would enable 'workers to participate more actively and widely in the administration of affairs of State through soviets, unions, worker self-management and other [...] organs of direct sovereignty.'[55] This appeared to imply a rejection, in the long term, of the existing system of parliamentary representation. In short, the whole legacy of the reforms was rejected in favour of a system inspired by the Soviet past, justified in terms of the Tsarist past.

The programme did not represent a convincing policy for a future KPRF government. Like the party's other ideological statements, it was largely a hybrid rhetorical document, whose function was to inspirit and rally the party's disparate forces, while appealing to voters' utopian and nostalgic aspirations. The KPRF's nationalist socialism was in many respects indebted to post-war Stalinism's chauvinism, imperialism and hostility to the West. This debt was acknowledged by the Party's leader, Gennady Zyuganov.[56]

b) Zyuganov and His Outlook

Zyuganov, like the Party he led, appeared to have evolved dramatically in the post-Soviet period. He had spent his life working up the ranks of the CPSU *apparat* – a career which committed him, at least in theory, to opposing imperialism and supporting internationalism. That Zyuganov in fact belonged to the Greater Russian neo-Stalinist wing of the Party is suggested by his signature of the Appeal to the People before the August 1991 coup and the series of alliances he concluded with nationalist and imperialist opponents of reform in 1992 and 1993.[57] He appears to have been strongly influenced by Sergei Kurginyan, who had recommended jettisoning classical Marxism in favour of messianic Russian nationalism and whose ideas closely resembled the KPRF's declarations and Zyuganov's own works in their attacks on Western plutocracy and support for a high-tech, green, collectivist Russian model of development competing for influence against the capitalist West.

Kurginyan's influence on Zyuganov is seen most clearly (though not acknowledged) in the Communist leader's work, *Russia and the Modern World* (1995). This outlines a view of history unorthodox in the extreme for one who might have been expected to espouse Marxist-Leninist ideology. History moves in cycles, pitching civilisations against each other, Zyuganov explained, citing the unexpected authority of the nineteenth-century arch-conservatives Danilevsky and Leontiev and the twentieth-century writers, Spengler and Toynbee.[58] (Given that in 95 pages, he could squeeze in only three references to Lenin,[59] one of them critical, the numerous citations of religious and nationalist opponents of socialist revolution will come as a surprise to anyone familiar with Party tradition: not only were the thinkers he cites banned, under the Soviet regime, but every political and academic argument had to be bolstered by innumerable references to Lenin).

Not just contemporary Russia but global civilisation was beset by crisis, according to Zyuganov. The clash of civilisations – not that of ideologies or classes – was the engine of history.[60] The Western model of development was on the point of expiry: it survived only by the voracious consumption and aggressive exploitation of its colonies' resources and workforces; this approach was no longer sustainable in a world whose resources had been polluted and plundered to the point of extinction.[61] With the new world order, which followed the collapse of the Soviet Union, the West hoped to find a solution to this dilemma and continue its expansionism:

> [...] The plan of the 'New World Order' in practice is nothing other than [...] the establishment of the global dictatorship of the West [...] It is a universal, messianic, eschatological, religious project [...] based on post-Christian religiosity.[62]

Happily, more sober forces were ready to stay the rash experiments of these hotheads.

Russia represented a different path of development and a different type of civilisation:

> [...] Russia is a particular type of civilisation, following on from and continuing the millennial tradition of Kievan Rus', the Muscovite kingdom, the Russian empire and the USSR; geopolitically, Russia is the core and chief pillar of the Eurasian continental bloc, whose interests are opposed to the hegemonic tendencies of the 'oceanic power' of the USA and the Atlantic 'Great Space'; in world outlook and ideology Russia is the expression of cultural-historical and moral traditions, whose fundamental values are conciliarism [*sobornost'*], collectivism, state power [*derzhavnost'*] and the striving to realise the highest ideals of good and justice; [...] Russia is an autonomous economic organism, fundamentally different [...] from the Western model of the 'free market'.[63]

Russia thus could not follow the Western path of development: liberalism had twice proved bankrupt and destructive on Russian soil: capitalism would undermine the spiritual and material bases of Russian society and State and ran counter to her historical traditions.[64] The attempt to adopt Western models, fostered by Gorbachev and Yeltsin, was misguided and ruinous.[65] Besides, Russia did not want to succumb to the general conflagration of Western civilisation; hence, she must return to her traditions and build on them.

The alliance between State power and spiritual authority, fundamental to the historical Russian State, continued to be essential to the well-being of contemporary Russia:

> The Russian State was based on the 'symphony of powers' – spiritual, moral-religious, State and social [*svetskii*]. As soon as this symphonic principle was broken, the internal contradictions in society immediately became deeper.[66]

The Orthodox church could take heart from the communists' pronouncements. The Russian idea (the power and integrity of the empire) was always based on these principles. Soviet Russia was the 'successor and custodian of the imperial, great-power inheritance' and, hence, of the Russian State's religious-historical role, as expressed in the formula 'Moscow is the Third Rome':

> [...] The thesis of 'Moscow – the Third Rome', the historical movement from Rome through Byzantium to Moscow, celebrated [...] the foundation of the three main principles of imperial statehood: Roman legal, sovereign unity was enriched by Byzantine spiritual-moral, Christian unity and, finally, was completed in the national unity of Muscovite Rus' – Russia. This was reflected in the formula 'Autocracy, Orthodoxy, Nationality'.

The essential tradition, lost in the early years of the Revolution, was recovered during the war and in the late Stalinist period, when the Party elite returned to national values and renounced Russophobia and unbridled campaigns against the Church.[67] It was this tradition that Russia needed to recover and build on in order to mobilise healthy patriotic forces in society and save the country. In the inevitable conflict between Western and Eurasian culture, Russia could look forward to rising from the ashes and surviving the collapse of Western civilisation.[68]

Zyuganov therefore claimed imperial tradition for Russian communism. However incongruous it was for a communist leader to see himself as the heir of the tsars, the contradictions between the two traditions are, perhaps, more apparent than real: Stalin and his heirs adapted the authoritarian, imperialist and chauvinist elements in late tsarist political culture and exploited them to build up Russian State power. Zyuganov thus emerged as a professed neo-Stalinist, not only on matters of State power and foreign relations but also in his commitment to economic collectivism and rejection of Western liberalism

and capitalism. However, he had also persuaded the KPRF to participate in the 1993 elections, despite the Party's antipathy to Yeltsin and
his political system.[69] How far he accepted the principle of democracy
– as opposed to being ready to exploit it – was open to question.

c) Constituency

If the leadership adopted this nationalist socialist ideology in the
expectation that it would prove popular and bring the party to power,
were they correct in making this assumption? What evidence is there
to suggest that their supporters and voters subscribed to the party's
new ideology? The KPRF's members and voters were older and
poorer than average (and hence may be presumed to have had an
interest in socialism): in the mid-1990s, 49 per cent of its voters were
over 55 years old and a further 32 per cent were between 40 and 54;
only 19 per cent were under 39. However, the party worked hard after
1993 to attract younger voters and were to some extent successful in
1995. By February 1998, Zyuganov claimed that 70 000 of the party's
500 000 members were under 40. Although predominantly older, not
all the party's supporters were poorly educated: the party's constituency included not only the predictable pensioners, blue-collar and
farm workers, but soldiers, students and academics also. Previously
well-funded sectors of the economy (such as higher education, as well
as the army and the defence industry) were now starved of resources
and populated by increasingly disaffected employees and students,
who were often unpaid for months. Hence, academics featured as a
distinct caucus in Zyuganov's 1996 election campaign, while the
KPRF began to make inroads into the youth vote.[70] It should not be
assumed, therefore, that the party's support was based simply on
nostalgia and ignorance.

KPRF voters were much less likely to switch allegiance than other
voters.[71] While this may be ascribed, to some extent, to age, it also suggests support for the party's perceived positions.[72] In Timmermann's
opinion, the relative weakness of the party's neo-Stalinists and relative
strength of the nationalist socialists (whose support within the party he
estimates at 75 per cent) may be ascribed to their respective popularity
among KPRF voters, who were principally preoccupied with falling
living standards, rising crime and, to a lesser extent, with Russia's decline
as a great power.[73] Stephen White and his colleagues found that the
party's rhetoric coincided with its voters' attitudes to authoritarianism

and socialism. Not surprisingly, they were more likely than other voters to have been members of the CPSU, to approve of communism and authoritarian rather than democratic models of government.[74] The communist electorate was also, on occasion, more xenophobic and nationalist than most other voters, judging by their readiness to express hostility to the West, ethnic minorities such as Jews and gypsies and their resentment of some of their new neighbours in the CIS.[75] The political instincts and views of KPRF supporters, in the mid-1990s, would appear not to have been wholly out of line with the party's nationalist socialism and its lack of enthusiasm for western democracy. Under these circumstances, the leadership enjoyed some latitude in determining the KPRF's tactics.

d) Duma Record

How should the party's record of participation in the Duma then be seen? Did it furnish evidence of its conversion to democracy? The KPRF's approach to the Duma may be explained as convincingly in terms of opportunism as of principle: the Duma was potentially useful to it, but this did not mean that the party was committed to preserving it in the long term. The KPRF's admittedly rhetorical programme documents spoke of the need to return to the soviet system, implicitly rejecting the bourgeois idea of liberal, representative democracy, while the party leaders' statements about democratic principles were contradictory and apparently dictated by circumstance.[76] Arguably, in participating in the Duma, the party hoped to strengthen the party machine, establish its image as a potential party of power, service key lobbies and court the electorate.

In the short term, the Duma, like the civil liberties that the party now defended,[77] provided the KPRF with valuable resources. The party used the privileges and support given to deputies to build up its organisation. Every deputy was entitled to five assistants paid by the state: hence, the party ensured that each deputy had his full quota of assistants, one in Moscow and four in the regions, to run the local party network. The state therefore paid for the party's regional machine, which, after the 1995 elections, consisted of about eight hundred full-time officials. In addition, the party's main organiser was based in the parliament as a consultant. All these assistants benefited from free public transport, privileged access to state institutions and information.[78] This was an appreciable boon for a party whose finances were problematic and the KPRF made more efficient use of these resources than other parties in the Duma.

By working in the Duma, the party was able to distance itself from the extreme opposition, with its propensity for violent street demonstrations. By contrast, the KPRF faction in the Duma seemed responsible, hard-working and professional, thanks to its readiness to ensure that the Parliament functioned with at least an appearance of efficiency.[79] There were additional reasons for this pragmatism: in the case of conflict between the President and the Duma, only the President could win, according to the constitution, either by imposing his choice as prime minister or by dissolving the parliament. In either case, his parliamentary opponents stood to lose.

In practice, the KPRF's approach to parliamentary business, and especially to economic issues, was less straightforward than might have been expected. The power to legislate offered the party a chance to court two constituencies, whose interests did not always coincide: its core electorate, those hurt by the reforms (pensioners, women, unskilled workers, students and academics) and those in the new business elite whose wealth depended on limiting liberalisation and continued state subsidies of industry.[80] Thus, the party criticised draft budgets, supported laws raising the minimum pensions and wages, compensating those whose savings had been eroded by inflation, and opposed privatisation, especially of land.[81]

However, the parliament was dominated as much by competing oligarchies as by parties. Journalists noted the influence exercised by lobbies such as banking, finance and trade; the agro-industry; the military-industrial complex; the coal, minerals, gas and oil industries. All parties were believed to come under pressure on issues such as budget finance, credits, import and export privileges, tax concessions, trade licences, bank registrations and privatisation. The Agrarians were the fraction which most openly and successfully defended sectoral interests, extracting concessions from the government on agricultural spending in the 1994 and 1995 budgets and supporting Prime Minister Chernomyrdin in the 27 October 1994 no-confidence vote, in exchange for the agricultural portfolio in the cabinet.[82] Similarly, the KPRF reportedly lobbied for increased expenditure on the heavy and defence industries in 1994. The communists frequently cooperated with the Agrarians in opposing the government and in promoting the interests of lobbies important to them. The party supported the Agrarians in approving a draft law opposing privatisation but enabling farm directors to exercise and acquire ownership of land, under the guise of retaining collective property rights over it.[83] Viewed in this perspective, the KPRF could hardly have afforded to ignore the Duma, if it hoped to be a serious contender for power.

On the other hand, the adoption of a new Civic Code and progress on a new Criminal Code were seen as major achievements for the Duma, enhancing its credentials as a democratic legislature.[84] But the Duma's commitment to the principle of civic liberties seemed uncertain at best. While ready to endorse measures on freedom of association and electoral rights,[85] the opposition-dominated Duma was just as ready as the President to contravene individual and press freedoms in practice. In April 1995, it passed a law extending the powers of the Federal Security Service (formerly the Counter-Intelligence Service) to include telephone tapping without a court order and opening private correspondence (a measure which democrats in the parliament also supported). In November and December 1994, the Duma passed a series of laws controlling advertising and the media, finally voting to take control of a television station in March 1995, so as to convey the opposition's point of view. These measures were adopted in the light of the forthcoming elections: the opposition was anxious to counter the President's influence over the media, which was exerted partly through the selective allocation of state funds.[86] If these measures may be explained by circumstance, others betrayed a tendency to subordinate the individual's rights to those of the state. A presidential decree on crime was opposed by Russia's Choice as unconstitutional and infringing the individual's rights, and by the communists for not being sufficiently resolute. The draft favoured by the KPRF envisaged special courts and ignored the presumption of innocence.[87] The Duma's record on the legality and respect for human rights which underpin democracy, was therefore inconsistent, and reflected the rhetorical attitudes of the main opposition parties.

Disregard for the constitution was evident also in the Duma's reaction to the war in Chechnya. The decision to intervene militarily was unconstitutional, as a Presidential decree should have been issued and approved by the Federal Council (while no decree was issued and the Federal Council had, on 8 December, called for negotiations and rejected the use of force), a point most fractions in the Duma chose to ignore. The Duma did not take the President to task for launching the war without parliamentary approval, while he happily ignored the Duma's calls in mid-December for an end to hostilities. Instead, the Duma chose, on 23 December, to rally to the government's contention that force had been used against illegal military formations.[88] The problem for the opposition was that the President's policies might have been inspired by their Great Power rhetoric: they could not conveniently explain how resolute measures to hold the state together were now to be deemed inappropriate. For the KPRF, the war was particularly problematic because it cut across the interests of its key supporters: the defence industry chiefs, who had found a powerful supporter in the deputy premier, Oleg Soskovets, and who had an interest in the war; and regional leaders in the north Caucasus and lower Volga, who supported the KPRF but who viewed the fighting and the government's assault on regional autonomy with disquiet. In addition, the war was deeply unpopular. The KPRF therefore confined itself to criticising the conduct rather than the principle of the war, while discreetly voting funds to continue it and pleasing the army by extending the draft.[89] The war justified measures, supported by the KPRF, to increase the parliament's control over the power ministries (which were directly subordinated to the President).[90] By contrast, the LDPR acted with perfect, if ill-judged, consistency in supporting the war.[91]

The KPRF's opposition was, therefore, sometimes more rhetorical than practical, as its conduct in a number of parliamentary votes also showed. On 27 October 1994, the government survived a no-confidence vote initiated by the LDPR in response to the 11 October fall of 25 per cent in the value of the rouble. The KPRF supported the vote, but the Agrarians' defection to the government ensured its survival. However, Zyuganov was reported to have persuaded the Women of Russia fraction to support the government to prevent a crisis, enabling the KPRF's continued use of the Duma to prepare for the presidential elections.[92] In the event, a protest against government incompetence had been duly registered. If the opposition ignored the opportunity to protest in a similar manner against the outbreak of war in Chechnya or against economic policy as enshrined in the 1995 budget, it resumed its attack in late June and early July 1995. The parliamentary elections were now imminent and deputies had less to lose. The war in Chechnya remained highly unpopular and the army's conduct of it was manifestly incompetent, an ineptitude demonstrated by the Budennovsk hostage crisis on 14–19 June (as a result of which 166 people were killed and over 400 wounded). In response, the Duma, with KPRF support, passed a vote of no-confidence in the Chernomyrdin government on 21 June 1995 by 241–72 votes.[93] According to the constitution, the President was obliged to react only if a second no-confidence vote were passed within three months, when he could either replace the Prime Minister or dissolve the parliament. Chernomyrdin forced the issue by calling a second no-confidence vote on 1 July, which the government won thanks to the support of some Agrarians. Following this, on 12 July, a KPRF-sponsored move to impeach the President was supported by only 168 deputies, with Zhirinovsky's LDPR rallying to the President's side.[94] However, if the KPRF had voted against the government's conduct of the war in successive confidence votes, it failed to support a motion to dismiss the power ministers (who were primarily responsible for declaring and pursuing the war) lest it alienate the military-industrial lobby.[95] The KPRF's record in no-confidence votes was consistent with the image of uncompromising opposition to the government it wished to project, but behind this lay a more complex approach to the government's parliamentary business. Characterised as professional by some observers,[96] this approach seemed to be shaped by expediency rather than by principle.

In fact, there was no consistent opposition within the Duma, while the government's base was also shifting and insecure.[97] Both democratic parties found much to criticise in the government's and President's conduct of affairs, even before their definitive break with him over Chechnya. Other parties' and fractions' positions were less easy to predict, even in the case of those rhetorically committed to relentless opposition: the LDPR increasingly supported the President in the Parliament, as, frequently, did the Agrarians in pursuit of narrow sectoral advantage, while the KPRF's sharp denunciations of the regime and government masked a readiness to work with them, when this served the party's purposes.[98] Hailed as a heartening instance of a growing culture of compromise, this ostensible pragmatism reflected the sometimes cynical opportunism of many parliamentarians and their awareness of the many ways in which the Parliament could be used to build up their power base. The Duma was not a bastion of democracy nor did participation in it mean that the KPRF had become a consciously democratic party. However, the party's leaders were increasingly aware that the road to power lay through Russia's new political institutions – the competitive electoral system and the Duma. This awareness and the mere fact of the Duma's existence (whatever its record as a legislature) represented progress in Russia's road to democracy. If, in the long term, the party refrained from committing itself unambiguously to democracy, it was ready to exploit an ostensibly democratic system, whose limitations, with regard to effective pluralism and liberty, were all too evident and not necesssarily uncongenial to the KPRF.

CONCLUSION

The KPRF's participation in the work of the Duma did not therefore provide conclusive evidence of its having evolved into a social democratic party by 1995 or early 1996.[99] Neither were the declarations of the party's putative social democrats always convincing. Valentin Kuptsov's insistence, in April 1994, on the need for greater party discipline and democratic centralism suggested that he was, at heart, a traditional, if effective, party manager, which his subsequent evolution appeared to confirm.[100] Similarly, Gennady Seleznev's failure to notice the famine in North Korea, when he visited the republic in early 1996, and his professed admiration for its independent patriotism were hardly indicative of social-democratic inclinations, any more than his belief in the need, in the event of a Zyuganov victory in the presidential elections, for a new constitution replacing the Parliament with a system of soviets.[101] Only after the failure of the patriotic front strategy advocated by Zyuganov was part of the parliamentary party to argue for the adoption of social democratic policies and norms, although Zyuganov's line also came under attack simultaneously from the hardline orthodox left, which wanted a return to Soviet Marxism.[102]

In many ways, Zyuganov's communists were an essentially nostalgic conservative, nationalist force. Their designation as a party of the classical left derives from a number of assumptions, whose applicability to the contemporary Russian Communist Party must be questioned. The supposedly left-wing characteristics of communism include its historically revolutionary vocation, as a movement which traditionally challenged the old order; in modern Russia, however, communists long sought to retain or restore, as far as practicable, the *ancien régime*. Similarly, communism's classically internationalist, anti-chauvinist, anti-imperial ideology has been largely renounced. Finally, to the extent that the KPRF still preached communism's egalitarian, collectivist economic ideals, the inspiration for these policies arguably lay as much in electoral opportunism as in unswerving devotion to the ideals of Marx and Lenin. Hence, the extent to which Zyuganov's communists in the mid-1990s might be described as the classical socialist left is open to question.

This leaves the problem of how far the KPRF deserved to be qualified as a nationalist party. Mainstream communists' affinity with the broad spectrum of Russian nationalism in the post-Soviet period was evident in the alliances they formed between 1991 and 1993: in the United Opposition and the National Salvation Front, many communists joined forces with right-wing nationalists in a programme of opposition to Yeltsin and his Western-oriented economic and political reforms, espousal of a return to Great Russian, imperial policies and an economic course favouring heavy industry and collectivisation. In 1995 and 1996, the party remained committed to winning power at the ballot-box but the ticket on which it chose to run was, significantly, neither that of social democracy nor classical Marxism, but of nationalist socialism, which rejected reform and Westernisation. It was no accident that Russian nationalism should have occupied so large a place in the renewed KPRF's policy documents and in its strategy: it was opportune in the prevailing political climate and it corresponded to much in the background and outlook of many party conservatives. The party's transformation into a social democratic political force, if it was to happen, would involve an arduous and prolonged metamorphosis, as neither its supporters nor many of its leaders or ideologues were social democrats at heart.

8 The Quest for Power: the 1995–96 Elections

If the Liberal Democrats had failed to grasp the opportunities afforded by the December 1993 elections, Zyuganov's KPRF had used the intervening two years to build up its party machine and prepare for the parliamentary and presidential elections of December 1995 and June 1996. For the first time, the radical opposition had a realistic chance of challenging the President's hold on power, although more because of the authorities' miscalculations than of the opposition's growing appeal.

A. THE 1995 DUMA ELECTIONS

The Yeltsin regime's satisfaction ratings before the December 1995 elections were low: in Spring 1995 (and Spring 1996), polls indicated that only 25 per cent of Russians approved of it, as opposed to 36 per cent in 1993 and 1994. Between 1994 and 1995, only one-fifth of those polled gave a positive rating to the new economic system.[1] The party of power, Chernomyrdin's *Nash Dom Rossiya* (Our Home is Russia) had been formed in summer 1995 to fight the elections but was hampered by the Prime Minister's bland image and the widespread impression that it represented the energy lobby. A pseudo-party of power-brokers, it lacked a popular base and symbolised Yeltsin's oligarchic regime. As in 1993, the democrats were disorganised and disunited, fielding several competing parties, principally Gaidar's Russia's Democratic Choice and Yavlinsky's *Yabloko*, on pro-reform, anti-war tickets. This inevitably divided the democratic vote, while the centre and government forces were also disunited. This gave the opposition its chance, for the electoral system (which reserved half the seats for parties which won a minimum of 5 per cent of the vote) punished small parties and disproportionately rewarded consolidated forces.[2]

However, the opposition were also divided in 1995. Leading the field was Zhirinovsky's LDPR, advocating an anti-Western foreign policy, defence of Russians in the 'near abroad', promotion of Russian state power and influence and state protection of domestic producers, the defence sector, the poor, the elderly and the security services. Contrary to expectation, Zhirinovsky's vote did not collapse in the 1995 Duma elections, when divisions in his party, his own ever more bizarre antics and increased competition from the rest of the opposition were expected to decimate his support.[3] The LDPR won 11.2 per cent of the vote and 51 seats in parliament, to become the third largest faction in the Duma (after Zyuganov's communists, with 22.3 per cent of the vote and the government's Our Home is Russia, with 10.13 per cent of the vote but more seats than the LDPR). However, his vote dropped from 12.3 million in 1993 to 7.7 million in 1995, closer to his score of 6.2 million votes in the 1991 presidential elections.[4] This did not augur well for the presidential campaign in 1996, for it pointed to a consistent support base of only six to eight million votes, which, while they yielded a disproportionate number of seats in the Duma (on account of the electoral system), would not suffice to ensure for Zhirinovsky a place in the final run-off in the Presidential elections.

Competing for the nationalist vote was Alexander Rutskoi, the former Vice-President, who had emerged from prison in the February 1994 amnesty to establish a new nationalist movement, *Derzhava* (Great Power).[5] Rutskoi now professed to believe Orthodox Russia to be incompatible with rationalist, individualistic Western civilisation and the political heritage of the French Revolution. Russia was communitarian, more concerned with justice than wealth. Her adoption of Western European liberalism had accomplished what Hitler had planned: the destruction of the state and the impoverishment of the Russian people.[6] However, Russia could recover culturally, spiritually and politically by returning to traditional principles: 'The Orthodox faith – strong authority – Russian conciliarism will save us from death and will again reintegrate the Russian people.' Russia should reincorporate the Ukraine and Belarus and regain its maritime borders on the Black Sea and the Baltics.[7]

Rutskoi now preached state control of key sectors of the economy, protectionism and omitted all mention of private farming from his economic policies.[8] If anything, he was more hostile to the West, democracy and civic freedoms than the communists,[9] calling for limits on press freedom. The media should be subject to popular control and prevented from promoting anti-state and anti-national values: instead, they should help to popularise the official ideology. Order and Orthodox revival, not liberty, were the priority.[10] The 1995 elections were seen by Rutskoi and his supporters as a chance to prove his popular credentials in advance of the 1996 presidential elections. Contrary to expectation, however, *Derzhava* won only 2.57 per cent of the vote and hence no seats in the parliament, which effectively excluded Rutskoi from the presidential race.[11]

Another contender for the nationalist vote was Alexander Lebed, a career soldier who first attracted attention in 1992 as the flamboyant commander of the forces which defended the Russian minority in Pridnestrovie. More successfully than Rutskoi, Lebed exploited his image as a simple honest soldier, an outsider in the political establishment, untainted by corruption and ambition. Sometimes viewed as a political chameleon,[12] he seems at heart to have been a Russian nationalist and *gosudarstvennik*. Ultimately, however, Lebed neither knew nor cared unduly how he was classified: 'I don't know who I am,' he confessed, 'a liberal, a socialist or a democrat'. Nor, he believed, were ordinary Russians concerned with such pedantic distinctions: 'Most Russians don't care whether they are ruled by fascists, or communists, or even Martians, as long as they are able to buy six kinds of sausage in the stores and lots of cheap vodka.'[13]

The end of the Soviet regime inspired in Lebed neither hope nor relief but regret. Of the Soviet Union, he wrote:

> He who does not regret its collapse has no heart and whoever thinks it can be restored in its previous form has no brains. There is something to regret: between being the Citizen of a Great Power, with many defects, but Great, or of an impoverished 'developing' country, there is a *big* difference.[14]

The fact that the Soviet citizen had few rights and that the concept of citizenship was virtually absent from Soviet legal and political practice seems to have escaped the General. He deplored the loss of power and prestige that followed the end of the Soviet regime – attacking Shevardnadze for the withdrawal from Eastern Europe, which had helped to ruin a great army. The destruction of the Soviet Union had been artificially engineered by its enemies, Lebed suggested in 1993. The August 1991 coup had been a provocation inspired by those who had wanted to destroy the Soviet Union and the CPSU, despite the wishes of the majority of the population.[15] To prevent the disintegration of post-Soviet Russia, Russian troops should remain in place from the Baltics to the Caucasus, as they were the last defence and refuge of millions of Russians abandoned by the new authorities.[16] By the mid-1990s, however, he came to accept the demise of the USSR, advocating a Greater Russia, composed of the Ukraine, Russia and Belarus.[17] He continued to emphasise the need for Russia to re-establish itself as a great power, while stressing the role of the army as a constructive force. Unlike other exponents of these themes, however, he rejected both racism and violence.[18] His devotion to Russian imperialism was thus gradually tempered by ambition and realism.

Elevated to high rank within the conservative Russian Communist Party, Lebed lost faith in the Soviet regime only on the eve of its destruction. Although as a presidential candidate Lebed appeared to endorse *glasnost'*, in 1995 he deplored the cultural changes wrought in the late eighties and early nineties: the replacement of pleasant light music with offensive rock, the ubiquity of demagogy, populism, attacks on the army and its officer corps.[19] These developments had destroyed a great power and led to the impoverishment of its citizens:

> The Union was ruined. Now, Russia is being ruined [...] Through political babble about reforms, democracy and human rights, we somehow lost former Soviet man, who is now needed by no-one. And now the overwhelming majority of the Soviet people has fallen into abject poverty [...][20]

Lebed did not find Russia's new regime congenial. Yeltsin's team of corrupt turncoats were interested only in enriching themselves at the expense of ordinary Russians and the state, Lebed averred.[21] Russia's democrats were not patriots: they experimented with the country and would leave it when it suited them.[22]

The goals of liberty and democracy inspired little enthusiasm in him: he frequently expressed his preference for authoritarian to liberal democratic models of government, praising Pinochet's Chile and Deng's China for combining strong rule with a flourishing economy. Pinochet had pulled Chile out of the abyss.[23] Democracy could not be introduced into Russia overnight: 'Democracy is a good word [...] It is still early to speak about it. We will achieve it in two or three generations. I won't live to see that time [...]'[24] In the meantime, democracy threatened Russia and might lead to tyranny and slavery. 'Power in Russia has always been severe,' Lebed commented.[25] Authoritarian rule was needed to put order on the chaos of contemporary Russia. What was required was a reinterpretation of Russian autocracy:

> There can be no return to monarchy; a single-party system did not prove itself, just as a parliamentary republic did not. Only a presi-

dential form of government remains. A tsar, a general secretary and a president are all the same – a form of authoritarian government.[26]

At times, his insistence on the importance of the army in guaranteeing national security, order and harmony in society suggested that he would not have been averse to a political role for the military.[27] 'What's wrong with a military dictator?' he asked in September 1994. 'In all its history, Russia has prospered under the strictest possible control. Consider Ivan the Terrible, Peter the Great, Catherine the Great or Stalin.'[28] Lebed appeared to have reservations about democracy, at least in its application to Russia, and to have accepted the Slavophile thesis that Russia had to find her own way forward, on the basis of her unique, autocratic traditions.

Certainly, he seemed to have little regard for the West (which he visited for the first time in 1996). Russians had spent too much time denigrating their history and achievements and copying the West, he suggested.[29] But the West was alien and even ill-disposed. Foreigners came to exploit Russia's wealth and people. Russia had vanquished her former enemies, but her new foe was more dangerous, because it was unseen and insidious, undermining the 'Spirit of the People' and destroying the 'moral bases bequeathed to us by our ancestors and replacing them with the imported surrogates of alien ideas'. The new enemy encouraged the development of 'every possible sect, party, confused political organisation', thereby 'creating political and economic chaos' and weakening Russia as a great power.[30] Although careful to moderate his language during the Presidential campaign, once in the Kremlin, Lebed's xenophobia reasserted itself. Mormons he viewed as 'mould and scum [...] artificially brought into our country to pervert, corrupt and break up our state'.[31] As state security chief, he explained that Russia needed to defend itself from foreign secret services which had learned the art of manipulating people's consciousness and subconscious, introducing them to ideas alien to Russia in order to prevent the emergence of a new, restorative national idea.[32] Only a return to national tradition would enable Russia recover from the upheavals it had undergone:[33]

> In their gigantic, millennial project, Russia's creators based themselves on three great buttresses – the spiritual power of the Orthodox Church, the creative genius of the Russian people and the power of the Russian army.[34]

The army embodied Russian spirituality, originality and national pride. Russians were suffering from spiritual AIDS but if her spiritual and state traditions – as represented by the Church and the army – were restored, the Russian nation and state would recover.[35]

The tract in which Lebed expressed many of these views, *Za derzhavu obidno*, was written in anticipation of the 1995 parliamentary election campaign because it was felt that a major contender for power could not afford to be without a 'philosophy' and an 'autobiography'. The function of ideology in the later Soviet regime was to camouflage the squalid realities of power and privilege and Lebed's backers at this point were formed in the old political culture. They sought to exploit the resentment caused by economic reform. The credibility of the General's musings mattered less than the appearance they created of a leader, capable of defending Russia's interests. It is, nonetheless, significant that Lebed was ready to lend his name to these positions.

More important than these documents in forming his popular image, however, was his stance on the main issue of the moment: Lebed succeeded in broadening his appeal by criticising the war in Chechnya, which he regarded as unwinnable and as exemplifying the irresponsible leadership of the Defence Minister, Pavel Grachev.[36] His growing popularity[37] and disagreements with Grachev, whom he accused of corruption and the collapse of army morale and organisation, led him to resign from the army in 1995 and launch himself on a political career, running for election in December 1995 as a leader of the Congress of Russian Communities (*KRO*).[38] Originally concerned with the fate of the Russian diaspora in the 'near abroad', the KRO was established as an all-Russian organisation in October 1994 to fight the 1995 Duma elections. Led initially by the epitome of the Red–Brown directors, Petr Romanov from Krasnoyarsk, it was reportedly backed by the directors of the military-industrial complex, including the former Security Council chief Yuri Skokov and several Duma deputies. Committed to a 'state-patriotic' programme, it opposed all forms of separatism and hoped to restore the territorial integrity of the traditional Russian state (the USSR).[39] By the time Lebed joined it as a leader, it was dominated by the ambitious and well-connected Yuri Skokov, who attempted to moderate its language, presenting the KRO as a populist, nationalist organisation, that would defend the economic and political rights of the little man while rebuilding Russia as a stable and formidable power, restoring law and order, eradicating corruption.[40] A coalition of opponents of reform, from communists to nationalists, the KRO was an uneasy hybrid. Skokov, Yeltsin's Security Council chief in 1992 and the parliament's favourite to succeed Gaidar as Prime Minister in December 1992, met with Yeltsin's approval for his discretion and flexibility.[41] Not forthcoming on his political connections, Skokov clearly hoped to exploit the rising tide of Russian nationalism and the charismatic Lebed to take power on behalf of the conservative defence industry lobby he represented. Although the KRO was expected to do well, it won only 4.3 per cent of the list vote and only Lebed and four other KRO candidates were elected to the Duma.[42]

Not only the non-communist nationalists but the communists too ran on a variety of tickets in the 1995 elections. On the extreme left of the spectrum, the neo-Stalinist Viktor Anpilov, despite his rejection of bourgeois democracy, decided to run in the elections, because he believed the KPRF had strayed from the path of true communism. Demanding the immediate restoration of the Soviet system, a return to a wholly planned economy and a one-party state,[43] Anpilov and his followers in the Communists for the USSR bloc came very close to crossing the 5 per cent barrier, winning 4.54 per cent of the list vote and one constituency seat in the Duma.[44] Power to the People, another neo-communist electoral bloc, led by the former Soviet Premier Nikolai Ryzhkov and Sergei Baburin, called for a return to a centralised economy and measures to relieve poverty. Despite winning only 1.6 per cent of the list votes, it succeeded in winning nine seats. Close in outlook to the KPRF and generally allied to it, the Agrarian Party cooperated with the KPRF in the 1993 and 1995 campaigns, enabling them to maximise their vote: in 1995, however, the Agrarians were vulnerable to the pragmatism and ambition of some of its leaders, which resulted in its losing some of its key figures. Partly as a result, the Agrarians' share of the list vote fell from 7.9 per cent in 1993 to 3.78 per cent in 1995, but it performed well locally, winning 20 seats in the constituencies.[45]

However, by far the largest and best organised party of the neo-communist parties was the KPRF. Its 1995 election manifesto was pitched to appeal to the party's key electorate, those who had suffered from the reforms and to attract voters of nationalist outlook. The Party burnished its socialist image by advocating higher social security payments but it was careful to indicate that it did not intend to abolish all private property, calling only for the nationalisation of strategically important industries and natural resources (including land). Its recipe for economic recovery was familiar, envisaging a large measure of state control. The manifesto made it clear that the Party viewed the Duma elections as part of a campaign to replace

Yeltsin as President and that, as a first step, it wanted to establish a popular, patriotic majority in the Duma. The KPRF clearly hoped to take votes from its main nationalist rival, Zhirinovsky's LDPR, whose record the KPRF attacked sharply, while emphasising its own nationalist credentials. Throughout, references to classical Marxism were avoided in favour of nationalism. The Fatherland's independence and unity should be restored, the Belovezha Accords abrogated and a single, united state gradually and peacefully restored. Rejecting Yeltsin's constitution, Zyuganov was vague about what should replace it – referring to the need for the restoration of 'Soviet democracy'. The 1995 election platform nonetheless represented a significant departure from classical and Soviet Marxism, with the emphasis it laid on the Party's parliamentary record, its tolerance of some private property and its rejection of internationalism. Its main gesture to neo-Stalinists came in its references to the need to restore the Soviet homeland.[46]

This strategy worked. Not only did the KPRF replace the LDPR as the party with the highest share of the list vote, but the electoral system rewarded it disproportionately. The KPRF, with 22.3 per cent of the vote commanded 34.9 per cent of the seats in the Duma and 44 per cent of the seats reserved for candidates elected by proportional representation from the party lists.[47] Conversely, overt nationalists wasted some of their votes – their 20.6 per cent of the vote yielding only 12.4 per cent of the seats. The chief beneficiary of the LDPR's loss was the KPRF, whose vote increased from 6.6 million (12.4 per cent) in 1993 to 15.4 million (22.3 per cent) in 1995. The overall neo-communist vote increased from 20.4 per cent (for the KPRF and Agrarians) in 1993 to 32.2 per cent in 1995.[48] Nationalists and socialists broadly opposed to reform and liberalisation thus won over half the vote.[49]

B. THE 1996 PRESIDENTIAL ELECTIONS

Victory in the 1995 elections meant that Zyuganov could aspire to be the leading opposition candidate in the 1996 presidential elections. The Red–Brown coalition was now at the height of its popularity and power seemed to be within its reach, if Zyuganov could manage to unite its disparate and often rival components and consolidate his vote. Yeltsin's popularity, already eroded by economic hardship and the confrontation with the parliament in 1993, slumped when he decided in December 1994 to declare war on Chechnya. By June 1995, his support in opinion polls had fallen to 6 per cent.[50] Having spent most of the second half of 1995 in hospital recovering from heart attacks, Yeltsin seemed to have little chance of success when the campaign opened in February 1996, while Zyuganov, at this point, enjoyed an approval rate of 20 per cent. As late as May 1996, some of the President's advisers warned against holding the elections at all, so doubtful did the outcome seem.

However, Zyuganov faced not only the formidable resources at the President's disposal but also competition from nationalist candidates, notably the maverick Zhirinovsky and General Alexander Lebed.[51] Zhirinovsky's popularity was waning and he was unable to make an impact on the campaign, as a determined effort was made to marginalise him and limit his media exposure.[52] Like other opposition candidates, Zhirinovsky, in 1996, had little opportunity to show his talents as a television performer and was swamped by Yeltsin's superior resources and command of the media. He was no longer a refreshing novelty but a familiar maverick. If in the past he had benefited from a protest vote, it did not follow that all his supporters wanted to entrust him with the government of Russia.[53] Zhirinovsky's support in June 1996 (4.3 million votes, 5.7 per cent) was the worst result he ever recorded and suggested that his star was finally waning.[54] The clever exponent of revanchist nationalism had been overshadowed by the ambitious General Alexander Lebed.

However, Lebed was an unpredictable force. He appeared to enjoy public support but he lacked an effective machine. Taken up and funded by Skokov in 1995 and then as rapidly discarded at the start of 1996, Lebed seemed in a weak and isolated position when he ran for the presidency in Spring and Summer 1996.[55] Again, the details of his position seemed less important than the image he projected. There was some confusion about what his programme actually was. Initially Lebed was left in the hands of ex-army officers, who devised for him an election platform resembling that of Vladimir Zhirinovsky. His 'Ideology of Common Sense' threatened to crack down on the 'criminal ethnic groups' who were responsible for the lawlessness on Russia's streets. It promised to defend Russian national interests and encourage the reunification of Russia and the states of the CIS, by exerting economic pressure on its neighbours. Russians abroad would be defended and the civil rights of non-Russians in Russia would be curtailed. The army, defence sector and agriculture would all be protected from irresponsible experiments and cutbacks. Russians should unite to create a great Russian power.[56] Then it emerged that Lebed's real programme differed from this – at least on foreign and economic policy. The second programme, which elaborated on his campaign slogan 'Truth and Order', was reportedly the work of a team assembled by the magnate Boris Berezovsky[57] (a representative of the new business class Lebed constantly castigated) and was designed to cast Lebed as a liberal nationalist and undercut Zhirinovsky's vote. The liberalism of this programme was largely confined to economic policy, where Lebed promised tax cuts and more entrepreneurial freedom to encourage small business (although poorly controlled big business was best placed to exploit these measures). The state was to guarantee free medical care and education, the payment of pensions and attend to the needs of the army and defence industries. As before, Lebed promised a crackdown on crime and corruption in high places and the bureaucracy.[58]

As with most candidates' material, this 'liberal' programme was not readily available to the electorate, which had to make its choice on the basis of what it saw on television or read in the press. It seemed, at times, that few people were interested enough in the elections to subject the General's assertions to rigorous scrutiny and that his laconic denunciations of crime, corruption and the deeply unpopular war in Chechnya, which he was almost alone in condemning, sufficed to define and recommend him to the electorate.

Zyuganov was less charismatic than Lebed. To maximise his support, he needed to appeal both to the wide spectrum of views covered by the Red–Brown opposition to Yeltsin and to more moderate, pragmatic voters. The priority was to unite the opposition around the communist candidate. This meant rallying patriots as well as socialists of various hues to his banner. The result was a platform of nationalist tenor, whose sweeping promises on social security were open to socialist interpretation and whose economic programme was contradictory. 'The Fatherland is in danger', it warned, reciting the habitual catalogue of ills: the Soviet Union had been dismembered and a large Russian population had been stranded 'abroad'; the Russians were dying out as a nation; the old were left undefended; the nation's wealth had been plundered; traditional culture was under attack. Zyuganov promised to renounce the Belovezha accords and work for the voluntary and peaceful restoration of the Soviet Union, to pursue an independent foreign policy and devote extra resources to the army and security services, to end crime and corruption, increase social security payments and guarantee security of employment. More innovatively, in an indication of its new respectable image, the party tried to exploit its record in parliament, suggesting that only the KPRF had attempted to stay the government's irresponsible hand, adopting measures in the Duma to increase social security payments, eradicate crime and restore a measure of state regulation of the economy and aid to defence, agriculture and science. A further indication of its movement away from classical Marxism and desire to attract a wider vote was its support for both an elected president and a parliament to which the government would be responsible. This represented a significant modification of its position as expressed in the party programme and the 1995 election manifesto, which had spoken of the need to restore the system of soviets to control the president and government and expressed the long-term goal of abolishing the Presidency.[59] This change reflected the Party's growing confidence in its electoral strength. To reinforce this new profile, the platform stressed that Zyuganov's aim was freedom and justice.[60]

Zyuganov's platform contained enough familiar nationalist rhetoric to retain the support of the 'patriotic' opposition but its gestures to the classical and Stalinist left were minimal. Neither Marx nor Lenin figured, while communism was mentioned only once, as being 'consonant with the centuries-old Russian traditions of conciliarity [*sobornost'*] and collectivism' and as corresponding 'to the fundamental interests of the Fatherland'. Instead, Zyuganov chose to emphasise his nationalism, his Russian blood and devotion to the Motherland.[61] Nonetheless, the ambiguities and patriotic rhetoric of this document enabled most leading figures and organisations of the nationalist and socialist opposition to rally to Zyuganov and present him as the candidate not of the KPRF but of the 'popular patriotic bloc'.[62] This was simply the latest form taken by the Red–Brown coalition since 1992 and it corresponded closely to the party's declared orientation. However, few of these supporters were democrats: several had been associated with earlier attempts to forestall or overthrow democratic rule. Their support, while necessary to guarantee a minimum vote, had the disadvantage of alienating potential moderate voters whom the KPRF needed to attract.

Zyuganov's reticence about the party's supposed ideals inspired doubts in the wider public, especially when the KPRF parliamentary fraction voted to reject the Belovezha accords, on 15 March 1996, and when General Valentin Varennikov ill-advisedly referred to the existence of a secret 'maximum' programme.[63] Yeltsin's campaign chose to exploit these fears, by stressing the divisions within the KPRF and the supposed dominance within it of neo-Stalinists.[64] In vain, Zyuganov reiterated that he did not intend to put the clock back. He declared:

> Our party is quite distinct from the Communist Party of the Soviet Union. We recognise a mixed economy, pluralism of opinion and freedom of religion.

However, he chose to reinterpret these differences when addressing the Congress of National Patriotic Forces on 8 June 1996, when he insisted that: 'We are not from the same party as Trotsky and Beria but from the other party of Marshal Zhukov and Stakhanov.'[65] The same ambiguity haunted his declarations on the economy. A moderate economic programme, carefully worded to present the KPRF's economic priorities in Keynesian guise, was published to reassure the elites and non-communist voters:[66] but Zyuganov was unable to give precise commitments on privatisation and the extent of state control he envisaged, because of the need to placate his left-wing.[67] Given Yeltsin's measures to neutralise the Chechnya issue (by at least appearing to attempt to end the war) and given that the deeply unpopular war had been a source of conflict with the President not for the chauvinist opposition (which favoured 'strong' measures to retain state unity) but for the democrats, who eventually felt obliged to rally behind Yeltsin, the economy was the biggest issue in the campaign, and, on this, Zyuganov was vulnerable to accusations of equivocation.[68] The party lost the support of elites, as its economic programme remained unclear.

The failure to broaden his core support (of around 30 per cent) beyond the socialist and nationalist opposition ensured Zyuganov's defeat. He had been hampered by several factors: his lacklustre personality and limited access to the media, along with the KPRF's negative image, prevented him from communicating effectively with the electorate.[69] Voters had not forgotten the past (of whose worst features the Yeltsin-controlled media assiduously reminded them) and, whatever their reservations about Yeltsin's regime, they did not want a return to communist rule, which was associated with shortages and, crucially, lack of freedom. The 1996 vote was above all a vote against the Soviet regime rather than a vote in favour of Yeltsin. Yeltsin compounded Zyuganov's problems by using his office to assist his re-election: he toured the country, ordering his officials to pay the enormous backlog of wages and pensions (as though he had no previous responsibility for these problems), promising higher pensions and stipends and insisting that budget expenditure be increased to allow for this. Nor did Yeltsin neglect key power brokers, moving to court provincial governors (signing 15 federal agreements with them, granting the regions and local elites more power in return for their support). Above all, Yeltsin's control of the media and the enormous resources which he was able to allocate to the campaign were decisive.[70]

Nonetheless, Zyuganov ran Yeltsin a close race in the first round (gaining 24.2 million votes or 32 per cent of the vote as opposed to Yeltsin's 26.6 million votes or 35.3 per cent). Lebed performed much better than expected, coming third with almost eleven million votes (14.5 per cent of the vote) and attracting 47 per cent of the army electorate, at the expense of Zhirinovsky.[71] This result was surprising, as Lebed had trailed in opinion polls and complained of the difficulty of getting his message across to the electorate. Soon after the first round of the elections, it emerged that Lebed had benefited from the assistance of Yeltsin's aides and money, especially in the final week of the campaign, when he appeared frequently on television and when many previously undecided voters were won over to him.[72] Anxious to attract his votes in the run-off on 4 July, Yeltsin made Lebed security chief, giving him the poisoned chalices of crime and the settlement of the Chechnya conflict, while apparently endorsing him as his heir apparent for the year 2000. He also used his position as President to have the second round of voting held on a weekday, rather than on a Sunday as should have been the case, to obtain the high turnout he needed to be re-elected. Meanwhile, the dispirited Zyuganov's campaign ran out of steam, as he failed to exploit the scandals and infighting in the Kremlin (which pointed to corruption and electoral malpractice) and the sudden absence of the President from the scene (due to an unannounced heart-attack).[73] Despite these tactical advantages Zyuganov failed to attract the key centrist votes: in the second round of voting on 3 July, he won 30.1 million votes (40.3 per cent of the vote) against Yeltsin's 40.2 million votes (53.8 per cent).[74]

Yeltsin's victory was remarkable, given his popularity ratings at the start of the campaign and the fact that the country was in the midst of a prolonged economic and social crisis and an unpopular war. Nonetheless, Zyuganov's score pointed to a formidable degree of alienation from the new regime: not only had 30 million voters sided with a coalition whose commitment to democratic principles was at best ambiguous and many of whose luminaries had in the past voiced xenophobic and quasi-fascist sentiments, but over a third of the electorate chose either to abstain or to vote against both candidates.

Commentators took solace from the fact that communist voters tended to be older, less well-educated and more marginalised (being based mainly in small provincial towns and the countryside) than the pro-reform voters and from the fact that Zhirinovsky had been squeezed by Lebed. The result, it was hoped, would settle the issue of who ruled Russia for long enough for the reforms to take root, while the opposition's vote would diminish as demography and modernisation took effect.

Should the 1996 presidential elections and their outcome be seen as a step on Russia's path to democracy? The fact that the elections were held and their results respected certainly helped to develop and consolidate democratic practice in Russia. However, neither the conduct of the elections nor the character of all the participants were fully democratic. Large numbers of voters were agnostic about or opposed to the new regime and, by extension, the principles which it professed, while many in the political and cultural elite proclaimed their hostility to democracy. How significant was the prevalence of anti-democratic ideologies and the electoral scores of nationalist and communist critics of the Western political practice and did they pose a threat to Russia's fledgling democracy?

The importance of ideology, for the public, should not be overestimated. Candidates' platforms were neither widely distributed nor well-known; instead, media image and local reputation played an important role in influencing how people voted.[75] Party loyalty has hitherto been weak, which suggests that voters lack ideological commitment. A tendency to vote negatively was evident in 1996: the public voted against the KPRF (which had the highest negative rating as well as the most consistent core support in the country)[76] rather than for Yeltsin. The close vote in the first round was arguably a more accurate reflection of the electorate's real preferences than the outcome of the second round, where the electorate was confronted with the uncongenial alternative of the unpopular incumbent and an unpredictable challenger. Almost a third of the electorate voted against both Yeltsin and Zyuganov in the first round and almost 4 million voters opted to vote against both candidates in the second round.[77] Whereas the parliamentary elections were not going to result in systemic change, a vote for Zyuganov in 1996 could have unforeseeable consequences. Under these circumstances, the electorate voted for the relative stability represented by Yeltsin. One should therefore hesitate before seeing the elections as unqualified statements of popular support for alternative ideologies.

Similarly, the elite's commitment to ideology can also be overstated. The 1996 elections were not primarily or simply a contest between democrats and communists. On the one hand, Yeltsin's power-base was not composed exclusively of full-blooded democrats, but included many ideologically neutral pragmatists drawn from the old establishment. Conversely, Zyuganov's supporters included not only proponents of orthodox Marxist-Leninism and authoritarian nationalism but also a business elite of directors and farm-managers who wanted to resist a deepening of reform and to retain and develop the current system of state patronage.[78] Not all of Zyuganov's backers were true believers in the Russian Idea: his allies in the business elite needed a relatively closed, corporative system to protect their interests in agriculture and heavy industry. Yeltsin's financial and business barons, conversely, required a more open, libertarian regime, enjoying Western support, to pursue their interests. For many pragmatic oligarchs confronted with the choice between Yeltsin and Zyuganov, what was at issue was not ideology but interests: competing networks of patronage and privilege, closed or open economic systems.

The bipolar model of conflict between the government and the opposition masks a more complex pattern of distribution and contestation of power, Lilya Shevtsova has observed.[79] The opposition and the legislature have been increasingly marginalised since the inception of the regime. Instead, especially since the end of 1993, when the problem of power ceased to be formulated in institutional terms, power has been disputed within the ruling elite, rather than between formal institutions or political parties and ideologies. Where these structures were drawn into the conflict, as in the struggle between Khasbulatov and Yeltsin, their principal function was to justify the ambitions and pretensions of the participants in the power struggle. More important than the formal mechanisms of political pluralism in determining how power has been exercised have been the new elites in the presidential administration, the government and the regions and cartels which have built up links with them. The competition between these circles, rather than elections or parties, is widely seen as having determined policy.[80] The weakness of political parties and institutions (the Duma above all) and the accumulation of power in the hands of a small minority have led to the emergence of a libertarian rather than a fully democratic regime, in which ideology occupies a secondary place.

Conclusion

After the defeat of Zyuganov and his popular-patriotic bloc in the Presidential elections in 1996, was left- and right-wing nationalism henceforth to be discounted as a factor in Russian politics and culture? Was its appeal within the intelligentsia, which had furnished Yeltsin's radical opponents with the arsenal of nationalist and authoritarian ideas with which to attack him, to be dismissed as a curiosity of no cultural significance? Was the rise of collectivist and authoritarian nationalism after 1991 merely a temporary phenomenon, provoked by economic and social crisis and unrelated to the long-term preferences of the Russian people, or did it reflect a growing and profound public alienation from democratic and liberal ideals?

Three factors – precipitous economic decline, loss of empire and political and social chaos at home – gave the nationalists and national-communists an opportunity to establish themselves, initially winning public attention with their strident street demonstrations in 1992 and 1993 and subsequently, significant support at the polls. The radical opposition was able to exploit growing disenchantment with the reforms to install itself, in late 1993, in the new political institutions and constitute the official opposition. They held this position not by virtue of unequivocal popular enthusiasm for their ideas but through a series of protest votes by a citizenry which increasingly felt it had nothing to lose.

Living standards had already started to decline sharply in the late Soviet period and this trend was intensified after 1991, when Yegor Gaidar attempted to liberalise the economy: GNP is estimated to have fallen by 50 per cent and real wages by 66 per cent between 1989 and 1995.[1] Between 1992 and 1995, agricultural production dropped by almost 24 per cent, industry and construction by over 46 per cent and GDP by 31.6 per cent. Unemployment, although masked, doubled in these years. As prices were liberalised, without anti-monopoly laws being introduced and with privatisation still a distant prospect, inflation soared and the rouble lost nine-tenths of its value against the dollar. The retail price index increased by over 900 per cent in 1993, by 315 per cent in 1994, by over 230 per cent in 1995 and a further 114.4 per cent in the first five months of 1996. Hence, although average money incomes increased sharply, they failed to prevent declining living standards.[2] By 1992, demand for meat, milk, fish, fruit and vegetables had fallen significantly in relation to 1980 consumption levels, with only bread and potatoes still being consumed to the same extent.[3]

Many Russians were not exclusively dependent on wages and state handouts, which was fortunate, given the growing tendency, from 1994 on, to delay their payment by several months. Late payment of wages (prompted by attempts to introduce some budgetary discipline) became an acute problem in 1995; by early 1996, 20 per cent of the population were experiencing delays, sometimes of several months, in receiving their wages. Statisticians noted the growing differentiation of Russian society, with the formation of a very wealthy elite, while a large proportion of the population experienced hardship. Every third Russian was calculated to live below the poverty line in the mid-1990s. In January 1993, 52.8 million people (35.5 per cent of the population) were estimated to be in poverty, although this figure fell to 39.6 million (26.7 per cent) by the end of the year. Another 19.3 million people (13 per cent of the population) had only subsistence level incomes, while 8 million (5 per cent) did not have enough money to buy sufficient food: these included single pensioners, invalids, children from large families and refugees.[4] Polls conducted in 1994 established that while fewer than 10 per cent of respondents continuously went without essential food, clothing and heating, only 43 per cent never went short of food and 22 per cent of necessary clothes. Only 19 per cent of Russians experienced no hardship, while two-thirds of respondents were dissatisfied with their living standards, which many believed to have declined since the Soviet period.[5] The situation had hardly improved by 1996, as the erratic stabilisation of 1994 was squandered by the war in Chechnya and the 1996 Presidential elections. Around one-third of the population was still estimated to live below the poverty line in 1996.[6]

The economic crisis was reflected in demographic changes: increased mortality rates, a decline of almost 200 000 in the total population, and, as during the Civil War, a movement away from the cities to the country.[7] As Matthew Wyman has observed, the economic collapse was worse than the Great Depression.[8] Not surprisingly, these changes were not greeted with enthusiasm: by 1994, only one Russian in seven had a favourable opinion about Yeltsin's reformed economy, while three in five felt positively about the Soviet command economy (even if they realised they could not return to it). They hoped, and 44 per cent believed, that things would improve in the future.[9] Although most people supported the market economy and free enterprise in principle, by the mid-1990s, socialist attitudes were still deeply embedded in popular opinion, with polls pointing to widespread support for the state regulation of prices, a comprehensive social security system, and opposition to unemployment, private and foreign ownership of the largest enterprises.[10]

Another factor influencing public opinion was the decline of the state. Russia was reduced approximately to its late seventeenth-century borders and its centre of gravity moved, as Geoffrey Murrell has noted, one thousand miles to the East, provoking a sense of humiliation comparable to a defeat in war.[11] Neither the dissolution of the Soviet Union nor the launching of economic shock therapy were formally endorsed by the Russian electorate when Yeltsin decided to adopt these policies in December 1991 and January 1992. As recently as March 1991, 53.5 per cent of Russians had voted in a referendum to retain a reformed Soviet Union. If they supported Russian republican sovereignty, this was not because they wished or expected the entire state to be swept away. Many believed that it needed to be reformed.[12] Only in 1991, however, were Russians willing to accept the dissolution of the USSR: public opinion in post-Soviet Russia consistently condemned the break-up of the USSR, with polls showing two-thirds of Russians regretting its demise, until 1994. Many wanted a return to Greater Russia and there was a 'responsive constituency' for politicians who wanted to re-create a reformed Soviet Union, according to Matthew Wyman.[13] Most people accepted, however, that the USSR could not be reconstituted: only one-fifth to one-third of Russians approved this option in polls.[14] The changes nonetheless left people disorientated: people were no longer certain or in agreement about where the country's boundaries should be drawn. Many Russians were unsure of their identity, what it meant to be Russian and where the country began and ended.[15] In the late 1970s and early 1980s, most Russians (70 per cent) had identified their homeland as the Soviet Union and it was not until 1993–94 that people started to identify with the Russian Federation instead and call themselves Russian (*rossiyan*) rather than Soviet citizens.[16] Support for the new Russian state increased from 20 per cent in 1992 to 41 per cent in 1994. This still left a majority who felt unanchored in the new system and without any deeper loyalty towards it.[17]

Yeltsin's policies were thus both materially and psychologically traumatic. From the outset, they provoked deep controversy within the political elite as well as in society, intensifying and embittering the power struggle between the President and the Parliament in 1992–93. Nonetheless, in the mid-1990s, most Russians continued to reject authoritarian options, such as an army takeover, a return to Soviet communism or rule by a 'strong leader', and a substantial majority supported democracy even at the height of the economic and political crisis in 1992 and 1993.[18] However, support for democracy and liberal values and for the system that purported to proclaim them soon began to be eroded.[19] By 1994, the new regime was thought to enjoy less popular support than the Soviet system. Disillusionment with and alienation from the state and politics became profound by the mid-1990s, with many people holding democratic politics to be ineffective and sterile, according to Matthew Wyman. His detailed study of public opinion in the post-Soviet period led him to conclude that the Russian electorate was particularly volatile and hence susceptible to the appeal of populism or even fascism.[20] Stephen White and his colleagues found that civic and state institutions were widely distrusted in 1994, with the Church and the army faring best and political parties, market institutions, the police, civil service and justice system and patriotic groups faring worst.[21] Popular distrust of the government was also gauged to be widespread. The new state appeared to command limited respect or loyalty, while the electorate was unanchored in political parties.[22] While polls showed no significant increase in the number of people opposing democracy, between 1993 and 1995, those ready to support it fell by 8 per cent.[23]

As enthusiasm for the new regime waned, Russians became increasingly agnostic about the merits of democratic politics: up to a quarter of the population, according to polls in the early 1990s, opposed competitive elections, while one-third were uncertain about their merits.[24] In polls in June 1993 and again in October 1994, 45 and 48 per cent of respondents agreed that Western democracy and the Russian way of life were incompatible, with only 29 and 27 per cent disagreeing.[25] This did not mean these Russians were necessarily hostile to democracy *per se*. Many saw it as a premature but nonetheless desirable goal: 35 per cent of respondents in a poll in November 1994 felt that Russia was not yet ready for democracy, while only 8 per cent thought democracy was wrong for Russia; more ominously, perhaps, a majority (41 per cent) were unable to answer.[26] The New Russian Barometer suggested that, in 1994, 22 per cent of Russians favoured abolishing parliament, while 39 per cent wanted to retain it and an equal number (39 per cent) were uncertain whether a parliament was desirable or not.[27] Matthew Wyman and Stephen White, analysing the December

1993 election results found that while 48 per cent of Russians accepted democratic principles, 16 per cent believed that there were better options, while 25 per cent preferred a one-party or no party system.[28] Polls therefore indicated that while a majority of Russians were ready to endorse democracy in principle, many were ambivalent, confused or had reservations about it in practice.

Polls suggested that authoritarian attitudes (if not consciously anti-democratic political preferences) were common. Yuri Levada believed that by the mid-1990s there was a widespread desire for order to be restored at any price. In a November 1994 poll, 81 per cent agreed that the state should restore order 'immediately and by any means'. The previous July, 70 per cent of those polled believed Russia needed a ruler who would restore order 'with an iron hand'.[29] Matthew Wyman found that while people were enthusiastic about their new-found rights and civic liberties, many were ready to accept their suspension to solve crime and separatism, while a large minority opposed them on principle – with 40 per cent ready to approve government control of the media and 30 per cent opposed to all forms of demonstration and protest. He found that large numbers of Russians were attracted by undemocratic options, including that of the authoritarian leader, who would impose order.[30] A poll of February 1996 suggested that 70 per cent of Russians wanted a strong leader, although 56 per cent also thought democratic procedures important (which left a large number of people who were insensitive or indifferent to their importance). Almost a fifth (19 per cent) wanted to close the parliament. A similar proportion adopted chauvinist positions, favouring special status for Russians in the state. If 17 per cent favoured democrats and another 17 per cent supported centrists, 24 per cent preferred nationalists or communists and most people (41 per cent) had no political allegiances. This political agnosticism was reflected in attitudes to the law, which did not bode well for the development of the civic and lawful society many Russians said they wanted: 54 per cent believed social justice to be more important than law, while 72 per cent said they would obey the law only when officials did.[31] People showed a consistent and overwhelming tendency to attach more importance to restoring order (75–79 per cent) than to building democracy (6–12 per cent).[32]

Many Russians toyed with more unequivocally authoritarian options. In July 1994, Yuri Levada found that up to 35 per cent of people were ready to support dictatorship, with a third favouring a military ruler and the same percentage ready to resist one. Other polls in 1994 put support for dictatorship lower, at 25 per cent in April, and 23 per cent in November, down from the high levels of support expressed for it in April and October 1992 (31 and 36 per cent respectively). Almost as worrying as the extent of declared support for dictatorship was the fact that many people seemed unable to make up their minds about its supposed advantages: between 20 and 36 per cent of Russians in successive polls were unable to decide whether or not dictatorship offered the only solution to Russia's problems.[33] Stephen White and his colleagues estimate support for dictatorship to have been much lower than this, with only 10 per cent supporting army rule in 1994.[34] These inconsistencies in findings may be partially explained by the alternatives people were asked to choose between. Matthew Wyman found that support for authoritarianism varied with the wording of the question: over half of the respondents endorsed an iron hand in preference to anarchic democracy (which 30 per cent nevertheless preferred) but only 25 per cent wanted dictatorship (while 50 per cent opposed it). He concluded that there was strong support for both options.[35] In short, polls suggested that a substantial minority endorsed authoritarian positions, while large numbers were alienated from the existing system and had few clear political allegiances. Others (as many as 30 per cent) were ready to endorse authoritarian rule at least for a time to restore order, despite their declared support for democratic and liberal principles.

In addition, a substantial minority of Russians professed their support for authoritarian rule (and to varying extents for imperialism, economic collectivism and racism). A survey conducted in Summer and Autumn 1995 indicated that while there was a consistent majority in favour of liberal, democratic ideas, many opposed these options: 28 per cent favoured a single state ideology (60 per cent supported diversity), 33 per cent thought a multi-party system harmful to society (45 per cent were in favour), 35 per cent supported the equal division of wealth by the state to avoid inequality (56 per cent favoured free enterprise). The collectivist third also thought strong one-man rule, untrammelled by representative bodies, good for the people (while 50 per cent opposed this).[36] Polls revealed consistent support for rule by a charismatic and powerful leader. Wyman and White discovered that significant minorities in 1993 believed in a form of populist authoritarian rule: 21 per cent felt that a strong popular leader should not be constrained by law; more thought the government should not be restrained by institutions such as a parliament (28 per cent) or the constitutional court (18 per cent). Many (76 per cent) agreed that the government should be able to suspend civic liberties to fight crime or slander of the government (36 per cent in favour). Worse still, these researchers found that Gaidar's supporters were more likely to support these propositions, with the communist voters and Zhirinovsky's supporters expressing most concern for civic liberties and parliamentary prerogatives.[37] While this survey revealed lamentably undemocratic attitudes to have been prevalent in the 'democratic' camp at the time of the Autumn 1993 crisis, it does not follow that the communists and nationalists were really better democrats than their rivals – only that they were pragmatic in their pursuit of power and perceived that the new system gave them a chance to win it legally.

Russian authoritarians could draw comfort from the confusion and ambiguity of public attitudes (as well as from a significant core of potential sympathisers) and from the absence of those factors which are necessary for a stable democracy – acceptance of the rule of law and the lack of full accountability of the Presidency and government.[38] The collectivist and authoritarian nationalists' success at the polls in 1993 and 1995 cannot be said to have been unrelated to trends in public opinion. If their ideas were not enthusiastically endorsed by a majority of the population, enough people felt sufficiently at a loss to vote for them and the consequences of this protest vote were unpredictable. It pointed to a political culture insecurely rooted in democratic and liberal values and a widespread social malaise open to exploitation by political adventurers. However, neither the depth of popular commitment to the varieties of authoritarianism on offer, nor the sincerity of their leading exponents was unambiguous. The stability of authoritarian or collectivist nationalism in Russian politics was thus open to question, but this, perhaps, was not the issue: what counted was whether, while it enjoyed temporary advantages, it could enable the radical opposition to dislodge the putative reformers and Westernisers and if not, why not.

Was there, then, a demonstrable connection between the economic and political crisis and Russians' political preferences? Was the rise of Zhirinovsky and Zyuganov precipitated by the collapse of the state and the economy or did it correspond to Russian's deep-seated political preferences and Russian political culture? The question posits a false alternative, in that both circumstance and culture sustained the opposition. On the one hand, Zhirinovsky and Zyuganov supporters came disproportionately from those who had suffered most from the reforms: the economic context was therefore important in understanding the development of the politics of alienation. To some extent, the opposition benefited from a protest vote. Although Zyuganov's predominantly elderly supporters were distinguished by their consistency, Zhirinovsky's young male voters were volatile: they voted against Yeltsin and his government rather than for a realistic alternative; in 1995, the communists attracted some of his supporters in provincial towns, while the LDPR won votes in the countryside from the Agrarians. However, if the opposition parties reaped a protest vote against the reforms, their support also corresponded to political attitudes in society, where the post-Soviet order was greeted with growing disenchantment, scepticism and hostility. A substantial minority of Russians held authoritarian and collectivist views and their support for the national-communist and nationalist opposition was hardly coincidental. In addition, enough people so disliked Yeltsin and his perceived allies as either to vote for the communists and nationalists in 1993 and 1995 or to refuse to vote tactically, to minimise their presence in the Duma. Hence, public alienation and political indifference, combined with the nationalists' and communists' core support, threatened Russia's uncertain democracy, as neither Zyuganov nor Zhirinovsky and their followers were committed democrats and their readiness to retain democratic institutions, if elected to power, was open to question. What prevented the opponents of Westernisation from capitalising on the opportunity presented to them by the support they enjoyed and public disenchantment with the reforms was their inability to cooperate and the fact that they were even more distrusted by the electorate than Yeltsin and his regime: when faced with the alternative of Zyuganov and Yeltsin, more Russians voted against Zyuganov than against Yeltsin.

In the light of this defeat, are the varieties of authoritarianism and exclusive nationalism on offer in Russia without significance? Ideas are important not only insofar as they influence government policy but also because they reflect and help to create the moral and intellectual atmosphere in which public life develops. The growth of nationalism has corresponded to a new mood in Russia, to a retreat from the liberal, democratic ideals of the late 1980s. The careers of charismatic politicians such as Lebed and Zhirinovsky point to this change in atmosphere. A new political discourse has developed, in which hitherto neglected themes (including Orthodoxy, national and imperial tradition) figure prominently. It has become clear that neo-fascism and racism are only the most extreme manifestations of a widely accepted and promulgated alternative vision of Russian statehood and destiny, founded not on individualism, liberty and democracy but on authoritarian rule and the quasi-mystical community of nation. Initially confined to the intelligentsia, these ideas have been relentlessly aired and popularised in a climate of social and political crisis, until they have become part of the common currency of political rhetoric. The emergence of new ideological themes in modern Russia has coincided with a transformation of the terms of the political game in post-Soviet Russia: the polarities of Soviet socialism and liberal democracy, which briefly dominated the late 1980s, have been replaced by the alternative of collectivist nationalism and oligarchic liberalism, characteristic of the post-Soviet period.

It is in this atmosphere that the political culture of post-Soviet Russia is being formed and nationalism would seem likely to influence it. As Russian nationalism tends towards collectivism and authoritarianism, this influence is unlikely to be wholly benign, yet its respectability has been questioned only by the dwindling cohort of the Westernised intelligentsia. Its prestige has grown rather than diminished, in recent years: while it may enjoy only limited support, it has won a measure of legitimacy thanks to its apparent endorsement in successive elections. Can a flourishing liberal, democratic political culture grow in the stony soil of Russia's Weimar? The emergence of exclusive right- and left-wing nationalism militates against it, proposing illusory and ultimately destructive ideals to an increasingly disenchanted population. After the Second World War, historians held nationalism to be an essentially obscurantist and maleficent force, seducing its adherents with myths of racial superiority, distorted accounts of history and visions of a utopian future, with which to redeem the unsatisfactory present and the often inglorious past.[39] In the context of contemporary Russia, there seems little reason to amend or jettison this assessment. True, elements of nationalism's and national-communism's critique of Russian modernity are understandable, even partially justifiable but, for the most part, their proponents have succumbed to the temptation of ideas which offer no solutions to Russia's present problems.

Although the critics of reform and Westernisation may have been divided and therefore weak, it does not follow that democracy in Russia is strong. Possibly more worrying for the future of democracy in Russia than the appeal of the authoritarian and collectivist ideologies of nationalism and national-communism is the weakness of democratic institutions and political culture, both among the political elite and the general population. The contempt for legality, the perception of a corrupt and inefficient bureaucracy, the lack of regional political organisations and weakness of democratic parties, the slow development of civil society all point to the virtual absence in Russia of the kind of social and cultural infrastructure which an effective democratic system presupposes. The concentration of executive, administrative and legislative powers in the office of President, in the context of the contempt shown for parliament since 1991, the tendency to rule by cabal and to inhibit press freedom do not provide a model of democratic practice and have done little to inculcate it. The superficiality and cynicism of the democratic revolution leave it vulnerable to nostalgia and ambition. Democracy, as a norm, risks being associated, for many contemporary Russians, with the failure of the economic reform, over which Russia's putative democrats have presided. The crime, corruption and private tragedies associated with it may yet fatally compromise the attempt to break free from the legacy of authoritarianism, under which Russia has laboured. The gap between rhetoric and reality remains as wide as ever: the reform has done little to enhance the political influence and prosperity of the Russian people (as opposed to the new and part of the old elite). Power and wealth have remained concentrated in the hands of the few, who have shown little concern for the fate of the many. As the historian Kliuchevsky noted of an earlier attempt to reform Russia: 'Lost in admiration for the way in which the reform has transmuted Russian tradition, we have lost sight of the way in which Russian tradition has transmuted the reform.'

Notes

INTRODUCTION

1. For Benda's criticism of the intellectuals' betrayal of their responsibility to universal values of humanism in favour of exclusive nationalism, see J. Benda, *La Trahison des Clercs*, 3rd edn (Grasset, Paris, 1975).

2. R. Sakwa, *Russian Society and Politics*, 2nd edn (Routledge, London and New York, 1996) pp. 257–60; P. Rutland, 'The Economy' in S. White, A. Pravda and Z. Gitelman, *Developments in Russian and Post-Soviet Politics*, 3rd edn (Macmillan, London, 1994) pp. 152–5; P. Rutland, 'An Economy Running on Empty' in J. Schmidt (ed.), *OMRI Annual Survey 1995* (M.E. Sharpe, Armonk, NY, 1996) p. 195.

3. See especially A. Walicki, *The Slavophile Controversy* (OUP, Oxford, 1975).

4. See A. Yanov, *The Russian New Right* (IIS, Berkeley, 1978).

5. See E. Thaden, *Conservative Nationalism in Nineteenth-Century Russia* (University of Washington Press, Seattle, 1964); M. Petrovich, *The Emergence of Russian Pan-Slavism* (Columbia University Press, New York, 1956); H. Kohn, *Le Pan-Slavisme: son Histoire et son Idéologie* (Payot, Paris, 1963); D. Rawson, *Russian Rightists and the Revolution of 1905* (CUP, Cambridge, 1995).

6. See F. Barghoorn, *Soviet Russian Nationalism* (OUP, Oxford, 1956).

7. See J. Dunlop, *The Faces of Contemporary Russian Nationalism* (Princeton University Press, Princeton, 1983); V. Shlapentokh, *Soviet Intellectuals and the Powers* (I.B. Tauris, London and New York, 1990).

8. This was derived from a school of early émigré thought, known as National Bolshevism. See M. Agursky, *Ideologiya natsional'-bol'shevisma* (YMCA Press, Paris, 1980).

9. Roman Szporluk, recognising Russian nationalism's ambivalent character, nonetheless believed that it might stimulate liberal reform of the Soviet system. See R. Szporluk, 'Dilemmas of Russian Nationalism', *Problems of Communism* (July–August 1989) 21–7, 34; R. Szporluk, 'The National Question' in T. Colton and R. Legvold (eds), *After the Soviet Union* (Norton, NY and London, 1989) p. 95. For analyses reflecting his influence, see Lapidus, Zaslavsky and Goldman, 'Introduction' in G. Lapidus, V. Zaslavsky and P. Goldman (eds), *From Union to Commonwealth: Nationalism and Separatism in the Soviet Republics* (CUP, Cambridge, 1992) p. 9, who assert that: '[...] There has been a notable shift in recent years away from the former imperial consciousness' and a 'widespread conversion to the values of liberal Russian nationalism'; M. Rywkin, *Moscow's Lost Empire* (M.E. Sharpe, Armonk, NY, 1994) p. 14. Others took a less optimistic view, see J. Dunlop, *The Rise of Russia and the Fall of the Soviet Empire*

(Princeton University Press, Princeton, 1993) pp. 123–85 for an overview of late Soviet nationalism. See too S. Carter, *Russian Nationalism* (Pinter, London, 1990) pp. 103–31. More emphatic in presenting Russian nationalism as an anti-democratic, xenophobic force were Alexander Yanov and Walter Laqueur: W. Laqueur, *Black Hundred. The Rise of the Extreme Right in Russia*, pbk edn (Harper Collins, NY, 1994); A. Yanov, *Posle Yeltsina. 'Veimarskaya Rossiya'* (Krik, Moscow, 1995) for the post-Soviet period.

1. THE INTELLIGENTSIA AND THE NATIONALIST REVIVAL

1. For a survey of the ideology of the new right at the end of the 1980s, see W. Laqueur, *Black Hundred: the Rise of the Extreme Right in Russia*, pbk edn (Harper Collins, 1994) pp. 154–80.
2. Alexander Solzhenitsyn, in 1973, discerned in the West not a vigorous society but a culture on the brink of collapse and hence not a model for Russia to emulate: '[...] The catastrophic weakening of the Western world and the whole of Western civilisation [...] is [...] the result of the historical, psychological and moral crisis [...] of humanitarian Western culture and world outlook'. Solzhenitsyn, *Letter to the Soviet Leaders* (Collins Harvill, London, 1974) p. 12. This belief in the decadence and mortality of the West was shared by Mikhail Antonov: 'The people and States of the West have outlived their day and are dying [...] They will perish not by sudden attack but by virtue of the drying up of their vital forces. They are tired of living'. Cited in A. Yanov, *Russian New Right* (IIS, Berkeley, 1978) pp. 76–7.
3. S. Kunaev, *NS*, 2, 1985, 176–7.
4. N. Zuyev, *NS*, 1, 1987, 187. See also Kunaev, *NS*, 2, 1985, 172.
5. Yu. Bondarev, *SK*, 18 July 1987, 6. See also Yu. Tsagarelli, *SK*, 1 December 1987, 5; V. Pikul', *NS*, 2, 1989, 190 for other attacks on rock music.
6. A. Doronin, *MG*, 9, 1987, 228. See also I. Glazunov, *Den'*, 5 May 1991.
7. V. Rasputin, *NS*, 1, 1988, 171. The film 'Is it Easy to be Young?', which discussed the alienation of young people, also aroused the right wingers' indignation: V. Belov, Yu. Bondarev and V. Rasputin wrote to *Pravda* to complain about it on 9 November 1987. See also A. Solzhenitsyn, *Rebuilding Russia* (Harvill, London, 1991) p. 40.
8. S. Bondarchuk, *SK*, 18 July 1987, 6.
9. A. Lanshchikov, *Lit. Rossiya*, 28 October 1988, 4.
10. L. Karpinsky, *MN*, 51, 1989, 13.
11. A. Lanshchikov, *Lit. Rossiya*, 28 October 1988, p. 4.
12. See round table discussion in L. Karpinsky, *MN*, 51, 1989, 13.
13. A. Kazintsev, *NS*, 2, 1988, 186.
14. MBIO: Transcript of tape of the broadcast in folder on *Pamyat'*.
15. V. Belov, *SK*, 6 July 1991, 4. See also S. Nepobedimy, *NS*, 1, 1990, 2–3 for an attack on *perestroika*.

16. M. Antonov, *NS*, 7, 1987, 9–12.
17. See S. Kunaev, *Molodoi Leninets*, March 1989. See also for an attack on liberal opinion, editorial in *Russkoe tovarishchestvo*, September 1990, 1. *Pamyat'* also attacked *glasnost"*s leaders – including Korotich, Shatrov and Yakovlev. The MBIO archive includes cartoons showing these figures as Jews, trying to hide their identity – a thesis also promulgated by nationalist writers: folder *Russkoe natsional'noe patrioticheskoe dvizheniye: Pamyat'*. For attacks on *perestroika* see for example Yuri Bondarev's speech at the nineteenth Party Conference; V. Potanin, 'Sokrovennoe' in V. Sotsenko (ed.), *Pisatel' i vremya* (Sovetskii pisatel', Moscow, 1989) p. 336. I. Glazunov, *Izvestiya*, 3 November 1988 for an attack on *perestroika* for allowing international 'Satanic' modernism to be enthroned.
18. N. Eidelman, *Nauka i zhizn'*, 10, 1988, 99–100.
19. A. Sakharov, 'On Alexander Solzhenitsyn's "A Letter to the Soviet Leaders"' in N. Bethell and B. Rubin (eds), *Kontinent: the Alternative Voice of Russia and Eastern Europe* (Hodder and Stoughton, London, 1977) pp. 22, 26.
20. 'Russkaya idea', *Isskustvo kino*, 6, 1988, 126–7.
21. A. Lanshchikov, *Moskva*, 6, 1989, 13.
22. A. Tuskarev, *Russkii vestnik*, 11–18 March 1992, 13.
23. 'Yevraziiskoe soprotivleniya', *Den'*, January 1992, 2.
24. For further examples of nationalists' authoritarianism, see T. Parland, *The Rejection in Russia of Liberal Democracy* (Finnish Society of Sciences, Helsinki, 1993) pp. 221–3. He cites Kozhinov as writing that 'democracy liberates the forces of *evil* more than it promotes goodness', ibid., p. 142.
25. Cited in J. Dunlop, 'Soviet Cultural Politics', *Problems of Communism*, (November–December 1987) 35.
26. M. Antonov, *NS*, 7, 1991, 133.
27. See A. Prokhanov, *NS*, 5, 1990, 85–98; A. Kuz'min, *Lit. Rossiya*, 23 June 1989 for similar views.
28. See Yu. Tyurin, *NS*, 6, 1987, 180–81, for a rejection of the Orthodox contribution to Russian political culture and an interpretation of Russian history as a fight for unity. A. Kuz'min, *Lit. Rossiya*, 23 June 1989, for Russian colonialism.
29. I. Shafarevich, *NS*, 6, 1989, 173, 175.
30. Ibid., 187–190.
31. Shafarevich, *NS*, 11, 1989, 162–72 for his more extreme anti-Semitic remarks.
32. Shafarevich, *NS*, 6, 1989, 184.
33. Ibid., 176.
34. Ibid., 179, 191.
35. Ibid., 178.
36. 'We believe in a freedom true and complete, living and not formal and contractual, in the freedom of children in the family of a father who has confidence in the love of [his] children', Dostoevsky wrote in 1880. Cited in E. Thaden, *Conservative Nationalism* (Univ. of Washington Press, Seattle, 1964) p. 79.

37. See K. Aksakov, 'Memorandum [...] on the Internal State of Russia' (1855) in W. Leatherbarrow and D. Offord (eds), *A Documentary History of Russian Thought* (Ardis, Ann Arbor, 1987) pp. 95–107; A. Galaktionov and P. Nikandrov, *Russkaya filosofiya* (Izdatel'stvo Leningradskogo universiteta, Leningrad, 1989) pp. 309–10.

38. See for example M. Lobanov, *MG*, 4, 1968 and V. Chalmaev, *MG*, 9, 1968. See J. Dunlop, *Contemporary Russian Nationalism* (Princeton University Press, Princeton, 1983) pp. 312–24; A. Yanov, *Russian New Right* (IIS, Berkeley, 1978) pp. 42–59; P. Duncan, 'The Party and Russian Nationalism' in P. Potyichnyj (ed.), *The Soviet Union: Party and Society* (CUP, Cambridge, 1988) pp. 232–3 for discussion of the ensuing controversies.

39. V. Osipov, *NS*, 1991, 127.

40. S. Kunaev, *NS*, 7, 1991, 124. See also A. Kuz'min, *NS*, 2, 1988, 156.

41. V. Kozhinov, *NS*, 7, 1991, 133.

42. A. Kuz'min, *NS*, 9, 1985, 188.

43. A. Kuz'min, *Lit. Rossiya*, 23 June 1989.

44. A. Lanshchikov in *Perestroika: sotsializm ili kapitalizm?* (Otechestvo, Moscow, 1989) pp. 14–15.

45. The term, adopted by Stalin, is equivalent to *Führer*, in Russian political terminology.

46. M. Antonov in *Perestroika: sotsializm ili kapitalizm?* (Otechestvo, Moscow, 1989) pp. 16–20.

47. Ibid., pp. 18–19.

48. V. Chalmaev, *Moskva*, 4, 1988, 185.

49. See V. Sorokin, *NS*, 8, 1989, 168. See also V. Kozhinov, *NS*, 4, 1988, 170–71.

50. See resolution of the Joint Central Plenum of the Russian Communist Party, 15 November 1990.

51. Neumann points to the structural similarities between Bolshevism and nationalism at an intellectual level, I. Neumann, *Russia and the Idea of Europe* (Routledge, London and New York, 1996) p. 174. See also F. Barghoorn, *Soviet Russian Nationalism* (OUP, Oxford, 1956). It was the belief that only Lenin's party was capable of rebuilding the state as a great power that led one wing of the White movement, led by Nikolai Ustrialov, the National Bolsheviks, to rally to Soviet power in the 1920s. See M. Agursky, *Ideologiya natsional'-bol'shevizma* (YMCA Press, Paris, 1980); N. Ustrialov, *V bor'be za Rossiyu* (Harbin, 1920); *Pod znakom revolyutsii* (Harbin, 1925).

52. On the Interfronts, see J. Dunlop, *The Rise of Russia* (Princeton University Press, Princeton, 1993) pp. 136–9. N. Melvin, *Forging the New Russian Nation* (RIIA, London, 1994) p. 13 asserts that they were created mainly by the security ministries.

53. A. Prokhanov, *Lit. Rossiya*, 5 January 1990, 4.

54. A. Prokhanov, *NS*, 5, 1990, 92–8.

55. See G. Bondarenko, *Alexander Prokhanov* (Paleya, Moscow, 1992) pp. 10, 23–4. For an analysis, see A. Yanov, *Posle Yeltsina* (Krik, Moscow, 1995) p. 156.

56. Cited in B. Koval' (ed.), *Rossiya segodnya* (Mezhdunarodnye otnosheniya, Moscow, 1993) p. 26. See too A. Yanov and A. Prokhanov, *Lit. gaz.*, 2 September 1992, 13; A. Yanov, *Posle Yeltsina* (Krik, Moscow, 1995) p. 157 for Prokhanov's declared sympathy for Mussolini. For Prokhanov's rebuttal of Kurginyan's criticisms of *Elementy*'s celebration of national-socialism and his appeal for the unity of the communist and neo-fascist opposition, see Prokhanov, *Den'*, 1, 1–9 January 1993, 3.

57. See for example A. Prokhanov, *Russkoe tovarishchestvo*, September 1990, 6–7.

58. For this congress, see O. Bychkova, *MN*, 49, 1990, 6. V. Pribylovsky, *Slovar'* politicheskikh partii (Panorama, Moscow, 1991) pp. 89–90.

59. See O. Bychkova, *MN*, 49, 1990, 6, for Alksnis quote. V. Pribylovsky, *Slovar'* (Panorama, Moscow, 1991) pp. 89–90.

60. 'Zayavlenie uchreditel'nogo s''ezda [...] Soyuz', (December 1990) in V. Berezovsky *et al.* (eds), *Rossiya [...] dokumenty*, vol. IX (RAU, Moscow, 1993) pp. 136–7.

61. Cited in V. Berezovsky *et al.* (eds), *Rossiya [...] dokumenty*, vol. IX (1993) pp. 142–4.

62. Yu. Teplyakov, *MN*, 6, 1991, 7. See too V. Alksnis, *Den'*, 16, August 1991, where he implicitly supports the principle of a coup.

63. V. Berezovsky *et al.* (eds), *Rossiya [...] dokumenty* vol. IX (RAU, Moscow, 1993) pp. 131–2. For the similarly inclined *Interdvizheniya* (the Party-sponsored pro-Soviet movements, which united Russians opposed to republican independence in the Baltics and Moldova) see J. Dunlop, *The Rise of Russia* (Princeton University Press, Princeton, 1993) pp. 136–9. V. Berezovsky *et al.* (eds), *Rossiya [...] dokumenty*, vol. III (RAU, Moscow, 1992) pp. 20–21 for their documents and rules. V. Berezovsky and N. Krotov, *Rossiya: partii*, vol. I, part 2 (RAU, Moscow, 1991) pp. 234–5.

64. O. Böss, *Die Lehre der Eurasier* (Harrasiwitz, Wiesbaden, 1961). P. Milyukov, 'Eurasianism' in B. Yakovenko (ed.), *Festschrift T.G. Masaryk*, vol. I (Cohen, Bonn, 1930) pp. 225–36. For a sample of their ideas, see S. Trubetskoi, *Yevropa i chelovechestvo* (Sofia, 1920) and the collection of essays in *Na putyakh* (Moscow, Berlin, 1922).

65. See L. Gumilev, *Ethogenez i biosfera zemli* (C&T, Moscow, 1994); L. Gumilev, *NS*, 1, 1991, 132, 134 where he admits he is a Eurasian. For a brief sympathetic summary, see G. Bondarenko, *Lev Gumiliev* (Paleya, Moscow, 1992) pp. 8, 24–5. For a critical review, see A. Yanov, *Posle Yeltsina* (Krik, Moscow, 1995) pp. 202–12. B. Clarke, *Empire's New Clothes* (Vintage, London, 1995) pp. 13–14, 191–2.

66. Quoted in A. Yanov, *Posle Yeltsina* (Krik, Moscow, 1995) p. 207.

67. Quoted in A. Yanov, *Posle Yeltsina* (Krik, Moscow, 1995) p. 211.

68. See I. Torbakov, 'The Statists and the Ideology of Russian Imperial Nationalism', *RFE/RL Research Report*, 11 December 1992, 10–16 for a review of this fashion.

69. Quoted in A. Ignatow, 'Der "Eurasismus"', *Berichte des Bundesinstituts für ostwissenschaftliche und internationale Studien*, 15 (1992) 31–2. Mikhalkov switched allegiance from Rutskoi in 1992 to Yeltsin in 1996, but he continued to preach Ilyin's ideas, arguing in an open letter to

the President for an end to inter-party fighting, political chaos and journalistic *bezpridel'* and for unity and self-sacrifice in the cause of the Fatherland. The new Russia should be Orthodox, nationalist, Eurasian, for Russian culture was neither European nor Asian but Eurasian; see N. Mikhalkov, *NG*, 20 July 1996, 3.

70. S. Sultanov, *NS*, 7, July 1992, pp. 142–3. See too his comments in 'Yevraziiskoe soprotivlenie', *Den'*, 2, 10–18 January 1992, 2–3.
71. V. Shtep, *NS*, 8, 1992, 119, 123.
72. Interview with O. Bychkova, *MN*, 7, 1992, 14.
73. A. Andreev, *Moskva*, November–December 1992, 159–60.
74. S. Baburin, *NS*, 2, 1995, 174.
75. Cited in W. Laqueur, *The Long Road to Freedom* (Unwin Hyman, London, 1989) p. 122. See also V. Belov, 'Vozrodit' v krestianstve' in V. Sotsenko (ed.), *Pisatel' i vremya* (Sovetskii pisatel', Moscow, 1989) p. 57: 'The Russian peasant was the main pillar of the great State – in the economic, military and spiritual and cultural sense.'
76. Cited in J. Dunlop, *Contemporary Russian Nationalism* (Princeton University Press, Princeton, 1983) p. 220. S. Kunaev, *NS*, 2, 1985, 174.
77. V. Soloukhin, *NS*, 6, 1988, 132–3.
78. N. Zuyev, *NS*, 1, 1987, 186.
79. A. Trofimov, *NS*, 1988, 182.
80. Cited in J. Dunlop, *Contemporary Russian Nationalism* (Princeton University Press, Princeton, 1983) p. 142.
81. See, for example, V. Sorokin, *NS*, 8, 1989, 168–9. V. Shlapentokh, *Soviet Intellectuals* (I.B. Tauris, London and NY, 1990) p. 208.
82. For Russian nationalist writers' obsession with the 'myth of cultural murder' since *glasnost'*, see K. Parthe, 'The Empire Strikes Back', *Nationalities Papers*, vol. XXIV, no. 4 (December 1996) 610–24.
83. In his memoirs, Ligachev rejects the view which sees him as the chief instigator of the campaign, while regretting its failure and abandonment. See Ye. Ligachev, *Inside Gorbachev's Kremlin*, 2nd edn (Westview Press, Boulder and Oxford, 1996) pp. 335–9. For background, see S. White, *Russia Goes Dry* (CUP, Cambridge, 1996) pp. 66–9.
84. F. Uglov, *NS*, 7, 1989, 157.
85. F. Uglov, *NS*, 151–2.
86. V. Osipov, *NS*, 7, 1991, 127.
87. F. Uglov, *NS*, 7, 1987, 156. Uglov's views were shared too by the mathematician Vladimir Zhdanov. They had campaigned against alcoholism since the early 1980s, ascribing it to Zionism, Trotskyism and imperialism. One of Zhdanov's speeches on this theme was disseminated by *Pamyat'* in Moscow and is reported to have become a *samizdat* best seller in 1985: see V. Pribylovsky, *Pamyat'* (Panorama, Moscow, 1991) p. 3.
88. For a discussion of the fundamentalists' anti-semitic, patriotic views and their links with Novosibirsk *Pamyat'*, see S. White, *Russia Goes Dry* (CUP, Cambridge, 1996) pp. 169, 183–5. He believes their 'anti-Zionist' views to have been quite widely held in this milieu.
89. G. Pyatov, *Lit. Rossiya*, 16 November 1990.

212 *Notes*

90. A. Kazintsev, *NS*, 2, 1988, 186.
91. A. Trofimov, *NS*, 2, 1988, 181. For similar statements by Lemeshev and Vykhodtsev, see G. Petrov, *SK*, 24 November 1987, 3.
92. 'Slovo o Solzhenitsyne', *NS*, 1, 1990, 63–4.
93. See his remarks in a round table with Rasputin, Shafarevich and Soloukhin, 'Slovo o Solzhenitsyne', *NS*, 1, 1990, 65.
94. 'Pis'mo pisatelei', *Lit. Rossiya*, 2 March 1990.
95. A. Kuz'min, *Lit. Rossiya*, 23 March 1989.
96. Cited by N. Zuyev, *NS*, 1, 1987, 185.
97. See V. Kozhinov, *NS*, 4, 1988, 169 for example of this. See also Kozhinov, *Sud'ba Rossii* (Moscow, 1990) p. 15 for an attack on Sakharov. He was a representative of the left radical intelligentsia, according to Kozhinov, by virtue of his condemnations, in September 1989, of the neo-Stalinist United Workers' Front.
98. A. Nevzorov, *Narodnaya pravda*, 2, November 1991, 5.
99. This had been the case even in the late nineteenth century, when a policy of active discrimination against the Empire's Jewish population was conducted under Alexander III. Not merely were careers in the civil service and high office excluded, but permission to study, and even to reside outside the Pale of Settlement – a large zone in the west and south of Ukraine – was difficult to obtain. The first years of the twentieth century witnessed an upsurge in anti-Semitism – expressed in such Russian apocrypha as the Protocols of the Elders of Zion, the pogroms of the Ukraine, the Black Hundreds and the famous trial of Beilis for supposedly committing the ritual murder of a child. See S. Ettinger, 'The Jews in Russia' in L. Kochan (ed.), *Jews in Soviet Russia* (OUP, Oxford, 1978) pp. 18–19. Also A. Lindemann, *The Jew Accused* (CUP, Cambridge, 1993) pp. 174–93. As a result, many young Jews supported the cause of revolution and were well-represented in the social-democratic movement and subsequently in the leadership of the Bolshevik Party.
100. S. Schwartz, *Antisemitizm v Sovetskom Soyuze* (NY, 1952) pp. 14–16.
101. See J. Dunlop, *Contemporary Russian Nationalism* (Princeton University Press, Princeton, 1983) p. 42. S. Carter, *Russian Nationalism* (Pinter, London, 1990) p. 78.
102. V. Shlapentokh, *Soviet Intellectuals* (I.B. Tauris, London and New York, 1990) p. 217.
103. A. Kuz'min, *NS*, 3, 1985, 190.
104. A. Kuz'min, *NS*, 7, 1988, 192.
105. V. Kozhinov, *Moskva*, 11, 1986, 191–4.
106. S. Kunaev, *NS*, 8, 1988, 187–8. See also I. Vinogradov, *MN*, 18, 1989, 11.
107. See interview conducted with Valentin Pikul', in which the interviewer complained that Stalin was attacked by those who wanted to evade responsibility for their crimes. Pikul' agreed, saying that Jews really ran the country while Stalin was merely their agent. V. Pikul', *NS*, 2, 1989, 188–9.
108. M. Zarubezhny, *NS*, 11, 1990, 149–51.
109. V. Pikul', *NS*, 2, 1989, 188.
110. V. Pikul', *NS*, 2, 1989, 190–91.
111. See I. Glazunov, *Den'*, 5, 1991.

112. V. Pikul', *NS*, 2, 1989, 186–7.
113. See Norman Cohn, *Warrant for Genocide* (Scholars Press, Chicago, 1981) pp. 61–73, 103–7. Tsar Nicholas II annotated and approved the Protocols which seemed to him to explain the rot that had set in with the 1905 revolution.
114. S. Kunaev, *NS*, 6, 1989, 160. For another example of belief in the Jewish plan to dominate the world and Russia in particular, see Bondarenko's interview with Lev Gumilev, *Den'*, 22–8 March 1992, 6. For anti-Zionism in RSFSR Writers' Union see S. Kuryanov and G. Ivanov, *Moskovskii komsomolets*, 9 May 1988.
115. See N. Katerli, *Leningradskaya pravda*, 9 October 1988, p. 3 for the influence of official anti-Zionism on *Pamyat'* and in particular of Romanenko's book, *O klassovoi sushnosti zionizma*, which reportedly belittled the Holocaust. Romanenko sued Katerli and had the initial verdict against him overturned by the city court. On Romanenko's case, see *SK*, 27 April 1989; V. Azadovsky, *MN*, 37, 1989, 5. *Sovetskaya kul'tura*, on 18 June 1987, alleged that Begun and Romanenko were among *Pamyat'*'s chief sources of inspiration. Begun brought a case against the paper, alleging damage to his reputation and threats to his life. (The journalists involved received death threats and Begun was accompanied at the trial by the *Pamyat'* leader, Dmitri Vasiliev.) The successful defence proved that entire sections of Begun's 'academic' work was directly copied from *Mein Kampf*. S. Rogov and V. Nosenko, *SK*, 9 February 1989, 6; 'Chto zashchishchaem', *Izvestiya*, 5 June 1988; P. Gutionov, *Izvestiya*, 26 February 1988, 3; 'Simvoly', *Russkaya mysl'*, 6 December 1987. On Begun, see N. Levin, *Paradox of Survival: the Jews of the Soviet Union*, vol. 2 (New York University Press, NY, 1990) pp. 786–9. On Begun and Romanenko and their anti-Semitic writings, see S. Reznik, *The Nazification of Russia* (Challenge Publications, Washington, 1996) pp. 35–60.
116. A. Kazintsev, *NS*, 11, 1990, 157.
117. G. Petrov, *SK*, 24 November 1987, 3.
118. Ibid., 3.
119. 'Izbrannye', *Nedelya*, 20–26 November 1989, 16.
120. 'Izbrannye', *Nedelya*, 20–26 November 1989, 17.
121. *Russkii vestnik*, 18–25 March 1992.
122. For the controversy surrounding the views of B. Pinaev and the *Otechestvo* organisation in Sverdlovsk, see V. Kichin, *SK*, 18 April 1987, 3–4. V. Kichin, *SK*, 29 October 1987, 3. Ye. Losoto, *Komsomol'skaya pravda*, 19 December 1987. B. Pinaev, *NS*, 8, 1987, 188–9. 'Rezonnye voprosy', *NS*, 12, 1987, 187–8.
123. Cited in J. Dunlop, 'Soviet Cultural Politics', *Problems of Communism*, (November–December 1987), 46–7, 51. This article gives a detailed account of the political battles in the cultural elite in 1986 and 1987. See too R. Marsh, *History and Literature* (Macmillan, London, 1995) for a fuller treatment.
124. See Ya. Brudny in A. Hewett and V. Winston (eds), *Milestones in Glasnost' and Perestroyka* (Brookings Institution, Washington, 1991) pp. 153–90 for a helpful overview.

125. The most systematic account is R. Marsh, *History and Literature* (Macmillan, London, 1995) pp. 46–9, 61–81. V. Krasnov, *Russia beyond Communism* (Westview Press, Boulder and Oxford, 1991) pp. 110–12 for a treatment sympathetic to the nationalist critics of liberalisation.
126. For a discussion, see R. Pittman, 'Writers and Politics in the Gorbachev Era', *Soviet Studies*, vol. XLIV, no. 2 (1992) 677–82. See too R. Marsh, *History and Literature* (Macmillan, London, 1995) pp. 19–21.
127. 'Pisateli', *Lit. gaz.*, 15 March 1989, 2.
128. A. Malgin, *MN*, 38, 1989, 12. E. Vesyolova, *MN*, 12, 1989, 2. See also J. and C. Garrard, *Inside the Writers' Union* (I.G. Tauris, New York and London, 1990) pp. 230–31, 233–4.
129. A. Latynina, *MN*, 13, 1989, 2. *Ogonek*, 6, February 1990, 18.
130. Interview with V. Oskotsky, 4 December 1990. See also V. Berezovsky, N. Krotov, *Rossiya: partii* vol. I, part 2 (RAU, Moscow, 1991) pp. 184–5.
131. L. Fomina, *Moskovskaya pravda*, 4 February 1990.
132. 'Vmesto', *Den'*, 14 July 1991.
133. 'Izbrannye', *Nedelya*, 20–26 November 1989, 16.
134. Glushkova, at the same meeting, 'Izbrannye', *Nedelya*, 20–26 November 1989, 16.
135. For further information on this incident, see G.L., 'Draka', *Kommersant*, 1, 1990; A. Selikhovsky, *Krasnaya presnya*, 6, February 1990; Yu. Rakhaev, *Moskovskii komsomolets*, 12 and 15 August 1990; N. Smirnova, *Moskovskaya pravda*, 11 August 1990; *Ogonek*, 43, 1990, 32–3; A. Gerber, *Moskovskii komsomolets*, 13 July 1990; V. Kalugin, *Den'*, 9 May 1991.
136. *Ogonek*, 6 February 1990, 18. *Aprel'* also wrote on 14 February 1990 to the Central Committee to complain about *Pamyat*'s attack in the Writers' House.
137. Signatories included Petr Proskurin, T. Glushkova, Mikhail Lobanov, S. Kunaev, A. Znamensky, V. Rasputin, V. Kozhinov, A. Prokhanov, V. Sorokin and I. Shararevich.
138. 'Pis'mo pisatelei', *Lit. Rossiya*, 2 March 1990.
139. 'Pis'mo pisatelei', *Lit. Rossiya*, 2 March 1990.
140. See T. Parland, *The Rejection in Russia* (The Finnish Society of Sciences, Helsinki, 1993) p. 233, who believes that this brand of Russian nationalism was imperialistic, anti-Semitic and semi-fascist.

2. NEO-FASCISM

1. For neo-fascist groups in Moscow, Yekaterinburg and St Petersburg, see A. Chelnokov, *Izvestiya*, 5 May 1994, 5; A. Chelnokov, *Izvestiya*, 15 March 1995, 4; A. Pashkov, *Izvestiya*, 4 July 1995, 5.
2. F. Carsten, 'Interpretations of Fascism' in W. Laqueur (ed.), *Fascism: A Reader's Guide* (Penguin, London, 1979) p. 482. Z. Sternhell, 'Fascist Ideology' in ibid., p. 325. R. Griffin, 'Introduction' to R. Griffin (ed.), *Fascism* (OUP, Oxford, 1995) p. 2. S. Payne, *A History of Fascism 1914–45* (UCL, London, 1995) pp. 6–14.

3. S. Payne, *A History of Fascism 1914–45* (UCL, London, 1995) pp. 14–19. George Mosse also pointed to the primacy for fascists of ideology and the 'revolution of the spirit', in which they hoped to escape the problem of social and economic change, see his remarks cited in R. Griffin (ed.), *Fascism* (1995) p. 303.

4. See R. Griffin (ed.), *Fascism* (Oxford, OUP, 1995) pp. 293–6. K.-D. Bracher insists on national-socialism's revolutionary as well as its negative ideology. K.-D. Bracher, *The German Dictatorship* (Penguin, London, 1973) p. 23. The Russian opposition shared many of the negative traits identified by Bracher, including imperialistic nationalism, conservative-authoritarian glorification of the all-powerful State, nationalistic socialism.

5. The term 'neo-fascist' shall be used in this text to make the distinction between contemporary Russian and classical European fascism. See too Griffin's distinction between fascist and para-fascist groups (the latter lack regenerative vision), *Fascism* (1995) p. 9.

6. V. Pribylovsky, *Pamyat': dokumenty i teksty* (Panorama, Moscow, 1991) pp. 1–2. V. Berezovsky *et al.* (eds), *Rossiya [...] dokumenty i materialy* vol. V (RAU, Moscow, 1992) pp. 86–7. See also G. Grishaeva, *Metrostroevets*, 27 July 1983. Yu. Zolin, *Metrostroevets*, 24 June 1983. T. Sergeev, 'U Pamyati svoi zakony', *Moskovskaya pravda*, 19 May 1988.

7. V. Pribylovsky, *Pamyat': dokumenty i teksty* (Panorama, Moscow, 1991) p. 3.

8. V. Pribylovsky, *Pamyat': dokumenty i teksty* (Panorama, Moscow, 1991) pp. 3–4. S. Carter, *Russian Nationalism* (Pinter, London, 1990) pp. 109–10. V. Berezovsky and N. Krotov, *Rossiya: partii [...]* vol. I, part 1 (RAU, Moscow, 1991) p. 68.

9. The demonstrators favoured its replacement by the project submitted by the sculptor, Vyacheslav Klykov (whose statue to Marshall Zhukov was finally erected at the entrance to Red Square in 1995). Klykov's association with *Pamyat'* was not fortuitous: he provided a sculpture, (of St Sergei Radonezh) whose erection caused a subsequent *Pamyat'* scandal. His next claim to fame was his signature of the Appeal to the People, the ideological justification of the August 1991 coup. See V. Berezovsky *et al.* (eds), *Rossiya [...] dokumenty i materialy*, vol. V (RAU, Moscow, 1992) p. 87. V. Pribylovsky, *Pamyat': dokumenty i teksty* (Panorama, Moscow, 1991) pp. 5–6. 'Chto takoe [...] Pamyat'?' *Russkaya mysl'*, 31 July 1987, 6.

10. A. Kiselev and A. Mostovshchikov, *MN*, 20, 1987, 4.

11. B. Yeltsin, *Against the Grain* (Cape, London, 1990) pp. 99–100. He refers to *Pamyat'*'s slogans as having been of 'an entirely proper kind, something about *perestroika*, Russia, freedom, the rottenness of the *apparat* [...]'. The most detailed account of this meeting depicts Yeltsin as an authoritarian nationalist rather than as a liberal democrat, see 'Chto takoe [...] Pamyat'?', *RM*, 31 July 1987, 6.

12. See M. Urban, *The Rebirth of Politics in Russia* (CUP, Cambridge, 1997) p. 366, n. 45.

13. Ye. Losoto, *Komsomol'skaya pravda*, 22 May 1987; Ye. Losoto, *KP*, 24 June 1987; G. Alimev and R. Lynev, *Izvestiya*, 2 June 1987; A. Golovkov and A. Pavlov, *Ogonek*, 21, 1987, 4–5; P. Gutionov, *Sovetskaya Rossiya*, 17 July 1987; A. Cherkizov, *Sovetskaya kul'tura*, 18 June 1987.

14. 'Vozzvanie patrioticheskogo ob"edineniya 'Pamyat' k russkomu narodu', 8 December 1987 in V. Berezovsky *et al.* (eds), *Rossiya [...] dokumenty*, vol. V (RAU, Moscow, 1992) pp. 88–91.

15. '"Pamyat'" kak ona i yest", *Soglasie*, 4, 14 March 1989.

16. Cited in V. Pribylovsky, *Pamyat'* (Panorama, Moscow, 1991) p. 11.

17. Ye. Losoto, *Komsomol'skaya pravda*, 22 May 1987, p. 4. See also G. Alimev and R. Lynev, *Izvestiya*, 2 June 1987, p. 3. for a similar encounter.

18. 'K russkomu narodu', 8 December 1987 in V. Berezovsky *et al.* (eds), *Rossiya [...] dokumenty*, vol. V (RAU, Moscow, 1992) pp. 88–91.

19. See for example 'Obrashchenie po natsional'nomy voprosu', June 1990, in V. Berezovsky *et al.* (eds), *Rossiya [...] dokumenty*, vol. V (RAU, Moscow, 1992) p. 114. 'Chto takoe [...] Pamyat'?' *RM*, 31 July 1987, 6–7 for the declarations of its leaders on this theme in the meeting with Yeltsin.

20. 'Za dukhovnoe vozrozhdenie Rossii', 9 September 1989, in V. Berezovsky *et al.* (eds), *Rossiya: [...] dokumenty*, vol. V (RAU, Moscow, 1992), pp. 109–10. '"Pamyat'" kak ona i yest", *Soglasie*, 14 March 1989 for the cult of leadership.

21. 'There is no doubt that the "great" experiment was the result of the international conspiracy of Judaeo-Masonic forces who aimed to transform the last remnant of the Autocratic Russian Empire into a colonial structure with cheap labour and scrounged raw materials'. In 'Obrashchenie po natsional'nomy voprosu', June 1990, in V. Berezovsky *et al.* (eds), *Rossiya [...] dokumenty*, vol. V (RAU, Moscow, 1992) p. 113.

22. See 'Chto takoe Pamyat'" *RM*, 31 July 1987, 6. 'Obrashchenie', June 1990, in V. Berezovsky *et al.* (eds), *Rossiya [...] dokumenty*, vol. V (RAU, Moscow, 1992) pp. 112–17.

23. G. Alimev and R. Lynev, *Izvestiya*, 2 June 1987, 3. G. Petrov, *SK*, 24 November 1987, 3.

24. P. Gutionov, *SR*, 17 July 1987, 4.

25. P. Gutionov, *SR*, 17 July 1987, 4. G. Alimev and R. Lynev, *Izvestiya*, 2 June 1987, 3.

26. Ye. Losoto, *Komsomol'skaya pravda*, 19 December 1987, 4. I. Lugovsky, *Komsomol'skaya pravda*, 24 June 1987, 4. These included Party members: see MBIO: Folder on *Russkoe natsional'noe patrioticheskoe dvizhenie Pamyat'*.

27. I. Sidorov, *Leningradskaya pravda*, 6 September 1988, 3.

28. N. Gevorkyan and D. Radyshevsky, *MN*, 7, 1990, 14. The public were attracted by them, the authors believed, but *Pamyat'* lacked the organisation to build on this.

29. These included Sverdlovsk (*Otechestvo*), Novosibirsk (*Pamyat'*), Krasnoyarsk (*Pamyat'*), Chelyabinsk (*Rodina*), Tyumen' (*Otechestvo*),

Irkutsk (*Vernost'*) and Magnitogorsk. V. Pribylovsky, *Slovar'* [...] *politicheskikh partii* (Panorama, Moscow, 1991) pp. 4–5; 54–6; 58; 68–9.

30. I. Sidorov, *Leningradskaya pravda*, 6 September 1988, 2.
31. See N. Pasko, *Vechernaya Moskva*, 15 June 1987. V. Dobrynina *et al.*, *Samodeyatel'nye initsiativnye organizatsii* (Moscow, 1990) p. 43.
32. 'Pamyat', *Panorama*, 14 (December 1990) 1. For Vasiliev's faction in 1989 see '"Pamyat'" kak ona i yest", *Soglasiya*, 4, 14 March 1989. For general information, see A. Gurkov, *MN*, 7, 1988, p. 4. 'Pamyat', *Soviet Analyst*, 3 June 1987, 6–9. A. Nikolaev, *Komsomolets Tatarii*, 19 November 1989, 4.
33. 'Osnovnye polozheniya manifesta russkogo narodnogo fronta dvizheniya "Pamyat'"', 28 August 1989 in V. Pribylovsky, *Pamyat'* (Panorama, Moscow, 1991) p. 22.
34. 'Pozitsiya russkogo narodnogo fronta dvizheniya "Pamyat'"', 1 September 1989 in V. Pribylovsky, *Pamyat'* (Panorama, Moscow, 1991) pp. 23–4.
35. V. Yeremin, *Nedelya*, 12, 1990, 11. See too Yu. Kazarin and A. Russovsky, *Vechernaya Moskva*, 25 February 1988 for interview with Sychev and other *Pamyat'* leaders.
36. See A. Antonov, 'Pamyat', *Izmailovskii vestnik*, 2, January 1990, 3, for interview with Ostashvili. For the programme of Ostashvili's *Pamyat' Union*, see *Energetik*, 18 January 1990, 3–5. A fuller version is published in V. Berezovsky *et al.* (eds), *Rossiya [...] dokumenty*, vol. V (RAU, Moscow, 1992) pp. 132–40.
37. For Filimonov's programme, see *Sovetskii tsirk*, 29, 20 July 1989.
38. V. Pribylovsky, *Slovar'* (Panorama, Moscow, 1991) pp. 57–8. V. Berezovsky and N. Krotov, *Rossiya: partii [...]*, vol. I, part 1 (RAU, Moscow, 1991) pp. 109–10. Interview with Yevgeny Proshechkin, Anti-Fascist Centre, 18 November 1990. For interview with Yemelyanov, see A. Kudyakov, *Karetny ryad'*, December 1989, 6. See too Z. Pyl'd, *Rech'*, September–October 1990, 5–6.
39. Yu. Chernichenko, *Ogonek*, 43, 1990, 31–2. Ye. Dodolev, *Moskovskii komsomolets*, 27 October 1990. KGB Chairman Kryuchkov is reported to have commented positively on the work of some *Pamyat'* groups in a television interview in December 1990, see S. Reznik, *The Nazification of Russia* (Challenge Publication, Washington, 1996) p. 190; B. Clarke, *An Empire's New Clothes* (Vintage, London, 1995) p. 181.
40. A conclusion also drawn by Yevgeny Proshechkin in interview 18 November 1990. See also O. Morozova, *Moskovskii komsomolets*, 18 October 1990, 2. On national-Stalinism, M. Pochemukhin, *Rech'*, July 1990, 5.
41. V. Pribylovsky, *Pamyat'* (Panorama, Moscow, 1991) p. 8.
42. 'Davaite slovo', *Molodaya gvardiya*, 7, 1990, 143–4.
43. V. Kozhinov, *NS*, 10, 1987, 167–72.
44. A. Kuz'min, *NS*, 3, 1988, 154–6.
45. In a speech in Gorky to the Fifth VOOPIK Congress.
46. V. Rasputin, *NS*, 1, 1988, 170–71.
47. A. Kazintsev, *NS*, 6, 1988, 186–7.
48. S. Kunaev, *NS*, 6, 1989, 157–8.

49. S. Kunaev, *Molodoi leninets*, March 1989.
50. I. Glazunov, *Pravda*, 27 September 1987, 5.
51. V. Astafiev, *Pamyat'*, 1, 6 May 1990. Astafiev was later largely to abjure politics. He gradually distanced himself from *Nash sovremennik* and its views, denouncing the fascist threat on television in 1995 and pronouncing in favour of Yeltsin in 1996. See S. Reznik, *The Nazification of Russia* (Challenge Publications, Washington, 1996) pp. 89–93 for his controversy with Natan Eidelman over anti-Semitism and p. 142 for his later evolution.
52. S. Lezov, *Strana i mir*, 3, 1988.
53. 'Pis'mo', *Literaturnaya Rossiya*, 2 March 1990, 3. This letter was subsequently reproduced, with an approving introduction in the neo-fascist bulletin *Pamyat'*, 6 May 1990.
54. G. Petrov, *SK*, 24 November 1987, 3.
55. By A. Builov, see 'Izbrannye', *Nedelya*, 20–26 November 1989, 16.
56. D. Likhachev, *Lit. Gaz.*, 26 April 1989. F. Burlatsky, *Pravda*, 18 July 1989, 3. N. Ivanova, *Ogonek*, 11, 1988, 25–8 for polemics with right-wing intelligentsia. For condemnations of anti-Semitism see V. Bykov and A. Adamovich, *SK*, 10 December 1987, 6.
57. See W. Slater, 'Russia', *RFE/RL Research Report*, vol. III, no. 16 (22 April 1994) 27. R. Orttung, 'A politically-timed fight against extremism', *Transition*, vol. I, no. 10 (23 June 1995) 2–7.
58. R. Orttung, 'A politically-timed fight against extremism', *Transition*, vol. I, no. 10 (23 June 1995) 4–5.
59. Interviews with Ye. Proshchechkin, Moscow City Council deputy and head of the Anti-Fascist Centre, 17 July 1995, and A. Gerber, 14 July 1995.
60. For unsuccessful attempts to prosecute neo-fascists for racist propaganda, see V. Kornev, *Izvestiya*, 20 January 1995, 4; Ye. Solomenko, *Izvestiya*, 11 January 1995, 2; Ye. Solomenko, *Izvestiya*, 20 January 1995, 4; *Izvestiya*, 25 January 1995, 1. In two of three cases, the prosecutor's office initiated proceedings and in each instance the local court, despite the unambiguous evidence of the defendants' publications, rejected the prosecution's case.
61. A conference on this theme, in relation to the war in Chechnya, was held in Moscow on 20–22 January 1995. See *Fashizm v totalitarnom i posttotalitarnom obshchestve* (Moscow, Progress, 1995) esp. pp. 5–8 for Sergei Kovalev's intervention.
62. A number are described by V. Pribylovsky, 'A Survey of Right-Wing Radical Groups', *RFE/RL Research Report*, vol. III, no. 16 (22 April 1994) 28–37. See also *Soyuz russkikh venedov*, a pagan fascist group, whose programme is published in V. Berezovsky *et al.* (eds), *Rossiya: [...] dokumenty*, vol. IX (RAU, Moscow, 1993) pp. 146–7. 'Soyuz russkikh natsionalistov', *Russkii vestnik*, 12, 18–25 March 1992, 8–9; this group called for the revival of the Black Hundreds. Pribylovsky estimated that there were about fifteen strictly fascist groups in Russia in early 1995. See V. Pribylovsky, 'What awaits Russia', *Transition*, vol. I, no. 10 (23 June 1995) 7.

63. The RNU's co-founder, Viktor Yakushev, believed that Russia should seek salvation not in the West but in its Aryan racial energy. See interview published by Pribylovsky, *Panorama*, 28, July 1991, 1, 4. See too MBIO: Folder on *Yedinstvo*.
64. M. Gessen, *Novoe vremya*, 35, 1994, 16. See too V. Batuev, *AiF*, 9, 1995, 7. See too interview in *Moskovskii komsomolets*, 4 August 1993, 2, in which Barkashov is quoted as saying: 'I am not a fascist, I'm a Nazi'.
65. A. Barkashov, 'Printsipy Russkogo Natsional'nogo Yedinstva' in A. Barkashov, *Azbuka russkogo natsionalista* (Slovo, Moscow, 1994) pp. 28–9, 33–5.
66. A. Barkashov, 'Printsipy' in A. Barkashov, *Azbuka russkogo natsionalista* (Slovo, Moscow, 1994) p. 36.
67. A. Barkashov, 'Printsipy' in A. Barkashov, *Azbuka russkogo natsionalista* (Slovo, Moscow, 1994) pp. 26–7. NATO, the IMF and the UN were identified as other agents of this campaign. See A. Barkashov, *Russkii poryadok*, 2–3, 1994, 1.
68. A. Barkashov, 'Printsipy' in A. Barkashov, *Azbuka russkogo natsionalista* (Slovo, Moscow, 1994) p. 35.
69. Cited by V. Ostrosvetov, *MN*, 15, 1994, 7a.
70. A. Barkashov, 'Printsipy' in A. Barkashov, *Azbuka russkogo natsionalista* (Slovo, Moscow, 1994) pp. 38–9. Russian democrats were, he alleged, unrepresentative by virtue of their class (too many from the intelligentsia) and race (they were all Jewish, he asserted), semi-criminal and anti-national; pp. 30–33.
71. His apologia for the use of force was unabashed: 'Chat about "univeral values" and "civilised relations" are a simple deception'. A. Barkashov, 'Printsipy' in A. Barkashov, *Azbuka russkogo natsionalista* (Slovo, Moscow, 1994) pp. 40–41.
72. A. Barkashov, 'Printsipy' in A. Barkashov, *Azbuka russkogo natsionalista* (Slovo, Moscow, 1994) pp. 27–8. 'Osnovnye polozheniya programmy dvizheniya "Russkogo Natsionalnogo Yedinstva"', *Russkii poryadok*, December 1993–January 1994, 24–7. A. Barkashov, *Moskovskii komsomolets*, 4 August 1993, 2, where he comments that he would close this paper down.
73. V. Ostrosvetov, *MN*, 15, 1994, 7a.
74. See M. Gessen, *Novoe vremya*, 35, 1994, p. 16. A. Barkashov, *Moskovskii komsomolets*, 4 August 1993, 2.
75. A. Barkashov, 'Tol'ko molodaya natsional'naya elita', *Azbuka* (Slovo, Moscow, 1994) pp. 89–92. A. Barkashov, 'Printsipy' in ibid., p. 48.
76. A. Barkashov, 'Printsipy' in *Azbuka* (1994) pp. 46–50. For a good summary of its organisation see V. Gel'bras, *Kto yest' chto* vol. I (RAN, Moscow, 1994) pp. 430–37. V. Ostrosetov, *MN*, 15, 1994, 7a.
77. A. Barkashov, *Moskovskii komsomolets*, 4 August 1993, 2.
78. V. Ruga, *Vechernaya Moskva*, 17 December 1991. A. Barkashov, *Moskovskii komsomolets*, 4 August 1993, 2.
79. A. Chelnokov, *Izvestiya*, 4 January 1994, 1.
80. V. Gel'bras, *Kto yest' chto*, vol. I (RAN, Moscow, 1994) pp. 436–7. A. Chelnokov, *Izvestiya*, 4 January 1994, 1.

81. 'Sootechestvenniki', *Russkii poryadok*, December 1993–January 1994. A. Barkashov, *Russkii poryadok*, December 1993–January 1994, 4, 6. V. Gel'bras, *Kto yest' chto*, vol. I (RAN, Moscow, 1994) p. 437.

82. M. Deich, *Moskovskii komsomolets*, 11 May 1995, 2. A. Chelnokov, *Izvestiya*, 4 January 1994, 1.

83. L. Belin, 'Ultranationalist parties', *Transition*, vol. I, no. 10 (23 June 1995) 8; interview with Ye. Proshchechkin, 17 July 1995. By contrast, Pribylovsky downplayed its significance in: 'What awaits Russia', *Transition*, vol. I, no. 10 (23 June 1995) 7. Membership of the core RNU unit in early 1994 was usually set at 500: V. Ruga, *Vechernaya Moskva*, 17 December 1991. A. Chelnokov, *Izvestiya*, 4 January 1994, 1, thinks that it had about 2300 followers in all Russia. S. Simonsen, 'Alexander Barkashov and RNU', *Nationalities Papers*, vol. XXIV, no. 4 (December 1996) 625. V. Gel'bras, *Kto yest' chto*, vol. I (1994) p. 430; V. Ostrosetov, *MN*, 15, 1994, 7a believes that it enjoyed some support in the security services. Typical members, however, seem to have been unemployed, poorly educated young men. Barkashov himself, an electrician and karate instructor, belonged to the working class, V. Batuev, *AiF*, 36, 1993, 8; A. Chelnokov, *Izvestiya*, 15 January 1994, 7; V. Ostrosetov, *MN*, 15, 1994, 7a.

84. V. Ostrosetov, *MN*, 15, 1994, p. 7a.

85. S. Simonsen, 'Alexander Barkashov and RNU', *Nationalities Papers*, vol. XXIV, no. 4 (December 1996) 625. V. Tishkov, *Ethnicity, Nationalism and Conflict after the Soviet Union* (Sage Publications, London, 1997) p. 237.

86. Interview with Romanov, Irkutsk, 20 June 1996.

87. E. Limonov, interview in *Rossiya*, 24, 1994, 6. See Ye. Klepikova and V. Solovyov, *Zhirinovsky: the Paradoxes of Russian Fascism* (Viking, London, 1995) pp. 101–2. For Zhirinovsky's reply to Limonov's criticisms, see V. Zhirinovsky, *Posledny vagon na sever* 3rd edn (Conjou, Moscow, 1995) pp. 16–22. Zhirinovsky claims that he objected to Limonov's romanticising and celebrating violence and his calls to armed violence against the government.

88. E. Limonov, *MN*, 45, 1992, 16.

89. Limonov, *SR*, 20 June 1992, p. 3.

90. 'Deklaratsiya o sozdanii natsional'-bolshevistskoi partii' and 'Manifest rossiikogo natsionalizma' in *Programma natsional'-bolshevistkoi partii* (ndp) pp. 1–24. See too I. Torbakov, 'The Statists and the Ideology of Russian Imperial Nationalism', *RFE/RL Research Report*, vol. I, no. 49 (11 December 1992) 12 for discussion.

91. E. Limonov, *MN*, 45, 1992, 16.

92. See A. Dugin, 'Konservativnaya revolyutsiya', *Elementy*, 1, 1992, 15–16, 49–56.

93. A. Dugin, *Konservativnaya revolyutsiya* (Arktogeya, Moscow, 1994) pp. 136–7.

94. *Elementy*, 1, 1992.

95. A. Dugin, *Konservativnaya Revolyutsiya* (1994) pp. 137, 289–304, 340.

96. A. Dugin, *Tseli i zadachi* (Fravarti, Moscow, 1995) pp. 3–24.

97. A. Nevzorov, *Pole chesti* (Shans, St Petersburg, 1995) pp. 3–7, 13. For his defence of his programme, see ibid., pp. 107–9. 131.

98. A. Nevzorov, *Pole chesti* (Shans, St Petersburg, 1995) pp. 187–8.

99. A. Nevzorov, *Pole chesti* (Shans, St Petersburg, 1995) pp. 40, 13, 25, 38, 196.

100. A. Nevzorov, *Pole chesti* (Shans, St Petersburg, 1995) pp. 196–7.

101. 'It is our country, in which there should be one master, one president, one ruler. And in this terrible situation, it should be a very hard ruler [...] of genius, of universal attraction'. Nevzorov, *Pole chesti* (Shans, St Petersburg, 1995) p. 10.

102. A. Nevzorov, *Pole chesti* (Shans, St Petersburg, 1995) pp. 20–21, 144–5.

103. A. Nevzorov, *Pole chesti* (Shans, St Petersburg, 1995) p. 147.

104. A. Nevzorov, *Pole chesti* (Shans, St Petersburg, 1995) pp. 107–8, 118–19, 202–4, 261.

105. A. Nevzorov, *Pole chesti* (Shans, St Petersburg, 1995) p. 124.

106. See V. Pribylovsky, 'A Survey of Radical Right-Wing Groups in Russia', *The Politics of Intolerance: RFE/RL Research Report*, vol. III, no. 16 (22 April 1994) 31. A. Nevzorov, *Pole chesti* (Shans, St Petersburg, 1995) p. 19.

107. Cited by J. Dunlop, *The Rise of Russia* (Princeton University Press, Princeton, 1993) p. 182.

108. A. Nevzorov, *Pole chesti* (Shans, St Petersburg, 1995) p. 15.

109. V. Sirotkin, *MN*, 22, 1994, 8a. V. Nazarov, *Kuranty*, 28 March 1995, 1.

110. See A. Kuprach, *Lit. Rossiya*, 20 April 1990. *Golos Rossii*, 5, 1993, 1. The date on this paper looks questionable and both its content and style would suggest an earlier date. V. Gel'bras, *Kto yest' chto*, vol. I (RAN, Moscow, 1994) pp. 181–91 for an overview. V. Berezovsky *et al.* (eds), *Rossiya [...] dokumenty*, vol. VI (RAU, Moscow, 1992) pp. 145–69 for early documents and history.

111. N. Lysenko, 'Tret'ya sila' in V. Berezovsky *et al.* (eds), *Rossiya [...] dokumenty*, vol. VI (RAU, Moscow, 1992) p. 163. B. Koval' (ed.), *Rossiya segodnya* (Mezhdunarodnye otnosheniya, Moscow, 1993) pp. 317 ff.

112. N. Lysenko, *Golos Rossii*, 4, 1992, 3. He cites Kurginyan in this article. For more hostile remarks about the USA, see N. Lysenko, *MG*, 9, 1993, 201–3, where he also suggests that Russia, by contrast, incarnates the will of God and history. *Politicheskaya programma natsional'no-respublikanskoi partii Rossii* (no publisher, Moscow, 1992) pp. 7–8.

113. *Politicheskaya programma* (Moscow, 1992) p. 12.

114. N. Lysenko, *MG*, 9, 1993, 196–203.

115. *Politicheskaya programma* (Moscow, 1992) p. 8.

116. *Politicheskaya programma* (Moscow, 1992) p. 11.

117. See L. Belin, 'Ultranationalist Parties', *Transition*, vol. I, no. 10 (23 June 1995) 9–10.

118. *Politicheskaya programma* (Moscow, 1992) pp. 8–10, 13.

119. *Politicheskaya programma* (Moscow, 1992) pp. 8, 11–13, 18–19.

120. *Politicheskaya programma* (Moscow, 1992) pp. 13–15.

121. N. Lysenko, *Obshchaya gazeta*, 18–24 November 1994, 8 where he denies that he ever called himself a national-socialist but sees positive elements in national-socialism's programme. At the party's fourth congress in March 1995, he distanced himself from 'fascism, swastikas, germanophilia', partly on account of his disagreements with Barkashov, partly because of his desire to build up his parliamentary base. See L. Aleinik, *Sevodnya*, 20 March 1995, 1.

122. He served for some months on the NSF's coordinating committee, before resigning ostensibly on the grounds that it was a neo-communist organisation that wanted to restore the Soviet Union, and partly because of his incompatibility with one of the Front's leaders, the communist Chechen, Sazhi Umalatova. He broke with Sterligov over his alleged Eurasianism and acceptance of the loss of Belorussia and Ukraine. V. Gel'bras, *Kto yest' chto*, vol. I (RAN, Moscow, 1994) pp. 190–91. V. Pribylovsky, 'A Survey of Radical Right-Wing Groups in Russia', *The Politics of Intolerance: RFE/RL Research Report*, vol. III, no. 16 (22 April 1994) 30.

123. An exception to this was his relatively cordial relations with the LDPR, despite Lysenko's reservations about Zhirinovsky's personality. L. Aleinik, *Sevodnya*, 28 March 1995, 1. N. Lysenko, *Obshchaya gazeta*, 18–24 November 1994, 8.

124. This was ignored for a long time. See V. Sirotkin, *MN*, 22, 1994, 8a; V. Nazarov, *Kuranty*, 28 March 1995.

125. Attempts to attract attention and win votes included demonstrations on the floor of the parliament in April 1995, when he tore up the Ukrainian flag. Later efforts to moderate the party's rhetoric and the expulsion of some of its maximalists led to a split in the party. For Lysenko's election manifesto in 1995, see N. Lysenko, 'K bor'be', *Zavtra*, no. 49, 1995, 3.

126. M. Wyman, *Public Opinion* (Macmillan, London, 1997) pp. 134–6. G. Denisovsky, *Daidzhest*, 14, 1990, 10.

127. R. Brym and A. Degtarev, *Slavic Review*, vol. LII, no. 1, 1993, 4–5.

128. J. Gibson, *Slavic Review*, vol. LIII, no. 3, 1994, 796–805.

129. J. Gibson, *Slavic Review*, vol. LIII, no. 3, 1994, 797–8. B. Clarke, *An Empire's New Clothes* (Vintage, London, 1995) p. 149.

130. See S. Reznik, *The Nazification of Russia* (Challenge Publications, Washington, 1996) pp. 171–2. D. Gerasimov, *Pravda*, 5 May 1993, 4, for an example.

131. S. Carter 'The CIS and After' in L. Cheles, R. Ferguson and M. Vaughan (eds), *The Far Right in Western and Eastern Europe* (Longman, London and New York, 1995) p. 185. For the growth of racism, see J. Dunlop, 'Russia: in Search of an Identity?' in I. Bremmer and R. Taras (eds), *New States, New Politics: Building the Post-Soviet Nations* (CUP, Cambridge, 1997) pp. 60–61.

132. VTsIOM, *MN*, 20 1990, 9. J. Dunlop, 'Confronting Loss of Empire', *Political Science Quarterly*, vol. CVIII, no. 4 (Winter 1993–4) 625.

133. S. White, M. Wyman, O. Kryshtanovskaya, 'Parties and Politics in Post-Communist Russia', *Communist and Post-Communist Studies*, vol. XXVIII, no. 2, 1995, 190. For widespread recognition of *Pamyat'*

(and Cossacks, the LDPR and Nina Andreeva) see M. Wyman, *Public Opinion* (Macmillan, London, 1997) p. 142.

134. The Union of Patriots was established to fight the 1995 elections. The Russian Party was founded in May 1991 and was notorious for the suggestion, made by one of its ideologues, that Russia should establish a single 'racial space' from the Atlantic to the Pacific, with reservations for Yakuts, Jews and other minorities. They sold *Mein Kampf* and other anti-Semitic and fascist material. V. Gel'bras, *Kto yest' chto*, vol. I (RAN, Moscow, 1994) pp. 406, 408–11.

135. *Vybory deputatov Gosudarstvennoi Dumy 1995* (Ves' mir, Moscow, 1996) pp. 83, 90–91, 144, 163–98 for single seat results. S. Polivanov, *MN*, 10, 1996, 6, for an overview.

136. D. Chubukov, *MN*, 21, 1995, 7.

137. See G. Mosse, *The Crisis of German Ideology* (Weidenfeld and Nicolson, London, 1964) p. 10 who makes the same point about the rise of Völkish ideas in Germany.

3. RUSSIAN ORTHODOXY AND NATIONALISM

1. See P.D. Steeves, *Keeping the Faith: Religion and Ideology in the Soviet Union* (Holmes and Meir, NY and London, 1989) pp. 31–2.

2. See N. Davis, *A Long Walk to Church* (Westview, Boulder, San Francisco and Oxford, 1995) pp. 71–8, 94–7, 104–6. W. Laqueur, *Black Hundred* (Harper Collins, NY, 1994) pp. 225–43. B. Clarke, *An Empire's New Clothes* (Vintage, London, 1995) pp. 111–14. W. Slater and K. Engelbrecht, 'Eastern Orthodoxy defends its position', *RFE/RL*, vol. II, no. 35 (September 1993) 50–54. J. Dunlop, *The Rise of Russia* (Princeton University Press, Princeton, 1993) pp. 159–63.

3. For surveys which suggested that believers were more authoritarian than the rest of the population, see J. Anderson, *Religion, State and Politics* (CUP, Cambridge, 1994) p. 207. While about 41 per cent of Russians claimed, in the early 1990s, to be Orthodox believers, church attendance was low and ignorance and indifference common: see S. White, R. Rose and I. McAllister, *How Russia Votes* (Chatham House, Chatham, NJ, 1997) p. 65.

4. G. Yakunin, 'V sluzhenii kul'tu' in T. Ryabnikova (ed.), *K svobode sovesti* (Progress, Moscow, 1989) pp. 172–206, esp. 203–5. For his involvement in Democratic Russia, see Y. Brudny, 'The Dynamics of Democratic Russia', *Post-Soviet Russia*, Vol. IX, no. 2 (1993) pp. 156–7. B. Clarke, *An Empire's New Clothes* (Vintage, London, 1995) pp. 111–13, 143.

5. A. Men', *Panorama*, 13 December 1990, 1–2.

6. N. Davis, *Long Walk to Church* (Westview, Boulder, San Francisco and Oxford, 1995) p. 85.

7. A. Men', *Mirovaya dukhovnaya kul'tura* (Fond imeni A. Menya, Moscow, 1995) pp. 628–31.

8. A. Men', 'Religiya, kul't lichnosti i sekulyarnoe gosudarsto' in T. Ryabnikova (ed.), *K svobode sovesti* (Progress, Moscow, 1989) pp. 106–10.
9. A. Men', 'Religiya', in T. Ryabnikova (ed.), *K svobode sovesti* (Progress, Moscow, 1989) pp. 110, 101.
10. For a summary of subsequent developments, in the pursuit of his murderers, see V. Gomez, 'News from across the regions', *Transition* (12 July 1996) 2–3.
11. A. Chernov, *Ogonek*, 10, 5–12 March 1988, 9–12. See too D. Likhachev, *Lit. gaz.*, 9 Sep. 1987, p. 2.
12. See for example D. Likhachev, *Lit. gaz.*, 12 Dec. 1988, 5–6.
13. D. Likhachev, 'Memory Overcomes Time' in D. Likhachev, *Reflections on Russia* (Westview, Boulder, San Francisco and Oxford, 1991) pp. 156–7.
14. D. Likhachev, *Reflections on Russia* (Westview, Boulder, San Francisco and Oxford, 1991) pp. 54–9. 94.
15. An analogous group was Alexander Chuev's All-Russian Christian Democratic Party. See V. Gel'bras, *Kto yest' chto*, vol. I (RAN, Moscow, 1994) pp. 351–5.
16. V. Pribylovsky, *Slovar'* (Panorama, Moscow, 1991) pp. 97–8.
17. Rules of the CDUR, in *Khristiansko-demokraticheskii soyuz Rossii* (Overseas Publications Interchange, London, 1990) pp. 27–8; 33–4.
18. Basic Principles of the CDUR in ibid., pp. 7–9.
19. Rott, *AiF*, 13, 1990, p. 8.
20. Programme of the CDU in B. Koval' (ed.), *Rossiya segodnya* (Mezhdunarodnye otnosheniya, Moscow, 1991) p. 132.
21. Programme of the CDU in B. Koval' (ed.), *Rossiya segodnya* (Mezhdunarodnye otnosheniya, Moscow, 1991) pp. 133–4.
22. V. Pribylovsky, *Slovar'* (Panorama, Moscow, 1991) p. 99 for lower estimate. V. Berezovsky and N. Krotov, *Rossiya: partii*, vol. I, part 1 (RAU, Moscow, 1991) p. 120 give the figure of 3000. Sosnin, in an interview on 13 September 1991 estimated membership at 5000, V. Gel'bras, *Kto yest' chto* vol. I (RAN, Moscow, 1994) p. 510.
23. V. Pribylovsky, *Slovar'* (Panorama, Moscow, 1991) p. 99.
24. V. Gel'bras, *Kto yest' chto*, vol. I (RAN, Moscow, 1994) pp. 515–17.
25. A. Solzhenitsyn, 'Kak nam obustroit' Rossiyu', *Komsomolskaya pravda*, September 1990 (special supplement). Quotations here are taken from the English edition *Rebuilding Russia* (Harvill, London, 1991) pp. 9–10. Solzhenitsyn's major political writings are to be found in Russian in Solzhenitsyn, *Publitsistika*, vol. I, *Stat'i i rechi* (Verkhne-Volzhskoe knizhnoe izdatel'stvo, Yaroslavl', 1995).
26. A. Solzhenitsyn, *The Russian Question* (Harvill, London, 1995) pp. 104–7. See too interview with Solzhenitsyn, 'Wie ein Sekretär des Volkes', *Der Spiegel*, 44 (1994) 157.
27. A. Solzhenitsyn, 'Wie ein Sekretär des Volkes', *Der Spiegel*, 44 (1994) 157.
28. Solzhenitsyn, 'Wie ein Sekretär des Volkes', *Der Spiegel*, 44 (1994) 155.
29. A. Solzhenitsyn, Speech to the Duma, in *Russkaya mysl'*, 24 October 1994, 1. A. Higgins, *Independent on Sunday*, 19 May 1994, 13.

A. Solzhenitsyn, 'Wie ein Sekretär des Volkes', *Der Spiegel*, 44 (1994) 148, 152, 155. A. Solzhenitsyn, *The Russian Question* (Harvill, London, 1995) pp. 99–102, 106. A. Solzhenitsyn, *AiF*, 27, 1995, 3.

30. A. Solzhenitsyn, *Letter to the Soviet Leaders* (London, 1974) pp. 50–58. A. Solzhenitsyn, 'As Breathing and Consciousness Return', *From under the Rubble* (1974) pp. 19, 22–4.

31. A. Solzhenitsyn, *The Russian Question* (Harvill, London, 1995) p. 96.

32. A. Solzhenitsyn, *Rebuilding Russia* (Harvill, London, 1990) pp. 13–15, 20–21.

33. A. Solzhenitsyn, *Rebuilding Russia* (Harvill, London, 1990) p. 43. For similar views, see A. Solzhenitsyn, 'Wie ein Sekretär des Volkes', *Der Spiegel*, 44 (1994) 143.

34. Solzhenitsyn, *Rebuilding Russia* (Harvill, London, 1990) pp. 58–9. See A. Solzhenitsyn, 'Wie ein Sekretär des Volkes', *Der Spiegel*, 44 (1994) 141–2. A. Solzhenitsyn, *AiF*, 27, 1995, 3.

35. A. Solzhenitsyn, *Rebuilding Russia* (Harvill, London, 1990) pp. 71–3ff. See too *Der Spiegel*, 44 (1994) 143. A. Solzhenitsyn, *Rossiiskaya gazeta*, 11 March 1995, 1–2. A. Solzhenitsyn, *Russkaya mysl'*, 24 October 1994.

36. A. Galaktionov and P. Nikandrov, *Russkaya filosofiya* (Izdatel'stvo Leningradskogo universiteta, Leningrad, 1989) pp. 308–9. See F. Dostoevsky, *Diary of a Writer* (Ianmead, Haslemere, 1984) pp. 981–7.

37. A. Solzhenitsyn, *Rebuilding Russia* (Harvill, London, 1990) p. 44.

38. A. Solzhenitsyn, *Rebuilding Russia* (Harvill, London, 1990) p. 48.

39. Solzhenitsyn, *Rebuilding Russia* (Harvill, London, 1990), p. 44.

40. Ibid., pp. 43–4. For the reaction from the democratic camp see 'Kto poidet', *Panorama*, 12 October 1990, 1–2.

41. A. Solzhenitsyn, *The Russian Question* (Harvill, London, 1995) pp. 89–96. A. Solzhenitsyn, 'Wie ein Sekretär', *Der Spiegel*, 44 (1994) 160, 163. A. Solzhenitsyn, *Russkaya mysl'*, 24 October 1994, 2.

42. A. Solzhenitsyn, *AiF*, 27, 1995, 3.

43. See, for example, A. Solzhenitsyn, *The Russian Question* (Harvill, London, 1995) p. 96. Tolstaya, *NYRB*, 19 October 1995, 7–8 for an unenthusiastic review. Also A. Solzhenitsyn, *Russkaya mysl'*, 24 October 1994, 1; A. Solzhenitsyn, *Izvestiya*, 4 May 1994, 5.

44. A. Solzhenitsyn, *The Russian Question* (Harvill, London, 1995) pp. 39–40, 62.

45. See for example, his comments on the benefits of Russian rule of Siberia for the locals, and the Tsarist tradition of sacrificing the Russian heartland to the empire. A. Solzhenitsyn, *The Russian Question* (Harvill, London, 1995) pp. 66, 70–71.

46. A. Solzhenitsyn, *The Russian Question* (Harvill, London, 1995) p. 102. A. Solzhenitsyn, *AiF*, 27, 1995, 3.

47. Solzhenitsyn, 'Wie ein Sekretär', *Der Spiegel*, 44, 1994, p. 155.

48. See, for example, 'Repentance and Self-Limitation' (1973) in A. Solzhenitsyn, *From under the Rubble* (1974) pp. 138–40.

49. A. Solzhenitsyn, 'Address to the International Academy of Philosophy' (1993) in *The Russian Question* (Harvill, London, 1995) pp. 119, 127.

50. A. Solzhenitsyn, *The Russian Question* (Harvill, London, 1995) p. 108. Solzhenitsyn, 'Wie ein Sekretär', *Der Spiegel*, 44 (1994) 146.

51. See V. Krasnov, *Russia beyond Communism* (Westview Press, Boulder, San Francisco and Oxford, 1991) pp. 57–64.
52. For reactions to the Duma speech, see M. Gokhman and V. Yelseenko, *RM*, 24 October 1994; V. Vyzhutovich, *Izvestiya*, 1 November 1994; L. Timofeev, *RM*, 10–16 November 1994. For the meeting with Yeltsin, see A. Plutnik, *Izvestiya*, 17 November 1994. *Rebuilding Russia* (1990) sold 26.5 million copies in 1990, *Der Spiegel*, 44, 1994, 137.
53. See T. Tolstaya, *NYRB*, 19 October 1995, 7–8.
54. V. Aksyuchits, *Golos*, 32, 1993, 6.
55. *Put': Gazeta rossiiskogo khristianskogo demokraticheskogo dvizheniya*, 3 October 1990, 1. B. Koval' (ed.), *Rossiya segodnya* (Mezhdunarodnye otnosheniya, 1991) p. 137.
56. V. Pribylovsky, *Slovar'* (Panorama, Moscow, 1991) p. 74. *Put'* 3, October 1990, 1.
57. 'Osnovnye polozheniya politicheskoi programmy RKhDD' in *Rossiiskoe khristianskoe demokraticheskoe dvizhenie: sbornik materialov* (Vybor, Moscow, 1990) p. 38.
58. 'Deklaratsiya RKhDD' in *RKhDD: sbornik* (Vybor, Moscow, 1990) p. 26.
59. 'Deklaratsiya' in *RKhDD: sbornik* (Vybor, Moscow, 1990) pp. 33–4.
60. 'Deklaratsiya' in *RKhDD: sbornik* (Vybor, Moscow, 1990) pp. 34–5. See too for similar thoughts about the Russians as God's chosen people, V. Aksyuchits, 'Russkaya ideya' in Ye. Trotsky (ed.), *Russkaya ideya* (Assotsiatsiya po izucheniyu russkoi natsii, Moscow, 1992) pp. 49–51.
61. 'Deklaratsiya' in *RKhDD: sbornik* (Vybor, Moscow, 1990) p. 23.
62. 'Programma' in *RKhDD sbornik* (Vybor, Moscow, 1990) pp. 39–47.
63. 'Programma' in *RKhDD sbornik* (Vybor, Moscow, 1990) pp. 48–50.
64. By Autumn 1990, the RKhDD claimed 12 000 to 15 000 members. Interview with N. Setyukova, 27 November 1990. V. Aksyuchits, *MN*, 21, 1990, 6. V. Pribylovsky, *Slovar'* (Panorama, Moscow, 1991) p. 75 estimates that the Party might have counted 500 members. G. Satarov, *Partiinaya zhizn'* (conference paper, 1991, paper courtesy of the author) p. 1 doubts the claims about membership of all new parties, believing that most counted no more than a few hundred or a few thousand members.
65. In April 1991, the RKhDD formed, with Travkin's Democratic Party and Astafiev's Kadets, a united right-wing bloc within the democratic opposition, Popular Accord, pledged to defend strong State structures. They proclaimed their desire to retain the unity and territorial integrity of the Russian Federation and of the new Union State which would emerge from a transformed USSR. MBIO Archive: *Deklaratsiya [...] Narodnogo Soglasiya* (1991).
66. For example, holding talks with Sergei Baburin, of the *Rossiya* group and Viktor Alksnis, formerly of *Soyuz*, in October and November 1991.
67. In August 1991, Father Gleb Yakunin resigned, criticising the RKhDD's growing emphasis on the State. By February and March 1992, open dissension had broken out in the ranks over the increasingly authoritarian and nationalist positions adopted by the Movement and its dubious alliances. On 25 March 1992, Valery Senderov resigned,

observing that 'the Movement has degenerated into a red-brown pro-USSR political group'. N. Babasyan, *Ekspress khronika*, 13, (243) 1992, 7.

68. T. Mikhalskaya, *MN*, 34, 23–30 August 1992, 14.

69. 'Osnovnye polozheniya politicheskoi programmy RKhDD' in V. Aksyuchits (ed.), *Vozrozhdenie Rossii* (Vybor, Moscow, 1993) pp. 36–7.

70. 'Osnovnye polozheniya ' in V. Aksyuchits (ed.), *Vozrozhdenie Rossii* (Vybor, Moscow, 1993) pp. 40–41.

71. 'Osnovnye polozheniya' in V. Aksyuchits (ed.), *Vozrozhdenie Rossii* (Vybor, Moscow, 1993) pp. 41, 55. See too M. Razoronova, *Kentavr*, November–December 1992, 108 for an acid assessment of the June 1992 party congress.

72. See, for example, V. Aksyuchits, *Pravda*, 15 October 1992, 1.

73. V. Aksyuchits, *NG*, 23 October 1992, 2; V. Aksyuchits, *Golos*, 32, 1993, 6.

74. 'Deklaratsiya RKhDD' in V. Aksyuchits, *Vozrozhdenie* (Vybor, Moscow, 1993) pp. 17–22. V. Aksyuchits, *Pravda*, 15 October 1992.

75. V. Gel'bras, *Kto yest' chto*, vol. I (1994) pp. 404–5.

76. V. Aksyuchits, *Golos*, 32, 1993, 6. See too M. Razoroneva, *Kentavr*, November–December 1992, 107–8.

77. 'Osnovnye polozheniya ' in V. Aksyuchits (ed.), *Vozrozhdenie Rossii* (Vybor, Moscow, 1993) pp. 43, 46–9, 59. Aksyuchits's own writing contrasted the formal, negative and egotistical freedom of the West with Russia's superior inner creative freedom, 'Russkaya ideya' in Ye. Trotsky (ed.), *Russkaya ideya* (Assotsiatsiya po izucheniyu russkoi natsii, Moscow, 1992) pp. 55–6.

78. See V. Gel'bras, *Kto yest' chto*, vol. I (RAN, Moscow, 1994) pp. 130–32.

79. Z. Krakhmal'nikova, *Stolitsa*, 50, 1993, 8.

80. V. Lvov and D. Savin, *Sevodnya*, 3 September 1994.

81. M. Razoroneva, *Kentavr*, November–December 1992, 103. R. Sakwa, *Sotsis*, 7, 1993, 131 for another asessment.

82. V. Berezovsky and N. Krotov (eds), *Rossiya: partii*, vol. I, part 1 (RAU, Moscow, 1991) p. 118. The writer V. Soloukin was elected its leader.

83. M. Antonov, *Russkii vestnik*, 17–24 June 1992, 6. See too V. Berezovsky *et al.*, *Rossiya [...] dokumenty*, vol. IX (RAU, Moscow, 1993) pp. 153–4 for its manifesto. A similar outlook was expressed by the Orthodox-nationalist group, *Vernost'* in Irkutsk.

84. 'Izbrannye', *Nedelya*, 20–26 November 1989, 16.

85. See *Put'*, 7 October 1991, 6.

86. V. Shtep, *NS*, 8, 1992, 122.

87. S. Engelhardt-Yurkov, *AiF*, 16, 1990, 8. S. Engelhardt-Yurkov, *Dialog*, 17, 1990, 37–8. Berezovsky *et al.*, *Rossiya [...] dokumenty*, vol. VI (RAU, Moscow, 1992) pp. 85–8 for its manifesto.

88. Berezovsky *et al.* (eds), *Rossiya [...] dokumenty*, vol. VI (RAU, Moscow, 1992) p. 85, who estimates that its membership fell from a maximum of up to 70 to about 10 in 1992.

89. In December 1988, he founded the Christian Patriotic Union, inspired by the group 'For the spiritual and biological salvation of the Nation'. Its aims included: 'the spiritual and moral renewal of society and the rebirth of the national-patriotic self-consciousness of the Russian

peoples'. V. Pribylovsky, *Slovar'* (Panorama, Moscow, 1991) p. 100. V. Berezovsky and N. Krotov, *Rossiya: partii [...]*, vol. I, part 1 (RAU, Moscow, 1991) p. 120.

90. In one report, the group was said to view the period since 1917 as 'the reign of Anti-Christ' and to be concerned above all with preventing 'the coming catastrophe' by uniting all Orthodox believers to fight for the restoration of the monarchy, *Russkoe tovarishchestvo*, 3 (1990) 6.

91. Cited in V. Berezovsky *et al.* (eds), *Rossiya [...] dokumenty*, vol X (RAU, Moscow, 1993) pp. 67–8. See too V. Osipov, *Obozrevatel'*, 2–3, February 1992, 4.

92. S. Ivanenko, *MN*, 43, 1990, 8–9. G. Razh, *Panorama*, 12, October 1990, 7. Both the Union of the Russian People and the Black Hundreds have been revived in modern Russia, see V. Pribylovsky, 'A Survey of Radical Right-Wing Groups in Russia', *The Politics of Intolerance: RFE/RL Research Report*, vol. III, no. 16 (22 April 1994) 36.

93. In the obscure National-Orthodox Movement. See V. Pribylovsky, *Slovar'* (Panorama, Moscow, 1991) pp. 95–6, 100.

94. V. Pribylovsky, *Slovar'* (Panorama, Moscow, 1991) p. 82. V. Berezovsky *et al.* (eds), *Rossiya [...] dokumenty*, vol. VIII (RAU, Moscow, 1992) pp. 159–60.

95. Even more extreme than Osipov's Union was V. Demin's Union of the Russian People, founded in August 1991 and inspired by Viktor Ostretov's work on the pre-revolutionary organisation.) Demin published a *samizdat* newssheet *Zemshchina* which boasted the slogan: 'To hell with democracy but monarchy is of heaven!' It printed articles about the coming of Anti-Christ, supposedly edifying, apocalyptic scriptural readings and fulminating articles on current affairs (for example: 'The End of the West: The West is coming to the end of its days of Sodomite well-being; Babylonish America is on the threshold of its apocalyptic death!' with quotations from the Bible to prove the point). See *Zemshchina*, 7, 1990; *Zemshchina*, 14, 1990. See V. Pribylovsky, *Slovar'* (Panorama, Moscow, 1991) p. 95. Close in outlook to Demin was Anton Tuskarev, who proposed restoring the authoritarian nationalism associated with the reign of Nicholas I and elaborated by his Education Minister, Uvarov. '"Orthodoxy, Autocracy, Nationality" is the basis of Russian national consciousness', Tuskarev declared. For him, Russia's future did not lie in following the path taken by other countries. The Godless, democratic West was to be rejected: 'Christianity and democracy are as incompatible as genius and villainy [...] Democracy denies and destroys the hierarchy and world order established by God and it makes its appearance in the world amid the hellish flames of revolution and thus its fundamental principle is without question evil, demonic'. Democracy destroyed nations, while monarchy was natural and God-given: A. Tuskarev, *Russkii vestnik*, 11–18 March 1992, 12–13.

96. For Cossacks, see V. Berezovsky *et al.* (eds), *Rossiya [...] dokumenty*, vol. X (RAU, Moscow, 1993) pp. 3–37. V. Sergeev, *Dvizhenie za vozrozhdenie kazachestva* (Severo-Kavkazskii kadrovy tsentr, Rostov-on-Don, 1993). S. Dontsov, *Russkii vestnik*, 45–52, 1994, 8–9. See too

F. Belelyubski, *Pravda*, 17 November 1993, 4 for xenophobic, authoritarian views expressed at the 2nd Congress of the All-Russian Monarchist Centre.

97. V. Pribylovsky, *Slovar'* (Panorama, Moscow, 1991) p. 93. For a discussion of the Cossack revival, see W. Laqueur, *Black Hundred* (Harper Collins, NY, 1994) pp. 192–203.

98. V. Berezovsky *et al.* (eds), *Rossiya: [...] dokumenty*, vol. X (RAU, Moscow, 1993) pp. 3–37 for their early proclamations.

99. V. Sergeev, *Dvizhenie za vozrozhdenie kazachestva* (Severo-Kavkazskii kadrovy tsentr, Rostov-on-Don, 1993) pp. 36–40.

100. S. Dontsov, *Russkii vestnik*, 45–52, 1994, 8–9. This interview enumerates the main Cossack groups and discusses Yeltsin's attempts to win them to his side in 1994. For an account of their reorganisation and rearmament, intolerant nationalism and Yeltsin's decision to court them, see G. Mashtakova, *MN*, 17–18, 1996, 6.

101. For a similar rehearsal of classic Slavophile views, see V. Aksyuchits, 'Russkaya ideya' in Ye. Trotsky (ed.), *Russkaya ideya* (Assotsiatsiya po izucheniyu russkoi natsii, Moscow, 1992) pp. 55–6.

102. V. Rasputin, *Rossiya: dni i vremena* (Pis'mena, Irkutsk, 1993) pp. 151–4, 161, 191.

103. V. Rasputin, *Rossiya: dni i vremena* (Pis'mena, Irkutsk, 1993) pp. 50–51, 56–60, 64.

104. See *Antikhrist v Moskve* (Novaya kniga, Moscow, 1995) for a collection of its protests, mostly written by Father Alexander Shargunov.

105. See V. Krasnov,'Russian National Feeling' in R. Conquest (ed.), *The Last Empire* (Hoover Institution, Stanford, 1986) pp. 110–15. J. Dunlop, *Russian Nationalism* (Princeton University Press, Princeton, 1983) pp. 122–9. D. Pospielovsky, *Soviet Studies on the Church* (Macmillan, London, 1988) pp. 162–3. D. Spechler, 'Russian Nationalism' in L. Hajda and M. Beissinger (eds), *The Nationalities Factor in Soviet Politics* (Westview, Boulder, San Francisco and Oxford, 1990) p. 295.

106. I. Glazunov, *Pravda*, 27 September 1987.

107. Glazunov quoted in V.S. Novikov (ed.), *Ilya Glazunov* vol. I (Avrora, Leningrad, 1992) p. 7. See too I. Glazunov, *Pravda*, 11 June 1985; I. Glazunov, *Den'*, 5, March 1991; V.S. Novikov, *Ilya Glazunov* (Golos, Moscow, 1994) p. 52.

108. I. Glazunov, *Den'*, 5 March 1991.

109. M. Lemeshev, *Vozroditsya li Rossiya?* (Voronezh, Moscow, 1994) pp. 3–25, 59, 75, 151–2.

110. M. Lemeshev, *Vozroditsya li Rossiya?* (Voronezh, Moscow, 1994) p. 153.

111. M. Lemeshev, *Vozroditsya li Rossiya?* (Voronezh, Moscow, 1994) pp. 162–3.

112. Another example is the 1996 Presidential candidate, writer and Olympic champion, Yuri Vlasov, who moved from supporting democratic reform to authoritarian nationalism in the post-Soviet period. See Yu. Vlasov, *Rus' bez vozhdya* (Soyuz zhurnalistov, Voronezh, 1995) especially pp. 97–104, 495–512.

113. S. White, R. Rose and I. McAllister, *How Russia Votes* (Chatham House, Chatham, NJ, 1997) p. 47. Yuri Fedorovich Orlov ascribed the

intelligentsia's support for the Society of Russian Scientists for Socialism to the impoverishment of Russian science: interview, Irkutsk, 20 June 1996. Professor Rurik Salaev offered a similar analysis of support for the brands of nationalism offered by Zyuganov and Lebed, interview, Irkutsk, 21 June 1996.

114. For examples, including the Russian Party, see V. Gel'bras, *Kto yest' chto*, vol. I (RAN, Moscow, 1994) pp. 157–65, 406–11.

115. 'Opredeleniya', *Zhurnal' Moskovskoi Patriarkhii*, 12, December 1990, 8.

116. N. Babasyan, *NG*, 21 May 1992. By the following summer, 80 brotherhoods were said to exist, Babasyan, *NG*, 11 July 1992. Other estimates of the Union's membership were much lower, see O. Antic, 'Revival of Orthodox Brotherhoods', *RFE/RL Research Report*, vol. I, no. 11 (13 March 1992) 63.

117. O. Antic, 'Revival of Orthodox Brotherhoods', *RFE/RL Research Report*, vol. I, no. 11 (13 March 1992) 62.

118. N. Babasyan, *NG*, 11 July 1992.

119. N. Babasyan, *NG*, 21 May 1992.

120. D. Shusharin, *NG*, 21 May 1992.

121. The fundamentalists, in an open letter to the Patriarch in late 1995, attacked Roman Catholic expansionism which the authors discerned in the Uniates' seizure of Orthodox churches in the Ukraine and the 'bloody war' and 'genocide of Orthodox believers' in the Balkans. Russia had every reason to be on its guard against this pernicious neighbour, which had allies within Russia and even in the Church itself, in the shape of 'modernisers' and 'renewers'. Church reformers, such as Father Georgy Kochetkov and his congregation, belonged to the Vatican's fifth column in the Church. One of the brotherhood's leaders attacked him at a church conference in November 1994, accusing him of trying to provoke a schism in the Church and subverting Orthodoxy. Finally the Patriarch bent under the pressure and ended Kochetkov's innovatory ministry: see A. Shatov *et al.*, *RM*, 21–7 December 1995, 9; D. Pospielovsky, 'Impressions', *Religion, State and Society*, vol. XXIII, no. 3 (1995) 255; Yu. Tabak, *RM*, 24–30 November 1994, 8. G. Scorer, 'New Old Believers', Paper presented to the BASEES Conference, March 1996.

122. See D. Pospielovsky, 'The Russian Orthodox Church' in M. Bourdeaux (ed.), *Politics of Religion* (M.E. Sharpe, Armonk, NY, and London, 1995) p. 62. D. Pospielovsky, 'Impressions of the Contemporary Russian Orthodox Church', *Religion, State and Society*, vol. XXIII, no. 3 (1995) 253.

123. 'Molim vas', *SR*, 18 February 1993.

124. D. Pospielovsky, 'Impressions', *Religion, State and Society*, no. 3, 1995, 259.

125. P. Scorer, 'New Old Believers', Paper presented to BASEES Conference, March 1996, p. 3.

126. D. Pospielovsky in M. Bourdeaux (ed.), *Politics of Religion* (M.E. Sharpe, Armonk, NY, and London, 1995) pp. 47, 57. Bychkov, *MN*, 7 March 1993, 7b.

127. See J. Dunlop, 'The Russian Orthodox Church' in M. Bourdeaux, *Politics of Religion* (M.E. Sharpe, Armonk, NY, and London, 1995)

p. 34, for a campaign trip by anti-reform Russian parliamentarians reportedly funded by the diocese of St Petersburg and the monastery at Zagorsk.

128. See J. Dunlop, 'The Russian Orthodox Church' in M. Bourdeaux, *Politics of Religion* (M.E. Sharpe, Armonk, NY, and London, 1995) pp. 15–16. The Church's involvement in this forum was defended by the liberal priest Vsevolod Chaplin, see Chaplin in ibid., pp. 106–9. Chaplin quoted the Patriarch as condemning chauvinism and autocracy and pronouncing in favour of pluralism, civic rights and constitutional government (though not in this forum).

129. For his background, see *Zhurnal' Moskovskoi Patriarkhii*, 1, 1991, 22.

130. See Ioann, 'The West Wants Class War' reprinted in N. Nielsen (ed.), *Christianity after Communism* (Westview, Boulder, San Francisco and Oxford, 1994), pp. 108–11. J. Dunlop, 'The Russian Orthodox Church' in M. Bourdeaux, *Politics of Religion* (M.E. Sharpe, Armonk, NY, and London, 1995) p. 32; J. Anderson, *Religion, State and Politics* (CUP, Cambridge, 1994) pp. 212–13; V. Wozniuk, 'In search of Right-Wing Nationalism', *Nationalities Papers*, vol. XXV, no. 2, (June 1997) 197 for other examples of Ioann's xenophobic and authoritarian views.

131. Ioann, *Samoderzhavie dukha* (Tsarskoe delo, St Petersburg, 1995) pp. 340, 345–6.

132. Ioann, *Samoderzhavie dukha* (Tsarskoe delo, St Petersburg, 1995) pp. 343–5.

133. Ioann, *Samoderzhavie dukha* (Tsarskoe delo, St Petersburg, 1995) p. 345.

134. Ioann, *Samoderzhavie dukha* (Tsarskoe delo, St Petersburg, 1995) p. 339.

135. Ioann, *Tvorenie dobra i pravy* (RNS, Moscow, 1993) pp. 4–9.

136. Ioann, 'Pravoslavnaya revolyutsiya', *Elementy*, 4, 1993, 18–19.

137. Z. Krakhmal'nikova, *Stolitsa*, 50, 1993, 7.

138. See N. Davis, *Long Walk to Church* (Westview, Boulder, San Francisco and Oxford, 1995) pp. 106–7. K. Dashiwa and B. Parrott, *Russia and the New States of Eurasia* (CUP, Cambridge, 1994) pp. 96, 98–9 for clerical alliances with the extreme right.

139. J. Dunlop, 'The Russian Orthodox Church' in M. Bourdeaux (ed.), *The Politics of Religion* (M.E. Sharpe, Armonk, NY, and London, 1995) p. 35. See also J. Anderson, *Religion, State and Politics* (CUP, Cambridge, 1994) pp. 212–13; R. Sakwa, *Russian Politics and Society*, 2nd edn. (Routledge, London and New York, 1996) p. 377 for the undemocratic and romantic nationalism of Metropolitan Innokenty of Khabarovsk. For condemnations of anti-Semitism by Orthodox clergy and believers, see Fr Andrei Kurayev, *Religion, State and Society*, vol. XXIII, no. 1 (1995) 37–8; Fr Alexander Borisov in ibid., 33–5; Zoya Krakhmal'nikova in ibid., vol. XX, no. 1 (1992) 7–28.

140. See P. Reeves, *The Independent*, 23 September 1997. On deteriorating relations between Rome and Moscow, see B. Johnston and C. White, *The Catholic Herald*, 20 June 1997.

141. See 'V ozhidanii', *RM*, 1–7 December 1994, 1. For attempts by the political elite to court the Church and the Church's attempts to entrench

itself in the State, see V. Wozniuk, 'In Search of Right-Wing Nationalism', *Nationalities Papers*, vol. XXV, no. 2 (June 1997) 198–205.

142. The Church tried to dissociate itself from anti-Semitism however, as did Senderov, Yakunin and others. See the latter's 'Open Letter and Church Leaders' published in *Informatsionny bulleten' po problemam repatriatsii i yevreiskoi kul'tury*, July–August 1990, pp. 156–60.

143. The Union of Vedists, a proto-fascist Leningrad group, was interested in ancient Aryan religion, which they believed to be a form of ancient Slav paganism, see V. Pribylovsky, *Slovar'* (Panorama, Moscow, 1991) pp. 90–91. For Viktor Yakushev's *Yedinstvo*, see MBIO Folder on *Yedinstvo*; V. Ruga, *Vechernaya Moskva*, 17 December 1991; G. Satarov, *Partiinaya zhizn'* (Conference paper, Moscow, 1991) pp. 10–11.

144. A. Lanshchikov, *Perestroika* (Otechestvo, Moscow, 1989) pp. 13–14.

145. A. Prokhanov, *Russkoe tovarishchestvo*, September 1990, 7.

146. See I. Shafarevich, *Perestroika* (Otechestvo, Moscow, 1989) pp. 24–7. A. Solzhenitsyn, *Rebuilding Russia* (Harvill, London, 1991) pp. 44–7.

147. See General Lebed's dismissive remarks on this vogue, in A. Lebed, *Za derzhavu obidno* (Gregory Page, Moscow, 1995) p. 364.

4. THE GENESIS OF THE AUGUST COUP

1. Y. Brudny, 'The Heralds of Opposition to Perestroyka', in A. Hewett and V. Winston (eds), *Milestones in Glasnost and Perestroyka* (The Brookings Institution, Washington, 1991) pp. 178–9; V. Shlapentokh, *Soviet Intellectuals and Political Power* (I.B. Tauris, London and New York, 1990) pp. 81–3.

2. J. Devlin, *The Rise of the Russian Democrats* (Edward Elgar, Aldershot, 1995) p. 129.

3. On 13 June 1989, its first meeting was held in Leningrad. A month later on 15–16 July 1989 the all-Union OFT was established (with 83 delegates from 18 cities and six Union Republics attending, including the Russian Inter-Movements from the Baltics). This was followed up on 8–9 September 1989 by the foundation of the RSFSR (or Russian Republic) OFT, at which 103 delegates represented 39 towns. Finally, on 2 December 1989, the Moscow OFT was founded. See V. Berezovsky and N. Krotov, *Neformal'naya Rossiya* (Molodaya gvardiya, Moscow, 1990) pp. 309–10; A. Gromov and O. Kuzin, *Neformaly: kto yest' kto* (Mysl', Moscow, 1990) pp. 222–3; V. Pribylovsky, *Slovar' novikh politicheskikh partii* (Panorama, Moscow, 1991) p. 53.

4. Western analysts have pointed to the movement's officious character, observing that Party leaders in Leningrad had taken part in its foundation and that a number of provincial Party officials were elected to its coordinating council. Soviet commentators also claimed that the OFT was supported by leaders of the official trade unions. V. Tolz, *The USSR's Emerging Multi-Party System* (Praeger, New York and London, 1990) pp. 61–2; A. Roxburgh, *The Second Russian Revolution* (BBC Books, London, 1991) p. 153; B. Kagarlitsky, 'Yeshcho odno zharkoe

leto' in S. Yushenkov (ed.), *Neformaly, sotsial'nye initsiativy* (Moskovskii rabochii, Moscow, 1990) p. 135, n. 1.

5. 'Dveri', *Leningradskaya pravda*, 8 June 1989.
6. Cited in A. Gromov and O. Kuzin, *Neformaly: kto yest' kto* (Mysl', Moscow, 1990) p. 214; 'OFT', *Leningradskaya Pravda*, 14 June 1989 for further details.
7. Cited in A. Gromov and O. Kuzin, *Neformaly: kto yest' kto* (Mysl', Moscow, 1990) p. 226.
8. It demanded changes to the electoral system (factory-based elections and Soviets), monetary reform aimed at confiscating unearned incomes, an end to market reforms and a restoration of the command economy. See V. Pribylovsky, *Slovar' novikh politicheskikh partii* (Panorama, Moscow, 1991) p. 53; V. Berezovsky and N. Krotov, *Rossiya: partii*, vol. I, part 2 (RAU, Moscow, 1991) pp. 327–8, where the coincidence between the OFT's demands and Prime Minister Pavlov's subsequent policies emerges clearly; A. Levikov, *MN*, 32, 1989, p. 10 for a leaflet by A. Pyzhkov for an apologia of the command system.
9. A. Gromov and O. Kuzin, *Neformaly: kto yest' kto* (Mysl', Moscow, 1990) pp. 216–17.
10. A. Gromov and O. Kuzin, *Neformaly: kto yest' kto* (Mysl', Moscow, 1990) pp. 215–17.
11. A similarity in atmosphere may also be noted. One Leningrad OFT leader was reported as crying: 'Around us are enemies. Enemies are springing up like mushrooms [...]'. Cited in V. Churbanov and A. Nelyubin, 'Neformalnye ob"edineniya i perestroika' in V. Pechenev and V. Vyunsky (eds), *Neformaly: kto oni, kuda zovut?* (Politizdat, Moscow, 1990) p. 36.
12. At a meeting in Moscow on 15 November 1990, Rumyantsev's draft Russian Constitution was denounced by the OFT as a bourgeois document, heralding counter-revolution, the exploitation of workers and their loss of social security rights.
13. For its 1 December 1990 meeting, critical of the reforms, see V. Berezovsky and N. Krotov, *Rossiya: partii*, vol. I, part 2 (RAU, Moscow, 1991) p. 328. Its third Congress, in March 1991, characterised Gorbachev's policies as 'right-opportunist, capitulationist, fatal for the Party' (and expelled Yarin for having associated himself with Gorbachev's policies), V. Pribylovsky, *Slovar' novikh politicheskikh partii* (Panorama, Moscow, 1991) p. 53.
14. R. Orttung, 'The Russian Right and the Dilemmas of Party Organisation', *Soviet Studies*, vol. XLIV, no. 3, (1992) 450, 456–7; M. Urban, *The Rebirth of Politics in Russia* (CUP, Cambridge, 1997) pp. 179–82. A. Pyzhkov got less than 1 per cent of the vote, when he stood for election in Leningrad on what was essentially the OFT's platform, V. Tolz, *Russia's Emerging Multi-Party System* (Praeger, London and New York, 1990) p. 66. Its programme was entitled *Rodina bol'na. Kak ei pomoch?*, dated December 1989.
15. I. Malyarov, *Lit. Gaz.*, 20 March 1991, 3.
16. Alexei Sergeev was elected to the Central Committee of the CPSU by the Twenty-eighth Party Congress in July 1990, while other OFT

leaders, like Victor Tyulkin and Ivan Boltovsky, were elected to the newly formed Russian Party Central Committee. Veniamin Yarin, one of the Presidents of the Russian OFT, was selected by Gorbachev for his Presidential Council on its creation in March 1990.

17. B. Kagarlitsky, 'Yeshcho odno zharkoe leto' in S. Yushenkov (ed.), *Neformaly, sotsial'nye initsiativy* (Moskovskii rabochii, Moscow, 1990) p. 135, n. 1.

18. V. Tolz, *Russia's Emerging Multi-Party System* (Praeger, London and New York, 1990) p. 67.

19. V. Berezovsky and N. Krotov, *Neformal'naya Rossiya* (Molodaya gvardiya, Moscow, 1990) p. 61 assimilate the Russian Centre with various *Pamyat'* organisations. The Centre was founded after a split within *Pamyat'* in 1987, according to V. Berezovsky and N. Krotov, *Rossiya: partii*, vol. I, part 1 (RAU, Moscow, 1991) p. 69. V. Pribylovsky, *Pamyat'* (Panorama, Moscow, 1991) pp. 2, 6–7, asserts that the Russian Centre was originally part of Igor Sychev's branch of *Pamyat'*.

20. See T. Sergeeva, 'U Pamyati svoi zakony', *Moskovskaya pravda*, 19 May 1988. Sergeeva conducted an extensive interview with leaders of Sychev's *Pamyat'* including Ponomareva: Ponomareva explained *Pamyat'*'s work in cultural terms and, with Sychev (a *Pamyat'* leader and member of the Artists' Union) praised *Pamyat'*'s cultural activities in this interview. V. Pribylovsky, *Pamyat'* (Panorama, Moscow, 1991) pp. 2, 6–7, affirms that the Moscow Party ordered Ponomareva to 'normalise the situation' in *Pamyat'*. See too Yu. Kazarin and A. Russovsky, *Vechernaya Moskva*, 25 February 1988.

21. V. Surkova, *Vechernaya Moskva*, 7 December 1988.

22. See J. Dunlop, *The Rise of Russia* (Princeton University Press, Princeton, 1993) pp. 131–2, who quotes an appeal published by its organisers in *Moskovskii literator* on 16 December 1988.

23. *Russkoe tovarishchestvo*, September 1990, 1.

24. Ibid., p. 1.

25. Communists and non-communists, imperialists and village-writers supported the Fellowship. The editorial board of its paper, *Russian Fellowship*, included the former political prisoner and novelist Leonid Borodin, the imperialist writer of war novels, Alexander Prokhanov, the village writers Valentin Rasputin and Vasily Belov. Other supporters included the critics Eduard Volodin, Vadim Kozhinov and Alexander Kazintsev and the film-maker Sergei Bondarchuk. 'Tovarishchestvo', *Literaturnaya gazeta*, 29 March 1989, 7. V. Berezovsky and N. Krotov, *Neformal'naya Rossiya* (Molodaya gvardiya, Moscow, 1990) pp. 339–40. Some numbers of the paper may be consulted at the MBIO: Folder *Russkoe tovarishchestvo*.

26. For the Intermovements, which were among the most successful Russian nationalist movements, see Dunlop, *The Rise of Russia* (Princeton University Press, Princeton, 1993) pp. 136–9.

27. *Moskovskaya pravda*, 15 June 1990; *Literaturnaya Rossiya*, 28 July 1989; V. Pribylovsky, *Slovar' novikh politicheskikh partii* (Panorama, Moscow, 1991) p. 22. For its reaction to the 1991 coup, see *Sovetskaya Rossiya*, 20 August 1991. See too V. Berezovsky *et al.* (eds), *Rossiya; [...] doku-*

menty, vol. II (RAU, Moscow, 1992) pp. 98–105 for a selection of its programme documents.

28. See J. Dunlop, *Contemporary Russian Nationalism* (Princeton University Press, Princeton, 1983) pp. 65–81 for their involvement in these campaigns under Brezhnev and in conservation generally. See too A. Gromov and O. Kuzin, *Neformaly: kto yest' kto*, (Mysl', Moscow, 1990) pp. 94–5; W. Laqueur, *The Long Road to Freedom* (Unwin Hyman, London, 1989) p. 51; N. Petro, 'The Project of the Century', *Studies in Comparative Communism*, vol. XX, nos. 3–4 (Autumn–Winter 1987) 238–45.

29. V. Pribylovsky, *Slovar' novikh politicheskikh partii* (Panorama, Moscow, 1991) p. 52; V. Berezovsky *et al.* (eds), *Rossiya: [...] dokumenty*, vol. V (RAU, Moscow, 1992) pp. 7–10 for some of its programme documents.

30. According to Vladimir Pribylovsky, many of these candidates were also members of *Pamyat'*: V. Pribylovsky, *Slovar' novikh politicheskikh partii* (Panorama, Moscow, 1991) pp. 51–2.

31. An *Otechestvo* society had been founded in Tyumen' in 1987 and in Sverdlovsk in December 1986. Sverdlovsk *Otechestvo* – despite its blatant anti-Semitism and the fact that its activities and ideology were indistinguishable from that of Vasiliev's *Pamyat'* – maintained links with the CPSU, helping to organise the founding conference of the Russian United Workers' Front (*OFT*) and joining that movement (although it did not take an active part in it thereafter). Other *Otechestvo* societies were established in Leningrad (25–26 March 1989) and Novosibirsk (16–17 March 1989). For the Tyumen' *Otechestvo* society, which started as an ecological-cultural protest group see V. Berezovsky and N. Krotov, *Rossiya: partii*, vol. I, part 2 (RAU, Moscow, 1991) p. 222. For the controversial Sverdlovsk society, which had neo-fascist connections, see V. Pribylovsky, *Slovar' novikh politicheskikh partii* (Panorama, Moscow, 1991) p. 55. Leningrad *Otechestvo* was founded 24–26 March 1989 at a conference of extreme nationalist and proto-fascist groups held in the Smolny Cathedral in the hope of establishing an All-Russian National-Patriotic Front. Most of Leningrad's right-wing groups attended: *Pamyat'* (Nikolai Lysenko, Yuri Riverov), a small monarchist group, *Vityaz'*; a group called *Patriot*, founded in May 1987 to promote the 'patriotic education of the young, and the propaganda of the fighting, working and revolutionary traditions of the Soviet people' and led by Alexander Romanenko, an anti-Semitic ideologist; and the Cossack Centre. The conference split over whether to accept or reject the CPSU's leading role: the anti-Communists (or Whites) left the meeting and the pro-socialist groups founded the Leningrad Russian Patriotic Movement 'Fatherland' (*Otechestvo*). Subsequently, the Leningrad *Otechestvo* was riven by quarrels and dissensions – but that it was broadly neo-fascist in character was evident, just as was the case in Sverdlovsk. See V. Pribylovsky, *Slovar' novikh politicheskikh partii* (Panorama, Moscow, 1991) pp. 54–5. For *Patriot* see V. Berezovsky and N. Krotov, *Rossiya: partii*, vol. I, part 2 (RAU, Moscow, 1991) p. 174.

32. V. Berezovsky and N. Krotov, *Rossiya: partii*, vol. I, part 2 (RAU, Moscow, 1991) p. 194; A. Kuz'min, *Literaturnaya Rossiya*, 23 June 1989.

33. V. Pribylovsky, *Slovar' novikh politicheskikh partii* (Panorama, Moscow, 1991) p. 54.
34. A. Kuz'min, *Literaturnaya Rossiya*, 23 June 1989.
35. P. Sergeev, *Literaturnaya Rossiya*, 23 June 1989. V. Berezovsky and N. Krotov, *Rossiya: partii*, vol. I, part 2 (RAU, Moscow, 1991) p. 194; A. Kuz'min, *Literaturnaya Rossiya*, 23 June 1989: a special section of the society's work was to be devoted to military-patriotic affairs.
36. A. Kuz'min, *Literaturnaya Rossiya*, 23 June 1989.
37. V. Berezovsky and N. Krotov, *Rossiya: partii*, vol. I, part 2 (RAU, Moscow, 1991) p. 194; V. Pribylovsky, *Slovar'* (Panorama, Moscow, 1991) p. 54 says that 14 *Otechestvo* members were elected to the Council. For the defence vote, see R. Sakwa, *Russian Politics*, 2nd edn (Routledge, London, 1996) p. 318.
38. After March 1990, there was discontent within the ranks about *Otechestvo*'s 'too moderate' approach and, in some quarters, about its support for Stalinism: 'Iz zhizni "Otechestva"', *Perestroika: sotsializm ili kapitalizm?* (Otechestvo, Moscow, 1989) p. 41; V. Pribylovsky, *Slovar' novikh politicheskikh partii* (Panorama, Moscow, 1991) p. 54; MBIO: *Linia*, December 1990.
39. Not to be confused with the *Union for the Regeneration of the Fatherland*, founded on 17–18 March 1990 by, *inter alia*, Leningrad's *Patriot*, Sverdlovsk and Tyumen's *Otechestvo*, Moscow's Sobriety, Chelyabinsk's *Rodina*. This body, which was led by the former CPSU member and anti-Semitic theorist, Alexander Romanenko, drew on the support of the National-Bolshevik wing of *Pamyat'* and stressed the importance of the fight against capitalism, Zionism and Baltic secession. Despite its connections with proto-fascism, it was represented at the February 1991 nationalist meeting, organised by the Russian Communist Party, 'For a Great, United Russia'. V. Pribylovsky, *Slovar' novikh politicheskikh partii* (Panorama, Moscow, 1991) p. 91.
40. V. Berezovsky *et al.* (eds), *Rossiya: [...] dokumenty*, vol. IX (RAU, Moscow, 1993) pp. 152–5.
41. V. Berezovsky and N. Krotov, *Rossiya: partii*, vol. I, part 1 (RAU, Moscow, 1991) pp. 114–15; V. Pribylovsky, *Slovar' novikh politicheskikh partii* (Panorama, Moscow, 1991) p. 92.
42. For the voters' and deputies' club *Rossiya*, see V. Pribylovsky, *Slovar' novikh politicheskikh partii* (Panorama, Moscow, 1991) pp. 75–6, who erroneously gives February 1990 as the founding date. See also *Literaturnaya Rossiya*, 29 December 1989, 2. The club seems to have inspired the formation of the similarly named deputies' fraction in the Russian Federation parliament in June 1991. Its founders included *Sovetskaya Rossiya*, *Literaturnaya Rossiya*, *Nash sovremennik*; the Russian Writers' Union, the All-Russian Cultural Fund, *Yedinenie*, the Committee for the Saving of the Volga and the *OFT*. The sponsors of the Patriotic Bloc included the All-Russian Society for the Preservation of Monuments, the Committee for Saving the Volga, the Committee for the Restoration of Christ the Saviour, the Fellowship of Russian Artists, the United Council of Russia, the OFT and several deputies from the *Rossiya* club.

43. *Literaturnaya Rossiya*, 29 December 1989, 2.
44. *Literaturnaya Rossiya*, 29 December 1989, 2. For a similar 'patriotic agenda', accompanied by calls for martial law, presidential rule and action against separatism, see 'S nadezhdoi i veroi', *Sovetskaya Rossiya*, 22 December 1989, 1.
45. *MN*, 12, 1990, 4; J. Dunlop, *The Rise of Russia* (Princeton University Press, Princeton, 1993) pp. 142–3; M. Urban, *The Rebirth of Politics in Russia* (CUP, Cambridge, 1997) pp. 179–82 for a discussion of the 1990 elections from the nationalists' perspective. They were poorly organised and short of local activists. Their campaign emphasised anti-capitalism and anti-Semitism.
46. T. Colton, 'The Moscow Election of 1990' in A. Hewett and V.H. Winston (eds), *Milestones in Glasnost and Perestroyka* (Brookings Institution, Washington, 1991) pp. 356–7, 362, 368.
47. L. Byzov and G. Gurevich, *Argumenty i fakty*, 7, 1990, 6, estimate support for the national-patriots at 5 per cent in Moscow, as opposed to 27 per cent for *gosudarstvenniki* and 15 per cent for Westernisers. An Autumn 1988 poll gave the patriots 11 per cent, *gosudarstvenniki* 28 per cent; renewers 41 per cent and Westernisers 14 per cent, see Kuz'min, *Perestroika: sotsializm ili kapitalizm?* (Otechestvo, Moscow, 1990) p. 21.
48. Nevzorov's propensities may be judged from his support for General Albert Makashov and Vladimir Zhirinovsky in the 1991 Presidential elections. For his background, see A. Chernov, 'Secret Spring', *Moscow News*, 30, 1991, 6.
49. E. Volodin, *Den'*, 3 February 1991.
50. 'Obrashchenie', *Den'*, 5 March 1991.
51. Ya. Yermakov, T. Shavshukova and V. Yakunechkin, *Kentavr*, 3, 1993, 67–8.
52. S. Smirnov, *Russkii vestnik*, 20 March 1991, 2.
53. Ya. Yermakov, T. Shavshukova and V. Yakunechkin, *Kentavr*, 3, 1993, 68.
54. J. Morrison, *Boris Yeltsin* (Penguin, London, 1991) p. 299, n. 1. 'Patrioty', *Postfaktum*, 25 February 1991, 6. The Pavlov government issued a special decree on 12 February 1991 on the Centre's activities, granting it the privileges of a corporation, exempting it from taxes as well as granting it equipment and freedom of foreign travel. The Centre was established by the Council of Ministers in February 1989 although, according to Ovchinsky, it was already functioning at the end of 1988. See too V. Berezovsky, N. Krotov *et al.* (eds), *Rossiya: [...] dokumenty*, vol. VI (RAU, Moscow, 1992) p. 54 for official support. Also Kurginyan's 1991 interview with *Sobesednik* in S. Kurginyan, *Sed'moi tsenarii*, vol. 1. *Do putcha* (Eksperimental'ny tvorcheskii tsentr, Moscow, 1992) pp. 116–19. In this, Kurginyan acknowledges his links with the Interior Ministry, KGB and the army.
55. S. Kurginyan, *Moskovskaya pravda*, 28 March 1991. *Postfaktum*, 25 February 1991, 6–7.
56. Kurginyan was reputed to have sent his notes and analyses on a regular basis to the Central Committee of the Party for information, and he was thought by some to have been involved in the preparation of the 1991

coup. S. Kordonsky, 'Pervy voenny povorot', *3 Dnya* (Postfaktum, Moscow, 1991) p. 71.

57. S. Kurginyan, *Moskovskaya pravda*, 1 March 1991.
58. V. Ovchinsky, one of the Centre's analysts, was identified as a department head in the Ministry of Internal Affairs by *Moskovskaya pravda*, 28 March 1991.
59. V. Ovchinsky, *Den'*, 3, February 1991.
60. S. Kurginyan, *Sed'moi tsenarii*. vol. 2. *Posle putcha* (Eksperimental'ny tvorcheskii tsentr, Moscow, 1992) pp. 10–106 for Kurginyan file as it allegedly appeared in the Central Committee archive, especially pp. 87–9, 96–8.
61. Alexander Prokhanov agreed with Ovchinsky's analysis: in an interview with John Morrison, he suggested that the real struggle, in this period, was between the old structures of the Union (the army, KGB, CPSU and the government) and the new 'criminal bourgeoisie' and the intellectuals. If Gorbachev were to be removed, order would be restored, J. Morrison, *Boris Yeltsin* (Penguin, London, 1991) pp. 275–6.
62. S. Kurginyan, *Sed'moi tsenarii*. Vol. 1. *Do putcha* (Eksperimental'ny tvorcheskii tsentr, Moscow, (1992) pp. 104, 107–9, 114, 121–2, 219–23.
63. S. Kurginyan, *Moskovskaya pravda*, 28 March 1991.
64. S. Kurginyan, *Moskovskaya pravda*, 28 March 1991.
65. S. Kurginyan, *Moskovskaya pravda*, 28 March 1991.
66. The October revolution was justified, he asserted, because it prevented the collapse into chaos of the Russian State, S. Kurginyan, *Moskovskaya pravda*, 26 July 1991.
67. Kurginyan's definition of the nation suggests that he had delved into the literature of the early nineteenth century: 'The determining factor for the concept of the nation is a common cultural and psychological mentality, arising from the unity of national culture as a fundamental system of values and common historical destiny determining the peculiarity of the nation's collective identity and creating its own and world history.' S. Kurginyan, *Moskovskaya pravda*, 26 July 1991.
68. S. Kurginyan, *Moskovskaya pravda*, 26 July 1991.
69. V. Bondarenko, *Den'*, 14 July 1991.
70. J. Morrison, *Boris Yeltsin* (Penguin, London, 1991) p. 267.
71. G. Razh, *Den'*, 12, June 1991, 3; A. Prokhanov, *Den'*, 9, May 1991, 1.
72. A. Prokhanov, *Den'*, 9, May 1991, 1.
73. A. Prokhanov, *Den'*, 9, May 1991, 1.
74. An accurate reference to the session of 17 June 1991.
75. A. Golovanov, *Den'*, 16, August 1991, pp. 1, 5.
76. That close contacts existed between the Party and Prokhanov was suggested not only by the contents of *Den'* but also by the anecdotal evidence of a series of photographs, procured by *Literaturnaya gazeta*, which showed the editor of *Den'*, in the Central Committee office of Oleg Baklanov, head of the military-industrial complex, member of the coup committee and widely seen as one of its masterminds. Kurginyan claimed to have been the ideologue of the coup and he certainly prepared the ground for it ideologically, see S. Kurginyan, 'Ya – ideolog', in Ye. Rasshivalova and N. Seregin (eds), *Putch. Khronika trevozhnykh dnei* (Progress, Moscow, 1991) p. 233.

77. 'Slovo k narody', *Sovetskaya Rossiya*, 23 July 1991. Pribylovsky believed Volodin to have been one of the authors of this text. Bondarenko suggests (a less likely candidate) Igor Shafarevich: see Bondarenko, 'Smena vekh', *Den'*, 18 September 1991, 2.

78. Klykov subsequently won fame as the author of the statue to Marshal Zhukov erected at the entrance to Red Square in 1995 to commemorate victory in the Second World War.

79. V. Zhirinovsky, *Sovetskaya Rossiya*, 30 July 1991.

80. For example by the board of *Yedinenie*, see A. Semyonov, *Moscow News*, 34–5, 1991, 2. R. Pittmann, 'Writers and the Coup', *Rusistika*, 4 (December 1991) p. 23, affirms that the Secretaries of the Writers' Union failed to back the coup and questioned its legality, although Yanaev's deputy had held a secret meeting with them in an attempt to obtain such an endorsement. This meeting caused a furore in the literary establishment after the coup.

81. V. Kryuchkov, *Den'*, 27, December 1991.

82. According to Alexander Rahr, 'Kryuchkov, the KGB and the 1991 Putsch', *RFE/RL Research Report*, vol. II, no. 31 (30 July 1993) 16–23, the KGB, whose powers had been augmented steadily throughout the previous Winter and Spring, was its chief instigator; he suggests the planning started in early August.

83. See M. Gorbachev, *Zhizn' i reformy* vol. II (Novosti, Moscow, 1995) pp. 559–60; M. Sixsmith, *The Moscow Coup: the Death of the Soviet System* (Simon and Shuster, London and New York, 1991) pp. 144–6.

84. M. Gorbachev, *The August Coup: the Truth and the Lessons* (Harper Collins, London, 1991) pp. 31–4. J. Dunlop, *The Rise of Russia* (Princeton University Press, Princeton, 1993) pp. 153–5 for assessment of the reasons for its failure. For support for the coup in the KGB and republican leadership, see J. Billington, 'A New Time of Troubles?' in R. Daniels (ed.), *Soviet Communism from Reform to Collapse* (D.C. Heath, Lexington, MA, 1995) pp. 380–81.

85. 'Obrashchenie k sovetskomu narodu' cited in Yu. Kazarin and V. Yakovlev (eds), *Smert' zagovora: belaya kniga* (Novosti, Moscow, 1992) p. 12. For restrictions on political and civic liberties, see 'Postanovlenie no 1' in ibid., pp. 27–36.

86. 'Postanovlenie no 1' in Yu. Kazarin and V. Yakovlev (eds), *Smert' zagovora: belaya kniga* (Novosti, Moscow, 1992) pp. 10–11.

87. 'Obrashchenie k sovetskomu narodu' cited in Yu. Kazarin and V. Yakovlev (eds), *Smert' zagovora: belaya kniga* (Novosti, Moscow, 1992) p. 12, 16.

88. A. Lukyanov later noted that the coup was inspired by the desire to save both the 'socialist orientation of society' and the Soviet system and constitution. In opposing capitalism and the dismantling of the USSR, he insisted that they had not envisaged a return to totalitarianism and the reversal of the reforms, A. Lukyanov, *Perevorot: mnimy i nastoyashchii* (Soyuz zhurnalistov, Voronezh, 1993) pp. 6–9. Pavlov also denied that they intended to revert to Stalinism (as Gorbachev believed). He claims that there was no programme, beyond opposition to the Union Treaty, which he calls 'anti-constitutional and anti-State', devotion to the

Motherland and forcing Gorbachev to adopt policies in the country's interests, V. Pavlov, *Gorbachev – putch – avgust iznutri* (Delovoi mir, Moscow, 1993) pp. 68, 70, 73, 97. Boldin too saw the revised Union Treaty as the culmination of a failed reform policy and the ruin of a great power's statehood. See V. Boldin, *Khrushchenie p'edestala* (Respublika, Moscow, 1995), pp. 393–5. Varennikov also claims to have acted in defence of the USSR constitution, territorial integrity, great power status and statehood, V. Varennikov, *Sud'ba i sovest'* (Paleya, Moscow, 1993) pp. 27, 41.

5. THE NATIONAL SALVATION FRONT 1991–93

1. See Yeltsin's comments on the Gaidar government at the time of the April 1992 crisis in B. Yeltsin, *The View from the Kremlin* (Harper Collins, London, 1994) pp. 166–7. From this, it emerges that Gaidar heard about Yeltsin's proposal to dismiss several ministers indirectly, through State Secretary Burbulis. See too S. White, 'The Presidency and Political Leadership in Post-Communist Russia' in P. Lentini (ed.), *Elections and Political Order in Russia* (Central European University Press, Budapest, London, New York, 1995) p. 220 for other examples.
2. See P. Koltsoe, *Russians in the Former Soviet Union* (Hurst, London, 1995) pp. 120–26.
3. Between a quarter and a third of the population were estimated to have been reduced to poverty. See conclusion.
4. Article 104 of the amended RFSFR Constitution of 1977 invested the Parliament with supreme power: 'The Congress of People's Deputies is the highest body of state power in the Russian Federation'. This provision was contradicted by Article 121.1, which was amended in May 1991 to read: 'The Presidency is the highest office in the Russian Federation.' See E. Teague, 'Yeltsin disbands the Soviets', *RFE/RL Research Report*, vol. II, no. 43 (29 October 1993) pp. 1–5.
5. See B. Yeltsin, *The View from the Kremlin* (Harper Collins, London, 1994) p. 188 for his very dismissive views not only on the Russian parliament but on parliaments and parliamentarians in general.
6. On the successor parties, see the summary in J. Barth Urban and V. Solovei, *Russia's Communists at the Crossroads* (Westview, Boulder and Oxford, 1997) pp. 21–9.
7. 'Skol'ko my imeem', *Lit. gaz.*, 25 March 1992. Ya. Yermakov, T. Shavshukova and V. Yakunechkin, *Kentavr*, 3, 1993, 70–72, 78; B. Slavin, *Pravda*, 25 December 1992, 1–2; V. Gel'bras, *Kto yest' chto*, vol. I (RAN, Moscow, 1994) pp. 239–47 for the Union of Communists; pp. 315–20 for the RPK.
8. 'Cherny peredel', *Molnya*, 61, 1993, 2; See too *Programma i ustav rossiiskoi kommunisticheskoi rabochei partii* (Riviera, Leningrad, 1993) pp. 11–24; V. Gel'bras, *Kto yest' chto*, vol. I (RAN, Moscow, 1994) pp. 301–8.

9. V. Sirotkin, *MN*, 28, 1994, 11. Sirotkin claims that Anpilov had links with the Popov brothers and Smirnov-Ostashvili of *Pamyat'* in 1990. This is not implausible, given his membership, at the time, of *Otechestvo*. He and his followers were not immune from anti-Semitism.

10. *Materialy uchreditel'nogo s"ezda vsesoyuznoi kommunisticheskoi partii bol'shevikov* (n.p. , Leningrad, 1991); 'Programma vsesoyuznoi kommunisticheskoi partii bol'shevikov' in *Vneshnepoliticheskaya platforma VKPB* (1992) pp. 31–5; *Materialy martovskogo plenuma ts.k VKPB* (n.p., Leningrad, 1994); 'Skol'ko my imeem', *Lit. Gaz.*, 25 March 1992; 'Right–Left Opposition', *MN*, 29, 1992, 7. See too J. Lester, *Modern Tsars and Princes* (1995) pp. 213–23 for a discussion of the successor parties.

11. Supporters of Labouring Moscow included Marxist and Bolshevik Platforms, the Initiative Movement, the Intermovement, the OFT, *Yedinstvo*. See V. Berezovsky *et al.* (eds), *Rossiya: partii [...] dokumenty*, vol. X (RAU, Moscow, 1993) pp. 72–81 for a sample of their leaflets. See too Ya. Yermakov, T. Shavshukova and V. Yakunechkin, *Kentavr*, 3, 1993, 75; V. Gel'bras, *Kto yest' chto*, vol. I (RAN, Moscow, 1994) pp. 47–9.

12. The Constitutional Court had been founded only the previous year (in July 1991). It had an impossible task, in that it was the guardian of a contradictory and much amended constitution, which had been drafted under a different regime but which it was now meant to interpret in the spirit of the new age and in accordance with the democratically expressed wishes of the electorate (although this meant that it had to make a political choice in deciding which of the competing pretenders to the democratic mandate, President or parliament, had precedence).

13. For its inception, see N. Garifulina, interviews with Baburin, Volkov and Pavlov, *SR*, 12 December 1991, 2; N. Garifulina, *SR*, 25 December 1991; S. Baburin, *Rossiya*, 18–24 March 1992, 4. ROS should not be confused with RONS, founded in 1990–92 by Igor Artemov and Alexander Tyurik, and which was distinguished from ROS mainly by the Orthodox, as opposed to communist, sympathies and background of its leaders, see V. Gel'bras, *Kto yest' chto*, vol. I (RAN, Moscow, 1994) pp. 424–9; *ROS: programmnye dokumenty* (n.p., Moscow, 1993) p. 3: reprinted in *Russkii vestnik*, 8–10, 1993, 5.

14. Most of ROS's initial supporters belonged to the *Rossiya* parliamentary faction, while Viktor Alksnis, Alexander Prokhanov, Igor Shafarevich and the writer Vasily Belov also showed interest in it. It included communists and nationalists fiercely hostile to communist influence in Russia. A. Andreev, 'ROS: god bor'by i ego uroki', *Moskva*, 11–12, 1992, 159.

15. Baburin was a more moderate figure than some of his associates: Nikolai Pavlov, his co-leader, was close to the neo-fascist National Republican Party. For his antecedents, see Baburin, *Rossiya*, 18–24 March 1992, 4.

16. Most of the December 1991 congress delegates were, according to one observer, hostile to market reform of the economy but felt they would

lose support if they said so openly: see I. Muravieva, *Rossiiskaya gazeta*, 24 December 1991, 3.

17. V. Todres, *NG*, 9 January 1992, 2.
18. The movement was allegedly based on ' [...] The recognition of the Russian Federation as the successor state not only of the USSR but also of historical Russia [...]', see A. Andreev, 'ROS: god bor'by', *Moskva*, 11–12, 1992, 158. Andreev was chairman of the Moscow of ROS, according to V. Gel'bras, *Kto yest' chto*, vol. I (RAN, Moscow, 1994) p. 364.
19. Gel'bras, *Kto yest' chto* vol. I (RAN, Moscow, 1994) p. 360.
20. 'K vozrozhdeniyu Rossii', December 1991, p. 3 in MBIO: Folder on ROS. Gel'bras dates this document from the founding conference in October 1991, see V. Gel'bras, *Kto yest' chto*, vol. I (RAN, Moscow, 1994) p. 356.
21. I. Muravieva, *Rossiiskaya gazeta*, 24 December 1991, 3.
22. V. Todres, *NG*, 9 January 1992 for its early orientation. See also Baburin's later remarks: 'The history of the USSR is finished. It's a crime but it's finished. The state which today is called the Russian Federation is not Russia for me. It is the remains of Russia [...] For me, Russia is something bigger than the Russian Federation' – a state including Belorussia, the Ukraine and Kazakhstan; V. Batuev, *AiF*, 31, 1994, 3.
23. A. Andreev, 'ROS: god bor'by', *Moskva*, 11–12, 1992, 158.
24. N. Garifulina, *SR*, 12 December 1991, 2.
25. V. Todres, *NG*, 9 January 1992, 2.
26. Quoted in V. Todres, *NG*, 9 January 1992, 2.
27. A. Andreev, 'ROS: god bor'by', *Moskva*, 11–12, 1992, 160.
28. S. Baburin, *NS*, 2, 1995, 175.
29. 'K vozrozhdeniyu Rossii', December 1991, pp. 2–3 in MBIO: Folder on ROS. V. Pribylovsky, 'A Survey of Radical Right-Wing Groups in Russia', *The Politics of Intolerance: RFE/RL Research Report*, vol. III, no. 16 (22 April 1994) 33.
30. V. Khamraev, *Sevodnya*, 56, 1995, 2 for a reiteration of this line at the March 1995 Congress; S. Baburin, *NS*, 2, 1995, 177.
31. See A. Andreev, 'ROS: god bor'by', *Moskva*, 11–12, 1992, 159: 'ROS is concerned with [...] Russia's winning a leading position in the scientific-technical field. To achieve this aim, we propose using the "locomotive principle" – to give priority to the development of high technology sectors, which can pull behind it the whole economy which is falling into ruin.'
32. Quoted in V. Batuev, *AiF*, 31, 1994, 3.
33. Baburin's tactical error in backing the parliament in October 1993 condemned ROS to oblivion: unable to compete in the 1993 elections, it was outflanked on the left by the KPRF and on the right by Zhirinovsky.
34. S. White, M. Wyman and O. Kryshtanovskaya, 'Parties and Politics in Post-Communist Russia', *Communist and Post-Communist Studies*, vol. XXVIII, no. 2 (1995) 190.
35. V. Gel'bras, *Kto yest' chto*, vol. 1 (Moscow, 1994) pp. 335–65; R. Sakwa, 'The Development of the Russian Party System' in P. Lentini (ed.),

Elections and Political Order (Central European University Press, Budapest, London and New York, 1995) p. 179.

36. For these two bodies see *Soyuz ofitserov. Kratkaya spravka* (ndp: 1992 or 1993). For Officers for the Revival of the Fatherland, see *Obozrevatel'*, February 1992, 28–30. For a short characterisation, see V. Pribylovsky, 'A Survey of Radical Right-Wing Groups in Russia', *The Politics of Intolerance: RFE/RL Research Report*, vol. III, no. 16 (22 April 1994) 32, 36.

37. See J. Dunlop, 'Russia: in Search of an Identity?' in I. Bremmer and R. Taras (eds), *New States, New Politics* (CUP, Cambridge, 1997) p. 62. Up to 40 per cent of the military, in some areas, voted for Zhirinovsky and 20 per cent for Zyuganov's communists in 1993, R. Sakwa, *Russian Politics and Society*, 2nd edn (Routledge, London, 1996) p. 318.

38. R. Sakwa, *Russian Politics and Society*, 2nd edn (Routledge, London, 1996) p. 318. 'Meuterei der Empörten', *Der Spiegel*, 36/1994, 147–8.

39. A. Zhilin, *MN*, 14, 1996, 4.

40. P. Sirotkin, *MN*, 24, 1994, 6a; N. Krotov, 'Rutskoi', in D. Maiorov (ed.), *Neizvestny Rutskoi* (Obozrevatel', Moscow, 1994) p. 31; N. Gul'binsky and M. Shakina, *Afghanistan ... Kreml'... Lefortovo* (Lada-M, Moscow, 1994) p. 169.

41. The Slavic Assembly included: Viktor Korchagin's anti-Semitic, nationalist Russian Party of Russia, which declared itself to be 'anti-communist, anti-Marxist, anti-Christian and anti-Zionist' and considered 'the Jewish issue' to be Russia's main problem; D. Vasiliev's Russian Party of National Revival; N. Lysenko's National Republican Party; Alexander Barkashov's Russian National Unity which called for a military nationalist dictatorship; *Otechestvo* (Moscow and Yekaterinburg branches); Fedor Uglov's Sobriety Union. See V. Pribylovsky, 'A Survey of Radical Right-Wing Groups in Russia', *The Politics of Intolerance: RFE/RL Research Report*, vol. III, no. 16 (22 April 1994) 34; P. Sirotkin, *MN*, 24, 1994, 6a who lists some other groups of neo-fascist orientation as helping to found the RNS. Bruce Clarke is inclined to view the RNS as partly officious, enjoying the support not only of elements in the security services but also of 'hard men' in Yeltsin's circle, B. Clarke, *An Empire's New Clothes* (Vintage, London, 1995) pp. 166–73. For the Slavic Assembly's extremist programme, see *Mezhdunarodnoe obshchestvennoe ob"edinenie 'Slavyanskii Sobor'* (np. Moscow, 1992) pp. 2–12, which refers to the 'total attack of world forces of evil on Slavic civilisation' (p. 2). The writers Bondarev and Proskurin were on its council.

42. A. Sterligov, *Pravda*, 8 September 1993, 1; V. Khamraev, *Sevodnya*, 10 February 1995. His publishing house was also alleged to have issued the Protocols of the Elders of Zion, P. Sirotkin, *MN*, 24, 1994, 6a.

43. A. Sterligov, *Pravda*, 8 October 1992, p. 2.

44. See preface to Ioann of St Petersburg, *Tvorenie dobra i pravdy* (RNS, Moscow, 1993). See also P. Sirotkin, *MN*, 24, 1994, 6a; V. Gel'bras, *Kto yest' chto*, vol. I (RAN, Moscow, 1994) pp. 412, 414–16.

45. A. Sterligov, *Pravda*, 8 October 1992, 2.

46. M. Yuzhakov, *Yedinstvo*, 5 May 1993, 4.

47. A. Frolov, *SR*, 20 June 1992, 1.

48. A. Sterligov, *Pravda*, 8 September 1993, 4; V. Gel'bras, *Kto yest' chto*, vol. I (RAN, Moscow, 1994) pp. 414–17.

49. N. Musienko, *Pravda*, 30 May 1995, 1; V. Khamraev, *Sevodnya*, 10 February 1995, 2.

50. A. Frolov, *SR*, 20 June 1992, 1.

51. See 'Obrashchenie k russkomu narodu' in *Mezhdunarodnoe obshchestvennoe ob"edinenie, 'Slavyanskii sobor'* (n.p., Moscow, 1992) pp. 11–12; 'Vystuplenie General-Maiora A.I. Sterligova' in *Obozrevatel'*, February 1992, 23, 25; V. Todres, *NG*, 16 June 1992.

52. 'Obrashchenie k russkomu narodu' in *Slavyanskii sobor* (n.p., Moscow 1992) p. 12; 'Zadachi RNS' in *Kentavr*, September–October 1992, 72–8; P. Sirotkin, *MN*, 24, 1994, 6a for a summary of its programme. *RNS: tretii s"ezd* (n.p., Suzdal', 1994) pp. 20, 26–7; G. Orekhanova, *SR*, 16 June 1994, p. 1 for the third congress, which reaffirmed these views.

53. V. Gel'bras, *Kto yest' chto*, vol. I (RAN, Moscow, 1994) pp. 420–21. The RNS also had bad relations with Zhirinovsky, *Pamyat'* and later Barkashov's RNU, *RNS: tretii s"ezd* (1994) p. 9; A. Yanov, *Vremya*, 23, 1993, 8–10.

54. See B. Clarke, *An Empire's New Clothes* (Vintage, London, 1995) pp. 171–3; Ye. Krasnikov, *MN*, 30, August 1997, 3.

55. V. Gel'bras, *Kto yest' chto*, vol. I (RAN, Moscow, 1994) pp. 412–23.

56. Tsentrizbirkom, *Vybory deputatov Gosudarstennoi Dumy 1995* (Ves' mir, Moscow, 1996) p. 174.

57. Even this seems an overestimate: only 84 delegates from 17 regions attended its September 1992 conference. While it purportedly managed to collect the 100 000 signatures necessary to form an electoral bloc with the ultra-nationalist Slavic Assembly and the Writers' Union in 1993, the Central Electoral Commission challenged their validity and barred them from presenting a nationwide list of candidates in the proportional voting, while the bloc did not field any candidates in local constituencies. See V. Gel'bras, *Kto yest' chto*, vol. I (RAN, Moscow, 1994) pp. 121–32.

58. Astafiev's Kadets showed a propensity to qualify noble promises in a way that nullified the impressive rhetoric: 'Supporting the right of the peoples inhabiting the Russian Federation to national-cultural autonomy and recognising the need for decentralisation, the departure from unitarian structures, the party supports a unified Russian State structure.' The party stressed 'its duty to defend the interests of Russians living on the territory of other Union Republics' and even suggested that it might be necessary to redraw Russia's frontiers: V. Berezovsky and N. Krotov (eds), *Rossiya: partii, [...]*, vol. I, part 2 (RAU, Moscow, 1991) p. 299.

59. V. Berezovsky and N. Krotov (eds), *Rossiya: partii, [...]*, vol. I, part 2 (RAU, Moscow, 1991) p. 299.

60. V. Gel'bras, *Kto yest' chto*, vol. I (RAN, Moscow, 1994) pp. 127–9.

61. W. Slater, 'The Centre Right in Russia', *RFE/RL Research Report*, vol. II, no. 3 (27 August 1993) 8; D. Rogozin, *Obozrevatel'*, February 1992, 3, saw it as an attempt to unite *'demokraty-gosudarstvenniki'*. It

has been suggested that Alexander Podberezkin and the RAU corporation sponsored this gathering. RAU allegedly had both Party and
American funding, Ye. Krasnikov, *MN*, 30, 1997, 3.

62. They included Baburin's national communists from ROS and *Rossiya*;
Cossack and Orthodox groups; centrist factions like *Smena*; extreme
nationalist groups representing the Russian diaspora in the Baltics,
Ukraine and Moldova; and neo-fascists, like Lysenko's National
Republican Party and Vasiliev's *Pamyat'*. W. Slater, 'The Centre Right
in Russia', *RFE/RL Research Report*, vol. II, no. 3 (27 August 1993)
pp. 8–9. Cultural luminaries included Shafarevich, Rasputin, V. Klykov
(a signatory of the Appeal to the People in July 1991, who was elected a
Co-Chairman); and Alexei Senin, a former Central Committee official
who converted to monarchism and edited *Russkii vestnik*): G. Razh,
Panorama, 31, April 1992, 6. General Alexander Rutskoi unintention-
ally shared the platform with *Pamyat'*'s Dmitri Vasiliev and distinguished himself with his anti-Western comments, although a curtain
was rapidly drawn over this nonetheless eloquent indiscretion. See
N. Gul'binsky and M. Shakina, *Afghanistan ... Kreml' ... Lefortogo*
(Lada-M, Moscow, 1994) pp. 184–6; G. Bondarenko, *Obozrevatel'*,
February 1992, 2; G. Razh, *Panorama*, 31, April 1992, 5–7.

63. 'RNS: politicheskie printsipy i blizhaishie zadachi', *Obozrevatel'*,
February 1992, 11. See too G. Koval'skaya and A. Dubnov, *Novoe
vremya*, 7, 1992, 7.

64. 'RNS: politicheskoe zayavlenie' in *Obozrevatel'*, February 1992, 16;
'Vystuplenie [...] Aksyuchitsa' in ibid., 2–4; D. Rogozin, in ibid., 3.

65. G. Koval'skaya and A. Dubnov, *Novoe vremya*, 7, 1992, 6–7;
T. Yakhlakova, *MN*, 7, 1992, 3.

66. 'Spravedlivost'', *SR*, 10 March 1992; *Literaturnaya Rossiya*, 13 March 1992.

67. Signatories included ROS; the Russian National Council (Aksyuchits);
Sterligov's Russian National Assembly; *Yedinenie*; Sterligov and
Terekhov's officers' groups; *Otchizna*, *Otechestvo*, Osipov's Russian
Party of National Regeneration; the Russian Communist Workers'
Party (Anpilov), the Russian Party of Communists, the Socialist Party
of Workers (Roy Medvedev), the Union of Communists: *SR*, 10 March
1992. The Russian National Assembly withdrew its support on
11 March (although individual members like Konstantinov and Astafiev
continued to belong to it). See W. Slater, 'The Centre Right in Russia',
RFE/RL Research Report, vol. II, no. 3 (27 August 1993) 10.

68. They included the Communists of Russia (67 seats) who believed that
Russian history and national traditions disposed Russia to collective
ownership and that 'our realistic goal must be socialism'; *Otchizna* (51
seats), which united patriotic army officers; Agrarian Union (130
members); initially All-Russian Union (Aksyuchits and Astafiev) and
Rossiya (53 seats) which was opposed to the disintegration of both the
Soviet Union and the Russian Federation. See A. Ostapchuk, *NG*,
7 April 1992; J. Steele, *Eternal Russia* (Faber, London and Boston,
1994) p. 279; A. Ostapchuk, *Spravochnik: politicheskie partii, dvizheniya i
bloki sovremennoi Rossii* (Leto, Nizhni Novgorod, 1993) p. 25.

69. V. Pribylovsky, *Panorama*, 32, 1992, 17–18; V. Pribylovsky, *Politicheskie fraktsii i deputatskie gruppy rossiiskogo parlamenta* (Panorama, Moscow, 1993) pp. 19–23.

70. A. Ostapchuk, *Spravochnik: politicheskie partii, dvizheniya i bloki sovremennoi Rossii* (Leto, Nizhni Novgorod, 1993) pp. 25–6; G. Saenko, *Oppozitsiya [...] oppozitsiya?* (MGSU, Moscow, 1995) pp. 180–92, 197–9 for texts of their declarations in June and September 1992.

71. Among the participants were Shafarevich, Osipov, Belov, Astafiev, Alksnis, Terekhov, Baburin, Makashov, Zyuganov, R. Kosopalov and Prokhanov. See J. Steele, *Eternal Russia* (Faber, London and Boston, 1994) p. 326; J. Dunlop, *The Rise of Russia* (Princeton University Press, Princeton, 1993) p. 299. Aksyuchits refused to join because of the inclusion of hardline communists.

72. A. Frolov, *SR*, 27 October 1992, 1; V. Vyzhutovich, *Izvestiya*, 26 October 1992, 2. For a list of signatories of its initial declaration, see 'Obrashchenie k grazhdanam Rossii orgkomiteta FNS', *SR*, 1 October 1992, 1. Only Sterligov, the neo-Stalinist Anpilov and two religious nationalists opposed to the communist presence in the body (Aksyuchits and Artemov) finally decided not to participate, V. Gel'bras, *Kto yest' chto*, vol. I (RAN, Moscow, 1994) pp. 499–500.

73. I. Konstantinov, *Yuridicheskaya gazeta*, 28, 1993, 9.

74. 'Obrashchenie', *SR*, 1 October 1992, 1.

75. 'Obrashchenie', *SR*, 1 October 1992, 1; the translation here is from W. Slater, 'Russia's "National Salvation Front" on the Offensive', *RFE/RL Research Report*, vol. II, no. 38 (24 September 1993) 2.

76. 'Obrashchenie', *SR*, 1 October 1992, 1. The economic provisions of this programme were qualified by Konstantinov in November 1992, when he suggested that the planned economy was necessary only in the short term: I. Konstantinov, *Pravda*, 25 November 1992.

77. See for example I. Konstantinov, *Yuridicheskaya gazeta*, 28, 1993, 9.

78. I. Konstantinov, *Yuridicheskaya gazeta*, 28, 1993, 9. See too I. Konstantinov, *Pravda*, 25 November 1992.

79. For Zyuganov's comments, which stressed the need for 'stabilisation' and state unity to reform economic and social policy, see *Literaturnaya Rossiya*, 6 November 1992, 2, 5. For Makashov, see *Den'*, 26, 1992.

80. J. Steele, *Eternal Russia* (Faber, London and Boston, 1994) pp. 325, 328–30.

81. G. Charodeev, *Izvestiya*, 27 October 1992, 1. See too N. Garifulina, *SR*, 31 October 1992 for the Front's reaction.

82. Yu. Feofanov, *Izvestiya*, 16 February 1993, 2; 'Front', *Izvestiya*, 1 April 1993, 1.

83. T. Clark, 'The Zhirinovsky Electoral Victory', *Nationalities Papers*, vol. XXIII, no. 6 (December 1995) 769–70.

84. S. White, M. Wyman and O. Kryshtanovskaya, 'Parties and Politics in Post-Communist Russia', *Communist and Post-Communist Studies*, vol. XXVIII, no. 2 (1995), 190, 195–7. The authors note that nationalists drew their support from all social groups, without reference to age or education, and that, unlike communist voters, they were neither poorer nor older than average, see ibid., pp. 194–5.

85. M. Wyman, B. Miller, S. White and P. Heywood, in P. Lentini (ed.), *Elections and Political Order* (Central European University Press, Budapest, London and New York, 1995) p. 131. Their findings suggested that one in two Russians believed that Russia should own part of other countries, and one in four that military action should be threatened to defend Russians abroad, if necessary.

86. See S. White, R. Rose and I. McAllister, *How Russia Votes* (Chatham House Publishers, Chatham, NJ, 1997) pp. 69–86.

6. THE RISE OF VLADIMIR ZHIRINOVSKY

1. A. Rahr, '"Power Ministries" support Yeltsin', *RFE/RL Research Report*, vol. II, no. 40 (8 October 1993) 9.

2. For Yeltsin's speech to the parliament on 10 December, see M. Gorshkov, V. Zhuravlev, L. Dobrokhotov (eds), *Yeltsin–Khasbulatov* (Terra, Moscow, 1994) pp. 235–8.

3. See M. Gorshkov, V. Zhuravlev and L. Dobrokhotov (eds), *Yeltsin–Khasbulatov* (Terra, Moscow, 1994) p. 153: 60 per cent of deputies were concerned with the social price of reforms, according to a poll of deputies at the sixth plenary session of the parliament in April 1992, although a majority of deputies supported the principle of radical economic reform. See also G. Murrell, *Russia's Transition to Democracy* (Sussex Academic Press, Brighton, 1997) p. 127, who estimates that the opposition could muster up to 679 votes in December 1992 and notes the centre's gradual move to the right in 1992.

4. The referendum asked four questions of the electorate: had they confidence in the President? 58.7 per cent voted yes; did they support the government's economic policies? 53 per cent again voted confidence; did they favour early parliamentary elections? 67.2 per cent were in favour; did they want early presidential elections? only 49.5 per cent agreed. Further analysis, however, suggested that support for Yeltsin was far less enthusiastic than these figures indicated. Surveys revealed that only 7 per cent fully endorsed the President and his government's policies, while 21 per cent gave them qualified approval and 43 per cent expressed little and 30 per cent no support for them. The President's personal approval ratings also suggested lack of enthusiasm: 33 per cent trusted him to some extent while 39 per cent tended to distrust him. See S. White, R. Rose, I. McAllister, *How Russia Votes* (Chatham House, Chatham, NJ, 1997) pp. 77–86 for a discussion of the referendum and its meaning.

5. From March 1993, Khasbulatov's speeches became more bitter and aggressive in their denunciation of Yeltsin, whom he accused of trying to restore totalitarian or dictatorial rule. In May, he started to exploit the 'Russian idea', defend 'Russian state interests' in foreign policy and attempted to strike an uneasy balance between the centralism of the *derzhavniki*, on whom he was increasingly dependent in the parliament, and the federalism he needed to espouse to win the support of regional

elites. In September 1993, he gave interviews to *Den'* and *Literaturnaya Rossiya* in the style of a Greater Russian nationalist, interested in the re-creation of the Union, see M. Gorshkov, V. Zhuravlev and L. Dobrokhotov (eds), *Yeltsin–Khasbulatov* (Terra, Moscow, 1994) pp. 326–7, 414–53, 497–515; *MN*, 39, 1993.

6. V. Pribylovsky, *Slovar'* (Panorama, Moscow, 1991) p. 54.

7. N. Krotov, 'Alexander Rutskoi' in D. Maiorov (ed.), *Neizvestny Rutskoi* (Obozrevatel', Moscow, 1994) pp. 23–4. N. Gul'binsky and M. Shakina, *Afghanistan ... Kreml' ... Lefortovo* (Lada-M, Moscow, 1994) p. 48.

8. 'Vitse-Prezident Rossii', *Panorama*, 28, July 1991, p. 1. Also cited in N. Gul'binsky and M. Shakina, *Afghanistan* (Lada-M, Moscow, 1994) p. 46.

9. Interview with *KP* of May 1989 in D. Maiorov (ed.), *Neizvestny Rutskoi* (Obozrevatel', Moscow, 1994) pp. 11–12.

10. Reprinted in D. Maiorov (ed.), *Neizvestny Rutskoi* (Obozrevatel', Moscow, 1994) p. 24.

11. See J. Devlin, *The Rise of the Russian Democrats* (Edward Elgar, Aldershot, 1995) pp. 202–4.

12. Reprinted in B. Koval' (ed.), *Rossiya segodnya* (Mezhdunarodnye otnosheniya, Moscow, 1991) pp. 70–71.

13. N. Krotov, 'Alexander Rutskoi', in D. Maiorov (ed.), *Neizvestny Rutskoi* (Obozrevatel', Moscow, 1994) p. 24.

14. For background, see N. Gul'binsky and M. Shakina, *Afghanistan* (Lada-M, Moscow, 1994) pp. 177–8. For similar comments, see too A. Rutskoi, *Rossiya ustala ot slov* (Golos, Moscow, 1992) p. 10.

15. 'Prichastie u Makdonaldsa', *Izvestiya*, 31 January 1992; 'Yest' li vykhod iz krizisa?', *Pravda*, 8 February 1992; 'Sil'naya vlast' – dlya demokratii', *NG*, 13 February 1992. All quotes here taken from D. Maiorov (ed.), *Neizvestny Rutskoi* (Obozrevatel', Moscow, 1994) who reproduce the articles in full.

16. Speech to Centre for Global Energy Problems, September 1991, in D. Maiorov (ed.), *Neizvestny Rutskoi* (Obozrevatel', Moscow, 1994) p. 121.

17. A. Rutskoi, 'Sil'naya vlast'' in D. Maiorov (ed.), *Neizvestny Rutskoi* (Obozrevatel', Moscow, 1994) pp. 49–50. A. Rutskoi, 'Prichastie u Makdonaldsa' in ibid., pp. 299–300.

18. A. Rutskoi, 'Yest' li vykhod' in D. Maiorov (ed.), *Neizvestny Rutskoi* (Obozrevatel', Moscow, 1994) pp. 121–2, 134. Speech to the Congress of Civic and Patriotic Forces in ibid., p. 277.

19. A. Rutskoi, 'Prichastie u Makdonaldsa' in D. Maiorov (ed.), *Neizvestny Rutskoi* (Obozrevatel', Moscow, 1994) pp. 297–9. Rutskoi had already expressed opposition to the dissolution of the USSR at the end of 1991, see A. Rutskoi, *Rossiya ustala ot slov* (Golos, Moscow, 1992) pp. 4–5, 8–9.

20. A. Rutskoi, 'Sil'naya vlast'', in D. Maiorov (ed.), *Neizvestny Rutskoi* (Obozrevatel', Moscow, 1994) pp. 52–3.

21. A. Rutskoi, 'Yest' li vykhod', in D. Maiorov (ed.), *Neizvestny Rutskoi* (Obozrevatel', Moscow, 1994) p. 121.

22. Speech to the Congress of Civic and Patriotic Forces cited in D. Maiorov (ed.), *Neizvestny Rutskoi* (Obozrevatel', Moscow, 1994) pp. 280–81.

23. N. Gul'binsky and M. Shakina, *Afghanistan* (Lada-M, Moscow, 1994) pp. 184–6.

24. Interview with *AiF*, 37, 1992 in D. Maiorov (ed.), *Neizvestny Rutskoi* (Obozrevatel' Moscow, 1994) p. 187. Travkin and Volsky shared his concern about the collapse of the USSR. For Volsky on this, see I. Torbakov, 'The Statists and the Ideology of Russian Imperial Nationalism', *RFE/RL Research Report*, vol. I, no. 49 (11 December 1992) 12–13.

25. N. Krotov, 'Alexander Rutskoi' in D. Maiorov (ed.), *Neizvestny Rutskoi* (Obozrevatel', Moscow, 1994) pp. 27–9, 34.

26. V. Orlov, *MN*, 35, 29 August 1993, 5a.

27. See his speech to the seventh Congress of Peoples' Deputies in December 1992, in D. Maiorov (ed.), *Neizvestny Rutskoi* (Obozrevatel', Moscow, 1994) pp. 64–5. Speech to the Supreme Soviet in late March 1993, see ibid., pp. 67–9. For his opposition to Yeltsin in the April referendum, see ibid., pp. 72–9. His political credo at this time is also outlined in Rutskoi, *Mysli o Rossii* (June 1993) in ibid., pp. 417–73. See especially his statements on Russian statehood, pp. 423–4, 427; on the integration of the CIS countries into Russia, pp. 416–17. For his attempt to exploit his image as a military man, see Rutskoi, *O chesti i bezchesti* (Paleya, Moscow, 1993) p. 20; J. Kampfner, *Inside Yeltsin's Russia* (Cassell, London, 1993) p. 133.

28. Rutskoi's relations with his own party (the People's Party of Free Russia) had never recovered from his early criticisms of the reforms, at the start of 1992, and he had little to do with it and ignored its positions. For Rutskoi's relations with the party, see M. Shakina, *Novoe vremya*, 44, 1993, 8–10. S. Zaslavsky, *Kentavr*, 1, 1993, pp. 39–45. Ye. Pestrukhina, *MN*, 42, 1994, 9.

29. V. Tolz, 'The Moscow Crisis and the Future of Democracy in Russia', *RFE/RL Research Report*, vol. II, no. 42 (22 October 1993) 4; V. Orlov, *MN*, 35, 1993, 5a; N. Gul'binsky and M. Shakina, *Afghanistan* (Lada-M, Moscow, 1994) p. 255; J. Lester, *Modern Tsars and Commissars* (Verso, London and New York, 1995) pp. 161, 200–10.

30. A. Prokhanov, *Den'*, 1–7 October 1993, 2.

31. In April 1993, the first signs of this were in the collaboration against Yeltsin in the referendum campaign, in the Committee to Defend the Constitution and the Constitutional Structure, which included Russian Unity, the LDPR, NSF, and the Union of Officers.

32. At its second congress, on 24–25 July 1993, both moderates like Baburin and neo-fascists like Lysenko and Pavlov (Lysenko over disagreements with the Communist chair Umulatova, a Chechen, who took exception to Lysenko's racist comments) departed, see W. Slater, 'Russia's "National Salvation Front" on the Offensive', *RFE/RL Research Report*, vol. II, no. 38 (24 September 1993) 3. See too A. Zhukov, *Rossiiskaya gazeta*, 29 July 1993, who affirms that the differences between communist and neo-Slavophile imperialists were accentuated at this meeting; G. Orekhanova, *SR*, 27 July 1993, 1; G. Saenko, *Oppozitsiya … oppozitsiya?* (MGSU, Moscow, 1995) p. 97.

33. A. Lugovskaya, *Izvestiya*, 29 July 1993; G. Saenko, *Oppozitsiya ... oppozitsiya?* (MGSU, Moscow, 1995) pp. 241–75 for its political resolutions and declarations, especially pp. 273–4.

34. G. Orekhanova, *SR*, 27 July 1993, 1.

35. 'Politicheskoe reshenie vtorogo kongressa FNS' in G. Saenko, *Oppozitsiya ... oppozitsiya?* (MGSU, Moscow, 1995) pp. 272–3.

36. Cited in W. Slater, 'Russia's "National Salvation Front" on the Offensive', *RFE/RL Research Report*, vol. II, no. 38 (24 September 1993) 3. See too his calls for military readiness in *SR*, 24 July 1993.

37. 'Politicheskoe reshenie vtorogo kongressa FNS' in G. Saenko, *Oppozitsiya* (MGSU, Moscow, 1995) pp. 254, 274–5. W. Slater, 'Russia's "National Salvation Front" on the Offensive', *RFE/RL Research Report*, vol. II, no. 38 (24 September 1993) 3.

38. See I. Konstantinov, *SR*, 24 July 1993, 1. NSF members participated with Civic Union in the 'All-Russian Meeting of Public Forces and Movements in Support of the Constitutional System, the Parliament and Democracy' held on 20 August. The meeting supported the demand for a strong parliament to prevent Yeltsin exceeding his powers.

39. See G. Murrell, *Russia's Transition to Democracy* (Sussex Academic Press, Brighton, 1997) p. 179.

40. See *MN*, 41, 8 October 1993, 2 for interviews with Rutskoi, Dunaev and Achalov which reflect this intransigeance.

41. Rutskoi rapidly appointed as Security and Interior Ministers Viktor Barannikov and Andrei Dunaev – both recently sacked by Yeltsin – and as Defence Minister, Vladislav Achalov, formerly in charge of the 1991 crackdown in the Baltics and active in the August coup. These appointments helped to keep the security ministries on the President's side during the ensuing crisis.

42. See E. Teague, 'Yeltsin's Difficult Road towards the Elections', *RFE/RL Research Report*, vol. II, no. 41 (15 October 1993) 4.

43. See G. Saenko, *Oppozitsiya ... oppozitsiya?* (MGSU, Moscow, 1995) pp. 280–95 for texts of their declarations and appeals.

44. V. Tolz, 'Russia's Parliamentary Elections', *RFE/RL Research Report*, vol. III, no. 2 (14 January 1994) 1.

45. S. Foye, 'Confrontation in Moscow', *RFE/RL Research Report*, vol. II, no. 42 (22 October 1993) 11.

46. Ibid., 12–13. See also *MN*, 41, 1993, 2–3 for chronology of these events.

47. J. Barth Urban and V. Solovei, *Russia's Communists at the Crossroads* (Westview, Boulder and Oxford 1997) pp. 86–9.

48. For the view that Khasbulatov and Rutskoi lost control to the hardliners, who directed the military defence of the White House, see O. Poptsov, *Khronika vremen 'Tsarya Borisa'* (Sovershenno sekretno, Moscow, 1996) pp. 331, 333; B. Clarke, *An Empire's New Clothes* (Vintage, London, 1995) p. 259; L. McDonnell, *October Revolution* (Spellmount, Staplehurst, 1994) pp. 70, 129, 135; N. Zheleznova, A. Panova and A. Surkov (eds), *Moskva – osen' 1993* (Respublika, Moscow, 1994) p. 282, citing Shumeiko; p. 365 for their calls to the crowd on 3 October. M. Gorshkov, V. Zhuravlev and L. Dobrokhotov

(eds), *Yeltsin–Khasbulatov* (Terra, Moscow, 1994) pp. 521–3 for Khasbulatov's carefully framed, relatively moderate response to Yeltsin's decree dissolving the parliament. R. Sakwa, *Russian Politics and Society*, 2nd edn (Routledge, London and New York, 1996) p. 127 for the gradual desertion of many parliamentarians to Yeltsin, thanks to a policy of judicious inducements.

49. *Pravda*, 20 June 1991, 1.

50. R. Sakwa, *Russian Politics and Society*, 2nd edn (Routledge, London and New York, 1993), p. 283.

51. A. Corning, 'Public Opinion and the Russian Parliamentary Elections', *RFE/RL Research Report*, vol. II, no. 48 (3 December 1993) 22.

52. Rutskoi had been a prominent leader of the centre-right Civic Union, a coalition of statist democrats and directors of state and military industries and enterprises, which advocated an end to radical economic reform, a partial return to central planning and the peaceful reconstruction of the USSR. See A. Rahr, 'Preparations for the Parliamentary Elections', *RFE/RL Research Report*, vol. II, no. 47 (26 November 1993) 5–6.

53. Neither side took the rhetoric of either democracy or authoritarianism entirely seriously, see for example a poll of December 1993, which suggested that Yeltsin's supporters were less democratic than KPRF and LDPR supporters: M. Wyman, B. Miller, S. White and P. Heywood, 'Parties and Voters in the Elections', in P. Lentini (ed.), *Elections and Political Order* (Central European University Press, Budapest, London and New York, 1995) pp. 132, 134–5.

54. Consisting of a Council of the Federation (178 seats) and the State Duma, or lower house, with 450 seats, 50 per cent elected by PR from party lists and 50 per cent elected in constituencies by simple majority. See A. Rahr, 'Preparations for the Parliamentary Elections', *RFE/RL Research Report* (26 November 1993) 1; R. Sakwa, *Russian Politics and Society*, 2nd edn (Routledge, London, 1996) pp. 417–23 for chapter 5 of the constitution.

55. See M. Cline, A. Corning and M. Rhodes, 'The Showdown in Moscow', *RFE/RL Research Report*, vol. II, no. 43 (29 October 1993) 13, 15–16 for opinion polls in October showing support for Yeltsin.

56. The People's Party of Free Russia: the ban was soon lifted but the party split. Civic Union performed poorly in the elections, failing to get any candidates elected on the list. See V. Tolz, 'Russia's Parliamentary Elections', *RFE/RL Research Report*, vol. III, no. 2 (14 January 1994) 3. A. Rahr, 'Preparations for the Parliamentary Elections', *RFE/RL Research Report*, vol. II, no. 47 (26 November 1993) 5.

57. The full list included, in addition: *OFT*, *Shchit*, Russian Communist Youth League, Labouring Russia, the Russian Communist Workers' Party (Anpilov and Tyulkin), Andreeva's All-Russian Communist Party of Bolsheviks, *Pamyat*', Patriotic Youth Front, Party of the Rebirth of Russia; see *NG*, 6 October 1993.

58. There were three main democratic blocs: Gaidar's Russia's Choice; *Yabloko*, the Yavlinsky–Boldyrev–Lukin bloc, which favoured less radical economic policies and a less pro-Western foreign policy; Sergei

Shakhrai's Russian Party of Unity and Concord, which united frustrated ambitious former Yeltsin protégés (Shakhrai, Shokhin, Stankevich) under a 'conservative' platform, which stressed the importance of the state, family, property and Russian tradition. Sobchak's MDR and Travkin's DPR were also in the democratic camp.

59. Tsentrizbirkom, *Vybory Deputatov Gosudarstvennoi Dumy 1995* (Ves' mir, Moscow, 1996) pp. 94, 202 with slightly lower figures (66 seats) for Russia's Choice in 1993 than the usually cited 70, as in R. Sakwa, *Russian Politics and Society*, 2nd edn (Routledge, London and New York, 1996) p. 393.

60. V. Tolz, 'Russia's Parliamentary Elections', *RFE/RL Research Report*, vol. III, no. 2 (14 January 1994) 2, n. 10. J. Kampfner, *Inside Yeltsin's Russia* (Cassell, London, 1994) p. 179.

61. See 'Constitution Watch', *East European Constitutional Review*, vol. V, no. 2 (Spring 1994) 19–20; White *et al.*, *How Russia Votes* (Chatham House, Chatham, NJ, 1997) pp. 116–18, 127–9; pp. 99–101 for reservations about the status of the new constitution.

62. See, for example, the sympathetic portrait presented in Ye. Kocherina (ed.), *Fenomen Zhirinovskogo* (Kontrolling, Moscow, 1992) pp. 82–3.

63. V. Zhirinovsky, *Posledny brosok na yug* (Rait, Moscow, 1993) pp. 5–18. See too Ye. Klepikova and V. Solovyov, *Zhirinovsky: the Paradoxes of Russian Fascism* (Viking, London and New York, 1995) pp. 69–74.

64. For example, his travels to Hungary as a student; his election as class leader at the institute; his *stages* at GKS and Radio Moscow; his subsequent assignment to a capitalist, NATO country as a young man are all indicative of his links with the security services. Oleg Kalugin believed him to be a former security worker, J. di Giovanni, 'Mad Vlad and Dangerous to Know', *Sunday Times Magazine*, 1 May 1994, 27, as did Gorbachev, G. Frazer and G. Lancelle, *Absolute Zhirinovsky* (Penguin, New York, 1994) pp. 126–7.

65. He was expelled from Turkey, where he had been sent to work with a trade delegation, for communist propaganda. See V. Kartsev, *!Zhirinovsky!* (Columbia University Press, New York, 1995) pp. 60–62; Ye. Klepikova and V. Solovyov, *Zhirinovsky: the Paradoxes of Russian Fascism* (Viking, London and New York, 1995) pp. 62, 70–72 for discussion of this incident and of his links with the KGB.

66. V. Kartsev, *!Zhirinovsky!* (Columbia University Press, New York, 1995) pp. 65–81; Ye. Klepikova and V. Solovyov, *Zhirinovsky: the Paradoxes of Russian Fascism* (Viking, London and New York, 1995) pp. 75–7.

67. LDP Programme in B. Koval' (ed.), *Rossiya segodnya* (Mezhdunarodnye otnosheniya, Moscow, 1991) pp. 185–6; V. Zhirinovsky, *Dialog*, 8, 1990, 34–6; see too N. Izyumova, *MN*, 17, 1990, 7; *AiF*, 12, 1990. Its first congress was held on 31 March 1990 and its founding congress on 13 December 1989. It was officially registered in April 1991, allegedly in contravention of regulations and on the instructions of the Deputy Minister of Justice, as the party could not gather the required 5000 signatures, 'Gospodin nezavisimy', *Ogonek*, 2, 1992. For its later more nationalist programme, see *Programma LDPR* (ndp); V. Gel'bras, *Kto yest' chto*, vol. I (RAN, Moscow, 1994) pp. 146–7.

68. V. Voronin, *Dialog*, 16, 1990, 47–8, 50; V. Pribylovsky, *Slovar'* (Panorama, Moscow, 1991) pp. 100–1; V. Todres, *NG*, 21 February 1991; V. Vyunitsky, *Dialog*, 17, 1990, p. 32.

69. N. Izyumova, *MN*, 17, 1990. See too V. Zhirinovsky, *Dialog*, 8, 1990, 36.

70. 'Gospodin nezavisimy', *Ogonek*, 2, 1992.

71. G. Frazer and G. Lancelle, *Absolute Zhirinovsky* (Penguin, New York, 1994) p. 9. See also J. Dunlop, *The Rise of Russia* (Princeton University Press, Princeton, 1993) p. 156.

72. Quoted in J. Dunlop, *The Rise of Russia* (Princeton University Press, Princeton, 1993) pp. 156–7. For similar sentiments see his remarks on Russian TV, 23 November 1993, cited by G. Frazer and G. Lancelle, *Absolute Zhirinovsky* (Penguin, New York, 1994) p. 12: 'Just look who has suffered most today. Again, it is pensioners of Russian nationality. [...] Or take servicemen. They have served their term and are now outside the borders of Russia. Not only can they not receive their service pension but they are not allowed into any form of activity since they served, allegedly, in an army of occupation'. Also V. Zhirinovsky, *Posledny brosok na yug* (Rait, Moscow, 1993) p. 40; V. Kalita, *Literaturnaya Rossiya*, 28, 1991, 3.

73. G. Frazer and G. Lancelle, *Absolute Zhirinovsky* (Penguin, New York, 1994) pp. 8–9. See too his declarations in Yu. Orlik, *Izvestiya*, 30 November 1993, 4.

74. See Yu. Orlik, *Izvestiya*, 30 November 1993, 4.

75. J. Dunlop, *The Rise of Russia* (Princeton University Press, Princeton, 1993) p. 156.

76. V. Zhirinovsky, *Posledny brosok na yug* (Rait, Moscow, 1993) pp. 32–3, 36–7; *Programma LDPR* (ndp) p. 9; P. Bruno, *Besedy na chistotu* (Rait, Moscow, 1995) pp. 51–2.

77. G. Frazer and G. Lancelle, *Absolute Zhirinovsky* (Penguin, New York, 1994) pp. 68–9; Yu. Orlik, *Izvestiya*, 30 November 1993, 4; V. Zhirinovsky, *Posledny vagon na sever* (Conjou, Moscow, 1995) pp. 68–70, 98–100; P. Bruno, *Besedy* (Rait, Moscow, 1995) pp. 56–8.

78. V. Zhirinovsky, 'My dolzhny uchest' uroki', *Pravda Zhrinivoskogo*, 7 (30), 1994, 1.

79. V. Zhirinovsky, *Posledny brosok* (Rait, Moscow, 1993) pp. 38–9.

80. V. Zhirinovsky, *Posledny vagon* (Conjou, Moscow, 1995) p. 12.

81. 'Millions of southerners will go home and you will breathe freely. Because it is not so much commercial kiosks that irritate you as those inside them. When healthy Russian lads, from your regions, are standing there with honest Russian faces, they are too ashamed to deceive you. For [...] it is mainly aliens and fly-by-night southern mafiosi who are the swindlers, burglars, rapists and killers': Mayak radio, 8 December 1993, cited by G. Frazer and G. Lancelle, *Absolute Zhirinovsky* (Penguin, New York, 1994) p. 97.

82. P. Bruno, *Besedy* (Rait, Moscow, 1995) pp. 9–10; A. Higgins, *The Independent*, 15 December 1993, 8; for his comments on this theme in the 1993 campaign, see Yu. Orlik, *Izvestiya*, 30 November 1993, 4.

83. *Pravda*, 20 June 1991, 1.

84. He planned to make Russia prosperous by selling arms abroad and hiring out its army. He called for more spending on social welfare, the army and the defence industries as well as for tax cuts, see: V. Zhirinovsky, *Posledny brosok* (Rait, Moscow, 1993) pp. 70–71; V. Zhirinovsky, *Posledny vagon* (Conjou, Moscow, 1995) pp. 15, 25–6, 106–7; V. Zhirinovsky, *O sud'bakh Rossii: s moei tochki zreniya* (Rait, Moscow, 1993) pp. 48–9; *Programma LDPR* (ndp) pp. 5–8.

85. K. Fedarko, 'Rising Czar?', *Time*, 11 July 1994, 33.

86. *Programma LDPR* (ndp) pp. 4–5. V. Zhirinovsky, *Posledny brosok* (Rait, Moscow, 1993) p. 70. V. Gel'bras, *Kto yest' chto*, vol. I (RAN, Moscow, 1994) pp. 150–54. The original programme was changed in 1991 and 1993.

87. P. Bruno, *Besedy* (Rait, Moscow, 1995) pp. 17–18; V. Zhirinovsky, *Posledny brosok* (Rait, Moscow, 1993) p. 14; *Slovo Zhirinovskogo*, 4 (17) 1995, 2, for the extension of the powers of the police and the president.

88. P. Bruno, *Besedy* (Rait, Moscow, 1995) p. 17.

89. V. Zhirinovsky, *Posledny brosok* (Rait, Moscow, 1993) pp. 29, 52; V. Zhirinovsky, *Posledny vagon* (Conjou, Moscow, 1995) p. 23; P. Bruno, *Besedy* (Rait, Moscow, 1995) p. 10; Ye. Klepikova and V. Solovyov, *Zhirinovsky* (Viking, London and New York, 1995) pp. 20, 120, 161.

90. V. Zhirinovsky, *Posledny vagon* (Conjou, Moscow, 1995) pp. 15–16.

91. V. Zhirinovsky, *Posledny vagon* (Conjou, Moscow, 1995) pp. 25–6, 106–7.

92. See, for example, Gaidar, whom Zhirinovsky sued. See Ye. Gaidar, *Izvestiya*, 18 June 1995, 2; and quoted by D. Hearst, *The Guardian*, 14 December 1993; R. Service, *The Independent*, 14 December 1993; N. Stone and Campbell, *The Sunday Times*, 19 December 1993; J. Kampfner, *The Daily Telegraph*, 14 December 1993.

93. J. Steele, *The Guardian*, 14 December 1993.

94. As one of his associates, Alexei Mitrofanov, remarked, 'Zhirinovsky is a mood, he is a state of the soul.' Quoted by K. Fedarko, 'Rising Czar?', *Time*, 11 July 1994, 34.

95. V. Zhirinovsky, *Posledny vagon* (Conjou, Moscow, 1995) p. 41.

96. See Limonov on his use of street language, quoted in Ye. Klepikova and V. Solovyov, *Zhirinovsky* (Viking, London and New York, 1995) p. 165. Zhirinovsky's famous parallel between Soviet history and sex, first presented in his paper *Liberal* in June 1990 and often used thereafter, is characteristic. See B. Koval', *Rossiya segodnya* (Mezhdunarodnye otnosheniya, Moscow, 1991) pp. 189–90.

97. See V. Kartsev, *!Zhirinovsky!* (Columbia University Press, New York, 1995) pp. 92–3 who gives several illustrations.

98. G. Frazer and G. Lancelle, *Absolute Zhirinovsky* (Penguin, New York, 1994) p. 133. P. Bruno, *Besedy* (Rait, Moscow, 1995) p. 42 for similar reminiscences about his mother.

99. For analyses of his support, see V. Shokarev, *Izvestiya*, 30 December 1993; A. Yanov, *Izvestiya*, 23 December 1993; M. Reshetnikov and V. Vassiliev, *Rossiiskie vesti*, 30 December 1993; L. Navrozov, *Rossiiskie vesti*, 20 April 1994; A. Chelnokov, *Izvestiya*, 4 January 1995. The last two analysts observe that many candidates and LDPR party members

were young men with a higher education, but the party's support drifted from the provincial towns, in 1993, to the poorer and less educated countryside in 1995. See also M. Wyman, 'Developments in Voting Behaviour: 1993 and 1995 Compared' (Paper delivered to BASEES Conference, Cambridge, 1996) pp. 4, 9, 16. For Zhirinovsky's attempts to court young businessmen, see V. Zhirinovsky, *Posledny vagon* (Conjou, Moscow, 1995) pp. 25–6. See M. Savin and A. Shagin, *NG*, 18 December 1993, 2 on the support of the Russian diaspora; V. Tolz, 'Russia's Parliamentary Elections', *RFE/RL Research Report*, vol. III, no. 2 (14 January 1994) 8, n. 29: Yeltsin, at a press conference, said one-third of the military voted for Zhirinovsky: the army had not been paid for several months and about 130 000 men were living in huts, according to J. Kampfner, *Inside Yeltsin's Russia* (Cassell, London, 1994) p. 182. See too Ye. Klepikova and V. Solovyov, *Zhirinovsky* (Viking, London and New York, 1995) pp. 178–80, 182–3 and S. Plekhanov, *Zhirinovsky: kto on?* (Yevraziya-nord, Moscow, 1994) pp. 137–8 for analysis of his vote in 1993 and especially his support in the army.

100. See M. Wyman, B. Miller, S. White and P. Heywood, 'Parties and Voters in the Elections', in P. Lentini (ed.), *Elections and Political Order* (Central European University Press, Budapest, London and New York, 1995) p. 127.

101. See A. Rahr, 'Preparations for the Parliamentary Elections', *RFE/RL Research Report*, vol. II, no. 47 (26 November 1993) 2–5 for discussion of their programmes.

102. A. Corning, 'Public Opinion', *RFE/RL Research Report*, vol. II, no. 48 (3 December 1993) 19. See also A. Rahr, 'Preparations for the Parliamentary Elections', *RFE/RL Research Report*, vol. II no. 47 (26 November 1993) 2.

103. D. Skillen, 'Media Coverage in the Elections', in P. Lentini (ed.), *Elections and Political Order* (Central European University Press, Budapest, London and New York, 1995) p. 121.

104. See S. White, R. Rose and I. McAllister, *How Russia Votes* (Chatham House, Chatham, NJ, 1997) pp. 121–2; M. Wyman, B. Miller, S. White and P. Heywood, 'Parties and Voters in the Elections', in P. Lentini (ed.), *Elections and Political Order* (Central European University Press, Budapest, London and New York, 1995) p. 129.

105. Zhirinovsky won 59 seats in the lists as opposed to Russia's Choice's 40. By contrast, he won only 5 constituencies, as opposed to Russia's Choice's 30 constituency seats. The communists were more consistent (KPRF winning 32 seats in the lists and 16 in the constituencies; the Agrarians won 21 and 12 respectively). Tsentrizbirkom, *Vybory deputatov Gosudarstvennoi Dumy* (Ves' mir, Moscow, 1996) p. 202; S. White, R. Rose and I. McAllister, *How Russia Votes* (Chatham House, Chatham, NJ, 1997) p. 123.

106. S. White, R. Rose, I. McAllister, *How Russia Votes* (Chatham House, Chatham NJ, 1997) pp. 122–5. A. Uglanov, *AiF*, 50, 1993, 1. V. Tolz, 'Russia's Parliamentary Elections', *RFE/RL Research Report*, vol. III, no. 2 (14 January 1994) p. 2.

7. ZYUGANOV'S COMMUNISTS AND NATIONALISM, 1993–95

1. See for example T. Clark, 'The Zhirinovsky Electoral Victory', *Nationalities Papers*, vol. XXIII, no. 24 (December 1995) 775–6.
2. V. Gel'bras, *Kto yest' chto*, vol. I (RAN, Moscow, 1994) p. 148; M. Savin and A. Shagin, *NG*, 18 December 1993, 1.
3. L. Navrozov, *Rossiiskie vesti*, 20 April 1994, 7; E. Schneider, 'Die nationalistischen und kommunistischen Fraktionen der russlandischen Duma', *Berichte des Bundesinstituts für ostwissenschaftliche und internationale Studien*, 28 (1995) p. 32; T. Clark, 'The Zhirinovsky Electoral Victory' *Nationalities Papers*, vol. XXIII, no. 24 (December 1995) 771; D. Slider, V. Gimpelson and S. Chugrov, 'Political Tendencies in Russia's Regions', *Slavic Review*, vol. LIII, no. 3 (Fall 1994) 731; M. McAuley, *Russia's Politics of Uncertainty* (CUP, Cambridge, 1997) pp. 273–5, 299–300.
4. W. Oshlies, *Wladimir Shirinowski* (Böhlau, Cologne, 1995) pp. 53–8; J. Morrison, *Vladimir Zhirinovsky: an Assessment* (Institute for National Strategic Studies, Washington, 1994) pp. 13–16; I. Malov, 'Skol'ko "stoit" Vladimir Zhirinovsky?', *MN*, 24, 1994, 7a.
5. See W. Oshlies, *Wladimir Shirinowski* (Böhlau, Cologne, 1995) pp. 25–6. The biography of his deputy, Vengerovsky, is suggestive in this respect. See E. Schneider, 'Die nationalistischen und kommunistischen Fraktionen der russlandischen Duma', *Berichte des Bundesinstituts für ostwissenschaftliche und internationale Studien*, 28 (1995) p. 11: Vengerovsky's background was in radio-engineering in its applications to space and defence and his links with the defence industry were reportedly good. Schneider also believed him to have been involved in counter-intelligence. Zavidiya, who funded several nationalist papers, including *SR, Den'* and *Literaturnaya Rossiya*, was alleged to have been a former bureaucrat turned businessman, who had been lent three million roubles, interest free, until December 1991, by the Central Committee of the CPSU. See W. Laqueur, *Black Hundred*, pbk edn (Harper Collins, 1994), p. 257; 'Gospodin nezavisimy', *Ogonek*, 2, 1992, 23.
6. This conclusion is also drawn by W. Oshlies, *Wladimir Shirinowski* (Böhlau, Cologne, 1995) p. 57.
7. V. Zhirinovsky, *LDPR: Ideologiya* (LDPR, Moscow, 1995) p. 14; J. Dunlop, 'Russia: in Search of an Identity?' in I. Bremmer and R. Taras (eds), *New States, New Politics* (CUP, Cambridge, 1997) p. 91.
8. He wanted fraction leaders to have the right to deprive deputies of their voting rights, should they refuse to obey the whip – an idea resisted by other deputies and fellow-LDPR members: E. Schneider, 'Die nationalistischen und kommunistischen Fraktionen der russlandischen Duma', *Berichte des Bundesinstituts für ostwissenschaftliche und internationale Studien*, 28 (1995) p. 14.
9. V. Gel'bras, *Kto yest' chto*, vol. I (RAN, Moscow, 1994) p. 148. Most were Moscow-based businessmen or, they claimed, employed in the

party apparat: E. Schneider, 'Die nationalistischen und kommunistischen Fraktionen der russlandischen Duma', *Berichte des Bundesinstituts für ostwissenschaftliche und internationale Studien*, 28 (1995) pp. 8–9, 32.

10. Among the defectors were V.A. Marychev, the party organiser in St Petersburg, Alexei Pronin, the party treasurer, the party organisers for Urdmurtia and Orenburg and Alexei Zavidiya. Other well-known figures resigned from the party, including the famous television hypnotist, Anatoly Kashpirovsky, the rock star Sergei Zharikov, the writer Eduard Limonov and the former journalist, Arkhipov. A. Chelnokov, *Izvestiya*, 4 January 1995, 7; V. Gel'bras, *Kto yest' chto*, vol. I (RAN, Moscow, 1994) p. 148; K. Fedarko, *Time Magazine*, 11 July 1994, 33. See also *RG*, 2 February 1994 for an open letter of protest from the party organiser in Kursk.

11. J. Lester, *Modern Tsars and Princes* (Verso, London and New York, 1995) p. 166; G. Luchterhand, 'Von der radikalen Opposition zur Beteiligung der Macht', *Osteuropa*, vol. XLIV, no. 10 (1996) 972.

12. V. Zhirinovsky, *LDPR: Ideologiya* (LDPR, Moscow, 1995) pp. 17–18; *V.V. Zhirinovsky i fraktsiya LDPR* (LDPR, Moscow, 1995) pp. 33–4, 49; S. White, M. Wyman and S. Oates, 'Parties and Voters in the 1995 Duma Elections', *Europe-Asia Studies*, vol. XLIX, no. 5 (1997) 774; E. Schneider, 'Die nationalistischen und kommunistischen Fraktionen der russlandischen Duma', *Berichte des Bundesinstituts für ostwissenschaftliche und internationale Studien*, 28 (1995) 13 who cites INDEM's analysis of voting patterns in the Duma from January to July 1994, and concludes that they voted more often against economic reform than the KPRF and Agrarians. The LDPR agreed to support the 1994 budget by having a criminal investigation into the Dutch GMM firm suspended and its being permitted to open in Moscow; the firm was believed to have financial links with the party, see A. Lugovskaya, *Izvestiya*, 21 June 1994; S. Chugaev, *Izvestiya*, 25 June 1994, 1. S. Chugaev, *Izvestiya*, 14 January 1995; S. Chugaev, *Izvestiya*, 22 June 1995.

13. Yu. Orlik, *Izvestiya*, 30 November 1993, 4; *V.V. Zhirinovsky i fraktsiya LDPR* (LDPR, Moscow, 1995) pp. 95–6.

14. V. Zhirinovsky, *Moi garantii izbiratelyam* (LDPR, Moscow, 1995) p. 12.

15. On the army's political profile, see J. Dunlop, 'Russia: in Search of an Identity?' in I. Bremmer and R. Taras (eds), *New States, New Politics* (CUP, Cambridge, 1997) pp. 62–4. Between 1992 and 1994, in opinion polls, army officers consistently expressed their regret over the dissolution of the USSR, the withdrawal from Eastern Europe and the Baltics. In summer 1994, 80 per cent hoped Russia would once more become a great power, while 62 per cent thought that authoritarian rule would solve the country's problems. See also R. Sakwa, *Russian Politics and Society*, 2nd edn (Routledge, London and NY, 1997) p. 318: in November 1992, 19 per cent of servicemen supported the government, while 56 per cent opposed it; 1995 surveys pointed to continued support for national-patriotic movements in the army, which, with the security forces and their families, accounted for 40 million voters, in Sakwa's estimate out of 110 million.

16. D. Slider, V. Gimpelson and S. Chugrov, 'Political Tendencies in Russia's Regions', *Slavic Review*, vol. LIII, no. 3 (Fall 1994) 730; L. Navrozov, *Rossiiskie vesti*, 20 April 1994, p. 7; M. Wyman, B. Miller and S. White, 'Parties and Voters in the Elections', in P. Lentini (ed.), *Elections and Political Order in Russia* (Central European University Press, Budapest, London and New York, 1995) p. 129; E. Schneider, 'Die nationalistischen und kommunistischen Fraktionen der russlandischen Duma', *Berichte des Bundesinstituts für ostwissenschaftliche und internationale Studien*, 28 (1995) pp. 31–2; M. Savin and A. Shagin, *NG*, 18 December 1993, 1; M. Reshetnikov and V. Vassiliev, *RG*, 30 December 1993, 4.

17. S. White, R. Rose and I. Mc Allister, *How Russia Votes* (Chatham House, Chatham, NJ, 1997) p. 137: only 35 per cent of LDPR voters identified with the party, unlike more loyal KPRF voters.

18. Yu. Levada, *Democratic Disorder and Russian Public Opinion Trends* (University of Strathclyde, Glasgow, 1995) pp. 8–9; S. Whitefield and G. Evans, 'Support for Democracy and Political Opposition in Russia', *Post-Soviet Affairs*, vol. XII, no. 3 (July–September 1996) 236, 239, who find their authoritarian and xenophobic attitudes shared by KPRF voters; M. Savin and A. Shagin, *NG*, 18 December 1993, 2; S. White, R. Rose and I. Mc Allister, *How Russia Votes* (Chatham House, Chatham, NJ, 1997) pp. 230–31, 145.

19. V. Zhirinovsky, *Moi garantii izbiratelyam* (LDPR, Moscow, 1995) p. 12; *V.V. Zhirinovsky i fraktsiya LDPR* (LDPR, Moscow, 1995) pp. 20, 33–4.

20. M. Wyman, *Public Opinion in Post-Communist Russia* (Macmillan, London and NY, 1997) pp. 142, 144–5; T. Clark, 'The Zhirinovsky Electoral Victory', *Nationalities Papers*, vol. XXIII, no. 24 (December 1995) 776.

21. *The Sunday Times*, 31 March 1996.

22. Ye. Krasnikov, *MN*, 13, 1996, 3. See the very useful monograph by R. Sakwa, *Communist Party of the Russian Federation and the Electoral Process* (University of Strathclyde, Glasgow, 1996) for a slightly different assessment of the weight of the hardliners and the reformers. Differences within the party were much reported in the press during the presidential elections, probably because it was felt that this would help to frighten voters away from Zyuganov. See *OMRI Russian Presidential Election Survey*, 1, 3 May 1996. See too S. Roy, *MN*, 14, 1996 as an example of this kind of report. See too J. Barth Urban and V. Solovei, *Russia's Communists at the Crossroads* (Westview, Boulder and Oxford, 1997) p. 5. They suggest that the Marxist-Leninists are best seen as modernisers, since they were less doctrinaire than other groups on the left and wanted to revivify workers' democracy. See G. Luchterhand, 'Von der radikalen Opposition zur Beteiligung der Macht', *Osteuropa*, vol. XLIV, no. 10 (1996) 979; A. Ostapchuk and Ye. Krasnikov, *MN*, 33, 1997, 1–2 for later developments.

23. See G. Luchterhand, 'Von der radikalen Opposition zur Beteiligung der Macht', *Osteuropa*, vol. XLIV, no. 10 (1996) 979.

24. J.-B. Naudet, *Le Monde Hebdomadaire*, 21 December 1995; J. Barth Urban and V. Solovei, *Russia's Communists at the Crossroads* (Westview, Boulder and Oxford, 1997) pp. 128–9.

25. S. White, R. Rose and I. Mc Allister, *How Russia Votes* (Chatham House, Chatham, NJ, 1997) p. 223.

26. W. Slater, 'The CPSU Today', *RFE/RL Research Report*, vol. III, no. 31 (12 August 1994) 2; I. Rybkin, *Mirovaya ekonomika*, 7, 1995, 44. The party's professional image was enhanced by its Duma attendance record: KPRF deputies had the best attendance record and went on fewer foreign trips than other deputies.

27. A. Zhukov, *Obshchaya gazeta*, 22–8 July 1994, 6, who insists on the orthodox parties' hostility to Zyuganov. Ya. Yermakov, T. Shavshukova and V. Yakunechkin, *Kentavr*, 3, 1993, pp. 71–3 for the support the orthodox parties enjoyed and their development, pp. 77–80 for how the socialists were overshadowed by nationalists in the preparations for the congress. B. Slavin, *Pravda*, 25 December 1992, 1–2.

28. V. Vyzhutovich, *Izvestiya*, 16 February 1993; V. Gel'bras, *Kto yest' chto*, vol. I (RAN, Moscow, 1994) pp. 104–5 says that membership increased from 500 000 in February 1993 to 600 000 later that year. R. Sakwa, 'Development of the Russian Party System', in P. Lentini (ed.), *Elections and Political Order in Russia* (Central European University Press, Budapest, London and New York, 1995) p. 180 believes that membership was about 550 000. Yermakov estimates membership in early 1993 at 400 000, *Kentavr*, 3, 1993, 65. V. Sirotkin, *MN*, 34, 1994, 8 believed membership had reached 600 000 at the end of the following year.

29. For documents which reveal the struggle between the Stalinists and democrats in the KP RSFSR in summer and autumn 1990, see B. Koval', *Rossiya segodnya* (Mezhdunarodnye otnosheniya, Moscow, 1991) pp. 52–64.

30. *Programmnoe zayavlenie IIogo chrezvychainogo s"ezda KPRF* (Paleya, Moscow, 1993) pp. 18–20.

31. *Programmnoe zayavlenie [...] KPRF* (Paleya, Moscow, 1993) p. 20.

32. *Programmnoe zayavlenie [...] KPRF* (Paleya, Moscow, 1993) p. 20.

33. *Programmnoe zayavlenie [...] KPRF* (Paleya, Moscow, 1993) p. 24.

34. *Programmnoe zayavlenie [...] KPRF* (Paleya, Moscow, 1993) pp. 23–4.

35. *Programmnoe zayavlenie [...] KPRF* (Paleya, Moscow, 1993) pp. 21–2.

36. See its appeal 'Za yedinstvo' in *Pravda*, 26 February 1993, 2.

37. *Programmnoe zayavlenie [...] KPRF* (Paleya, Moscow, 1993) p. 20.

38. *Programmnoe zayavlenie [...] KPRF* (Paleya, Moscow, 1993) p. 23.

39. *Programmnoe zayavlenie [...] KPRF* (Paleya, Moscow, 1993) p. 22.

40. *Programmnoe zayavlenie [...] KPRF* (Paleya, Moscow, 1993) p. 23.

41. These included Prigarin's Union of Communists, Anpilov and Andreeva's parties and some of the RKP.

42. *Programmnoe zayavlenie [...] KPRF* (Paleya, Moscow, 1993) p. 25.

43. See for example *ST*, 31 March 1996.

44. 'Programma KPRF', *Dialog*, 3, 1995, 25–6.

45. 'Programma KPRF', *Dialog*, 3, 1995, 27.

46. 'The Great October Socialist Revolution was for Russia the only chance of national-state self-preservation in a situation of military, political and economic collapse [...]', 'Programma KPRF', *Dialog*, 3, 1995, 25.

47. 'Programma KPRF', *Dialog*, 3, 1995, 25.

48. See for example, N. Ustrialov, *V bor'be za Rossiyu* (Harbin, 1920); N. Ustrialov, *Pod znakom revolyutsii* (Harbin, 1925).

49. 'Programma KPRF','Programma', *Dialog*, 3, 1995, 22–4.
50. 'Programma KPRF', *Dialog*, 3, 1995, 25.
51. Zyuganov explicitly flirted with Eurasianism in 1992 and 1993. See his remarks to the effect that: '[...] Into a state of Eurasian character, a synthesis of Slav and Muslim culture, [...] people are attempting to introduce a type of Western democracy, which entirely fails to correspond to the traditions, habits or possibilities of our society', G. Zyuganov, *Literaturnaya Rossiya*, 6 November 1992, 2. See too G. Zyuganov, *Drama vlasti* (Paleya, 1993) pp. 4, 174–9.
52. 'The Soviet Union was the geopolitical heir of the Russian Empire. As a state and social system, it saw itself as an indissoluble unity. [...] Therefore, the rebirth of our Fatherland and the return to the path of socialism are inseparable', 'Programma KPRF', *Dialog*, 3, 1995, 25.
53. On the economy, the Party promised: price reductions on food and essential manufactured goods; the restoration of nationalised property and state socialism in the long term, with tolerance of some private property in the short term; state controls over banks, foreign exchange, the defence industry; state subsidies and planning to assist selected economic sectors; protectionism; minimum pensions and social security benefits; free education; the promotion of large families; progressive income tax; the prevention of private farming and provision of high living standards for the security services: 'Programma KPRF', *Dialog*, 3, 1995, 27–9.
54. 'Programma KPRF', *Dialog*, 3, 1995, 28.
55. 'Programma KPRF', *Dialog*, 3, 1995, 22, 27–8.
56. G. Zyuganov, *Rossiya i sovremenny mir* (Obozrevatel', Moscow, 1995) pp. 58–9.
57. Zyuganov signed the Appeal to the People in July 1991; joined the United Opposition, was one of the leaders of General Sterligov's Russian National Council in 1992, which he left for the National Salvation Front in Autumn 1992. See 'Skol'ko my imeem kompartii?', *Lit. gaz.*, 25 March 1992, 11 and V. Sirotkin, *MN*, 34, 1994, 8, for his background in Orel province Komsomol and later in the propaganda department of the CPSU and as CC Secretary for Ideology of the KP RSFSR. See also A. Yanov, *MN*, 10, 1996, 4 for Zyuganov's position within the various trends in the Brezhnevite party.
58. G. Zyuganov, *Rossiya i sovremenny mir* (Obozrevatel', Moscow, 1995) pp. 16–18, 65–6.
59. G. Zyuganov, *Rossiya i sovremenny mir* (Obozrevatel', Moscow, 1995) pp. 22, 66, 91.
60. G. Zyuganov, *Rossiya i sovremenny mir* (Obozrevatel', Moscow, 1995) pp. 23, 65, 69–70.
61. G. Zyuganov, *Rossiya i sovremenny mir* (Obozrevatel', Moscow, 1995) pp. 77–8. He also cites Spengler at some length on this theme, ibid., p. 17.
62. G. Zyuganov, *Rossiya i sovremenny mir* (Obozrevatel', Moscow, 1995) p. 75.
63. G. Zyuganov, *Rossiya i sovremenny mir* (Obozrevatel', Moscow, 1995) p. 20.

64. G. Zyuganov, *Rossiya i sovremenny mir* (Obozrevatel', Moscow, 1995) pp. 4, 94.
65. G. Zyuganov, *Rossiya i sovremenny mir* (Obozrevatel', Moscow, 1995) pp. 33, 36.
66. G. Zyuganov, *Rossiya i sovremenny mir* (Obozrevatel', Moscow, 1995) p. 56.
67. G. Zyuganov, *Rossiya i sovremenny mir* (Obozrevatel', Moscow, 1995) pp. 57–8.
68. G. Zyuganov, *Rossiya i sovremenny mir* (Obozrevatel', Moscow, 1995) pp. 23, 78–9, 87, 93.
69. G. Zyuganov, *Derzhava* (Informpechat, Moscow, 1994) pp. 75–6.
70. H. Timmermann, 'Die Wiederkehr der KP Russlands', *Berichte des Bundesinstituts für ostwissenschaftliche und internationale Studien*, 12 (1996) 10, 31–2; M. Wyman, 'Developments in Voting Behaviour: 1993 and 1995 Compared', Paper delivered to BASEES Conference, Cambridge 1996, pp. 8–9; J. Ishiyama, 'Red Phoenix? The Communist Party in Post-Soviet Russian Politics', *Party Politics*, vol. II, 2 (1996) 156.
71. Sixty-six per cent of its 1993 voters voted for the party again in 1995, as opposed to 19 per cent of LDPR voters, H. Timmermann, 'Die Wiederkehr der KP Russlands', *Berichte des Bundesinstituts für ostwissenschaftliche und internationale Studien*, 12 (1996) 11.
72. S. White, R. Rose and I. Mc Allister, *How Russia Votes* (Chatham House, Chatham, NJ, 1997) p. 144; M. Wyman, 'Developments in Voting Behaviour: 1993 and 1995 Compared', Paper delivered to BASEES Conference, Cambridge 1996, pp. 13–14 on voter fidelity and its programmatic basis.
73. H. Timmermann, 'Die Wiederkehr der KP Russlands', *Berichte des Bundesinstituts für ostwissenschaftliche und internationale Studien*, 12 (1996) 12–13, 21.
74. S. White, R. Rose and I. McAllister, *How Russia Votes* (Chatham House, Chatham, NJ, 1997) pp. 144–5, 229–34.
75. See M. Wyman, B. Miller, S. White and P. Heywood, 'Parties and Voters in the Elections', in P. Lentini (ed.), *Elections and Political Order in Russia* (CEUP, Budapest, London and NY, 1995) pp. 138–9.
76. See J.-B. Naudet, *Le Monde Hebdomadaire*, 21 December 1995, where Zyuganov professes his support for political pluralism and presidential power. His deputy, Kuptsov, addressing the April 1994 party conference insisted, however, that the party's participation in the Duma did not mean that it had rejected the 'revolutionary and democratic traditions of communism': J. Barth Urban and V. Solovei, *Russia's Communists at the Crossroads* (Westview, Boulder and Oxford, 1997) pp. 127–8.
77. For laws on civic liberties passed by the Duma in 1994 and 1995, see I. Rybkin, *Mirovaya ekonomika*, 7, 1995, 44–5.
78. See R. Sakwa, *The CPRF and the Electoral Process* (University of Strathclyde, Glasgow, 1996) pp. 20–21; G. Luchterhand, 'Von der radikalen Opposition zur Beteiligung der Macht', *Osteuropa*, vol. XLIV,

no. 10 (1996) 973; J. Barth Urban and V. Solovei, *Russia's Communists at the Crossroads* (Westview, Boulder and Oxford, 1997) pp. 138–9.

79. See T. Remington and S. Smith, 'The Early Legislative Process in the Russian Federal Assembly' in D. Oleson and P. Norton (eds), *The New Parliaments of Central and Eastern Europe* (Frank Cass, Portland and London, 1996), pp. 174–8, 186–7; T. Remington and S. Smith, 'The Development of Parliamentary Parties in Russia', *Legislative Studies Quarterly*, vol. XX, no. 4 (1995) 474.

80. These included figures such as Aman Tuleev from Kemerovo and Petr Romanov from Krasnoyarsk. Factory directors constituted one of the biggest professional groups among the 1995 intake of KPRF deputies. See R. Sakwa, *The CPRF and the Electoral Process* (University of Strathclyde, Glasgow, 1996) pp. 7–8; G. Luchterhand, 'Von der radikalen Opposition zur Beteiligung der Macht', *Osteuropa*, vol. XLIV, no. 10 (1996) 976, 979–80.

81. I. Rybkin, *Mirovaya ekonomika*, 7, 1995, 44; G. Luchterhand, 'Von der radikalen Opposition zur Beteiligung der Macht', *Osteuropa*, vol. XLIV, no. 10 (1996) 973.

82. I. Lugovskaya, *Izvestiya*, 21 June 1994, 4; 'Komu prinadlezhit vlast'', *Izvestiya*, 7 July 1994, 5; I. Savvateeva, *Izvestiya*, 25 January 1995, 1; I. Rybkin, *Mirovaya ekonomika*, 7, 1995, 46; E. Schneider, 'Die national-istischen und kommunistischen Fraktionen der russlandischen Duma', *Berichte des Bundesinstituts für ostwissenschaftliche und internationale Studien*, 28 (1995) 15.

83. See I. Savvateeva, *Izvestiya*, 3 June 1994; V. Konovalev, *Izvestiya*, 11 February 1995.

84. T. Remington and S. Smith, 'The Early Legislative Process in the Russian Federal Assembly' in D. Oleson and P. Norton (eds), *The New Parliaments of Central and Eastern Europe* (Frank Cass, Portland and London, 1996) pp. 186–7.

85. I. Rybkin, *Mirovaya ekonomika*, 7, 1995, 45.

86. S. Chugaev, *Izvestiya*, 10 March 1995; A. Platkovsky, *Izvestiya*, 18 March 1995, 1–2; 'Constitution Watch', *East European Constitutional Review*, vol. IV, no. 1 (Winter 1995) 28; C. Dmitriev, 'KGB Successor Organisations Wield Wide Powers' in J. Schmidt (ed.), *The OMRI Annual Survey 1995 of Eastern Europe and the Former Soviet Union: Building Democracy* (M.E. Sharpe, Armonk, NY, and London, 1996) pp. 233–4.

87. A. Larin, *Izvestiya*, 22 June 1994, 2.

88. See E. Schneider, 'Die nationalistischen und kommunistischen Fraktionen der russlandischen Duma', *Berichte des Bundesinstituts für ostwissenschaftliche und internationale Studien*, 28 (1995) 17–20, 33–4.

89. L. Telen, *MN*, 50, 1995, 1.

90. E. Schneider, 'Die nationalistischen und kommunistischen Fraktionen der russlandischen Duma', *Berichte des Bundesinstituts für ost-wissenschaftliche und internationale Studien*, 28 (1995) pp. 18–19. He depicts the party of war in the Duma as the LDPR, Baburin's Russian Way, 80 per cent of the KPRF, 82 per cent of the Agrarians, most of DPR and PRES.

91. For Zhirinovsky's *rapprochement* with the government over Chechnya, see S. Chugaev, *Izvestiya*, 14 January 1995, 1.

92. S. Chugaev, *Izvestiya*, 28 October 1994, 2; J. Barth Urban and V. Solovei, *Russia's Communists at the Crossroads* (Westview, Boulder and Oxford, 1997) p. 137; 'Constitution Watch', *East European Constitutional Review*, vol. IV, no. 1 (Winter 1995) 23.

93. S. Chugaev, *Izvestiya*, 22 June 1995, 1.

94. 'Constitution Watch', *East European Constitutional Review*, vol. IV, no. 3 (Summer 1995) 25; S. White, R. Rose and I. McAllister, *How Russia Votes* (Chatham House, Chatham, NJ, 1997) pp. 184–5.

95. O. Latsis, *Izvestiya*, 23 June 1995, p. 2.

96. T. Remington and S. Smith, 'The Early Legislative Process in the Russian Federal Assembly' in D. Oleson and P. Norton (eds), *The New Parliaments of Central and Eastern Europe* (Frank Cass, Portland and London, 1996), pp. 178, 186–7.

97. I. Rybkin, *Mirovaya ekonomika*, 7, 1995, 44; T. Remington and S. Smith, 'The Development of Parliamentary Parties in Russia', *Legislative Studies Quarterly*, vol. XX, no. 4 (1995) 474; S. Chugaev, *Izvestiya*, 14 January 1995, 1.

98. Examples include *Yabloko*'s support for no-confidence votes in June and July 1995; *Yabloko* and Russia's Choices condemnation of the war in Chechnya; the LDPR and Agrarians' support for the budgets in 1994 and 1995; the LDPR's support for the war in Chechnya and for Yeltsin in July 1995.

99. This is also the view of G. Murrell, *Russia's Transition to Democracy* (Sussex Academic Press, Brighton, 1997) pp. 32–3, 220. R. Sakwa, *The CPRF and the Electoral Process* (University of Strathclyde, Glasgow, 1996) pp. 28–31 for its ambiguities, especially in relation to *narodovlastie*.

100. J. Barth Urban and V. Solovei, *Russia's Communists at the Crossroads* (Westview, Boulder and Oxford, 1997) pp. 127–8; G. Luchterhand, 'Von der radikalen Opposition zur Beteiligung der Macht', *Osteuropa*, vol. XLIV, no. 10 (1996) 980, for his desire to build up his power in the *apparat*. See too S. Simonsen, 'Still Favouring the Power of the Workers', *Transitions*, vol. IV, no. 7 (December 1997) 52–6, who presents Kuptsov as an essentially conservative communist.

101. G. Seleznev, *AiF*, 24, 1996, 3.

102. The party initially consolidated the patriotic bloc with which it had fought the elections by forming, on 7 August 1996, the National-Patriotic Union of which Zyuganov was elected the chairman. This alignment was the source of renewed controversy in 1997. Ye. Krasnikov, *MN*, 31, 1996, 3; Ye. Krasnikov, *MN*, 33, 1996, 4; Ye. Krasnikov, *MN*, 30, 1997, 3; I. Kuzmin, *MN*, 31, 1997, 3; A. Ostapchuk and Ye. Krasnikov, *MN*, 33, 1997, 1–2.

8. THE QUEST FOR POWER: THE 1995–96 ELECTIONS

1. S. White, R. Rose and I. McAllister, *How Russia Votes* (Chatham House, Chatham, NJ, 1997) pp. 181, 183.

2. L. Belin and R. Orttung, 'Parties Proliferate', *Transition*, vol. I, no. 17 (22 September 1995) 42–50, 67 for review of the main electoral blocs;

also S. White, R. Rose and I. McAllister, *How Russia Votes* (Chatham House, Chatham, NJ, 1997) pp. 204–12.

3. For campaign statements, see V. Zhirinovsky, *LDPR: ideologiya i politika* (LDPR, Moscow, 1995) pp. 14–18; V. Zhirinovsky, *Moi garantii izbiratelyam* (LDPR, Moscow, 1996) pp. 10–12. His party was famous for its splits, see Ye. Klepikova and V. Solovyov, *Zhirinovsky* (Viking, London and New York, 1995) pp. 101–2; Ye. Kocherina (ed.), *Fenomen Zhirinovskogo* (Kontrolling, Moscow, 1992) pp. 28–9; S. Plekhanov, *Zhirinovsky: kto on?* (Yevraziya-nord, Moscow, 1994) pp. 130–34; L. Belin and R. Orttung, 'Parties Proliferate', *Transition*, vol. I, no. 17 (22 September 1995) 24; A. Chelnokov, *Izvestiya*, 4 January 1995, 1; A. Chubur, *Rossiiskie vesti*, 2 February 1994, 2; I. Malov, *MN*, 24, 1994, 7a, on party funding.

4. Tsentrizbirkom, *Vybory deputatov Gosudarstvennoi Dumy* (Ves' mir, Moscow, 1996) p. 94.

5. Rutskoi's People's Party of Free Russia, which many extreme nationalists had joined in Autumn 1993, had split, with the nationalist wing following Rutskoi into the 'social-patriotic movement *Derzhava*' in April 1995. It was believed to have been backed by the fund *Vozrozhdenie*, whose finances were the source of constant controversies in 1993. In 1994 and early 1995, Rutskoi was backed by the RAU corporation and its subsidiary the Spiritual Heritage Foundation. Ye. Pestrukhina, *Kuranty*, 6 April 1995, 4; M. Shakina and N. Gul'binsky, *Novoe vremya*, 44, 1993, 10; Ye. Pestrukhina, *MN*, 42, 1994, 9.

6. *Sotsial'-patrioticheskoe dvizhenie Derzhava* (np, Irkutsk, 1995) pp. 14–16.

7. A. Rutskoi, *Obretenie veru* (np, Moscow, 1995) p. 4; *Sotsial'-patriotich-eskoe dvizhenie Derzhava* (np, Irkutsk, 1995) pp. 66–8, 70–71; Ye. Krasnikov, *NG*, 1 April 1995, 1; S. Klishina, *MN*, 32, 1994, 6.

8. A. Rutskoi, *Obretenie veru* (np, Moscow, 1995) pp. 14–15.

9. A. Rutskoi, *Obretenie veru* (np, Moscow, 1995) pp. 49–50, 55, 58, 72.

10. A. Rutskoi, *Obretenie veru* (np, Moscow, 1995) pp. 22–3, 43, 89–91, 94, 117–26.

11. Tsentrizbirkom, *Vybory deputatov Gosudarstvennoi Dumy* (Ves' mir, Moscow, 1996) p. 92; Rutskoi's personality retained its appeal especially in his home province of Kursk, where he was elected governor with an overwhelming 79 per cent of the vote in Autumn 1996, despite attempts to prevent him standing and his consequent inability to campaign. This victory over the official candidate gave Rutskoi a seat in the upper house of the Russian parliament and a chance to rebuild his political career, R. Beeston, *The Times*, 23 October 1996.

12. A. Yuriev, *Sevodnya*, 31 May 1996, 4–5; A. Yanov, *MN*, 24, 1996, 1–2; *The Economist*, 26 October 1996, 41–2, portrays him as inconsistent while D. Lieven, *The Times*, 18 October 1996 tends to an optimistic assessment.

13. C. Freeland, *Financial Times*, 6 September 1994, 3.

14. A. Lebed, *Za derzhavu obidno* (Gregory Page, Moscow, 1995) pp. 409–10.

15. A. Lebed, *Za derzhavu obidno* (Gregory Page, Moscow, 1995) pp. 324, 408. A. Lebed, *Spektakl' nazyvalsya putch* (Lada, Tiraspol, 1993) pp. 43–4.

16. A. Lebed, *Spektakl' nazyvalsya putch* (Lada, Tiraspol, 1993) p. 45; A. Lebed, 'Hier müssen Köpfe rollen', *Der Spiegel*, 36, 1994, 148.

17. S. Simonsen, 'Going his Own Way: a Profile of General Alexander Lebed', *Journal of Slavic Military Studies*, vol. VIII, no. 3 (September 1995) 533–4, 540; B. Lambeth, *The Warrior who Would Rule Russia* (Brassey's Rand, Santa Monica and London, 1996) pp. 41–2.

18. S. Shihab, *Le Monde Hebdomadaire*, 21 December 1995. S. Simonsen, 'Going his Own Way: a Profile of General Alexander Lebed', *Journal of Slavic Military Studies*, vol. VIII, no. 3 (September 1995) 539–41.

19. A. Lebed, *Za derzhavu obidno* (Gregory Page, Moscow, 1995) pp. 320–21, 364–6.

20. A. Lebed, *Za derzhavu obidno* (Gregory Page, Moscow, 1995) p. 433.

21. 'Presidential hopefuls', *MN*, 23, 1996, 4. For a poorly veiled attack on Chernomyrdin, see A. Lebed, *Rossiiskaya federatsiya*, 9, July 1996, 1–2.

22. A. Lebed, *Za derzhavu obidno* (Gregory Page, Moscow, 1995) p. 442.

23. A. Lebed, *Izvestiya*, 20 July 1994, 1; A. Lebed, 'Hier müssen Köpfe rollen', *Der Spiegel*, 36, 1994, 149; A. Lebed, *Za derzhavu obidno* (Gregory Page, Moscow, 1995) p. 409; S. Simonsen, 'Going his Own Way: a Profile of General Alexander Lebed', *Journal of Slavic Military Studies*, vol. VIII, no. 3 (September 1995) 542; B. Lambeth, *The Warrior who Would Rule Russia* (Brassey's Rand, Santa Monica and London, 1996) pp. 68–9.

24. 'Democracy is a Good Word', *Transition*, vol. I, no. 22 (1 December 1995) 19.

25. A. Lebed, *Za derzhavu obidno* (Gregory Page, Moscow, 1995) pp. 436–7, 443.

26. 'Democracy is a Good Word', *Transition*, vol. I, no. 22 (1 December 1995) 19. See also his comments in C. Freeland, *FT*, 6 September 1994, 3; A. Lebed, *Za derzhavu obidno* (Gregory Page, Moscow, 1995) p. 434.

27. See A. Lebed, *AiF*, 22, June 1994, 6; A. Lebed, *Izvestiya*, 20 July 1994, 1.

28. C. Freeland, *FT*, 6 September 1994, 3. On the need for unity and the dangers of political pluralism, see A. Lebed, *NG*, 5 October 1995, 5.

29. A. Lebed, *Za derzhavu obidno* (Gregory Page, Moscow, 1995) pp. 432, 446–7.

30. A. Lebed, *Za derzhavu obidno* (Gregory Page, Moscow, 1995) pp. 435–6; A. Lebed, *Spektakl' nazyvalsya putch* (Lada, Tiraspol, 1993) p. 46. For his criticisms, during the 1995 campaign, of the Russian democrats, their denigration of Russia and concessions to the West, which had insisted, he claimed, on the dismemberment of the USSR, see S. Shihab, *Le Monde Hebdomadaire*, 21 December 1995.

31. P. Reeves, *The Independent*, 28 June 1996. A view also reflected in his first election manifesto, *AiF*, 23, 1996, 4.

32. A. Lebed, *Rossiiskaya federatsiya*, 9, July 1996, 2. On NATO expansion, he oscillated between threatening third world war and professing indifference, see V. Gomez, 'Russia: Lebed Resigns', *Transition*, vol. I, no. 11 (30 June 1995) 35–6; 'Russian Heir Presumptive', *The Times*, 10 October 1996; C. Freeland, *FT*, 25 July 1996, 19.

33. A. Lebed, *Spektakl' nazyvalsya putch* (Lada, Tiraspol, 1993) pp. 46–7.

34. A. Lebed, *Za derzhavu obidno* (Gregory Page, Moscow, 1995) p. 422.

35. A. Lebed, *Za derzhavu obidno* (Gregory Page, Moscow, 1995) pp. 422–4, 444–5.
36. See, for example, *The Times*, 10 October 1996; J. Schmidt (ed.), *Building Democracy* (M.E. Sharpe, New York and London, 1996) p. 246.
37. A. Lebed, *Obshchaya gazeta*, 18–24 March 1994, 8.
38. The KRO had its origins in the sharply anti-Yeltsin opposition, including the Union for the Regeneration of Russia and Sterligov's Russian National Council, whose emphasis on a strong State capable of defending Russians' interests the KRO shared. See V. Gel'bras, *Kto yest' chto*, vol. I (RAN, Moscow, 1994) pp. 482–6; W. Slater, 'The Center-Right in Russia', *RFE/RL Research Report*, vol. II, no. 34 (27 August 1993) 7, 10.
39. A. Stepovoi, *Izvestiya*, 29 October 1994, 4.
40. The KRO, which according to Skokov in November 1995, had social justice as its main aim, propounded 'the ideology of state patriotism, that is of the State for the people', unlike the 'plutocratic' democrats who ruled Russia in their own narrow interests, Yu. Skokov, *Zavtra*, 47, 1995, 1, 3. See too its 1995 election manifesto, *Kongress russkikh obshchin* (KRO, Moscow, 1995); A. Zhilin and S. Yastrebov, *MN*, 38–9 1995, 4; A. Mursaliyev, *MN*, 38–9, 1995, 2; L. Belin and R. Orttung, 'Parties Proliferate', *Transition*, vol. I, no. 17 (22 September 1995) p. 49; R. Orttung, 'Yeltsin's Most Dangerous Rival', *Transition*, vol. I, no. 22 (1 December 1995) 14–16.
41. B. Yeltsin *The View from the Kremlin* (Harper Collins, London, 1994) pp. 172–3.
42. Tsentrizbirkom, *Vybory deputatov Gosudarstvennoi Dumy* (Ves' mir, Moscow, 1996) p. 92.
43. L. Belin, 'Are the Communists Poised for Victory?', *Transition*, vol. I, no. 22 (1 December 1995) 25–6; C. Scott, *The Sunday Times*, 17 December 1995; D. Pushkar, *MN*, 37, 1995, 3; O. Bychkova, *MN*, 40–41, 1995, 2.
44. Tsentrizbirkom, *Vybory deputatov Gosudarstvennoi Dumy* (Ves' mir, Moscow, 1996) p. 92.
45. Tsentrizbirkom, *Vybory deputatov Gosudarstvennoi Dumy* (Ves' mir, Moscow, 1996) pp. 92, 154.
46. 'Za nashu sovetskuyu rodinu', *SR*, 31 August 1995, 3. For its rejection of NATO actions in Bosnia, the ratification of START II and calls for increased defence expenditure in September 1995, see J. Barth Urban and V. Solovei, *Russia's Communists at the Crossroads* (Westview, Boulder and Oxford, 1997) p. 163.
47. Tsentrizbirkom, *Vybory deputatov Gosudarstvennoi Dumy* (Ves' mir, Moscow, 1996) pp. 94, 202–3.
48. Tsentrizbirkom, *Vybory deputatov Gosudarstvennoi Dumy* (Ves' mir, Moscow, 1996) p. 94.
49. S. White, R. Rose and I. McAllister, *How Russia Votes* (Chatham House, Chatham, NJ, 1997) p. 235.
50. R. Sakwa, *Russian Politics and Society*, 2nd edn (Routledge, London, 1996) p. 113.

51. These included the former democrat, Duma deputy, writer and Olympic weight-lifter, Yuri Vlasov. By 1992, Vlasov had joined the right-wing of Aksyuchits's Christian Democratic Party and he became an increasingly xenophobic and bitter critic of the reforms, which he saw as a betrayal of Russia's interests. As a Presidential candidate, he was backed by Eduard Limonov, but lacking organisation and resources, he made no impact on the campaign and won only a little over 150 000 votes in the first round of the campaign. See *Rossiskaya federatsiya*, 9, 1996, 9; *Maximov's Companion to the Russian Presidential Elections* (Maximov Publishers, London, 1996) pp. 92–4. For a sample of his views, see Yu. Vlasov, *Rus' bez vozhdya* (Soyuz zhurnalistov, Voronezh, 1995).

52. For his declining support, see T. Clark, 'The Zhirinovsky Electoral Victory', *Nationalities Papers*, vol. XXIII, no. 4 (December 1995) 776. For his pronouncements at this time and a noticeable leftward shift in his position, see V. Zhirinovsky, *VII s"ezd LDPR* (LDPR, Moscow, 1996) pp. 62–5, 71.

53. See voter quoted by S. Erlanger, *The Guardian*, 31 December 1993.

54. R. Orttung, S. Parrish and P. Morvant, 'Yeltsin Campaigns Hard', *Transition*, vol. II, no. 14, (12 July 1996) 57–9.

55. A. Ostapchuk and Ye. Krasnikov, *MN*, 40–41, 1995, 4, discuss his relations with Skokov and his base support in *Chest' i rodina*, a group of patriotic army officers.

56. A. Lebed, *AiF*, 22–3, 1996. A variant of this programme was available in Irkutsk, see A. Lebed, *My yeshche gordimsya Rossiei* (Vostok, Moscow, 1996).

57. A. Chelnokov, *Izvestiya*, 11 July 1996, 5.

58. OMRI Russian Presidential Survey, no. 4, 22 May 1996; O. Latsis, *Izvestiya*, 29 May 1996; A. Lebed, *Programmnoe zayavlenie*, press release, 24 April 1996 (which stresses the need for honesty, law and order); A. Lebed, *Izvestiya*, 31 May 1996, 3; A. Lebed, *Vostochnaya-sibirskaya pravda*, 28 May 1996; A. Lebed, *RG*, 29 June 1996; A. Zhilin, *MN*, 25, July 1996, 2.

59. 'Za nashu sovetskuyu rodinu', *SR*, 31 August 1995.

60. *Predvybornaya platforma [...] Zyuganova* (ndp, 1996) pp. 1–22. This rhetoric was repeated on the campaign trail, see S. Scholl, *MN*, 19, 1996, 2.

61. *Predvybornaya platforma [...] Zyuganova* (ndp, 1996) pp. 1–2.

62. Those involved included Rutskoi and *Derzhava*, Baburin and *ROS*; Terekhov's Union of Officers, Miloserdov's Russian Party of Russia (an offshoot of *Pamyat'*); (Vasiliev backed Yeltsin, however, and attended his inauguration); the imperialist *Soyuz*; Anpilov and Working Russia, the orthodox Marxist Leninists of *Roskomsoyuz*, Ryzhkov's Power to the People; the Agrarian Party, Starodubtsev's Agrarian Union; the Society of Russian Scientists of Communist Orientation; and individuals such as the writers Alexander Prokhanov, Yuri Bondarev, Valentin Rasputin, Vadim Kozhinov, Alexander Kazintsev and the former dissident priest, Dmitri Dudko. See *Zavtra*, 10, March 1996, 1; *Zavtra*, 12, March 1996, p. 1; N. Ilyina (ed.), *Pochemu Zyuganov dolzhen stat' prezidentom*

(Zyuganov Election Fund, Moscow, 1996) pp. 7–10, 17–22. See too Yu. Lebedev, *MN*, 7 (should read 8) 1996, 2; Ye. Krasnikov, *MN*, 3, 1996, 2; L. Belin, 'Zyuganov Tries to Broaden an Already Powerful Coalition', *Transition*, vol. II, no. 11 (31 May 1996) 12–13.

63. Yu. Bogomolov, *MN*, 11, 1996, 1.

64. OMRI Russian Presidential Election Survey, 1, 3 May 1996. The Yeltsin-sponsored free paper, distributed in the provinces, *Ne dai Bog* depicted Zyuganov in various unflattering guises, for example, as Hitler and as rationing sausage.

65. *MN*, 10, 1996, 2. Ye. Rykovtseva, *MN*, 23, June 1996, 4.

66. 'Eto mozhno delat'', *NG*, 25 May 1996, 1, 6. This programme was reportedly prepared by Yuri Maslyukov, see A. Ostapchuk, *MN*, 23 June 1996, 2. Maslyukov's moderate position is outlined in an interview with N. Kirichenko and A. Galiyev, *MN*, 24, 1996, 9.

67. For Zyuganov's reluctance to identify himself as a social democrat, see interview in *Zavtra*, 15, 1996, 1, 2. For his nationalist television slots, see OMRI Russian Presidential Survey, 12, 2 July 1996.

68. For examples of his attempts to present himself as a social democrat, censorious of nationalism and anti-Semitism and supportive of a mixed economy see excerpts of his interview on NTV in Zyuganov, *Izbiratel'*, 13 June 1996 (supplement to *SR*); A. Pushkov, *MN*, 6, 1996, 1, 6; *MN*, 42–3, 1995, 2.

69. On the KPRF's negative rating, see polls cited in *Novoe vremya*, 23 July 1993, 13; *MN*, 26, 1996, 3. According to the 1996 poll, 44 per cent of respondents expected life to stay the same if Yeltsin won the elections, 7.7 per cent expected it to get worse and 28.8 per cent expected it to improve; the corresponding figures for Zyuganov were 23.1 per cent, 41.9 per cent and 10.1 per cent.

70. Officially, Yeltsin was reported to have spent $2.9 million but he is rumoured to have spent up to $100 million. For his use of his office to secure re-election, see L. Belin and R. Orttung, 'Electing a Fragile Political Stability', *Transitions*, vol. III, no. 2 (7 February 1997) 68; 'Constitution Watch', *East European Constitutional Review*, vol. V, nos. 2–3 (Spring–Summer 1996) 21; *Maximov's Companion to the Russian Presidential Elections* (Maximov Publishers, London, 1996) p. 37. Yeltsin secured the backing of media moguls Berezovsky of ORT, Vladimir Gusinsky and Igor Malashenko of NTV. On state and often on regional television, he received sympathetic and blanket coverage, unlike the marginalised Zyuganov. For Yeltsin's vastly superior access to the broadcast media and the pro-Yeltsin tenor of this coverage, see European Institute for the Media, *Media and the Russian Presidential Elections*, newsletter no. 2 (4 June 1996), 1–3.

71. Zhirinovsky came fourth with 4.3 million votes. *Rossiiskaya federatsiya*, 9, 1996, 9; *MN*, 24, 1996, 1.

72. A. Chelnokov, *Izvestiya*, 11 July 1996, 5; R. Beeston, *The Times*, 20 June 1996; C. Freeland, *FT*, 25 July 1995, 19; R. Orttung, S. Parrish and P. Morvant, 'Yeltsin Campaigns Hard', *Transition*, vol. II, no. 14 (12 July 1996) 59; S. Parrish, 'Enter Lebed', *Transition*, vol. II, no. 15 (26 July 1996) 8.

73. See S. White, R. Rose and I. McAllister, *How Russia Votes* (Chatham House, Chatham, NJ, 1997) pp. 263–6 for an account.
74. According to the Central Electoral Commission, Yeltsin won 40 208 384 votes to Zyuganov's 30 113 306 votes, see *Rossiiskaya federatsiya*, 9, 1996, pp. 9, 12; *Maximov's Companion to the Russian Presidential Elections* (Maximov Publishers, London, 1996) p. 254.
75. R. Sakwa, *Russian Politics and Society*, 2nd edn (Routledge, London, 1996) p. 111; D. Skillen, 'Media Coverage' in P. Lentini (ed.), *Elections and Political Order* (Central European University Press, Budapest, London and New York, 1995) p. 121.
76. See *MN*, 26, 1996, 3. *Novoe vremya*, 23, July 1993, 13. L. Belin, 'Are the Communists for Victory?', *Transition*, vol. I, no. 22 (1 December 1995) 27.
77. S. White R. Rose and I. McAllister, *How Russia Votes* (Chatham House, Chatham, NJ, 1997) p. xviii. M. Mendras, 'Interpreting the Russian Elections', *East European Constitutional Review*, vol. V, no. 2–3 (Spring–Summer 1996) 51. *Rossiiskaya federatsiya*, 9, 1996, 9.
78. See A. Fadin, 'Guennadi Ziouganov, un futur "président rouge" à la solde du capital?', *Courrier International*, 281 (21–7 March 1996), 18.
79. L. Shevtsova, *MN*, 22, 1996, 2.
80. For an excellent analysis of the new *nomenklatura* see R. Sakwa, *Russian Politics and Society*, 2nd edn (Routledge, London, 1996) pp. 159–63, 165, 171. See too 'Russia and Democracy', *The Economist*, 16 December 1995, 20; K. Maidanek, *Svobodnaya mysl'*, 9, 1994, p. 29; O. Poptsov, *Khronika vremen 'Tsarya Borisa'* (Sovershenno sekretno, Moscow, 1996) p. 393; T. Graham, *NG*, 23 November 1995, 5.

CONCLUSION

1. S. White, R. Rose and I. McAllister, *How Russia Votes* (Chatham House, Chatham, NJ, 1997) p. 178.
2. The World Bank, *Statistical Handbook 1996* (World Bank, Washington, 1996) pp. 404–5, 407.
3. *Novaya Rossiya: 1994: informatsionno-statisticheskii al'manakh* (Mezhdunarodnaya akademiya informatizatsii, Moscow, 1994) pp. 516–19.
4. *Novaya Rossiya: 1994: informatsionno-statisticheskii al'manakh* (Mezhdunarodnaya akademiya informatizatsii, Moscow, 1994) p. 533. Goskomizdat' Rossii, *Rossiiskii statisticheskii ezhegodnik* (Logos, Moscow, 1996) p. 30 for declining incomes and GDP.
5. S. White, R. Rose and I. McAllister, *How Russia Votes* (Chatham House, Chatham, NJ, 1997) pp. 60–62.
6. S. White, R. Rose and I. McAllister, *How Russia Votes* (Chatham House, Chatham, NJ, 1997) p. 179.
7. The World Bank, *Statistical Handbook 1996* (World Bank, Washington, 1996) pp. 379–81.
8. M. Wyman, *Public Opinion in Post-Communist Russia* (Macmillan, London and New York, 1997) p. 97.

9. S. White, R. Rose and I. McAllister, *How Russia Votes* (Chatham House, Chatham, NJ, 1997) p. 211.

10. See R. Sakwa, *The CPRF and the Electoral Process* (University of Strathclyde, Glasgow, 1996) p. 30; I. Mikhailovskaya, 'Russian Voting Behaviour', *East European Constitutional Review*, vol. V, no. 2–3 (Spring–Summer 1996) 61; M. Wyman, *Public Opinion in Post-Communist Russia* (Macmillan, London and New York, 1997) p. 211.

11. G. Murrell, *Russia's Transition to Democracy* (Sussex Academic Press, Brighton, 1997) p. 15.

12. See J. Devlin, *The Rise of the Russian Democrats* (Edward Elgar, Aldershot, 1995) p. 250.

13. J. Dunlop, 'Russia: in Search of an Identity?' in I. Bremmer and R. Taras (eds), *New States, New Politics* (CUP, Cambridge, 1997) p. 55; V. Tishkov, *Ethnicity, Nationalism and Conflict* (Sage Publications, London and Notre Dame, 1997) p. 252 cites a poll of November–December 1993 in which 70 per cent thought the break-up of the USSR was more bad than good; M. Wyman, *Public Opinion* (Macmillan, London and New York, 1997) pp. 173, 160–68 for evolution of these views in 1990–92; Yu. Levada, *Democratic Disorder and Russian Public Opinion Trends* (University of Strathclyde, Glasgow, 1995) p. 4.

14. J. Dunlop, 'Russia: in Search of an Identity?' in I. Bremmer and R. Taras (eds), *New States, New Politics* (CUP, Cambridge, 1997) p. 55.

15. See P. Goble, 'Three Faces of Nationalism' in C. Kupchan (ed.), *Nationalism and Nationalities in the New Europe* (Cornell University Press, Ithaca and London, 1995) p. 129.

16. L. Drobizheva 'Perestroika', in G. Lapidus, V. Zaslavsky and P. Goldman (eds), *From Union to Commonwealth* (CUP, Cambridge, 1992) p. 101; V. Tishkov, *Ethnicity, Nationalism and Conflict* (Sage Publications, London and Notre Dame, 1997) p. 264; J. Dunlop, 'Russia: in Search of an Identity?' in I. Bremmer and R. Taras (eds), *New States, New Politics* (CUP, Cambridge, 1997) pp. 55–7; M. Wyman, B. Miller, S. White and P. Heywood, 'Parties and Voters in the Elections', in P. Lentini (ed.), *Elections and Political Order* (Central European University Press, Budapest, London and New York, 1995) p. 132.

17. J. Dunlop, 'Russia: in Search of an Identity?', in I. Bremmer and R. Taras (eds), *New States, New Politics* (CUP, Cambridge, 1997) p. 55.

18. S. White, R. Rose and I. McAllister, *How Russia Votes* (Chatham House, Chatham, NJ, 1997) p. 48; M. Wyman, *Public Opinion* (Macmillan, London and New York, 1997) pp. 89–90; J. Gibson, 'The Resilience of Mass Support for Democratic Institutions' in V. Tismaneanu (ed.), *Political Culture and Civil Society in Russia* (M.E. Sharpe, Armonk, NY and London, 1995) pp. 77–81, 87; Yu. Levada, *Democratic Disorder and Russian Public Opinion Trends* (University of Strathclyde, Glasgow, 1995) p. 6.

19. See J. Devlin, *The Rise of the Russian Democrats* (Edward Elgar, Aldershot, 1995) pp. 241–3, 251–4, for declining support for democratisation and reform after 1990. See however J. Gibson, 'The Resilience of Mass Support for Democratic Institutions', in V. Tismaneanu (ed.),

Political Culture and Civil Society in Russia (M.E. Sharpe, Armonk, NY and London, 1995) pp. 77–81, 87–8 for a different view.

20. M. Wyman, *Public Opinion* (Macmillan, London and New York, 1997) pp. 236–7.

21. S. White, R. Rose and I. McAllister, *How Russia Votes* (Chatham House, Chatham, NJ, 1997) pp. 44–5, 51. See also Ye. Chinyaeva, 'The Search for the "Russian Idea"', *Transitions*, vol. IV, no. 1 (June 1997) 43.

22. M. Wyman, *Public Opinion* (Macmillan, London and New York, 1997) pp. 98–9; K. Dashiwa and B. Parrott, *Russia and the New States of Eurasia* (CUP, Cambridge, 1994) p. 130: polls indicated that most people (41 per cent in mid-1992 and 47 per cent in 1993) felt that no political party reflected their views.

23. S. Whitefield and G. Evans, 'Support for Democracy and Political Opposition in Russia', *Post-Soviet Affairs*, vol. XII, no. 3 (July–September 1996) 224.

24. J. Gibson, 'The Resilience of Mass Support for Democratic Institutions' in V. Tismaneanu (ed.), *Political Culture and Civil Society in Russia* (M.E. Sharpe, Armonk, NY and London, 1995) pp. 77–81.

25. Yu. Levada, *Democratic Disorder and Russian Public Opinion Trends* (University of Strathclyde, Glasgow, 1995) pp. 8–9.

26. Yu. Levada, *Democratic Disorder and Russian Public Opinion Trends* (University of Strathclyde, Glasgow, 1995) pp. 10–11.

27. S. White, R. Rose and I. McAllister, *How Russia Votes* (Chatham House, Chatham, NJ, 1997) p. 151.

28. M. Wyman, B. Miller, S. White and P. Heywood, 'Parties and Voters in the Elections', in P. Lentini (ed.), *Elections and Political Order* (Central European University Press, Budapest, London and New York, 1995) p. 134.

29. Yu. Levada, *Democratic Disorder and Russian Public Opinion Trends* (University of Strathclyde, Glasgow, 1995) p. 11.

30. M. Wyman, *Public Opinion* (Macmillan, London and New York, 1997) pp. 138–40, 131.

31. Cited by Ye. Chinyaeva, 'The Search for the "Russian Idea"', *Transition*, vol. IV, no. 1 (June 1997) 42–4.

32. Yu. Levada, *Democratic Disorder and Russian Public Opinion Trends* (University of Strathclyde, Glasgow, 1995) appendix P10.

33. Yu. Levada, *Democratic Disorder and Russian Public Opinion Trends* (University of Strathclyde, Glasgow, 1995) pp. 11–12, appendix P9.

34. S. White, R. Rose and I. McAllister, *How Russia Votes* (Chatham House, Chatham, NJ, 1997) p. 47.

35. M. Wyman, *Public Opinion* (Macmillan, London and New York, 1997) p. 131.

36. Quoted by I. Mikhailovskaya, 'Russian Voting Behaviour', *East European Constitutional Review*, vol. V, no. 2–3 (Spring–Summer 1996) 60–61.

37. M. Wyman, B. Miller, S. White and P. Heywood, 'Parties and Voters in the Elections', in P. Lentini (ed.), *Elections and Political Order* (Central European University Press, Budapest, London and New York, 1995) pp. 132, 134–5.

38. See S. White, R. Rose and I. McAllister, *How Russia Votes* (Chatham House, Chatham, NJ, 1997) pp. xiii–xiv.
39. See Elie Kedourie, *Nationalism*, 3rd edn. (Hutchinson University Library, London, 1969); H. Kohn, *The Mind of Modern Germany* (Macmillan, London, 1965); G. Mosse, *The Crisis of German Ideology* (Weidenfeld and Nicolson, 1964). For its mythopoeic tendencies, see E. Hobsbawm and T. Ranger (eds), *The Invention of Tradition* (CUP, Cambridge, 1983). For a short discussion of the historiography of nationalism, see A. Smith, 'Nationalism and the Historians' in G. Balakrishnan (ed.), *Mapping the Nation* (Verso, London and New York, 1996), pp. 175–97.

References

In addition to the works cited below, I have also referred to material on the informal movement of the late 1980s and early 1990s in the archive of the Moscow Bureau for Information Exchange (MBIO) founded by Vyacheslav Igrunov. The State Historical Library contains a valuable collection of party programmes from the early to mid-1990s.

Abramovich, Aron. 'Uchastie yevreev v vooruzhennikh silakh SSSR do voiny s Germanei', *NS*, 11, 1990, 151–6.

Agursky, Mikhail. *Ideologiya natsional'-bol'shevizma* (YCMA Press, Paris, 1980).

——. 'The Prospects of National-Bolshevism' in Conquest R. (ed.), *The Last Empire* (Hoover Institute, Stanford, 1986) pp. 87–108.

——. *The Third Rome: National-Bolshevism in the USSR* (Westview Press, Boulder, CO, London, 1987).

Akhromeev, Sergei. 'Polveka s nachala voiny', *Den'*, 12, June 1991.

Aksakov, Konstantin. 'Memorandum on the Internal State of Russia' in Leatherbarrow, W. and Offord, D. (eds), *A Documentary History of Russian Thought from the Enlightenment to Marxism* (Ardis, Ann Arbor, 1987) pp. 95–107.

Aksyuchits, Viktor. 'Russia's Christian Democrats', *MN*, 21, 3–10 June 1990, 6.

——. 'Ispytanie russkoi idei', *Pravda*, 15 October 1992, 1–2.

——. 'Russkaya ideya' in Trotsky Y. (ed.), *Russkaya ideya i sovremennost'* (APIN, Moscow, 1992) pp. 48–64.

——. V plenu novykh utopii', *NG*, 23 October 1992, 2.

——. 'Ya ne boyus' slovo diktatura', *Golos*, 32, 9–15 August 1993, 6.

——. (ed.) *Vozrozhdenie Rossii. Khristianskaya demokratiya i prosveshchenny patriotizm* (Vybor, Moscow, 1993).

——. *Miropraviteli temy veka sego* (Vybor, Moscow, 1994).

Aleinik, Lev. 'Natsional'-respublikantsy razrabotali sverkhideologiyu', *Segodnya*, 28 March 1995, 2.

Alekseev, N., Il'in, V., Savitsky *et al. Yevraziiskii sbornik: politika, filosofiya, rossievedenie* (Prague, 1929).

Alexeev, S. 'Tormoza perestroiki', *MG*, 9, 1989, 220–22.

Alexei, Patriarch of Moscow and All-Russia. 'Pis'mo: s lyubov'yu, nadezhdoi i trevogoi za vas', *SR*, 6 July 1991, 3.

——. 'Your Prophets are our Prophets', *MN*, 7, 16–23 February 1992, 16.

Alimev, G. and Lynev, R. 'Kuda uvodit Pamyat'?', *Izvestiya*, 2 June 1987, 3.

Alksnis, Viktor. 'Pora derzhat' otvet', *Den'*, 16, August 1991.

Anderson, Benedict. *Imagined Communities: Reflections on the Origins and Spread of Nationalism* (Verso, London and New York, 1983).

Anderson, John. *Religion, State and Politics in the Soviet Union and the Successor States* (CUP, Cambridge, 1994).

Andreev, A. 'ROS: god bor'by i ego uroki', *Moskva*, 11–12, 1992, 158–62.
Andreeva, N. 'Ne mogu postupat'sya printsipamy', *SR*, 13 March 1988, 3.
——. 'Glasnost' obyazyvaet', *MG*, 7, 1989, 272–7.
Anishchenko, G.A. and Aksyuchits, Viktor. 'Obrashchenie po povodu vzaimo-otnoshenii mezhdu dvumya chastami russkoi tserkvy', *Russkii kur'er*, 26 September 1991, 11.
Anisin, N. 'Tbiliskoe delo: lozh' i pravda', *Den'*, 9, May 1991.
Anpilov, Viktor. 'Za krasnoe yedinstvo', *Zavtra*, 7 February 1996, 1, 3.
——. 'Ostanovit' man'yakov Yeltsina', *Molnya*, 61, 1993, 1.
Antic, O. 'Revival of Orthodox Brotherhoods in Russia', *RFE/RL Research Report*, vol. I, no. 11 (13 March 1992) 62–3.
Antikhrist v Moskve (Novaya kniga, Moscow, 1995).
Antonov, A. 'Pamyat', *Izmailovskii vestnik*, 2, January 1990, 3.
Antonov, M. 'Uskorenie: vozmozhnosti i pregrady', *NS*, 7, 1986, 3–20.
——. 'Yest' li budushchee u sotsializma?', *NS*, 7, 1991, 132–3.
——. 'Davaite vnesem yasnost'. Otkrytoe pis'mo S.B. Stankevichu', *Russkii vestnik*, 23, 1992, 2.
'Are they house-trained?', *The Economist*, 16 December 1995, 27–8.
Arifdzhanov, R. 'Lozung "spasitelei": ni voiny, ni mira', *Izvestiya*, 2 November 1994, 2.
Aron, L. 'Russia between Revolution and Democracy', *Post-Soviet Affairs*, vol. II, no. 4 (October–December 1995) 305–39.
Astafiev, Viktor. 'Mesto dveistviya. Rasskazy', *NS*, 5, 1986, 123–41.
——. 'Slovo kandidata', *Lit. gaz.*, 1 February 1989, 1.
——. 'Ne znaem serdtse serediny', *Pravda*, 30 June 1989.
——. 'Ya budu s 'Pamyat'yu', *Pamyat'*, 6 May 1990.
Azadovsky, K. 'Ovations and Posters in Court', *MN*, 37, 10–17 September 1989, 15.
Azrael, Jeremy (ed.). *Soviet Nationality Policies and Practices* (Praeger, NY, 1978).
Babasyan, N. 'Raskol v RKhDD', *Express-khronika*, 13, 1992.
——. 'Soyuz pravoslavnikh bratstv', *NG*, 21 May 1992.
——. 'Kartinki s vystavki', *NG*, 11 July 1992.
Baburin, Sergei. 'Segodnya Popov mne strashen', *Rossiya*, 18–24 March 1992, 4.
——. 'Natsional'nye interesy na rubezhe dvatsat' pervogo veka', *NS*, 2, 1995, 173–6.
Balburov, D. '*MN* goes undercover among Nationalists', *MN*, 40–41, 20–26 October 1995, 3.
——. 'Rivalries among Russian Nazis', *MN*, 8, 29 February–6 March 1996, 3.
Baranova-Gorchenko, I. 'Vo blago', *MG*, 9, 1987, 222–6.
Baranovsky, Igor. 'Ot KGB do LDPR', *MN*, 36, 4–11 September 1994, 1, 11.
Barghoorn, F.C. *Soviet Russian Nationalism* (OUP, Oxford, 1956).
——. 'Russian Nationalism and Soviet Politics' in Conquest R. (ed.), *The Last Empire* (Hoover Institute, Stanford, 1986) pp. 30–77.
Barkashov, A.P. 'Ya ne fashist, ya natsist', *Moskovskii komsomolets*, 4 August 1993, 2.
——. *Azbuka russkogo natsionalista* (Slovo, Moscow, 1994).
——. 'Raz'yasnenie pozitsii', *Russkii poryadok*, December 1993–January 1994, 4–6.

——. 'Tol'ko molodaya natsional'naya elita [...] spaset Rossiyu ot pora-boshcheniya', *Russkii poryadok*, 2–3, 1994, 1.

Barsukov, A. 'Ob'edinennye demokraty', *NG*, 2 July 1991.

Batuev, V. 'Russkii natsist so svastikoi', *AiF*, 36, 1993, 8.

——. 'Baburin, kotory zhivet ne v SSSR', *AiF*, 31, August 1994, 3.

——. 'My natsional-sotsialisty', *AiF*, 9, 1995, 7.

Beeson, T. *Discretion and Valour: Religious Conditions in Russia and Eastern Europe* (Collins and Fontana, London and Philadelphia, 1982).

Beeston, R. 'Yeltsin made secret election pact with Lebed', *The Times*, 20 June 1996.

——. 'Former Anti-Yeltsin Plotter in Landslide Poll Victory', *The Times*, 23 October 1996.

——. 'Dismissed Lebed left to await his hour of destiny' *The Times*, 18 October 1996, 19.

Begun, V. and Borsh, V. 'Otluchenie ot perestroiki', *SK*, 10 December 1987, 6.

Belelyubsky, F. 'Monarkhisty uvazhayut zakonnost"', *Pravda*, 17 November 1993, 4.

——. 'Front ili tyl?', *Pravda*, 25 October 1994, 1.

Belin, Laura, 'Ultranationalist parties follow disparate paths', *Transition*, vol. I, no. 10 (23 June 1995) 8–12.

——. 'Zhirinovsky's Uphill Battle', *Transition*, vol. I, no. 22 (1 December 1995) 20–24, 68.

——. 'Are the Communists Poised for Victory?' *Transition*, vol. I, no. 22 (1 December 1995) 25–8.

——. 'An array of mini-parties wage futile parliamentary campaigns', *Transition*, vol. II, no. 4 (23 February 1996) 15–19.

——. 'Zyuganov Tries to Broaden an Already Powerful Left-Wing Coalition', *Transition*, vol. II, no. 11 (31 May 1996) 15.

—— and Orttung, R. 'Parties Proliferate on Eve of Elections', *Transition*, vol. I, no. 17 (22 September 1995) 42–50, 67.

——. 'Domestic Affairs' in Schmidt J. (ed.), *OMRI Annual Survey of Eastern Europe and the Former Soviet Union 1995. Building Democracy* (Sharpe, London and NY, 1996) pp. 210–23.

Belov, Vasily. 'Vozrodit' v krestianstve' in Stetsenko, V. (ed.), *Pisatel' i vremya* (Sovetskii pisatel', Moscow, 1989) pp. 55–70.

——. 'Zapiski na khodu', *SR*, 6 July 1991, 1, 4.

——. 'Khvatit' sidet' v temnote', *SR*, 20 June 1992, 2.

Belyakov, A. 'V nashem dome poselilsya zamechatel'ny sosed', *Stolitsa*, 29, 1992, 1, 3.

Benda, J. *La Trahison des Clercs*, 3rd edn (Grasset, Paris, 1975).

Berezovsky, V.N., Krotov, N.I. *Neformal'naya Rossiya* (Molodaya Gvardiya, Moscow, 1990).

Berezovsky, V., Krotov, N., Chervyakov, V. *Rossiya: partii, assotsiatsii, soyuzy, kluby. Spravochnik* 2 vols. (RAU Press, Moscow, 1991).

Berezovsky, V., Krotov, N., Solovei, V., Chervyakov, V. *Rossiya: partii, assotsi-atsii, soyuzy, kluby. Sbornik materialov i dokumentov*, 10 vols. (RAU Press, Moscow, 1992–3).

Berger, M. 'Zhelanie parlamenta pomoch' invalidam', *Izvestiya*, 14 February 1995, 1, 2.

Besançon, Alain. 'Nationalism and Bolshevism in the USSR' in Conquest R. (ed.), *The Last Empire* (Hoover Institute, Stanford, 1986) pp. 1–13.

Bethell, Nicholas and Rubin, Barry. *Kontinent: the Alternative Voice of Russia and Eastern Europe* (Hodder and Stoughton, London, 1977).

Bilinsky, Leonid. *Katekhizis monarkhizma* (Prestol', Moscow, 1991).

Billington, J. 'A New Time of Troubles?' in Daniels, R. (ed.), *Soviet Communism from Reform to Collapse* (D.C. Heath, Lexington, 1995) pp. 378–87.

Bobkov, V. and Sergeev, A. (eds) *Al'ternativa: Vybor puti. Perestroika upravleniya i gorizonty rynka* (Mysl', Moscow, 1990).

Bogomolov, G. *et al.*. 'Front bez flangov', *Leningradskaya pravda*, 25 July 1989, 2.

Bogomolov, Yuri. 'Znakomye vse litsa v tolpe', *Izvestiya*, 15 April 1994, 2.

——. 'General Shoots his Big Mouth', *MN*, 11, 21–27 March 1996, 1–2.

Boldin, V. *Khrushchenie p'edestala* (Respublika, Moscow, 1995).

Bondarenko, G. 'Sterzhnevaya slovesnost', *NS*, 12, 1989, 165–78.

——. 'Natsional'naya Rossiya', *Den'*, 14, July 1991.

——. 'Smena vekh', *Den'*, 18, September 1991, 1, 2.

——. 'Prosti, raspyataya Rossiya', *Obozrevatel'*, 2–3, February 1992, 2.

——. 'V gostyakh u L'va Gumileva', *Den'*, March 1992, 6.

——. *Lev Gumilev* (Paleya, Moscow, 1992).

——. *Alexander Prokhanov* (Paleya, Moscow, 1992).

Bondarev, Yuri. 'Istina mnogolika', *SR*, 18 July 1987, 6.

'Boris Goodenough?', *The Economist*, 4–10 November 1995, 37–8.

Borisov, Fr A. 'An Orthodox Priest Responds to the Appeal', *Religion, State and Society*, vol. XXIII, no. 1 (1995) 33–5.

Böss, Otto. *Die Lehre der Eurasier* (Harrasowitz, Wiesbaden, 1961).

Boulton, L. 'Neo-fascists benefit from reformist disunity', *FT*, 13 December 1993.

——. 'Voters back Yeltsin reforms', *FT*, 13 December 1993.

Bourdeaux, M. *Gorbachev, Glasnost' and the Gospel* (Hodder and Stoughton, London, 1990).

——. *The Politics of Religion in Russia and the New States of Eurasia* (M.E. Sharpe, Armonk, NY and London, 1995).

Bracher, K.-D. *The German Dictatorship: the Origins, Structure and Consequences of National Socialism* (Penguin, London, 1973).

Bremmer, Ian and Taras, Ray (eds). *Nations and Politics in the Soviet Successor States* (CUP, Cambridge, 1993).

——. *New States, New Politics: Building the Post-Soviet Nations* (CUP, Cambridge, 1997).

Brown, J. 'Extremism in Eastern Europe and the Former Soviet Union' in *The Politics of Intolerance, RFE/RL Research Report*, vol. III, no. 16 (22 April 1994) 1–4.

Brudny, Yitzhak M. 'The Heralds of Opposition to Perestroyka' in Hewett, A. and Winston, V.H. (eds), *Milestones in Glasnost and Perestroyka: Politics and People* (Brookings Institution, Washington, 1991), pp. 153–89.

Brym, R. and Degtaryev, A. 'Anti-Semitism in Moscow: Results of an October 1992 Survey', *Slavic Review*, vol. LI, no. I (1993), 1–12.

Buhl-Zedginidze, N. 'S tochki zrenii chetvertoi vlasti', *Strana i mir*, 2, March–April 1992, 22–36.

Bulychev, Yuri. 'Russkii konservatizm', *Moskva*, 2, February 1993, 122–35.

Burg, Steven L. 'The Calculus of Soviet Anti-Semitism' in Azrael, J. (ed.), *Soviet Nationality Policies and Practices* (Praeger, NY, 1978) pp. 189–222.

Buzgalin, Alexander and Kolganov. A. *Bloody October in Moscow* (Monthly Review Press, NY, 1994).

Bychkov, S. 'Voskresenie mifa', *MN*, 10, 7 March 1993, 7b.

Bychkova, Olga. 'Unruly Soyuz', *MN*, 49, 16–23 December 1990, 6.

——. 'Sergei Baburin', *MN*, 7, 16–23 February 1992, 14.

——. 'We shall propose a Constitution of Soviet Democracy', *MN*, 40–41, 20–26 October 1995, 1–2.

Byzov, L. and Gurevich, G. 'Peremeny politicheskoi soznaniya', *AiF*, 7, 1990, 6.

Carrère d'Encausse, Hélène. 'Determinants and Parameters of Soviet Nationality Policy' in Azrael, J. (ed.) *Soviet Nationality Policies and Practices* (Praeger, NY, 1978) pp. 39–59.

Carsten, F. 'Interpretations of Fascism' in Laqueur, W. (ed.) *Fascism: a Reader's Guide* (Penguin, London, 1979) pp. 457–87.

Carter, Stephen. *Russian Nationalism: Yesterday, Today, Tomorrow* (Pinter, London, 1990).

——. 'The CIS and After: the Impact of Russian Nationalism' in Cheles, L., Ferguson, R. and Vaughan, M. (eds), *The Far Right in Western and Eastern Europe* (Longman, London and New York) pp. 174–97.

Chaadaev, P.Y. *Stat'i i pis'ma* (Moscow, 1989).

Chalmaev, V. 'Ispytanie nadezhd', *Moskva*, 4, 1988, 183–96.

Chaplin, V. 'The Church in Contemporary Russia' in Bourdeaux, M. (ed.), *The Politics of Religion in Russia and the New States of Eurasia* (M.E. Sharpe, Armonk, NY, and London, 1995) pp. 95–112.

Charodeev, Gennady. 'Yeltsin gotov otbyt' ocherednuyu ataky neprimirimoi oppozitsii', *Izvestiya*, 27 October 1992, 1.

Cheles, L., Ferguson, R. and Vaughan, M. (eds) *The Far Right in Western and Eastern Europe* (Longman, London and New York).

Chelnokov, Alexei. 'Pulya prevala podpol'nuyu odisseyu glavnogo rossiiskogo fashista', *Izvestiya*, 4 January 1994, 1.

——. 'Boevye sokoly iz svity glavarya', *Izvestiya*, 4 January 1994, 7.

——. 'Russkii natsist dolzhen byt' v dorogikh botinkakh', *Izvestiya*, 5 May 1994, 5.

——. 'Ot naperstka i kart – k prezidentskomu kreslu', *Izvestiya*, 29 June 1994, 4.

——. 'Molodoi natsist p'et gor'kuyu i chitaet "Mein Kampf"', *Izvestiya*, 15 January 1995, 7.

——. 'Dobrye, milye lyudi', *Izvestiya*, 15 March 1995, 4.

——. 'Okruzhenie Lebeda', *Izvestiya*, 11 July 1996, 5.

Cherkizov, Andrei. 'O podlinnykh tsennostyakh', *SK*, 18 June 1987, 3.

——. *Khronograf 1991–1996* (Mart, Moscow, 1996).

Chernaev, A. 'Chelovek, kotory spas mir', *MK*, 11 April 1995.

Chernov, Andrei, 'Predvaritel'nye itogi tysyacheletnego opyta', *Ogonek*, 10, March 1988, 9–12.

——. 'Deti Sharikova', *Ogonek*, 3, January 1989, 31.
——. 'The Party which claims to be saving Marxism', *MN*, 17, 6–13 May 1990, 4.
——. 'Secret Spring', *MN*, 30, 28 July–4 August 1991, 6.
'Cherny peredel v Rossii: zayavlenie ispolkoma "Trudovaya Rossiya"', *Molnya*, 61, 1993, 2.
Chinaeva, Ye. 'A Eurasianist Model of Interethnic Relations could Help Russia Find Harmony', *Transition*, vol. II, no. 22 (1 November 1996) 30–35.
——. 'The Search for the "Russian Idea"', *Transitions*, vol. IV, no. 1 (June 1997) 40–46.
'Chto takoe ob"edinenie Pamyat'?', *Russkaya mysl'*, 31 July 1987, 6–7.
Chubukov, D. 'Fashizm v Rossii', *MN*, 21, 26 March–2 April 1995, 7.
Chubur, A. 'Partitura vtorogo prishestviya Sharikova napisana v programme LDPR', *Rossiiskie vesti*, 2 February 1994, 2.
Chugaev, S. 'Duma v tseitnote', *Izvestiya*, 21 June 1994, 2.
——. 'Napadaya na pravitel'stvo', *Izvestiya*, 29 October 1994, 2.
——. 'Duma ne namerena vstupat' v konflikt s prezidentom', *Izvestiya*, 11 January 1995, 2.
——. 'Duma', *Izvestiya*, 14 January 1995, 1.
——. 'Fraktsiya Zhirinovskogo', *Izvestiya*, 27 January 1995, 2.
——. 'Duma reshila pogovorit'', *Izvestiya*, 11 March 1995, 1.
——. 'Zhazhda', *Izvestiya*, 14 March 1995, 1, 4.
——. 'Prinyatoi Dumoi federal'ny byudzhet', *Izvestiya*, 17 March 1995, 2.
——. 'Gosudarstvennaya Duma ne reshilas' obsuzhdat' vopros', *Izvestiya*, 24 June 1995, 2.
——. 'Duma brosaet vyzov Prezidentu', *Izvestiya*, 22 June 1995, 1.
Chupakov, A. 'Politicheskie partii kommunisticheskoi orientatsii o russkoi gosudarstvennosti', *Izm*, vol. II, no. 10 (1996) 48–54.
Churbanov, V. and Nelyubin, A. 'Neformalnye ob"edineniya i perestroika: nadezhdy i trevogi' in Pechenev, V. and Vyunsky, V. (eds), *Neformaly: kto oni? kuda zovut?* (Politizdat, Moscow, 1990) pp. 9–47.
Clark, T. 'The Zhirinovsky Electoral Victory: Antecedents and Aftermath', *Nationalities Papers*, vol. XXIII, no. 4 (December 1995) 767–78.
Clarke, Bruce. 'Russian Roulette', *Prospect*, November 1995, 24–30.
——. *An Empire's New Clothes: the End of Russia's Liberal Dream* (Vintage, London, 1995).
Cline, M., Corning, A. and Rhodes, M. 'The Showdown in Moscow: Tracking Public Opinion', *RFE/RL Research Report*, vol. II, no. 43 (29 October 1993) 11–16.
Cohn, Norman. *Warrant for Genocide: the Myth of the Jewish World-Conspiracy and the 'Protocols of the Elders of Zion'*, rev. edn (Scholars' Press, Chicago, 1981).
Colton, T. 'The Moscow Election of 1990' in Hewett, A. and Winston, V. (eds), *Milestones in Glasnost' and Perestroyka: Politics and People* (Brookings Institute, Washington, 1991) pp. 326–81.
——. 'The Constituency Nexus in the Russian and other Post-Soviet Parliaments' in Hahn, J. (ed.), *Democratization in Russia: the Development of Legislative Institutions* (M.E. Sharpe, Armonk, NY, 1996) pp. 49–82.

—— and Levgold R. (eds) *After the Soviet Union: from Empire to Nations* (Norton, NY and London, 1992).

Conquest, Robert. (ed.) *The Last Empire. Nationality and the Soviet Future* (Hoover Institute, Stanford, 1986).

'Constitution Watch: Russia', *East European Constitutional Review*, vol. III, no. 2 (Spring 1994) 19–22; vol. IV, no. 1 (Winter 1995) 23–30; no. 2 (Spring 1995) 24–8; no. 3 (Summer 1995) 23–8; vol. V, no. 1 (Winter 1996) 21–5; no. 2–3 (Spring–Summer 1996) 21–3.

Corning, Amy. 'Public Opinion and the Russian Parliamentary Elections', *RFE/RL Research Report*, vol. II, no. 48 (3 December 1993) 16–23.

Dadiani, Lionel. 'Natsisty i "poputniki"', *Novoe vremya*, 36, 1994, 16–19.

'Daite slovo Pamyati', *MG*, 7, 1990, 143–5.

Dallin, A. (ed.) *Political Parties in Russia* (University of California, Berkeley, 1993).

Daniels, R. (ed.) *Soviet Communism from Reform to Collapse* (D.C. Heath, Lexington, 1995).

Dashiwa, Karen and Parrott, Bruce. *Russia and the New States of Eurasia. The Politics of Upheaval* (CUP, Cambridge, 1994).

Davis, Nathaniel. *A Long Walk to Church: A Contemporary History of Russian Orthodoxy* (Westview Press, Boulder, San Francisco and Oxford, 1995).

Davydova, N. 'The Road to Church', *MN*, 39, 7–14 October 1990, 4.

Deich, M. 'Legion "vervolf" i drugie', *MK*, 11 May 1995, 2.

'Deklaratsiya RKhDD', 20 June 1992, in Aksyuchits, V. (ed.), *Vozrozhdenie Rossii* (Vybor, Moscow, 1993) 8–35.

Denisovski, G. *et al.* 'Slovo sredi nas antisemitov?', *Daidzhest*, 14, 1990, 10.

Devlin, K. 'L'Unità on the Secret History of the Andreeva Letter', *RFE/RL*, 215/88, 26 May 1988, 1–6.

Dichev, T. 'Sionizm – eto fashizm', *Russkii vestnik*, 22, 1992, 8.

Dmitriev, A. and Toshchenko, Zh. 'Sotsiologicheskii opros i politika', *Sotsiologicheskoe issledovanie*, 5, 1994, 42–51.

Dmitriev, C. 'KGB Successor Organisations Wield Wide Powers' in Schmidt, J. (ed.) *The OMRI Annual Survey of Eastern Europe and the Former Soviet Union 1995. Building Democracy* (M.E. Sharpe, Armonk, NY and London, 1996) pp. 233–6.

Dmitriev, O. 'Staraya nomenklatura i novaya elita', *Rossiiskie vesti*, 3 June 1994, 2.

Dobrynina, V., Suslova, Ye. and Yuvkin, M. (eds) *Samodeyatel'nye initsiativnye organizatsii: problemy i perspektivy razvitiya* (Moscow, 1990).

Dodolev, E. 'Pamyat' i KGB', *MK*, 27 October 1990, 4.

Dolganov, V. 'Po raznym spiskam', *Izvestiya*, 12 January 1989.

Dontsov, S. 'Vozrodit' ob"edinennoe kazachestvo', *Russkii vestnik*, 45–52, 1994, 8–9.

Doronin, A. 'Kul'tura i kontrkul'tura', *MG*, 9, 1987, 226–9.

Doroshenko, N. 'Vo imya zdravogo smysla', *MG*, 9, 1987, pp. 233–7.

——. 'Kto vinovat i chto delat'?', *Moskovskii literator*, 19 January 1990.

Dostoevsky, F. *Diary of a Writer* (Ian Mead, Haslemere, 1984).

'Draka v tsentralnom dome literatorov', *Kommersant*, no. 3, 1, 1990.

Drobizheva, L. 'Perestroika and the ethnic consciousness of Russians' in Lapidus, G., Zaslavsky, V. and Goldman, P. (eds), *From Union to*

Commonwealth. Nationalism and Separatism in the Soviet Republics (CUP, Cambridge, 1992) pp. 98–113.

Drozdov, V.S. 'Pamyat' i russkoe natsional'noe dvizhenie' in Levichev (ed.), *Neformal'naya vol'na* (Moscow, 1990) pp. 109–23.

Dubnov, Vadim. 'S"ezd skuchnykh "pobeditelei"', *Novoe vremya*, 4, 1995, 16.

Dudinsky, I. 'Yantar' ili shcheben', *SK*, 14 November 1987, 4–5.

Dudko, Dmitri. 'Razlichenie dukhov', *Zavtra*, 5, February 1996, 5.

Dugin, Alexander. 'Kontinent Rossiya', *Kontinent Rossiya* (Znanie, Moscow, 1990) pp. 51–64.

——. 'Konservativnaya revolyutsiya: kratkaya istoriya ideologii tret'ego puti', *Elementy: evraziiskoe obozrenie*, 1, 1992, 15–16, 49–56.

——. *Konservativnaya revolyutsiya* (Arktogea, Moscow, 1994).

——. *Tseli i zadachi nashei revolyutsii* (Fravarti, Moscow, 1995).

Duncan, P. 'The Party and Russian Nationalism in the USSR: from Brezhnev to Gorbachev' in Potichnyj P. (ed.), *The Soviet Union: Party and Society* (CUP, Cambridge, 1988) pp. 229–44.

Dunlop, John. *The New Russian Revolutionaries* (Nordland, Mass., 1976).

——. *The Faces of Contemporary Russian Nationalism* (Princeton UP, Princeton, 1983).

——. *The New Russian Nationalism* (Praeger, NY, 1985).

——. 'Language, Culture, Religion and National Awareness' in Conquest, R. (ed.), *The Last Empire* (Hoover Institution, Stanford, 1986) pp. 265–89.

——. 'Soviet Cultural Politics', *Problems of Communism*, November–December 1987, 34–56.

——. 'Gorbachev and Russian Orthodoxy', *Problems of Communism*, July–August 1989, 96–116.

——. 'The Russian Orthodox Church and Nationalism after 1988', *Religion in Communist Lands*, vol. XVIII, no. 4 (Winter 1990) 292–306.

——. 'Russian Nationalism Today: Organisations and Programmes', *Nationalities Papers*, vol. XIX, no. 2 (Fall 1991) 146–66.

——. *The Rise of Russia and the Fall of the Soviet Empire* (Princeton UP, Princeton, 1993).

——. 'Russia: Confronting a Loss of Empire' in Bremmer, I. and Taras, R. (eds), *Nations and Politics in the Soviet Successor States* (CUP, Cambridge, 1993) pp. 43–72.

——. 'Confronting Loss of Empire 1987–91', *Political Science Quarterly*, vol. CVIII no. 4 (Winter 1993–4) 603–34.

——. 'The Russian Orthodox Church as an "Empire-Saving" Institution' in Bourdeaux, M. (ed.), *The Politics of Religion* (M.E. Sharpe, Armonk, NY, London, 1995) pp. 15–40.

——. 'Russia: in Search of an Identity?' in Bremmer, I. and Taras, R. (eds), *New States, New Politics* (CUP, Cambridge, 1997) pp. 29–95.

Dupeux, Louis. *National Bolshévisme. Stratégie Communiste et Dynamique Conservatrice*, 2 vols. (Champion, Paris, 1979).

Durnovtsev, V. 'Rossiya i zapad v vekhovoi ideologii' in Gusev K. (ed.), *Intelligentsiya i revolyutsiya* (Moscow, 1985) pp. 82–7.

'Dveri otkryty dlya vsekh: obrashchenie k trudyashchimsya Leningrada', *Leningradskaya pravda*, 8 June 1989.

Dzhunusov, M.S. 'Patriotizm v mnogomernom izmerenii', *Izm*, vol. II, no. 10 (1996) 61–9.

Engelgardt-Yurkov, S.V. 'Yest' li budushchee u monarkhicheskoi idei?', *Dialog*, 17, 1990, 37–40.

——. 'O konstitutsionno-monarkhicheskoi partii', *AiF*, 16, 1990, 8.

Erlanger, S. '"Disaffected men" backed Zhirinovsky', *The Guardian*, 31 December 1993, 10.

'Eto mozhno delat' segodnya!', *NG*, 25 May 1996, 1.

European Institute for the Media. *The Media and the Russian Presidential Elections*, Newsletter 2, 4 June 1996, 1–3.

Fadeev, V. 'A chto yesli bez "vashikh" i "nashikh"?', *Sovetskii tsirk*, 16 November 1989.

Fadin, A. 'Guennadi Ziouganov, un futur "président rouge" à la solde du capital?', *Le Courrier International*, 21–27 March 1996, 18.

Fashizm v totalitarnom i posttotalitarnom obshchestve (Moscow, Progress, 1995).

Fedarko, K. 'Rising Czar', *Time Magazine*, 11 July 1994, 26–34.

Fedorov, Boris, 'Byt' liberal'nym demokratom dano ne kazhdomu', *Izvestiya*, 24 May 1994, 2.

Feofanov, Yuri. 'Delo o prividenii v konstitutsionnom sude', *Izvestiya*, 16 February 1993, 5.

Fish, M. Steven. 'Who Shall Speak for Whom? Democracy and Interest Representation in Post–Soviet Russia' in A. Dallin (ed.), *Political Parties in Russia* (University California, Berkeley, 1993) pp. 34–47.

——. 'The Advent of Multipartism in Russia', *Post-Soviet Affairs*, vol. II, no. 4 (October–December 1995) 340–83.

Fomina, L. 'Poteri na pole brani', *Moskovskaya Pravda*, 4 February 1990.

Foye, S. 'Russia's Defence Establishment in Disarray', *RFE/RL Research Report*, vol. II, no. 36 (10 September 1993) 49–54.

——. 'Confrontation in Moscow: the Army backs Moscow for now', *RFE/RL Research Report*, vol. II, no. 42 (22 October 1993) 10–15.

Frazer, G. and Lancelle, G. *Absolute Zhirinovsky: A Transparent View of the Distinguished Russian Statesman* (Penguin, New York, 1994).

Freeland, Chrystia. 'General awaits the call of destiny', *FT*, 6 September 1994, 3.

——. 'A Fatalist in the Line of Fire', *FT*, 25 July 1996, 19.

——. 'Yeltsin sacks the "disruptive" Lebed', *FT*, 18 October 1996.

Frolov, A. 'Obezdolenny narod', *SR*, 20 June 1992, 1.

——. 'Otechestvo v opasnosti', *SR*, 27 October 1992, 1.

'Front natsional'nogo spaseniya uzakonen. Posledstviya nepredskazuemy', *Izvestiya*, 1 April 1993, 1, 5.

Gaidar, Yegor. 'Demokratiya v Rossii: real'nost' ili prognoz?', *RG*, 17 May 1995, 2.

——. 'Izbezhit li Zhirinovsky publichnogo suda?', *Izvestiya*, 18 June 1997, 2.

Galaktionov, A. and Nikandrov, P. *Russkaya filosofiya: IX–XIX vv.* (Izdatel'stvo Leningradskogo Universiteta, Leningrad, 1989).

Garifulina, N. 'Kto ty ROS?', *SR*, 12 December 1991, 2.

——. 'Yesli dorog tebe tvoi dom', *SR*, 25 December 1991, 2.

——. 'Otvet na zapret', *SR*, 31 October 1992, 1, 3.

—— and Gerasimov, D. 'My prodolzhim bor'bu', *SR*, 20 June 1992, 1.

—— and Ryabov, A. 'Miting trebuet: daite slovo narodu', *SR*, 16 June 1992, 1.

Garrard, J. and C. *Inside the Soviet Writers' Union* (I.B. Tauris, London and New York, 1990).

Gel'bras, V. *Kto yest' chto. Politicheskaya Moskva 1994*, 2 vols. (RAN, Moscow, 1994).

'General gets a slice of power', *MN*, 24, 27 June–3 July 1996, 1.

Gerasimov, D. 'Satanskoe plemya', *Pravda*, 5 May 1993, 4.

Gessen, Masha. 'V dome pod svastikoi', *Novoe vremya*, 35, 1994, 15–17.

Gevorkyan, N. 'Tipun mne na yazik', *MN*, 15, 26 February–5 March 1995, 4.

——. and Radyshevsky, D. 'Do we have to wait for bloodshed', *MN*, 7, 18 February 1990, 14.

Gibson, James. 'Understandings of Anti-Semitism in Russia: an analysis of the politics of anti-Jewish attitudes', *Slavic Review*, vol. LIII, no. 3 (Fall 1994) 796–806.

——. 'Misunderstandings of Anti-Semitism in Russia: an analysis of the politics of anti-Jewish attitudes', *Slavic Review*, vol. LIII, no. 3 (Fall 1994) 829–41.

——. 'The Resilience of Mass Support for Democratic Institutions and Processes in the Nascent Russian and Ukrainian Democracies' in Tismaneanu V. (ed.), *Political Culture and Civil Society in Russia and the New States of Eurasia* (M.E.Sharpe, Armonk, NY, and London, 1995) 53–111.

—— and Duch, Raymond. 'Emerging Democratic Values in Soviet Political Culture' in Miller, A., Riesinger, W. and Hesli, V. (eds), *Public Opinion and Regime Change* (Westview Press, Boulder, San Francisco and Oxford, 1993) pp. 69–94.

Gidaspov, B. 'U nas khvatit voli ...', *NS*, 5, 1990, 3–5.

Gill, Graeme. *The Collapse of a Single Party System. The Disintegration of the CPSU* (CUP, Cambridge, 1994).

Gimpelson, Vladimir. 'Russia's New Independent Entrepreneurs', *RFE/RL Research Report*, vol. II, no. 36 (10 September 1993) 44–8.

Di Giovanni, Janine. 'Mad Vlad and Dangerous to Know', *Sunday Times Magazine*, 1 May 1994, 20–7.

Gitelman, Zvi. 'Glasnost', perestroika and anti-Semitism', *Foreign Affairs*, vol. LXX, no. 2 (1991) 141–59.

Glazunov, Ilya. 'Chto pomnit'? Chem gordit'sya?', *Pravda*, 11 June 1985, 3.

——. 'Poisk cherez traditsiyu', *Pravda*, 27 September 1987.

——. 'Menya khotyat ubit'', *Den'*, 5, March 1991.

——. 'Russkii – tot, kto lyubit Rossiyu', *AiF*, 17, 1994, 1, 5.

Goble, Paul. 'Three Faces of Nationalism in the Former Soviet Union' in Kupchan C. (ed.), *Nationalism and Nationalities in the New Europe* (Cornell University Press, Ithaca and London, 1995), pp. 122–35.

Gokhman, M. and Yeliseenko, V. 'Otklyki na vystuplenie A.I. Solzhenitsyna', *Russkaya mysl'*, 24 October 1994, supplement, 3.

Golovanov, A. 'Pora derzhat' otvet', *Den'*, 16, August 1991, 1, 5.

Golovenko, A. *Sazhi Umalatova* (Paleya, Moscow, 1992).

——. Kokhanov, N. and Shirokov, V. 'Kongress narodov SSSR', *Pravda*, 21 September 1993, 1–2.

Golovkov, A. and Pavlov, A. 'O chem shumite vy?', *Ogonek*, 21, 1987, 4–5.

Gomez, V. 'News from Across the Regions', *Transition*, vol. II, no. 14 (12 July 1996) 2–3.

——. 'Russia: Lebed Resigns', *Transition*, vol. I, no. 11 (30 June 1995) 35–6.

Goncharov, A. 'Naiti i otkryt'', *SK*, 16 January 1986.

Gorbachev, M.S. *The August Coup: the Truth and the Lessons* (Harper Collins, London, 1991).

——. *Zhizn' i reformy*, 2 vols. (Novosti, Moscow, 1995).

Gorshkov, M., Zhuravlev, V., Dobrokhotov, L. *Yeltsin–Khasbulatov: Yedinstvo, kompromiss, bor'ba* (Terra, Moscow, 1994).

Goskomizdat Rossii, *Rossiiskii statisticheskii ezhegodnik: 1996* (Logos, Moscow, 1996).

'"Gospodin nezavisimy". Fenomen Zhirinovskogo v faktakh i dokumentakh', *Ogonek*, 2, 1992, 22–4.

Graham, Thomas. 'Novy russkii rezhim', *NG*, 23 November 1995, 5.

Griffin, R. (ed.), *Fascism* (OUP, Oxford, 1995).

Grigoriev, V. 'Na vystavke i vokrug nee', *Pravda*, 21 July 1986.

Grishaeva, G. 'Itogi i zamysly', *Metrostroevets*, 27 July 1983.

Gromov, A. and Kuzin, O. *Neformaly: kto yest' kto* (Mysl', Moscow, 1990).

Gubenko, V. and Piskarev. 'Samozvantsy i samodel'shchiki', *KP*, 31 January 1988, 2.

Gubanov, S. 'Kontseptsia sotsialisticheskoi perestroiki' in Bobkov, V. and Sergeev, A. (eds), *Al'ternativa: vybor puti* (Mysl', Moscow, 1990) pp. 186–209.

Gul'binsky, N. and Shakina, M. *Afghanistan ... Kreml' ... Lefortovo...? Epizody politicheskoi biografii Aleksandra Rutskogo* (Lada-M., Moscow, 1994).

Gumilev, L. 'Menya nazivayut yevraziitsem', *NS*, 1, 1991, 132–41.

——. *Etnogenez i biosfera zemli* (C&T, Moscow, 1994).

——. *Konets i vnov' nachalo* (C&T, Moscow, 1994).

Gurkov, A. 'Shadows off Screen', *MN*, 7, 1988, 14–21 February 1988.

Guroff, G. and A. 'The Paradox of Russian National Identity' in Szporluk R. (ed.), *National Identity and Ethnicity in Russia and the New States of Eurasia* (M.E. Sharpe, Armonk, NY, and London, 1994) pp. 78–100.

Gurvich, V. 'Russkii marsh k fashizmu', *Kentavr*, 2, March–April 1994, 128–32.

Gutionov, Pavel. 'Samozvannye radeteli "dukha"', *SR*, 17 July 1987, 4.

——. 'Podmena', *Izvestiya*, 26 February 1988, 3.

Hahn, Jeffrey (ed.) 'Changes in Contemporary Russian Political Culture' in Tismaneanu, V. (ed.) *Political Culture and Civil Society in Russia and the New States of Eurasia* (M.E. Sharpe, Armonk, NY, 1995) pp. 112–36.

——. *Democratization in Russia: the Development of Legislative Institutions* (M.E. Sharpe, Armonk, NY, 1996).

Hajda, L. and Beissinger, M. (eds) *The Nationalities Factor in Soviet Politics and Society* (Westview Press, Boulder, San Francisco and Oxford, 1990).

Hearst, David. 'Nationalist Vows to Return to Former Glory', *The Guardian*, 14 December 1993.

Hewett, A. and Winston, V. (eds) *Milestones in Glasnost and Perestroyka: Politics and People* (Brookings Institution, Washington, 1991).

Higgins, Andrew. 'One Day in the Stormy Life of Solzhenitsyn', *The Independent on Sunday*, 29 May 1994.

Hobsbawm, Eric, and Ranger T. (eds) *The Invention of Tradition* (CUP, Cambridge, 1983).

Hough, Jerry F. 'The Russian Elections of 1993: Public Attitudes towards Economic Reform and Democratisation', *Post-Soviet Affairs*, vol. X, no. 1 (January–March 1994) 1–37.

Hughes, Michael. 'The Never-Ending Story: Russian Nationalism, National Communism and Opposition to Reform in the USSR and Russia', *The Journal of Communist Studies*, vol. IX, no. 2 (June 1993) 41–61.

Hyams, Neil. 'Russian Nationalism' in Schöpflin, G. (ed.), *The Soviet Union and Eastern Europe* (New York and Oxford, 1986) pp. 232–43.

'I snova o "Shirmachakh"', *SK*, 27 April 1987.

Ignatow, Assen. 'Der 'Eurasismus' und die Suche nach einer neuen russischen Kulturidentität' (*Berichte des Bundesinstituts für ostwissenschaftliche und internationale Studien*, 15, 1992).

'Ihm muss man zuhören', *Der Spiegel*, 44, 1994, 136–9.

Ilyasov, Farkhad. 'Right-wing voters unruly', *MN*, 12, 28 March–3 April 1996, 2.

Ilyina, Natalya (ed.) *Pochemu Zyuganov dolzhen stat' prezidentom* (Zyuganov Election Fund, Moscow, 1996).

Innokenty, Igumen (Pavlov). 'Problemy religioznogo obrazovaniya v sovremennoi Rossii', *Russkaya mysl'*, 2–8 November 1995, 9.

Ioann, Metropolitan of St Petersburg and Ladoga. *Tvoreniem dobra i pravdy* (RNS, Moscow, 1993).

——. 'Pravoslavnaya revolyutsiya protiv sovremennogo mira', *Elementy*, 4, 1993, 18–19.

——. 'The West Wants Chaos' in Nielsen, Niels (ed.), *Christianity after Communism: Social, Political and Cultural Struggle in Russia* (Westview Press, Boulder, San Francisco and Oxford, 1994) pp. 107–12.

——. *Samoderzhavie dukha: ocherki russkogo samosoznaniya* (Tsarskoe delo, St Petersburg, 1995).

——. Obituary of, *Zavtra*, 45, November 1995, 1.

Isakov, V. 'Pochemu deti pobeditelei dali sebya obmanut'?', *Pravda*, 26 May 1995, 1–2.

Ishiyama, J. 'Red Phoenix? The Communist Party in Post-Soviet Politics', *Party Politics*, vol. II, no. 2 (1996) 147–75.

Ivanenko, S. 'They want to restore the Russian Monarchy', *MN*, 43, 4–11 November 1990, 8–9.

Ivanitsky, V. 'Izbiratel'nye bloki: pervy opyt', *Dialog*, 3, February 1990, 47–52.

'Iz zhizni Otechestva' in *Perestroika: sotsializm ili kapitalizm?* (Otechestvo, Moscow, 1989) pp. 41–7.

'Izbrannye mesta iz rechei pisatelei', *Nedelya*, 47, 20–26 November 1989, 16–17.

Izyumova, Natalya. 'LDP set to hold Congress in Kremlin', *MN*, 17, 6–13 May 1990, 7.

'K narodam Rossii', *Russkii vestnik*, 4, 1991, 2.

Kagarlitsky, B. 'Yeshcho odno zharkoe leto' in Yushenkov, S. (ed.), *Neformaly: sotsial'nye initsiativy* (Moskovskii rabochii, Moscow, 1990) pp. 121–35.

Kaiser, Robert. *The Geography of Nationalism in Russia and the USSR* (Princeton University Press, Princeton, 1994).

Kalita, V. 'Za menya progolosovala tselaya Shveitsariya', *Literaturnaya Rossiya*, 12 July 1991, 2–3.

Kalugin, V. 'Kto ubil Ostashvili?', *Den'*, 9, May 1991.

Kampfner, J. *Inside Yeltsin's Russia* (Cassell, London, 1994).

——. 'Neo-fascist challenge to Yeltsin', *The Telegraph*, 14 December 1993.

——. 'A whiff of Weimar in the air', *The Telegraph*, 14 December 1993.

Kartsev, V. *! Zhirinovsky! An Insider's Account of Yeltsin's Chief Rival* (Columbia University Press, New York, 1995).

Katerli, N. 'Dorogo k pamyatnikam', *Leningradskaya pravda*, 9 October 1988, 3.

Kazarin, Yu. and Yakovlev, V. (eds) *Smert' zagovora: belaya kniga* (Novosti, Moscow, 1992).

Kazarin, Yu. and Russovsky, A. 'Pamyat': vchera i segodnya', *Vechernaya Moskva*, 25 February 1988.

Kazintsev, A. 'Litsom k istorii: prodolzhateli ili potrebiteli,' *NS*, 11, 1987, 166–75.

——. 'Ochishchenie ili zloslovie', *NS*, 2, 1988.

——. 'Formula nestabil'nosti', *NS*, 6, 1988, 185–90.

——. 'Novaya mifologiya', *NS*, 5, 1989, 144–68.

——. 'Ya boryus' s pustotoi', *NS*, 11, 1990, 157–65.

Khamraev, V. 'Sterligov – Yeltsinu', *Segodnya*, 10 February 1995, 2.

——. 'Baburinsty po prezhnemu gotovy vzyat'sya za vozrozhdenie Otechestva', *Segodnya*, 28 March 1995, 2.

Khasbulatov, R. *The Struggle for Russia. Power and Change in the Democratic Revolution* (Routledge, London and New York, 1993).

——. 'Rossiya, trevogi i nadezhdy', *RG*, 13 April 1993, 3.

——. 'Russkaya ideya', *RG*, 17 June 1993, 3–4.

——. 'Zashchitim parlamentizm – spasem stranu i demokratiyu', *RG*, 21 August 1993, 3.

Khinstein, A. 'V parlament', *MK*, 4 April 1995, 1.

——. 'Ya mogu vse rasskazat'', *MK*, 4 May 1995, 3.

Khristiansko-demokraticheskii soyuz Rossii (Overseas Publications Interchange, London, 1990).

Kichin, V. 'Lozh' – ne tochka zreniya', *SK*, 29 October 1987, 3.

Kireev, R. 'Zhirinovsky kak zerkalo russkoi revolyutsii', *Moskovskaya pravda*, 16 April 1994, 3.

Kirichenko, N. and Galiyev, A. 'A Communist Vision of the Future Economy', *MN*, 24, 27 June–3 July 1996, 9.

Kiselev, A. and Mostovshchikov. 'Let's Talk on Equal Grounds', *MN*, 20, 17 May 1987, 4.

Klepikova, Ye. and Solovyov, V. *Zhirinovsky: the Paradoxes of Russian Fascism* (Viking, London and New York, 1995).

Klier, J.D. 'Pamyat' and the Jewish Menace: Remembrance of Things Past', *Nationalities Papers*, vol. XIX, no. 2 (Fall 1991), 214–27.

Klishina, S. 'Dlinny put' k shturvalu', *MN,* 32, 7–14 August 1994, 6.

Kochan, L. *The Jews in Soviet Russia since 1917,* 3rd edn (OUP, Oxford, 1978).

Kocherina, Ye. *Fenomen Zhirinovskogo* (Kontrolling, Moscow, 1992).

Kohn, Hans. *Pan-Slavism: its History and Ideology* (Notre Dame, Indiana, 1953).

——. *The Mind of Germany* (Macmillan, London, 1961).

Kolakowski, Leszek. *Main Currents of Marxism,* 3 vols (OUP, Oxford, 1982).

Kolganov, A. *et al.* 'Raspri pozabyv', *Partiinaya zhizn',* 20, October 1990, 8–11.

Kolosov, M. 'Otkrytoe pis'mo Yuryu Bondarevu', *Ogonek,* 1, 1990, 8.

Kolstoe, P. *Russians in the Former Soviet Union* (Hurst, London, 1995).

Kommunisticheskaya partiya rossiiskoi federatsii: vtoroi chrezvichainy s"ezd kompartii Rossiiskoi Federatsii (Paleya, Moscow, 1993).

'Kommunisty apparata Rossii', *AiF,* 23, 1990, 2.

'Komu prinadlezhit'sya vlast' v Rossii? 2. Pravitel'stvo ego prevoskhoditel'stva', *Izvestiya,* 5 July 1994, 5.

'Komu prinadlezhit'sya vlast' v Rossii? 3. Parlament – trudnoe ditya', *Izvestiya,* 7 July 1994, 5.

Kongress russkikh obshchin (NP, Moscow, 1995).

Konovalov, Valery. 'Duma nanosit sokrushitel'ny udar po agrarnoi reforme', *Izvestiya,* 11 February 1995, 1.

Konstantinov, Ilya. 'Front perekhodit v nastuplenie', *SR,* 24 July 1993, 1.

——. 'FNS: konfrontatsiya ili dialog?', *Pravda,* 25 November 1992, 1–2.

——. 'Vnutripoliticheskaya bor'ba i vneshnaya politika Rossii', *Yuridicheskaya gazeta,* 28, 1993, 4–5, 8–9.

Konstantinova, N. 'Dva goda rossiskogo parlamentarizma', *NG,* 2 December 1995, 1–2.

Kordonsky, S. 'Pervy voenny perevorot v SSSR', *Tri Dnya* (Postfaktum, Moscow, 1991) 70–74.

Kornev, V. 'Kolokol' sozyvaet chernosotentsev', *Izvestiya,* 20 January 1995, 4.

Kosolapov, R. 'K debatam o russkoi idee', *Izm,* vol. II, 10, 1996, 69–74.

Koval', B. (ed.) *Rossiya segodnya: politicheskii portret v dokumentakh 1985–91* (Mezhdunarodnye otnosheniya, Moscow, 1991).

——. (ed.) *Rossiya segodnya: politicheskii portret v dokumentakh 1991–2* (Mezhdunarodnye otnosheniya, Moscow, 1993).

Kovalevsky, P. *Zarubezhnaya Rossiya* (Librairie des Cinq Continents, Paris, 1971).

Koval'skaya, G. and Dubnov, A. 'Patrioty ne ponyali drug-druga?', *Novoe vremya,* 7, 1992, 6–7.

Koyré, A. *La Philosophie et le Problème National en Russie au début du XIXe Siècle,* reedn (Gallimard, Paris, 1976).

Kozhinov, Vadim. 'Uroki istorii: o leninskoi kontseptsii natsional'noi kul'tury', *Moskva,* 11, 1986, 183–98.

——. 'Pravda i istina', *NS,* 4, 1988, 160–75.

——. 'My menyaemsya?', *NS,* 10, 1987, 160–74.

——. *Sud'ba Rossii* (Moscow, 1990).

Krakhmal'nikova, Zoya. 'Russophobia, Anti-Semitism and Christianity: Some Remarks on an Anti-Russian Idea', *Religion, State and Society,* vol. XX, no. 1 (1992) 7–28.

——. 'Dvoiniki', *Stolitsa,* 50, 1993, 6–9.

—— (ed.) *Russkaya ideya i yevrei* (Nauka, Moscow, 1994).

Krasnikov, Ye. 'Rutskoi razoblachaet prezidenta Yeltsina', *NG,* 4 April 1995, 1.

——. 'Reds ready to unite', *MN,* 3, 26 January–1 February 1996, 2.

——. 'What price third force', *MN,* 10, 14–20 March 1996, 2.

——. 'New Communists Opt for Traditionalism', *MN,* 13, 4–10 April 1996, 3.

——. 'Communists Contest Ministerial Posts', *MN,* 21, 6–12 June 1996, 4.

——. 'Lebed Prepares for Presidential Elections in 2000', *MN,* 30, 7–13 August 1996, 2.

——. 'Is Gennady Zyuganov Switching Seats?', *MN,* 31, 14–20 August 1996, 4.

——. 'Communists afraid of Zyuganov straying', *MN,* 33, 28 August–3 September 1996, 4.

Krasnov, Vladislav. 'Russian National Feeling: an Informal Poll', in Conquest, R. (ed.), *The Last Empire* (Hoover Institution, Stanford, 1986), pp. 109–30.

——. *Russia beyond Communism: a Chronicle of National Rebirth* (Westview Press, Boulder, San Francisco and Oxford, 1991).

——. 'Pamyat': a force for change?', *Nationalities Papers,* vol. XIX, no. 2 (Fall 1991) 167–82.

Krotov, N. 'Alexander Rutskoi: politicheskii portret' in D. Maiorov (ed.), *Neizvestny Rutskoi* (Obozrevatel', Moscow, 1994) pp. 22–40.

Krotov, Ya. 'Dvoinoi standart', *MN,* 10, 7 March 1993, 7b.

Kudriavtsev, I. 'Vitse-Prezident Rossii dva goda nazad', *Panorama*, 28, July 1991, 1–2.

Kunaev, Stanislav. 'O vselenskikh drovakh i traditsii otechestvennoi poezii', *NS,* 2, 1985, 170–81.

——. 'Razmyshleniya na starom Arbate', *NS,* 7, 1988, 26–7.

——. 'Vse nachinalos' s Yarlykov', *NS,* 180–89.

——. 'Patriotizm – dvizhushchaya sila perestroiki', *Molodoi leninets,* March 1989.

——. 'Palka o dvukh kontsakh', *NS,* 6, 1989, 156–66.

——. ' Kto narushaet demokraticheskie normy?', *Russkoe tovarishchestvo,* 1, September 1990, 7.

Kupchan, C. (ed.) *Nationalism and Nationalities in the New Europe* (Cornell University Press, Ithaca and London, 1995).

Kuprach, A. 'Sozdana novaya partiya', *Literaturnaya Rossiya*, 20 April 1990.

Kurayev, Fr A. 'Anti-Semitism is a Sin', *Religion, State and Society,* vol. XXIII, no. 1 (1995) 37–8.

Kurginyan, S., Ovchinsky V. *et al.* 'Predotvratit' katastrofu, obespechit' razvitie obshchestva', *Moskovskaya pravda,* 28 March 1991, 1–4.

——. 'Finansovaya voina', *Moskovskaya pravda,* 1 March 1991, 2.

——. 'Sud'ba kommunizma', *Moskovskaya pravda,* 26 July 1991, 2–3.

Kurginyan, S. 'Rossiya ne mozhet ostat'sya v storone ot bor'by za mirovoe gospodstvo', *Narodnaya tribuna,* 2 November 1991.

——. 'Ya – ideolog chrezvychainogo polozheniya' in Rasshivalova, Ye. and Seregin, N. (eds), *Putch. Khronika trevozhnikh dnei* (Progress, Moscow, 1991) pp. 233–8.

——. 'Vernut'sya v istoriyu', *SR,* 18 June 1992, 2.

——. *Sed'moi tsenarii,* 3 vols. (Eksperimental'ny tvorcheskii tsentr, Moscow, 1992).

Kuryanov, S. and Ivanov, G. 'Pervye shagi. Kuda?', *MK,* 9 May 1988.

Kuz'min, Apollon. 'Prodolzhenie vazhnogo razgovora', *NS*, 3, 1985, 182–90.
——. 'Neozhidannye priznaniya', *NS*, 9, 1985, 182–90.
——. 'Meli v eksterritorial'nom potoke', *NS*, 9, 1987, 173–9.
——. 'K kakomu khramu ishchem my dorogu?', *NS*, 3, 1988, 154–64.
——. 'Chto pishem i chto v ume?', *NS*, 7, 1988, 191–2.
——. 'Otechestvo – glavnaya tsennost'', *Literaturnaya Rossiya*, 23 June 1989, 14.
——. 'Yest' li budushchee u sotsializma?', *NS*, 7, 1991, 123–5.
Kuzmin, I. 'Opposition: Appeasers Taming Radicals', *MN*, 31, 14–20 August 1997, 3.
Lambeth, B. *The Warrior who Would Rule Russia? A Profile of Aleksander Lebed* (Brassey's Rand, Santa Monica and London, 1996).
Lanshchikov, Anatoly. 'My vse glyadim v napoleony', *NS*, 7, 1988, 106–42.
——. 'Natsional'ny vopros v Rossii', *Moskva*, 6, 1989, 3–15.
Lapidus, Gail W. *The New Russia: Troubled Transformation* (Westview Press, Boulder, San Francisco and Oxford, 1995).
——. 'From democratization to disintegration: the impact of perestroika on the national question' in Lapidus, G., Zaslavsky, V. and Goldman, P. (eds), *From Union to Commonwealth: Nationalism and Separatism in the Soviet Republics* (CUP, Cambridge, 1992) pp. 45–70.
Lapshin, M. 'Nel'zya primirit' grabitelya i zhertvu', *Pravda*, 30 May 1995, 1–2.
Laqueur, Walter (ed.) *Fascism: A Reader's Guide* (Penguin London, 1979).
——. *The Long Road to Freedom: Russia and Glasnost'* (Unwin Hyman, London, 1989).
——. *Black Hundred: The Rise of the Extreme Right in Russia*, pbk edn (Harper Collins, New York, 1994).
Larin, A. 'Ne promenyat' by kukushku na yastreba', *Izvestiya*, 22 June 1994, 2.
Latsis, O. 'Mozhet li Boris Yeltsin proigrat' vybory?', *Izvestiya*, 3 June 1994, 4.
——. 'Vpered v proshloe: novaya programma kompartii Rossii', *Izvestiya*, 14 February 1995, 4.
——. 'Duma progolosovala za voinu', *Izvestiya*, 23 June 1995, 2.
——. 'General i Freiburgskaya shkola', *Izvestiya*, 29 May 1996.
Latynina, Alla, 'The Climate Won't Change', *MN*, 13, 26 March 1989, 2.
Lavrin, Janko, *Russia, Slavdom and the Western World* (Bles, London, 1969).
Lebed, Alexander. *Spektakl' nazyval'sya putch* (Lada, Tiraspol, 1993).
——. 'Ocherednoi voiny Rossiya ne perezhivet', *AiF*, 22, 1994, 6.
——. 'Hier müssen Köpfe rollen, gnadenlos', *Der Spiegel*, 36/1994, 148–50.
——. 'Sama zhizn' zastavlaet generalov zanimat'sya politikoi', *Izvestiya*, 20 July 1994, 4.
——. 'V lampasakh i s kharizmoi', *Obshchaya gazeta*, 18–24 November 1994, 8.
——. 'Rossiya seichas – mesto gde voruyut', *NG*, 5 October 1995, 5.
——. *Za derzhavu obidno* (Gregory Page, Moscow, 1995).
——. *My yeshche budem gordit'sya Rossiei: poryadok dlya vsekh* (Vostok, Moscow, 1996).
——. 'Moyu programmu nado obyasnit' vsem', *Vostochno-sibirskaya pravda*, 28 May 1996.
——. 'Ideologiya zdravogo smysla: kratkoe izlozhenie programmy kandidata v prezident A.I. Lebeda', *AiF*, 22, 1996, 5; *AiF*, 23, 1996, 4.

——. 'Programmnoe zayavlenie kandidata na dolzhnost' prezidenta Rossii Alexandra Lebeda', *Izvestiya*, 31 May 1996, 3.

——. 'Russkaya doroga', *Vostochno-sibirskaya pravda*, 13 June 1996.

——. 'Yesli delo tak dal'she poidet', *RG*, 29 June 1996.

——. 'Svoyu programmu ya pisal sam', *Russkii vostok*, 12, June 1996, 4.

——. 'Ya budu kontrolirovat' razvitie reform', *Rossiiskaya federatsiya*, 9, July 1996, 1–2.

——. 'How I Made Peace with the Chechens', *The Times*, 10 October 1996.

Lebedev, Yu. 'Presidential Ambitions not Easily Forgone', *MN*, 7, 23–8 February 1996, [erroneously numbered: should read: 8, 29 February–6 March] 2.

Legostayev, V. 'God 1987 – peremena logiki', *Den'*, 14, July 1991.

Lemeshev, Mikhail. *Vozrodit'sya li Rossiya?* (Voronezh, Moscow, 1994).

Leningradskoe russkoe patrioticheskoe dvizhenie 'Otechestvo'. Programma. Ustav (n.p., Leningrad, 1989).

Lentini, Peter. 'Overview of the Campaign' in Lentini, Peter, (ed.), *Elections and Political Order in Russia. The Implications of the 1993 Elections to the Federal Assembly* (Central European University Press, Budapest, London and New York, 1995) pp. 63–93.

Leonov, S. 'Uroki Zhirinovskogo', *AiF*, 50, 1993, 2.

Leonov, Y. 'O platforme marksistskoi rabochei partii', *AiF*, 14, 1990, 8.

——. 'Marksistskaya rabochaya partiya', *Dialog*, 13 September 1990, 41–4.

Lester, Jeremy. *Modern Tsars and Princes: the Struggle for Hegemony in Russia* (Verso, London and New York, 1995).

Levada, Yuri. 'And still they don't understand us', *MN*, 38, 22–9 September 1991, 5.

——. 'What February Left in its Wake', *MN*, 10, 8–15 March 1992, 16.

——. *Democratic Disorder and Russian Public Opinion Trends in VCIOM Surveys 1991–95* (Centre for the Study of Public Policy, University of Strathclyde, Glasgow, 1995).

Levikov, A. 'Are Leningraders any Worse?', *MN*, 32, 6 August 1989, 10.

Levin, Nora. *Paradox of Survival: the Jews in the Soviet Union since 1917*, 2 vols. (New York University Press, New York and London, 1990).

Lezov, S. 'Pogromy k tysyacheletiyu', *Strana i mir*, 3, 1988.

Lieven, A. 'Neo-Fascist Victory', *The Times*, 14 December 1993.

Lieven, D. 'Is Russia ready for a Cromwell?', *The Times*, 18 October 1996, 22.

Ligachev, Ye. *Izbrannye rechi i statii* (Politizdat, Moscow, 1989).

——. *Inside Gorbachev's Kremlin: the Memoirs of Yegor Ligachev*, 2nd edn (Westview Press, Boulder and Oxford, 1996).

Likhachev, Dmitri. *Reflections on Russia* (Westview Press, Boulder, San Francisco, Oxford, 1991).

Limonov, Eduard. 'Prava cheloveka: zhivye i mertvye', *SR*, 20 June 1992, 3.

——. 'Edichka the Samurai', *MN*, 45, 15–22 November 1992, 16.

——. 'Chelovek prishchii bez ocheredi', *Rossiya*, 24, 29 June–5 July 1994, 6.

Lindemann, Albert. *The Jew Accused: Three Anti-Semitic Affairs: Dreyfus, Beilis, Frank, 1894–1915* (CUP, Cambridge, 1991).

Linz, Juan. 'Some Notes towards a Comparative Study of Fascism' in Laqueur, W. (ed.), *Fascism: a Reader's Guide* (Penguin, London, 1979) pp. 13–78.

Lipatov, A. 'Russkaya Akademiya', *Den'*, 2 January 1992.

Lisichkin, G. 'Nina Andreeva: for and against', *MN*, 33 August 1989, 15.

Lobanov, Mikhail. 'Posleslovie', *NS*, 4, 1988, 154–9.

Loshak, V. 'Hope that Springs for the New People in Old Square', *MN*, 8, 20–26 July 1990, 4. (London edn).

——. 'New Leaders', *MN*, 16, 14–20 September 1990, 7. (London edn).

——. 'Underground Party Committee in Action', *MN*, 29, 19–26 July 1992, 3.

Losoto, Ye. 'V bezpamyat'stve', *Komsomol'skaya pravda*, 22 May 1987.

——. 'Slishkom pokhozhe', *Komsomol'skaya pravda*, 19 December 1987, 4.

Luchterhandt, Galina. *Die neuen politischen Parteien im neuen Russland* (Temmen, Bremen, 1993).

——. 'Von der radikalen Opposition zur Beteiligung der Macht. Die KP der Russlandischer Föderation', *Osteuropa*, vol. XLVI, no. 10 (October 1996) 968–86.

Lugovskaya, A. 'Dikii lobbizm', *Izvestiya*, 21 June 1994, 4.

——. 'Natsional'nye ryady FNS reduyut', *Izvestiya*, 27 July 1993, 2.

Lugovsky, I. 'O chem zabyla Pamyat'', *Komsomol'skaya pravda*, 24 June 1987.

Lukinykh, N. 'K zritelyu cherez ternii i lavry', *SK*, 17 February 1987, 4.

Lukyanov, Anatoly. *Perevorot. Mnimyi i nastoyashchii* (Soyuz zhurnalistov, Voronezh, 1993).

L'vov, V. and Savin, D. 'Khristiansko-demokraticheskie partii v sovremennoi Rossii', *Segodnya*, 3 September 1994, 14.

Lysenko, N. 'Nasha tsel' – velikaya imperiya', *Golos Rossii*, 4, 1992, 3.

——. 'Strategiya nashei bor'by', *MG*, 9, 1993, 175–203.

——. 'Otsel' grozit' nam budut turki', *Obshchaya gazeta*, 18–24 November 1994, 8.

——. 'Nikolai Lysenko – ul'tra-natsionalist ili politik zavtrashnego dnya?', *Zavtra*, 49, December 1995, 3.

——. Pavlov, N. and Ovchinnikov. 'K bor'be za rodinu', *Zavtra*, 49, December 1995, 3.

McAuley, Mary. *Russia's Politics of Uncertainty* (CUP, Cambridge, 1997).

McDonnell, L. *October Revolution* (Spellmount, Staplehurst, 1994).

McElvoy, Anne. 'Neo-Fascist sets sights on Yeltsin', *The Times*, 14 December 1993.

Maidanik, K. 'Levye dvizheniya v postavtoritarnom obshchestve', *Svobodnaya mysl'*, 9, 1994, 21–35.

Maiorov, D. (ed.) *Neizvestny Rutskoi: politicheskii portret* (Obozrevatel', Moscow, 1994).

Makarov, D. and Ragozin, D. 'Vokrug Zhirinovskogo', *AiF*, 2–3, 1994, 3.

Malashenko, A. 'Khilye pobegi ideologicheskogo dreva', *Rossiiskie vesti*, 16 May 1995, 2.

——. 'Islam i natsional'-kommunizm', *NG*, 21 March 1992, 3.

Malgin, A. 'Non-Governmental Literature', *MN*, 38, 17 September 1989, 12.

Malov, I. 'Skol'ko stoit Vladimir Zhirinovsky?', *MN*, 24, 12–19 June 1994, 7a.

Malukhin, V. 'Debaty pisatelei', *Izvestiya*, 20 January 1989.

Malyarov, I. and Yerinets, S. 'My ne dolzhny proigrat'', *Lit. Gaz.*, 20 March 1991, 3.

Malyutin, M. and Yusupovsky, A. *Rasstanovka sil v Rossii* (Moscow, 1993).

'Manifest kongressa narodov SSSR', *Pravda*, 25 September 1995, 1.

References   291

'Manifest soyuza "Khristianskoe vozrozhdenie"', *Russkoe tovarishchestvo*, 3 (c. December 1990), 6.
Marsh, Rosalind. *History and Literature in Contemporary Russia* (Macmillan, London, 1995).
Mashtakova, G. 'Cossacks on the March', *MN*, 17–18, 20–22 May 1996, 6.
Materialy uchreditel'nogo s"ezda vsesoyuznoi kommunisticheskoi partii bol'shevikov, 8 November 1991 (n.p., Leningrad, 1991).
Materialy martovskogo (1994 g.) plenuma, ts.k. VKPB (n.p., Leningrad, 1994).
'Materialy IIIgo s"ezda KPRF', *Izm*, vol. I, no. 6 (1995) 4–49.
Materialy IIIgo s"ezda Russkogo Natsional'nogo Sobora, 7 aprelya 1994 g. (n.p., Suzdal', 1994).
Materialy IIIoi vsesoyuznoi konferentsii marksistskoi platformy KPSS (n.p., Moscow, 1990).
Maximov's Companion to the 1996 Russian Presidential Elections in 1996: Election Results: Facts and Figures (Maximov Publications, London, 1996).
Melville, A. 'An Emerging Civic Culture?' in Miller, A., Reissinger, W. and Hesli, V. (eds) *Public Opinion and Regime Change* (Westview Press, Boulder, San Francisco and Oxford, 1993) pp. 56–68.
Melvin, Neil. *Forging the New Russian Nation* (RIIA, London, 1994).
——. *Russians beyond Russia: the Politics of National Identity* (RIIA, London, 1995).
Men', Fr Alexander. 'Religiya, kul't lichnosti i sekulyarnoe gosudarstvo' in Ryabnikova, T. (ed.), *K svobode sovesti* (Progress, Moscow, 1989) 88–111.
——. *Mirovaya dukhovnaya kul'tura. Khristianstvo. Tserkov'. Lektsii i besedy* (Fond imeni Alexandra Menya, Moscow, 1995).
Mendras, Marie. 'Interpreting the Russian Elections', *East European Constitutional Review*, vol. V, no. 2–3 (Spring–Summer 1996) 51–7.
Merkl, P. and Weinberg, L. *The Revival of Right-Wing Extremism in the Nineties* (Frank Cass, London and Portland, 1997).
'Meuterei der Empörten?', *Der Spiegel*, 36/1994, 146–8.
'Mezha v pisatel'skom stane', *SR*, 5 July 1991.
Mezhdunarodnoe obshchestvennoe ob"edinenie 'Slavyanskii sobor'. Materialy i dokumenty (n.p., Moscow, 1992).
Mezhuev, V. 'Parad dal'tonikov', *Pravda*, 1 February 1995, 4.
Midford, P. 'Pamyat's Political Platform, Myths and Realities', *Nationalities Papers*, vol. XIX, no. 2 (Fall 1991) 183–213.
Mikhailov, A. 'Perestroika istorii – razrushenie kul'tury', *Russkoe tovarishchestvo*, 3 (n.d., late 1990/early 1991) 7.
Mikhailov, N. 'Vybor – posle vyborov', *NG*, 20 July 1996, 1, 3.
Mikhailov, S. and Prokhanov, A. 'Ne na miting – na s"ezd', *Den'*, March 1991.
Mikailovskaya, I. 'Russian Voting Behaviour as a Mirror of Social-Political Change', *East European Constitutional Review*, vol. V, no. 2–3 (Spring–Summer 1996) 57–63.
Mikhalskaya, T. 'Viktor Aksyuchits', *MN*, 34, 23–30 August 1992, 14.
Miller, A., Reissinger, W. and Hesli, V. (eds) *Public Opinion and Regime Change* (Westview Press, Boulder, San Francisco and Oxford, 1993).
Milyukov, P. 'Eurasianism and Europeanism in Russian History' in Yakovenko, B. (ed.), *Festschrift T.G. Masaryk zum 80 Geburtstag*, vol. I (F. Cohen, Bonn, 1930) 225–36.

Mitrofanov, A. 'Rutskogo obokrali', *MK*, 4 April 1995, 1.

Mitrokin, S. 'Konservativny lager"', *Panorama*, 29, September 1991, 7.

'Molim vas – prislushaites'!', *SR*, 18 February 1993.

Morozova, O. 'Pamyat' obeshchala menya povesit"', *MK*, 18 October 1990, 2.

Morrison, James. *Vladimir Zhirinovsky: an Assessment of a Russian Ultra-Nationalist* (McNair Paper 30, April 1994; Institute for National Strategic Studies, National Defence University, Washington, 1994).

Morrison, John. *Boris Yeltsin: from Bolshevik to Democrat* (Penguin, London, 1991).

Morvant, Penny. 'Concern Mounts over Crime and Wage Arrears' in Schmidt, J. (ed.), *OMRI Annual Survey of Eastern Europe and the former Soviet Union 1995. Building Democracy* (M.E. Sharpe, Armonk, NY, and London, 1996) 224–6.

Mosse, George. *The Crisis of the German Ideology. Intellectual Origins of the Third Reich* (Weidenfeld and Nicolson, London, 1964).

Moynihan, B. 'From Russia with Hate', *The Sunday Times Magazine*, June 1996, 40–44.

Mukhin. G. 'Pervy vsetserkovny s"ezd pravoslavnoi molodezhi', *Zhurnal Moskovskoi Patriarkhii*, 5, May 1991, 23–9.

Muravieva, I. 'Prezhde chem poiti na marsh', *RG*, 24 December 1991, 3.

Murray, D. *A Democracy of Despots* (Westview Press, Boulder and Oxford, 1995).

Murrell, G. *Russia's Transition to Democracy. An Internal Political History 1989–96* (Sussex Academic Press, Brighton, 1997).

Mursaliev, A. 'Birds of a Feather?', *MN*, 38–9, 6–12 October 1995, 2.

Musienko, N. 'Za Rus' yedinuyu', *Pravda*, 30 May 1995, 1.

Na putyakh: utverzhdenie yevraziitsev (Gelikon, Moscow and Berlin, 1922).

'Nasha kul'tura i literatura v gody perestroiki', *Literaturnaya Rossiya*, 28 October 1988.

'Nashego polku pribylo', *Zavtra*, 12, March 1996, 1.

Naudet, J.-P. 'Guennadi Ziouganov veut donner tout le pouvoir aux soviets', *Le Monde Hebdomadaire*, 12 December 1995.

Navrozov, L. 'Vladimir Zhirinovsky: sverkh-Gitler i sverkh-Stalin?', *Rossiiskie vesti*, 20 April 1994, 7; 21 April 1994, 5; 27 April 1994, 2.

Nazarov, V. 'Vse smeshalos' v dome NRPR', *Kuranty*, 28 March 1995, 1.

Nelan, B. 'How much of a red is he?', *Time Magazine*, 8 January 1996, 10–11.

Nelson, L. and Kuzes, I. 'Coordinating the Russian Privatisation Programme', *RFE/RL Research Report*, vol. III, no. 20 (20 May 1994) 15–27.

Nenashev, S. 'United Workers' Front', *MN*, 26, 25 June 1989, 2.

Nepobedimy, S. 'Pora vozrazhdat' Rossiyu', *NS*, 1, 1990, 3–5.

Neumann, Iver. *Russia and the Idea of Europe* (Routledge, London and New York, 1996).

Nevzorov, A. 'Yest' takoe uzhasnoe ponyatie "intelligentsiya"', *Narodnaya tribuna*, 2 November 1991.

——. *Pole chesti* (Shans, St Petersburg, 1995).

Nielsen, Niels (ed.) *Christianity after Communism: Social, Political and Cultural Struggle in Russia* (Westview Press, Boulder, San Francisco and Oxford, 1994).

Nikolaev, A. 'Obshchestvo Pamyat': oppozitsiya perestroike?', *Komsomolets Tatarii*, 19 November 1989, 4.

Novaya Rossiya 1994: informatsionno-statisticheskii al'manakh (Mezhdunarodnaya akademiya informatsii, Moscow, 1994).

V.S. Novikov (ed.) *Ilya Glazunor* 2 vols. (Avrora, Leningrad, 1992). *Ilya Glazunor* (Golos, Moscow, 1994).

Novodvorskaya, V. 'Fashizm vtoroi svezhesti', *Moskovskaya pravda*, 16 April 1994, 3.

'O genotside russkogo naroda', *Russkii vestnik*, 9, 1992, 2–3.

Oates, S. 'Vying for Votes on a Crowded Campaign Trail', *Transition*, vol. II, no. 4 (23 February 1996) 26–9.

'Obedinenny Front Trudyashchikhsya', *Leningradskaya Pravda*, 14 June 1989.

'Obrashchenie k grazhdanam Rossii orgkomiteta FNS', *SR*, 1 October 1992.

'Obrashchenie k narodam Rossii', *Den'*, 5, March 1991.

'Obrashchenie k narodnym deputatam SSSR', *NS*, 12, 1989, 3–6.

Oittinen, V. 'Ein populistischer Zwitter: Russlands KP zwischen Leninismus und Staatspatriotismus', *Blätter für deutsche und internationale Politik*, vol. XL, no. 8, 946–55.

Omel'chenko, Ye. and Pilkington, H. 'Stabilization or Stagnation? A Regional Perspective' in Lentini, P. (ed.), *Elections and Political Order in Russia* (Central European University Press, Budapest, London and New York, 1995) pp. 143–66.

'Oppozitsiya i russkii vopros', *NS*, 6, 1993, 98–104.

'Opredeleniya Svyashchennogo Sinoda', *Zhurnal Moskovskoi Patriarkhii*, 12 December 1990, 8.

Orekhanova, G. 'K spaseniyu Otechestva', *SR*, 16 June 1992, 1.

——. 'Splachivaet trevoga', *SR*, 27 July 1993, 1–2.

——. Ovcharov , V. and Garifulina, N. 'Interv'yu v kulyarakh kongressa', *SR*, 27 October 1992, 1–2.

Orlik, Yu. 'Demokratiya tozhe predusmatrivaet nasilie', *Izvestiya*, 30 November 1993, 4.

Orlov, V. 'Protivnik, naslednik', *MN*, 35, 29 August 1993, 5a.

Orttung, R.W. 'The Russian Right and the Dilemmas of Party Organisation', *Soviet Studies*, vol. XLIV, no. 3 (1992) 445–78.

——. 'Congress of Russian Communities Fights for a Stable Niche', *Transition*, vol. I, no. 22 (1 December 1995) 14–6, 68.

——. 'Yeltsin's Most Dangerous Rival: a Profile of Alexander Lebed', *Transition*, vol. I, no. 22 (1 December 1995) 17–19.

——. 'Duma Elections Bolster Leftist Opposition', *Transition*, vol. II, no. 4 (23 February 1996) 6–11.

——. 'Duma Vote Reflects North–South Divide', *Transition*, vol. II, no. 4 (23 February 1996) 12–14.

——. 'Voters Face a Red and White Choice', *Transition*, vol. II, no. 11 (31 May 1996) 6–11.

——. 'Rejecting Communists, Voters Return Yeltsin to Office', *Transition*, vol. II, no. 15 (26 July 1996) 6–7.

——. 'From Confrontation to Cooperation in Russia', *Transition*, vol. II, no. 25, (13 December 1996) 16–20.

——. Morvant, P. and Parrish, S. 'Yeltsin Campaigns Hard to Secure Reelection', *Transition*, vol. II, no. 14 (12 July 1996) 57–9.

Oschlies, Wolf. *Wladimir Schirinowski. Der hässliche Russe und das postkommunistische Osteuropa* (Böhlau, Cologne, Weimar, Vienna, 1995).

Osipov, V. 'Yest' li budushchee u sotsializma?', *NS*, 7, 1991, 125–8.

——. 'Samoe strashnoe seichas – defitsit patriotizma', *Obozrevatel'*, 2–3 February 1992, 4.

'Osnovnye polozheniya programmy dvizheniya Russkogo Narodnogo Yedinstva po postroeniyu natsional'nogo gosudarstva', *Russkii poryadok*, December 1993–January 1994, 24–7.

Ostapchuk, A. 'Levo-pravye razrabotali dispozitsiyu', *NG*, 7 April 1992.

——. 'V Moskve sostoyalsya plenum ts.k', *NG*, 16 June 1992.

——. *Spravochnik: politicheskie partii, dvizhenii i bloki sovremennoi Rossii* (Leto, Nizhni Novgorod, 1993).

——. 'House of Pragmatists', *MN*, 9, 7–13 March 1993, 3.

—— and Krasnikov, Ye. 'General Lebed starts his own Movement', *MN*, 40–41, 20–26 October 1995, 6.

Ostashvili, K. 'Pamyat' – bez retushi', *Izmailovskii vestnik*, 2, January 1990.

Ostrosvetov, V. 'Russkii poryadok Alexandra Barkashova', *MN*, 15, 10–15 April 1994, 7a.

Ovchinsky, V. 'Natsional'no-politicheskii ekstremizm v SSSR', *Den'*, 3, February 1991, 2.

Ovrutsky, L. 'Rutskoism', *MN*, 12, 22–9 March 1992, 7.

'Pamyat': Gorbachev's Strange Friends', *Soviet Analyst*, 3 June 1987, 6–8.

'Pamyat' kak ona yest'', *Soglasiya*, 4, 14 March 1989.

'Pamyat': opyt predvratitel'nogo opisaniya', *Panorama*, 14 December 1990.

Parland, Th. *The Rejection in Russia of Totalitarian Socialism and Liberal Democracy: a Study in the Russian New Right* (The Finnish Society of Sciences and Letters, Helsinki, 1993).

Parrish, S. 'Enter Lebed', *Transition*, vol. II, no. 15 (26 July 1996) 8–10.

—— and Rutland, P. 'The Many Faces of Boris Yeltsin', *Transition*, vol. II, no. 11 (31 May 1996) 18–22.

Parthe, K. 'The Empire Strikes Back; How Right-Wing Nationalists Tried to Recapture Russian Literature', *Nationalities Papers*, vol. XXIV, no. 4 (December 1996) 601–24.

Pashkov, A. 'Prizrak Mussolini brodit po Uralu', *Izvestiya*, 4 July 1995, 5.

Pasko, N. 'Bredni: kto stoit v ryadakh Pamyati?', *Vechernaya Moskva*, 15 June 1987.

'Patriarch Accused of Insulting Religious Feelings', *MN*, 13, 29 March–5 April 1992, 2.

'Patrioty, tekhnokraty, voennye i reformisty idut na dvizhenie', *Pravaya al'ternativa* (Occasional Paper, Postfaktum, 25 Febraury 991) 4–7.

Pavlov, N. 'Teper' vmeste', *Obozrevatel'*, 2–3, February 1992, 2.

Pavlov, P. 'O byvshem V-P', *Segodnya*, 2 June 1994, 3.

Pavlov, Valentin. *Gorbachev – Putch – Avgust iznutri* (Delovoi mir, Moscow, 1993).

Payne, S. *A History of Fascism 1914–45* (UCL Press, London, 1995).

Pechenev, V. and Vyunsky, V. (eds) *Neformaly: kto oni? kuda zovut?* (Politizdat, Moscow, 1990).

Perestroika: sotsializm ili kapitalizm? (Otechestvo, Moscow, 1989).

'Perechitivaya vozhd'', *Izvestiya*, 14 June 1996.

Pestrukhina, Ye. 'Kak possorilis' Rutskoi s Lipitskim', *Kuranty*, 6 April 1995, 4.
—— and Skorobogat'ko, T. 'Derzhavnye sotsial-demokraty', *MN*, 42, 25 September–2 October 1994, 9.
Petro, N. 'The Project of the Century: a Case Study of Russian National Dissent', *Studies in Comparative Communism*, vol. XX, nos. 3–4 (Autumn–Winter 1987) 235–52.
Petrov, G. 'Tak vy probivaetes' k pravde?', *SK*, 24 November 1987, 3.
Petrovich, M. *The Emergence of Russian Pan-Slavism 1856–1870* (Columbia University Press, New York, 1956).
Pikul', V. and Zhuravlev, S. 'Chest' svoego imeni', *NS*, 2, 1989, 184–92.
Pinaev, B. 'Unizhenie klassiki', *NS*, 8, 1987, 188–9.
'Pis'mo pisatelei Rossii v VS SSSR, VS RSFSR, Ts.K KPSS', *Literaturnaya Rossiya*, 2 March 1990.
Pittman, R. 'Writers and Politics in the Gorbachev Era', *Soviet Studies*, vol. XLIV, no. 4 (1992) 665–85.
——. 'Writers and the Coup: the chronology of events in Summer 1991', *Rusistika*, 4, December 1991, 16–19.
Platkovsky, A. 'Pod novoi vyveskoi vozrazhaemsya KGB', *Izvestiya*, 18 March 1995, 1–2.
Plekhanov, S. *Zhirinovsky: kto on?* (Yevrazia-nord, Moscow, 1994).
Plutnik, A. 'Alexander Solzhenitsyn – Boris Yeltsin. Vstrecha na vyshem urovne', *Izvestiya*, 17 November 1994, 1.
Pochemukhin, M. (pseud.)'O ponyatii natsional'-stalinizma', *Rech'*, 1 July 1990, 5.
'Poderzhivaem pisatelei Rossii', *Pamyat'*, 6 May 1990.
Politicheskaya programma Natsional'no Respublikanskoi Partii Rossii (n.p., Moscow, 1992).
Polivanov, S. 'Fascists' Dismal Poll Failure', *MN*, 10, 14–20 March 1996, 6.
Polosin, V. 'Pravoslavie i novaya yevropeiskaya real'nost', *SR*, 29 July 1993, 6.
Polovodov, N. 'Na pozitsiakh rabochego cheloveka', *SR*, 3 July 1991, 3.
Ponomarev, G. 'Chto sluchilos' v ts.d.l.', *Vechernaya Moskva*, 20 February 1990.
Popov, M. 'Kak rozhdalas' rabochaya partiya', *Narodnaya pravda*, 1–10 January 1992, 3.
Poptsov, O. *Khronika vremen 'Tsarya Borisa'. Rossiya, Kreml'. 1991–1995* (Sovershenno sekretno, Moscow, 1996).
Pospielovsky, Dimitry. *A History of Soviet Atheism in Theory and Practice and the Believer. Vol. III. Soviet Studies on the Church and the Believer's Response to Atheism* (Macmillan, London, 1988).
——. 'Impressions of the Contemporary Russian Orthodox Church: its Problems and its Theological Education', *Religion, State and Society*, vol. XXIII, no. 3 (1995) 249–62.
——. 'The Russian Orthodox Church in the Post-Communist CIS' in Bourdeaux, M. (ed.), *The Politics of Religion in Russia and the New States of Eurasia* (M.E. Sharpe, Armonk, NY, and London, 1995) pp. 41–74.
Potanin, V. 'Sokrovennoe' in Stetsenko, V. (ed.), *Pisatel' i vremya* (Sovetskii pisatel', Moscow, 1989) pp. 325–37.
'Pravda o sionizme', *Lit. Gaz.*, 12 February 1986, 14.
'Predotvarim ugrozu demokratii i konstitutsionnomu stroyu v Rossii', *SR*, 21 September 1993, 1.

Predvybornaya platforma kandidata na dolzhnost' Prezidenta Rossiiskoi Federatsii Zyuganova Gennadiya Andreevicha (ndp [1996]). Also published in *Zavtra*, 12, March 1996, 3.

Prelovskaya, I. 'Test na terpimost'', *Izvestiya*, 4 July 1995, 2.

'Presidential Hopefuls about Each Other', *MN*, 23, 20–26 June 1996, 4.

Pribylovsky, Vladimir. 'Pamyat': opyt opisaniya', *Panorama*, 10 September 1990, 7.

——. 'Pamyat': opyt predvaritel'nogo opisaniya: VI. Novye tendentsii', *Panorama*, 14, December 1990, 1, 4.

——. *Slovar' novikh politicheskikh partii i organizatsii Rossii*, 3rd edn (Panorama, Moscow, 1991).

——. *Pamyat': dokumenty i teksty* (Panorama, Moscow, 1991).

——. 'Likurg, Chingis-Khan i Gitler', *Panorama*, 28, July 1991, 1, 4.

——. Bloki i fraktsii Rossiiskogo parlamenta', *Panorama*, 32, May 1992, 14–18.

——. *Politicheskie fraktsii i deputatskie gruppy rossiiskogo parlamenta* (Panorama, Moscow, 1993).

——. 'A Survey of Radical Right-Wing Groups in Russia', *The Politics of Intolerance. RFE/RL Research Report*, vol. III, no. 16 (22 April 1994) 28–37.

——. 'What Awaits Russia: Fascism or a Latin-American Style Dictatorship?', *Transition*, vol. I, no. 10 (23 June 1995) 6–7.

Programma i ustav Rossiiskoi Kommunisticheskoi Rabochei Partii (Riviera, Leningrad, 1993).

'Programma Kommunisticheskoi Partii Rossiiskoi Federatsii', *Dialog*, 3, 1995, 22–30.

Programma Liberal'no-Demokraticheskoi Partii Rossii (ndp) [c.1993].

Programma Natsional'-Bol'shevistskoi Partii (Paleya, ndp) [c.1993].

'Programma Soyuza Pamyat'', *Energetik*, 18 January 1990, 3–5.

Programmnoe zayavlenie A. I. Lebeda dlya pressy (24 April 1996).

'Programmnoe zayavlenie Rossiiskogo Narodnogo Sobraniya', *Obozrevatel'*, 2–3, February 1992, supplement, 12–17.

Programmnoe zayavlenie II chrezvychainogo s"ezda Kommunisticheskoi Partii Rossiiskogo Federatsii (Paleya, Moscow, 1993).

Prokhanov, Alexander. 'Tragediya', *Literaturnaya Rossiya*, 5 January 1990, 4–5.

——. 'Zametki konservatora', *NS*, 5, 1990, 85–98.

——. 'V poiskakh trekh kontseptsii', *Russkoe tovarishchestvo*, 1, September 1990, 6–7.

——. 'V gostyakh u Generala Rodionova', *Den'*, 9, May 1991, 1, 3.

——. 'Yesli khotim zhit'', *Den'*, 1–9 January 1993, 2–3.

——. 'Snachala – ipatievskii dom, a potom – vsyu Rossiyu', *Den'*, 1–7 October 1993, 1–2.

Prokhorov, V. and Orlov, S. 'Pervoaprel'skaya partiya', *Panorama*, 7 July 1990, 5.

'Protiv podmen', *NS*, 5, 1988, 189–90.

Pushkar, D. 'Communists do not Want to Build Communism', *MN*, 37, 22–28 September 1995, 3.

Pushkarev, S., Rusak, V. and Yakunin, Fr G. *Christianity and Government in Russia and the Soviet Union. Reflections on the Millennium* (Westview Press, Boulder and London, 1989).

Pushkov, A. 'Russian Neo-Communism at the Davos Forum', *MN*, 6, 15–21 February 1996, 1, 6.

Putnik, A. 'Smotrite kto prishel', *Izvestiya*, 23 December 1993, 4.

Pyanyk, G., Dubnov, A. and Safarova, T. 'Konstantin Ostashvili: moya babushka – nemka', *Kommersant*, 24 September–1 October 1990.

Pyl'd, Z. 'Natsional'-stalinisty za rabotoi. Ubiistvo o. A. Menya', *Rech'*, September–October 1990, 5–6.

——. 'Monarkhiya – mat' poryadka', *Novaya rech'*, 4, October–November 1990, 6.

Ra'anan, U., Mesner, M., Armes, K. and Martin, K. (eds) *State and Nation in Multi-Ethnic Societies; the Break-Up of Multi-National States* (Manchester University Press, Manchester and New York, 1991).

Rahr, A. 'Kryuchkov, the KGB and the 1991 Putsch', *RFE/RL Research Report*, vol. II, no. 31 (30 July 1993) 16–22.

——. 'The Future of the Russian Democrats', *RFE/RL Research Report*, vol. II, no. 39 (1 October 1993) 1–4.

——. 'Power Ministries Support Yeltsin', *RFE/RL Research Report*, vol. II, no. 40 (8 October 1993) 8–11.

——. 'The October Revolt: Mass Unrest or Putsch', *RFE/RL Research Report*, vol. II, no. 44 (5 November 1993) 1–4.

——. 'Preparations for the Parliamentary Elections in Russia', *RFE/RL Research Report*, vol. II, no. 47 (26 November 1993) 1–6.

Rakhaev, Yu. 'Nastoyashchaya familiya dedushki', *MK*, 12–15 August 1990.

Rasputin, V. 'Zhertvovat' soboyu dlya pravdy', *NS*, 1, 1988, 169–78.

——. 'Yesli po sovesti' in V. Kanunikova (ed.), *Yesli po sovesti* (Khudozhestvennaya literatura, Moscow, 1988), 224–36.

——. 'Simvol derzhavnosti', *Literaturnaya Rossiya*, 6 November 1992, 3.

——. *Rossiya: dni i vremena* (Pis'mena, Irkutsk, 1993).

Rasshivalova, Ye. and Seregin, N. (eds) *Putch: khronika trevozhnikh dnei* (Progress, Moscow, 1991).

Rawson, D. *Russian Rightists and the Revolution of 1905* (CUP, Cambridge, 1995).

Razh, G. 'Yazov', *Den'*, 12 June 1991, 3.

——. 'Syezd lubitelei rodiny', *Panorama*, 31 April 1992, 5–7.

Razorenova, M. 'Rossiiskoe khristiansko-demokraticheskoe dvizhenie', *Kentavr*, 6 November–December 1992, 101–8.

Reeves, P. 'Yeltsin's new ally reveals his darker side', *The Independent*, 28 June 1996.

——. 'Lebed plots next round', *The Independent*, 18 October 1996.

'Religiya v SSSR', *Russkaya mysl'*, 20 May 1988, 5.

Remington, Thomas F. 'Representative Power and the Russia State' in S. White, A. Pravda and Z. Gitelman, *Developments in Russian and Post-Soviet Politics* (Macmillan, London, 1994) pp. 57–88.

——. 'The Development of Parliamentary Parties in Russia', *Legislative Studies Quarterly*, vol. XX, no. 4 (1995) 457–89.

——. 'Ménage à Trois: the End of Soviet Parliamentarism' in Hahn, Jeffrey (ed.), *Democratization in Russia: the Development of Legislative Institutions* (M.E. Sharpe, Armonk, NY, 1996) pp. 106–39.

—— and Smith, S. 'The Early Legislative Process in the Russian Federal Assembly' in Olson, D. and Norton, P. (eds), *The New Parliaments of Central and Eastern Europe* (Frank Cass, London, Portland, 1996) 161–92.

Reshetnikov, M. and Vasiliev, V. 'Demokratiya. Natsional'-populizm. Ekstremizm. Fashizm?', *Rossiiskie vesti*, 30 December 1993, 4–5.

Reznik, S. *The Nazification of Russia: Anti-Semitism in the Post-Soviet Era* (Challenge Publications, Washington, 1996).

'Rezonnye voprosy', *NS*, 12, 1987, 187–8.

Rhodes, M. 'Diversity of Political Views among Russia's Believers', *RFE/RL Research Report*, vol. III, no. 11 (18 March 1994) 44–50.

Rogger, Hans. *National Consciousness in Eighteenth Century Russia* (Harvard University Press, Cambridge, Mass., 1960).

Rogov, S. and Nosenko, V. 'Chto skazal A', *SK*, 9 February 1989, 6.

Rogozin, D. 'Pravy tsentr – za vozrozhdenie Rossii', *Obozrevatel'*, 2–3, February 1992, 3.

Romanov, A. 'Zemlya russkaya', *Moskva*, 2, 1993, 201–4.

'Rossiiskii Obshchenarodny Soyuz', *Russkii vestnik*, 22, 1992, 9.

Rossiiskoe khristiansko-demokraticheskoe dvizhenie: sbornik materialov (Vybor, Moscow, 1990).

'Rossiiskoe Narodnoe Sobranie: politicheskie printsipy i blizhaishie zadachi', *Obozrevatel'*, 2–3, February 1992, Supplement, p. 11.

Rott, V. 'O KhDS Rossii', *AiF*, 13, 1990, 8.

Roy, S. 'Ghostly Cabinet', *MN*, 14, 11–17 April 1996, 1.

Roxburgh, A. *The Second Russian Revolution* (BBC Books, London, 1991).

Rtishchev, F. 'Za "derzhavu" obidno', *SR*, 25 April 1995, 1.

Rudensky, N. 'Russian Minorities in the Newly Independent States' in Szporluk, R. (ed.), *National Identity and Ethnicity in Russia and the New States of Eurasia* (M.E. Sharpe, Armonk, NY, 1994) pp. 58–77.

Ruga, V. 'Boeviki poka premiruyutsya', *Vechernaya Moskva*, 17 December 1991.

Rurikevich, A. 'Toxic Avenger', *Living Here*, 5 July 1996, 1–2.

'Russia and Democracy', *The Economist*, 16 December 1994, 19–23.

Russia: State Duma Election Report (IRI, Washington, and Moscow, 1996).

'Russian Heir Presumptive', *The Times*, 10 October 1996.

'Russkaya ideya; problemy kul'tury – problemy kinematografa', *Iskusstvo kino*, 6, 1988, 118–31.

Russkii National'ny Sobor: tretii s"ezd (n.p., Suzdal', 1994).

Russkii Obshchenarodny Soyuz. Programmnye dokumenty (n.p., Moscow, 1993).

'Russkoe Natsional'noe Yedinstvo namereno priti k vlasti', *NG*, 10 February 1995, 1–2.

Rutland, Peter. 'The Economy: the Rocky Road from Plan to Market', in S. White, A. Pravda and Z. Gitelman, *Developments in Russian and Post-Soviet Politics* (Macmillan, London, 1994) pp. 131–61.

——. 'An Economy Running on Empty' in Schmidt, J. (ed.), *The OMRI Annual Survey of Eastern Europe and the Former Soviet Union 1995: Building Democracy* (M.E. Sharpe, Armonk, NY, 1996) pp. 190–97.

——. 'Russia's Broken "Wheel of Ideologies"', *Transitions*, vol. IV, no. 1 (June 1997) 47–55.

Rutskoi, Alexander, *O chesti i beschesti* (Paleya, Moscow, 1993).
——. *Rossiya ustala ot slov: sbornik intervyu A.V. Rutskogo* (Golos, Moscow, 1993).
——. *Obretenie veru* (n.p., Moscow, 1995).
——. *O nas i o sebe* (Nauchnaya kniga, Moscow, 1995).
Ryabnikova, T. (ed.) *K svobode sovesti* (Progress, Moscow, 1989).
Rybkin, Ivan. 'Gosudarstvennaya Duma: pervyi god stanovleniya', *Mirovaya ekonomika i mezhdunarodnye otnosheniya*, 7, 1995, 42–9.
Rykovtseva, Ye. 'Open list a bit too open', *MN*, 17–18, 20–22 May 1996, 2.
Rywkin, M. *Moscow's Lost Empire* (M.E. Sharpe, Armonk, NY, and London, 1994).
Ryzhkov, Nikolai. *Perestroika: istoriya predatel'stv* (Novosti, Moscow, 1992).
——. 'Za nami – strana', *Zavtra*, 1, January 1996, 4.
'S nadezhdoi i veroi', *SR*, 22 December 1990, 1.
Saenko, G. *Oppozitsiya ... oppozitsiya? Da zdravstvuet oppozitsiya* (MGSU, Moscow, 1995).
Safarova, T. and Dubnov, A. 'Konstantin Ostashvili', *Kommersant*, 23–30 July 1990.
Sakharov, Andrei. 'On Alexander Solzhenitsyn's "A Letter to the Soviet Leaders"' in Bethell, N. and Rubin, B. (eds), *Kontinent: The Alternative Voice of Eastern Europe* (Hodder and Stoughton, London, 1977) pp. 19–30.
Sakwa, Richard. *Russian Politics and Society* (Routledge, London and New York, 1993).
——. 'Khristianskaya demokratiya v Rossii', *Sotsiologicheskoe issledovanie*, 4, 1993, 126–34; 7, 1993, 122–30.
——. 'The Development of the Russian Party System: Did the Elections Change Anything?' in Lentini, Peter (ed.), *Elections and Political Order in Russia* (Central European University Press, Budapest, London and New York, 1995) pp. 169–201.
——. *Russian Politics and Society*, 2nd edn (Routledge, London and New York, 1996).
——. *The Communist Party of the Russian Federation and the Electoral Process* (Studies in Public Policy, no. 265, University of Strathclyde, Glasgow, 1996).
Satarov, G. *Partiinaya zhizn' Rossii do i posle avgusta* (MSS courtesy of the author, 1991).
Savin, M. and Shagin, A. 'LDPR: slagaemye pobedy', *NG*, 18 December 1993, 1–2.
Savvateeva, I. 'Zemel'nyi kodeks', *Izvestiya*, 3 June 1994, 1–2.
Scammell, M. *Solzhenitsyn: a Biography* (Paladin, London, 1986).
Schapiro, L. 'Nationalism in the Soviet Empire: the Anti-Semitic Component' in Conquest, R. (ed.) *The Last Empire* (Hoover Institution, Stanford, 1986) pp. 78–86.
Schmidt, J. (ed.) *The OMRI Annual Survey of Eastern Europe and the Former Soviet Union 1995: Building Democracy* (M.E. Sharpe, Armonk, NY, 1996).
Schneider, E. Die nationalistischen und die kommunistischen Fraktionen der russlandischen Staatsduma (*Berichte des Bundesinstituts für ostwissenschaftliche und internationale Studien*, 28, 1995).
Scholl, S. 'Zyuganov, when do you tell the Truth?', *MN*, 19, 23–29 May 1993, 2.

300 References

Schöpflin, G. (ed.) *The Soviet Union and Eastern Europe*, rev. edn (Facts on File, New York and Oxford, 1986).

——. 'Nationalism and Ethnicity in Europe, East and West' in Kupchan, C. (ed.), *Nationalism and Nationalities in the New Europe* (Cornell University Press, Ithaca and London, 1995) 37–65.

Scorer, P. *New Old-Believers and Neo-Restorationists.* Paper presented to BASEES Conference March 1996.

Seide, G. 'Orthodoxie, Staatsmacht und Armee. Die neue Rolle der Russischen Orthodoxen Kirche', *Osteuropa*, vol. XLVI, no. 10 (October 1996) 1005–19.

Seleznev, G. 'U nas svoya doroga', *AiF*, 26, 1996, 3.

Semenov, A. 'Otkrovenie v korichnevykh tonakh', *MN*, 52, 30 October–6 November 1994, 6.

Semenov, D. 'Will the Writers' Union Disband Itself?', *MN*, 34–5, 1–8 September 1991, 2.

Semina, L. 'Po zakonam grazhdanskogo vremeni' in Pechenev, V. and Vyunsky, V. (eds), *Neformaly: kto oni? kuda zovut?* (Politizdat, Moscow, 1990) pp. 163–86.

Sergeev, A. 'Situatsiya chrezvychainaya', *SR*, 3 July 1991, 3.

Sergeev, P. Untitled note on the founding of Otechestvo, *Literaturnaya Rossiya*, 23 June 1989, 14.

Sergeev, T. 'U Pamyati svoi zakony', *Moskovskaya pravda*, 19 May 1988.

Sergeev, V. *Dvizhenie za vozrozhdenie kazachestva* (Severo-kavkazskii kadrovy tsentr, Rostov-on-Don, 1993).

Service, Robert. 'Liberal with his Threats', *The Independent*, 14 December 1993.

Seton-Watson, Hugh. 'Russian Nationalism in Historical Perspective' in Conquest, R. (ed.). *The Last Empire* (Hoover Institution, Stanford, 1986) pp. 14–29.

Shafarevich, Igor. 'Socialism in our Past and Future' in Solzhenitsyn, A., Agursky, M. and Shafarevich, I. *From under the Rubble* (Collins Harvill, London, 1975) pp. 26–66.

——. 'Rusofobiya', *NS*, 6, 1989, 167–92; 11, 1989, 162–72.

——. 'Fenomen emigratsii', *Literaturnaya Rossiya*, 8 September 1989, 4–5.

——. 'Prigovor: vinovna natsiya', *Den'*, 6, March 1991.

——. 'Ne vremya dlya sporov', *Literaturnaya Rossiya*, 6 November 1992, 3.

Shakina, M. and Gul'binsky, N. 'Partiya budet zhdat' svoego lidera', *Novoe vremya*, 44, October 1993, 8–11.

Shatov, Protoirei A., Shargunov, Prot. A., Sakharov, Ieromonakh Kirill *et al.* 'Pravoslavnye i katoliki', *Russkaya mysl'*, 21–27 December 1995, 9.

Sheinis, O. 'Kongress: vzglyad sleva', *Obozrevatel'*, 2–3 February 1992, 3.

Shepp, L. and Vellerov, Ye. 'Picasso and Co', *MN*, 16, 22 April 1990, 7.

Shevtsova, Lilia. 'Political Pluralism in Post-Communist Russia' in Dallin, A. (ed.), *Political Parties in Russia* (University of California, Berkeley, 1993) pp. 49–62.

——. 'Russia's Post-Communist Politics: Revolution or Continuity' in Lapidus, G. (ed.), *The New Russia* (Westview Press, Boulder, 1995) 5–36.

——. 'Elections: Hoax Time', *MN*, 22, 13–19 June 1996, 2.

——. 'Parliament and the Political Crisis in Russia 1991–1993' in Hahn, Jeffrey (ed.), *Democratization in Russia: the Development of Legislative Institutions* (M.E. Sharpe, Armonk, NY, 1996) pp. 29–48.

Shihab, Sophie. 'Sacha Lebed à l'Assaut du Kremlin', *Le Monde Hebdomadaire*, 21 December 1995.

Shlapentokh, V. *Soviet Intellectuals and Political Power: the Post-Stalin Era* (I.B. Tauris, London and New York, 1990).

Shokarev, V. 'Kto golosoval za LDPR', *Izvestiya*, 30 December 1993, 4.

Shtep, V. 'Departizatsiya', *NS*, 8, 1992, 117–23.

Shusharin, D. 'Vse k luchemu', *Russkii kurier*, 26, September 1991, 11.

——. 'Dissidenty i svyashchenniki', *NG*, 24 March 1992.

——. 'Zagovor fundamentalistov', *NG*, 1 April 1992, 6.

——. 'Ibo o tom, chto oni delayut taino', *NG*, 21 May 1992.

Schwartz, S. *Antisemitizm v Sovetskom Soyuze* (NY, 1952).

Sidorov, I. 'Pamyat' kak ona yest'', *Leningradskaya pravda,* 6 September 1988, 2–3.

Simonsen, Sven. 'Leading the Communists through the 1990s', *Transition*, vol. I, no. 12 (14 July 1995) 60–63.

——. 'Going his own Way: a Profile of General Alexander Lebed', *The Journal of Slavic Military Studies*, vol. VIII, no. 3 (September 1995) 528–46.

——. 'Aleksander Barkashov and the RNU: Blackshirt Friends of the Nation', *Nationalities Papers*, vol. XXIV, no. 4 (December 1996) 625–40.

——. 'Still Favouring the Power of the Workers', *Transitions*, vol. IV, no. 7 (December 1997) 52–6.

Sirotkin, V. 'Fyurer – s nami!', *MN*, 22, 29 May–5 June 1994, 8a.

——. 'Russkii Natsional'ny Sobor', *MN*, 24, 12–19 June 1994, 6a.

——. 'Natsional'-bol'sheviki', *MN*, 28, 10–17 July 1994, 11.

——. 'Natsional'ny kommunizm', *MN*, 34, 21–8 August 1994, 8.

Sivertsev, M. 'Civil Society and Religion in Traditional Political Culture: the Case of Russia' in Bourdeaux, M. (ed.), *The Politics of Religion in Russia and the New States of Eurasia* (M.E. Sharpe, Armonk, NY, and London, 1995) pp. 75–94.

Sixsmith, Martin. *The Moscow Coup: the Death of the Soviet System* (Simon and Schuster, London, 1991).

Skillen, D. 'Media Coverage in the Elections' in Lentini, Peter (ed.), *Elections and Political Order in Russia* (Central European University Press, Budapest, London and New York, 1995) pp. 97–123.

Skokov, Yu. 'Vlast' pod kontrol' naroda', *Zavtra*, 46, November 1995, 1.

——. 'Gosudarstvo dlya naroda', *Zavtra*, 47, November 1995, 1, 3.

'Skol'ko my imeem kompartii', *Lit. gaz.*, 25 March 1992, 11.

Skorobogatko, T. 'Communist fakirs reinvent Soviet Union', *MN*, 11, 21–27 March 1996, 2.

Slater, Wendy. 'The Center Right in Russia', *RFE/RL Research Report*, vol. II, no. 34 (27 August 1993) 7–14.

——. 'Russia's National Salvation Front on the Offensive', *RFE/RL Research Report*, vol. II, no. 38 (24 September 1993) 1–6.

——. 'The Church's Attempts to Mediate in the Russian Crisis', *RFE/RL Research Report*, vol. II, no. 43 (29 October 1993) 6–10.

------. 'The Trial of the Leaders of Russia's August 1991 Coup', *RFE/RL Research Report*, vol. II, no. 48 (3 December 1993) 24–30.

------. 'Russia's Plebiscite on a New Constitution', *RFE/RL Research Report*, vol. III, no. 3 (21 January 1994) 1–7.

------. 'Russian Duma Sidelines Extremist Politicians', *RFE/RL Research Report*, vol. III, no. 7 (18 February 1994) 5–9.

------. 'Russia', *The Politics of Extremism: RFE/RL Research Report*, vol. III, no. 16 (22 April 1994) 23–7.

------. 'The CPSU Today', *RFE/RL Research Report*, vol. III, no. 31 (12 August 1994) 1–6.

------ and Engelbrekt, K. 'Eastern Orthodoxy Defends its Position', *RFE/RL Research Report*, vol. II, no. 35 (3 September 1993) 48–58.

------ and Tolz, V. 'Yeltsin Wins in Moscow but Loses in the Regions', *RFE/RL Research Report*, vol. II, no. 40 (8 October 1993) 1–7.

Slavin, B. 'Chto tam, u kommunistov', *Pravda*, 25 December 1992, 1–2.

Slider, D., Gimpel'son, V. and Chugrov, S. 'Political Tendencies in Russia's Regions: Evidence from the 1993 Parliamentary Elections', *Slavic Review*, vol. LIII, no. 3 (Fall 1994) 711–32.

Slobodyanyuk, D. 'RNS poidet drugim putem', *RG*, 15 June 1992, 2.

'Slovo k narodu', *SR*, 23 July 1991, 1.

'Slovo o Solzhenitsyne', *NS*, 1, 1990, 58–67.

Smena vekh (Prague, 1921).

Smirnov, I. 'Playing with Cheats the Scientific Way: how accurate are we in appraising Russian national socialism?', *MN*, 30, 5–12 August 1989, 8.

Smirnov, S. 'Za yedinuyu veru', *Russkii vestnik*, 4, 1991, 2.

Smirnova, N. 'Delo Ostashvili: ataka na pressu', *Moskovskaya pravda*, 11 August 1990.

Smith, A. 'Nationalism and the Historians' in Balakrishnan, G. *Mapping the Nation* (Verso, London and New York, 1996) 175–97.

Smolowe, J. 'Clap of Thunder', *Time Magazine*, 27 December 1993, 14–19.

Sobyanin, A., Gel'man, E. and Kayunov, O. 'Kto golosoval za amnistiyu?', *AiF*, 11, 1994, 3.

'Soglashenie o sovmestnykh deistviakh v podderzhku yedinogo kandidata na dolzhnost' prezidenta RF G.A. Zyuganova ot narodno-patrioticheskikh sil Rossii', *Zavtra*, 10 March 1996.

Sokolov, A. 'Posledny polkovnik imperii', *Elementy*, 3, 1993, 10–12.

Sokolov, V. 'Nachinaetsya c publitsistiki', *Lit. gaz.*, 15 January 1986, 3.

Solodar, C. 'Sionizm – agressiya – lozh'', *KP*, 18 July 1986.

Solomenko, Ye. 'Propovednik natsizma', *Izvestiya*, 11 January 1995, 2.

------. 'Podsudimy ne skryval radosti', *Izvestiya*, 20 January 1995, 4.

Soloukhin, V. 'Motivy', *NS*, 6, 1988, 119–35.

Solzhenitsyn, Alexander. *Letter to the Soviet Leaders* (Collins Harvill, London, 1974).

------. *Rebuilding Russia* (Harvill, London, 1990).

------. 'Vybirat'sya iz pod oblomkov kommunizma', *Izvestiya*, 4 May 1994, 5.

------. 'Put' k istseleniyu Rossii ne zakryt', *Russkaya mysl'*, 28 October 1994.

------. 'Nuzhny li "malye dela"?', *AiF*, 27, 1995, 3.

------. 'Wie ein Sekretär des Volkes', *Der Spiegel*, 44, 1994, 139–63.

——. *The Russian Question at the End of the Twentieth Century* (Harvill, London, 1995).

——. 'Denezhki porovnu', *Zemstvo* (supplement to *RG*), 11 March 1995, 1–2.

——. *Publitsistika v trekh tomakh. vol. I. Stat'i i rechi* (Verkhne-volzhskoe knizhnoe izdatel'stvo, Yaroslavl', 1995).

——. Agursky, M. and Shafarevich, I. *From under the Rubble* (Collins Harvill, London, 1975).

'Sootvechestvenniki', *Russkii poryadok*, December 1993–January 1994, 2–3.

Sorgin, V. *Politicheskaya istoriya sovremennoi Rossii* (Progress-Akademiya, Moscow, 1994).

Sorokin, V. 'Svoi chuzhie', *NS*, 8, 1989, 168–74.

Sotseno, V. (ed.), *Pisatel' i vremya* (Sovetskii pisatel', Moscow, 1989).

Sotsial-patrioticheskoe dvizhenie Derzhava (n.p., Irkutsk, 1995).

Soyuz ofitserov. Kratkaya spravka (n.d.p.) [c.1992].

'Soyuz russkikh natsionalistov', *Russkii vestnik*, 12, 1992.

'Spravedlivost'. Narodnost'. Gosudarstvennost'. Patriotizm. Deklaritsiya v sozdanii ob"edinennoi oppozitsii', *Literaturnaya Rossiya*, 13 March 1992. Also published in SR, 10 March 1992, 1.

Spechler, D. 'Russian Nationalism and Soviet Politics' in Hajda, L. and Beissinger, M. (eds), *The Nationalities Factor in Soviet Politics and Society* (Westview Press, Boulder, San Francisco and Oxford, 1990) pp. 281–304.

Staravoitova, Galina. 'Nationality Policies in the Period of Perestroika' in Lapidus, G., Zaslavsky, V. and Goldman, P. (eds) *From Union to Commonwealth: Nationalism and Separatism in the Soviet Republics* (CUP, Cambridge, 1992) pp. 114–21.

Stavrou, T. and Nichols, R. (eds) *Russian Orthodoxy under the Old Regime* (University of Minnesota Press, Minneapolis, 1978).

Steele, Jonathan. 'The Bitter End of Empire', *The Guardian*, 14 December 1993.

——. *Eternal Russia. Yeltsin, Gorbachev and the Mirage of Democracy* (Faber, London and Boston, 1994).

Steeves, Paul. *Keeping the Faiths: Religion and Ideology in the Soviet Union* (Holmes and Meir, New York and London, 1989).

——. 'Christian Democrats in Russia 1989–1993' in Nielsen, Niels (ed.), *Christianity after Communism: Social, Political and Cultural Struggle in Russia* (Westview Press, Boulder, San Francisco and Oxford, 1994) pp. 63–74.

Stepanishin, V. 'S kem intelligentsiya?', *Vek XX i mir*, 12, 1989, 7–8.

Stepovoi, A. 'Yeshche odin Romanov sobiraetsya spasti Rossiyu', *Izvestiya*, 29 October 1994, 4.

Sterligov, Alexander. 'Vystuplenie Gen.-maiora A.I. Sterligova na otkrytiya RNS', *Obozrevatel'*, 2–3, February 1992, 23–6.

——. 'Ya nadeyus stat' merom Moskvy', *Pravda*, 8 October 1992, 2.

——. 'A otstupat'sya nekuda', *Pravda*, 8 September 1993, 1, 4.

Sternhell, Z. 'Fascist Ideology' in W. Laqueur (ed.), *Fascism, a Reader's Guide* (Penguin, London, 1979) 325–406.

Stone, N. and Campbell, M. 'Return of the Evil Empire', *The Sunday Times*, 19 December 1993.

Strukova, Ye. and Belenkin, B. *Listovki Belovo Doma: moskovskie letuchie izdaniya 22 sentyabrya–4 oktyabrya* (Logos, Moscow, 1993).

Sultanov, S. 'Dukh yevraziitsa', *NS*, 7, 1992, 143–8.

Sumovsky, V. 'Understanding Pamyat'', *MN*, 13, 26 March 1989, 4.

Suny, Ronald. 'State, civil society and ethnic cultural consolidation in the USSR' in Lapidus, G., Zaslavsky, V. and Goldman, P. (eds), *From Union to Commonwealth: Nationalism and Separatism in the Soviet Republics* (CUP, Cambridge, 1992) pp. 22–44.

———. *The Revenge of the Past. Nationalism, Revolution and the Collapse of the Soviet Union* (Stanford University Press, Stanford, 1993).

Surkov, A. 'Natsional'naya bezopasnost' v predvybornoi upakovke', *Rossiiskie vesti*, 4 April 1995, 1, 3.

Surkova, V. 'Russkii tsentr nachinaet deistvovat'', *Vechernaya Moskva*, 7 December 1988.

'Svobodu V. Anpilovu', *Sovetskoe informbyuro*, 1 November 1993.

Szporluk, Roman. 'Dilemmas of Russian Nationalism', *Problems of Communism*, July–August 1989, 15–35.

———. 'The Imperial Legacy and the Soviet Nationalities Problem' in Hajda, L. and Beissinger M. (eds), *The Nationalities Factor in Soviet Politics and Society* (Westview Press, Boulder, San Francisco and London, 1990) pp. 1–23.

———. 'The National Question' in Colton, T. and Levgold, R. (eds), *After the Soviet Union* (Norton, New York and London, 1992) pp. 84–112.

———. 'Introduction: Statehood and Nation-Building in the Post-Soviet Space' in Szporluk, R. (ed.), *National Identity and Ethnicity in Russia and the New States of Eurasia* (M.E. Sharpe, Armonk, NY, and London, 1994) pp. 3–17.

'S''ezd narodno-patrioticheskoi partii', *Kentavr*, 5, September–October 1992, 70–72.

Tabak, Yu. 'Khronika odnoi konferentsii', *Russkaya mysl'*, 24–30 November 1993, 8.

Tarasov, B. 'Otchizna zovet', *SR*, 10 July 1991.

Tatu, M. and Vernet, D. 'Un entretien avec le numéro deux soviétique', *Le Monde*, 4 December 1987, 1, 6.

Taylor, P. 'Solzhenitsyn: from Gulag to Gulag', *The Sunday Times Magazine*, 23 January 1994, 16–25.

Teague, Elizabeth. 'Yeltsin's Difficult Road towards Elections', *RFE/RL Research Report*, vol. II, no. 41 (15 October 1993) 1–4.

———. ' Yeltsin Disbands the Soviets', *RFE/RL Research Report*, vol. II, no. 43 (29 October 1993) 1–5.

———. 'North–South Divide', *RFE/RL Research Report*, vol. II, no. 47 (26 November 1993) 7–23.

———. 'Center–Periphery Relations in the Russian Federation' in Szporluk, R. (ed.), *National Identity and Ethnicity in Russia and the New States of Eurasia* (M.E. Sharpe, Armonk, NY, and London, 1994) pp. 21–57.

Telen, L. 'Welcome back Comrades!', *MN*, 50, 22–28 December 1995, 1–2.

———. 'Battling Hard for the Centre', *MN*, 8, 29 February–6 March 1996, 3.

———. 'Roosevelt not Marx', *MN*, 21, 6–12 June 1996, 4.

Telyakov, Yu. 'New Arms for the Army!', *MN*, 6, 10–17 February 1991, 7.

Thaden, E. *Conservative Nationalism in Nineteenth Century Russia* (University of Washington Press, Seattle, 1964).

Thorson, Carla. 'The Fate of the Communist Party in Russia', *RFE/RL Research Report*, vol. I, no. 37 (18 September 1992) 1–6.

——. 'Russia's Draft Constitution', *RFE/RL Research Report*, vol. II, no. 48 (3 December 1993) 9–15.

Timmermann, H. Die kommunistische Partei der Russischer Föderation. Aktuelle Analysen (*Berichte des Bundesinstituts für ostwissenschaftliche und internationale Studien*, 69–70, 1995).

——. Die Wiederkehr der KP Russlands. Programm, Struktur und Perspektiven der Sjuganov-Partei (*Berichte des Bundesinstituts für ostwissenschaftliche und internationale Studien*, 12, 1996).

Timofeev, Lev. '28 oktyabrya Gosudarstvennaya Duma ne sumela ponyat' programmnoi rechi', *Russkaya mysl'*, 10–16 November 1994.

Tishkov, V. *Ethnicity, Nationalism and Conflict after the Soviet Union* (Sage Publications, London and Notre Dame, 1997).

Tismaneanu, V. (ed.), *Political Culture and Civil Society in Russia and the New States of Eurasia* (M.E. Sharpe, Armonk, NY, and London, 1995).

Tochkin, G. 'Mrachnye prognozy OFT', *Panorama*, 10, September 1990, 6.

——. 'Kuda kommunisty podat'sya?', *Panorama*, 3, 30 December 1991, 12.

'To the Polls: Forward March', *MN*, 24, 27 June–3 July 1996, 3.

Todres, V. 'Natsional'-Patrioty', *NG*, 21 March 1991.

——. 'Situatsiya vzryvaet ushchemlennost' russkikh', *NG*, 9 January 1992, 2.

——. 'Rossiya dolzhna stat' normal'noi velikoi derzhavoi', *NG*, 16 June 1992.

Tolstaya, Tatyana, 'Russian Lessons', *New York Review of Books*, 19 October 1995, 7–9.

Tolz, Vera. *The USSR's Emerging Multi-Party System* (Praeger, London and New York, 1990).

——. 'Russia: Westernizers continue to challenge National Patriots', *RFE/RL Research Report*, vol. I, no. 49 (11 December 1992) 1–9.

——. 'The Moscow Crisis and the Future of Democracy in Russia', *RFE/RL Research Report*, vol. II, no. 42 (22 October 1993) 1–9.

——. 'The Thorny Road towards Federalism', *RFE/RL Research Report*, vol. II, no. 48 (3 December 1993) 1–8.

——. 'Russia's Parliamentary Elections: What Happened and Why', *RFE/RL Research Report*, vol. III, no. 2 (14 January 1994) 1–8.

——. 'Problems in Building Democratic Institutions in Russia', *RFE/RL Research Report*, vol. III, no. 9 (4 March 1994) 1–7.

——. 'The Civic Accord', *RFE/RL Research Report*, vol. III, no. 19 (13 May 1994) 1–5.

——. 'The Radical Right in Post-Communist Russian Politics' in Merkl, P. and Weinberg, L. (eds), *The Revival of Right-Wing Extremism in the Nineties* (Frank Cass, London and Portland, 1997) pp. 177–202.

—— and Wishnevsky, J. 'The Russian Media and the Political Crisis in Moscow', *RFE/RL Research Report*, vol. II, no. 40 (8 October 1993) 12–15.

Torbakov, I. 'The Statists and the Ideology of Russian Imperial Nationalism', *RFE/RL Research Report*, vol. I, no. 49 (11 December 1992) 10–16.

Toshchenko, Zh., Volkov, V. and Levanov, Ye. 'Kommunisty o partii', *AiF*, 25, 1990, 2.

'Tovarishchestvo russkikh khudozhnikov', *Lit. gaz.*, 29 March 1989, 7.

Treadgold, Donald. *The West in Russia and China. vol. I. Russia 1472–1917* (CUP, Cambridge, 1973).

——. 'Russian Orthodoxy and Society' in Stavrou, T. and Nichols, R., *Russian Orthodoxy under the Old Regime* (Minneapolis, 1978) pp. 21–43.

——. 'Nationalism in the USSR' in Conquest, R. (ed.), *The Last Empire* (Hoover Institution, Stanford, 1986) pp. 381–96.

'Tret'ya vsesoyuznaya konferentsiya Marksistskoi Platformy', *Golos kommunistov*, 1 January 1990, 1.

Tri dnya: 19–21 Avgust 1991 (Postfaktum, Moscow, 1991).

Trofimov, A. 'Otechestvo, pamyat' i my', *NS*, 2, 1988, 178–85.

Tropnikov, Ye. and Tochkin, G. 'Partiya diktatura proletariata', *Panorama*, 12, October 1990, 6.

Trotsky, Ye. (ed.) *Russkaya ideya i sovremennost'* (Assotsiatsiya po izucheniyu russkoi natsii, Moscow, 1992).

Trubetskoi, N. *Europa und die Menschheit* (Drei Masken Verlag, Munich, 1922).

Tsagarelli, Yu. 'Prepodnosit rok urok', *SK*, 1 December 1987, 5.

Tsentrizbirkom, *Vybory deputatov Gosudarstvennoi Dumy 1995* (Ves' mir, Moscow, 1996).

Tuskarev, A. 'Khristianskoe gosudarstvo', *Russkii vestnik*, 11, 1992, 12–13.

Tyurin, Yu. 'Dostovernost'i vymysel', *NS*, 6, 1987, 180–89.

Uchreditel'ny s"ezd kommunisticheskoi partii RSFSR: stenograficheskii otchet, 2 vols. (Politizdat, Moscow, 1991).

Uglanov, A. 'Demokratiyu khoronit' rano', *AiF*, 50, 1993, 1–2.

Uglov, F. 'Glyadya pravdu v glaza', *NS*, 7, 1987, 150–57.

Urban, M. 'The Politics of Identity in Russia', *Slavic Review*, vol. LIII, no. 3 (Fall, 1994) 733–65.

——. Igrunov, V. and Mitrokhin, A. *The Rebirth of Politics in Russia* (CUP, Cambridge, 1997).

Urban, Joan Barth and Solovei, V. *Russia's Communists at the Crossroads* (Westview Press, Boulder and Oxford, 1997).

Ustrialov, N. *V bor'be za Rossiyu* (Okno, Harbin, 1920).

——. *Pod znakom revolyutsii* (Russkaya zhizn', Harbin, 1925).

Varennikov, Valentin. *Sud'ba i sovest'* (Paleya, Moscow, 1993).

Verkhovsky, A. 'Kto poidet za Solzhenitsynym', *Panorama*, 12, October 1990, 1–2.

Vernikov, V. 'Eksportnaya glasnost'', *Izvestiya*, 3 November 1988.

Vesyolaya, Ye. 'Aprel: A Writers' Committee in Support of Perestroika', *MN*, 12, 19–26 March 1989, 2.

Vinogradov, I. 'Vassily Belov's Crossroads', *MN*, 18, 30 April 1989, 11.

Vlasov, Yu. *Rus' bez vozhdya* (Soyuz zhurnalistov, Voronezh, 1995).

'Vmesto epitafii', *Den'*, 14, July 1991.

Volodin, E. 'O natsional' bol'shevizme', *Den'*, 3 February 1991.

Voronin, V. 'Tsentristkii blok', *Dialog*, 16, November 1990, 47–50.

Voronin, Yu. and Lebedev, V. 'Nuzhny chrezvychainye mery', *SR*, 10 July 1991.

'V ozhidanii postanovlenii arkhieriskogo sobora russkoi pravoslavnoi tserkvy', *Russkaya mysl'*, 1–7 December 1994, 1–2.

VTsIOM. 'About Oneself and Others', *MN*, 20, 27 May–3 June 1990, 9.

Vujacic, Veljko. 'Gennady Zyuganov and the "Third Road"', *Post-Soviet Affairs*, vol. XII, no. 2 (1996) 118–54.

Vybory: programmy, kontseptsii: platforma OFT (n.p., Leningrad, 1989).

Vybory-93: partii, bloki, lidery: spravochnik (Itar-Tass, Moscow, 1993).

'Vystuplenie n.d. V.V. Aksyuchitsa na kongresse grazhdanskikh i patriotich-eskikh sil Rossii', *Obozrevatel'*, 2–3, February 1992, supplement, 2–4.

Vyunitsky, V. 'Ot dikii mnogopartiinosti k blokovoi sisteme', *Dialog*, 17 November 1990, 28–36.

Vyzhutovich, V. 'Dispensarizatsiya Generala Rutskogo', *Stolitsa*, 8, 1992, 1–3.

——. 'Front natsional'nogo spaseniya: kommunisty i patrioty, shag v pered!', *Izvestiya*, 26 October 1992, 2.

——. 'Front natsional'nogo spaseniya razoruzhat'sya ne nameren', *Izvestiya*, 29 October 1992, 1.

——. 'Kommunisty dolzhny vladet' ot oruzhiya slova i mysli do oruzhiya, kotorye strelyayut', *Izvestiya*, 16 February 1993, 2.

——. 'Alexander Solzhenitsyn kak zerkalo obshchestvennogo smyateniya', *Izvestiya*, 1 November 1994, 4.

Walicki, A. *The Slavophile Controversy* (OUP, Oxford, 1975).

White, Stephen. 'The Presidency and Political Leadership in Post-Communist Russia' in Lentini, Peter (ed.), *Elections and Political Order in Russia* (Central European University Press, Budapest, London and New York, 1995) pp. 202–25.

——. *Russia Goes Dry: Alcohol, State and Society* (CUP, Cambridge, 1996).

——. Pravda, A., Gitelman, Z. (eds) *Developments in Russian and Post-Soviet Politics*, 3rd edn (Macmillan, London, 1994).

——. McAllister, I. and Kryshtanovskaya, O. 'Religion and Politics in Post-Communist Russia', *Religion, State and Society*, vol. XXII, no. 1 (1994) 75–88.

—— and McAllister, I. 'The CPSU and its Members: between Communism and Post-Communism', *British Journal of Political Science*, vol. XXVI, no. 1 (1996) 105–22.

——. Wyman, M. and Kryshtanovskaya, O. 'Parties and Politics in Post-Communist Russia', *Communist and Post-Communist Studies*, vol. XXVIII, no. 2, pp. 183–202.

——. Wyman, M., Miller, B. and Heywood, P. 'Public Opinion, Parties and Voters in the December 1993 Russian Elections', *Europe-Asia Studies*, vol. XLVII, no. 4 (June 1995) 591–614.

——. Wyman, M. and Oates, S. 'Parties and Voters in the 1995 Duma Elections', *Europe-Asia Studies*, vol. XLIX, no. 5 (July 1997) 767–98.

——. Rose, R. and McAllister, I. *How Russia Votes* (Chatham House Publishers, Chatham, NJ, 1997).

Whitefield, S. and Evans, G. 'Support for Democracy and Political Opposition in Russia', *Post-Soviet Affairs*, vol. XII, no. 3 (July–September 1996) 218–42.

'Why Hasn't the Russian National Idea Seized the Masses Yet?', *MN*, 12, 27 March–2 April 1997, 5.

Williams, Christopher. *From the Black Hundreds to Zhirinovsky: the Rise of the Extreme Right in Russia*, Paper presented to the Russian Studies Group,

Renvall Institute of Historical Research, University of Helsinki, 28 February 1994.

Winbush, S. Enders. 'The Great Russians and the Soviet State: the Dilemmas of Ethnic Dominance' in Azrael, J. (ed.), *Soviet Nationality Policies and Practices* (Praeger, New York, 1978) pp. 349–60.

Wishnevsky, J. 'Liberal Opposition Emerging in Russia, *RFE/RL Research Report*, vol. II, no. 44 (5 November 1993) 5–11.

Woolf, S. *Fascism in Europe* (Weidenfeld and Nicolson, London, 1981).

World Bank, Statistical Handbook 1996: States of the Former USSR (World Bank, Washington, 1996).

Wozniuk, V. 'In Search of Right Wing Nationalism: the Politics of Religion and Nationalism in the New Russia', *Nationalities Papers*, vol. XXV, no. 2 (June 1997) 195–210.

Wyman, M., Miller, B., White, S. and Heywood, P. 'Parties and Voters in the Elections' in Lentini, Peter (ed.), *Elections and Political Order in Russia* (Central European University Press, Budapest, London and New York, 1995) pp. 124–42.

——. *Developments in Voting Behaviour: 1993 and 1995 Compared*, Paper delivered to BASEES Conference, Cambridge 1996.

——. *Public Opinion in Post-Communist Russia* (Macmillan, London and New York, 1997).

Yakhlakova, T. 'White Russia with a Streak of Black', *MN*, 7, 16–23 February 1992, 3.

Yakovlevna, Ye. 'Dlya vozrozhdeniya Orlovshchiny', *Izvestiya*, 24 June 1994, 5.

Yakunin, Fr Gleb. 'V sluzhenii kul'tu. Moskovskaya Patriarkhiya i kul't lichnosti Stalina', in Ryabnikova, T., *K svobode sovesti* (Progress, Moscow, 1989) pp. 172–206.

——. 'The Present State of the Russian Orthodox Church and the Prospects for Religious Revival in Russia' in Pushkarev, S., Rusak, V., Yakunin, Fr G., *Christianity and Government in Russia and the Soviet Union. Reflections on the Millennium* (Westview Press, Boulder and London, 1989) pp. 107–45.

Yakushev, V. 'Nuzhna li VChK perestroiki', *MG*, 7, 1989, 203–23.

Yanov, A. *The Russian New Right: Right-Wing Ideologies in the Contemporary Soviet Union* (IIS, Berkeley, 1978).

——. 'Dva vzglyada na russkuyu ideyu', *Lit. gaz.*, 2 September 1992, 13.

——. 'Opozdavshee na stoletie', *Novoe vremya*, 23, 1993, 8–13.

——. 'Dom modelei Kurginyana – Yanova', *Stolitsa*, 14, 1994, 6–8.

——. *Posle Yeltsina: 'Veimarskaya' Rossiya* (Krik, Moscow, 1995).

——. 'Gennady Zyuganov's Patriotic Communism', *MN*, 10, 14–20 March 1996, 4.

——. 'General Lebed's "Special Path"', *MN*, 24, 27 June–3 July 1996, 1–2.

Yashmann, V. 'The Role of the Security Agencies in the October Uprising', *RFE/RL Research Report*, vol. II, no. 44 (5 November 1993) 12–18.

Yelistratov, I. and Chugaev, S. 'Konservativny revansh', *Izvestiya*, 22 April 1992.

Yeltsin, B. *Against the Grain: an Autobiography* (Jonathan Cape, London, 1990).

——. *The View from the Kremlin* (Harper Collins, London, 1994).

——. 'He Has Made a Series of Mistakes', *The Times*, 18 October 1996, 19.

Yelymanov, Alexei. 'Pochemu ne rastet natsional-kommunisticheskaya oppozitsiya?', *Obshchaya gazeta*, 28 October–3 November 1994, 7.

Yemelyanenko, V. and Leonyeva, L. 'Provinces drive towards stability', *MN*, 9, 7–13 March 1996, 1, 3.

Yemelyanenko, V. 'Fashizm: na vstrechu vyboram', *MN*, 50, December 1994, pp. 1, 4.

Yeremin, V. 'Toska po khozyainu', *Nedelya*, 12, 1990.

Yermakov, Ya., Shavshukova, T. and Yakunechkin, V. 'Kommunisticheskoe dvizhenie v Rossii v period zapreta', *Kentavr*, 3, 1993, 65–80.

'Yest' li budushchee u sotsializma?', *NS*, 7, 1991, 122–33.

'Yest' takaya partiya!', *SR*, 16 February 1993, 1.

'Yevraziiskoe soprotivlenie', *Den'*, 2, 10–18 January 1992, 2–3.

Yuriev, A. 'Odinatsat' figur', *Sevodnya*, 31 May 1996, 4–5.

Yushenkov, S. (ed.), *Neformaly: sotsial'nye initsiativy* (Moskovskii rabochii, Moscow, 1990).

Yushin, M. 'Diplomatiya Zhirinovksogo', *Izvestiya*, 29 December 1993, 4.

Yushin, Y. 'Pora nakonets i Rossii vzyat' slovo', *Literaturnaya Rossiya*, 15 December 1989, 4–5.

Yuzhakov. 'Russkii natsional'ny sobor na puti bor'by', *Yedinstvo*, 5 May 1993, 4.

'Za nashu sovetskuyu rodinu', *SR*, 31 August 1995, 3.

'Za politiku narodnogo soglasiya', *Literaturnaya Rossiya*, 29 December 1989.

'Za yedinstvo deistvii kommunistov', *Pravda*, 26 February 1993, 2.

'Zadachi russkogo natsional'nogo sobora', *Kentavr*, 5, 1992, 72–8.

Zarubezhny, M. (pseud.), 'Yevrei v Kremle', *NS*, 11, 1990, 148–51.

Zaslavsky, S. 'Svobodnaya Rossiya', *Kentavr*, 1, (1993), 37–47.

Zaslavsky, V. *The Neo-Stalinist State: Class, Ethnicity and Consensus in Soviet Society* (M.E. Sharpe, Armonk, NY, 1982).

——. 'The evolution of separatism in Soviet society under Gorbachev' in Lapidus, G. (ed.) *From Union to Commonwealth* (CUP, Cambridge, 1992) pp. 71–97.

——. 'Success and Collapse: traditional Soviet nationality policy' in Bremmer, I. and Taras, R. (eds), *Nations and Politics in the Soviet Successor States* (CUP, Cambridge, 1993), 29–42.

'Zayavlenie koordinatsionnogo soveta patrioticheskikh sil Rossii', *Russkii vestnik*, 7 May 1991, 5.

'Zayavlenie kongressa grazhdanskikh i patrioticheskikh sil Rossii', *Obozrevatel'*, February 1991, supplement, 1.

Zernov, N. *The Russian Religious Renaissance of the Twentieth Century* (Longman and Todd, London, 1963).

Zheleznova, N., Panova, A. and Surkov, A. (eds) *Moskva, osen' – 93. Khronika protivostoyaniya* (Respublika, Moscow, 1994).

Zhilin, A. 'Lebed: Don't Cast me as a Political Killer', *MN*, 25, 4–10 July 1995, 1–2.

——. 'Generals divided over June elections', *MN*, 14, 11–17 April 1996, 4.

——. Reform according to Lebed', *MN*, 28, 24–9 July 1996, 2.

—— and Yastrebov, S. 'Yuri Skokov', *MN*, 38–9, 6–12 October 1995, 4.

Zhirinovsky, V. 'LDPR ot pervogo litsa', *Dialog*, 8, 1990, 34–6.

——. 'My ne pozvolim razrushit' nash dom', *SR*, 30 July 1991, 3.

——. *O sud'bakh Rossii. vol. I. Uroki istorii, vol. II. Posledny brosok na yug. vol. III. S moei tochki zrenii* (Rait, Moscow, 1993).

——. 'LDPR na puti k vlasti', *Sokol Zhirinovskogo*, 3 (11), 1994, 3.

——. 'My dolzhny uchest' uroki istorii', *Pravda Zhirinovskogo*, 7, 1994, 1–2.

——. 'V. Zhirinovsky otvechaet na voprosy zhurnalistov', *Slovo Zhirinovskogo*, 4 (17), 1995, 2.

——. *Posledny vagon na sever* (Conjou, Moscow, 1995).

——. *Moi garantii izbiratelyam* (LDPR, Moscow, 1995).

——. *LDPR: ideologiya i politika* (LDPR, Moscow, 1995).

——. *VII s"ezd LDPR* (LDPR, Moscow, 1996).

—— and Bruno, P. *Besedy na chistotu* (Rait, Moscow, 1995).

V.V. Zhirinovsky i fraktsiya LDPR v Gosudarstvennoi Dume (LDPR, Moscow, 1995).

Zhukov, A. 'Radikaly vsekh kompartii – ob"edinyaites'!', *Obshchaya gazeta*, 22–28 July 1994, 6.

——. 'Na dolgo li sokhranit'sya yedinstvo oppozitsiii?', *RG*, 29 July 1993, 3.

Zlobin, N. 'The Political Spectrum' in Dallin, A. (ed.), *Political Parties in Russia* (University of California, Berkeley, 1993) pp. 63–79.

Zolin, Yu. 'Vstrecha s poezei Rubtsova', *Metrostroivets*, 24 June 1983.

Zolotonosov, M. 'K probleme merzavtsev', *MN*, 15, 26 February–5 March 1995, 21.

Zorkin, V. and Prokhanov, A. 'Zakon rodiny', *Den'*, 30, August 1993, 1–2.

Zuyev, N. 'Prodol'zhenie zhizni', *NS*, 1, 1987, 185–7.

Zyuganov, Gennady, 'Ostanovit' vrazhdu i khaos', *Literaturnaya Rossiya*, 6 November 1992, 2, 5.

——. *Drama vlasti: stranitsy politicheskoi avtobiografii* (Moscow, 1993).

——. *Derzhava* (Informpechat', Moscow, 1994).

——. *Rossiya i sovremenny mir* (Obozrevatel', Moscow, 1995).

——. *Veryu v Rossiyu* ('Voronezh', Voronezh, 1995).

——. *Za gorizontom* (Vneshnye vody, Orel, 1995).

——. 'Znat' i deistvovat'', *Zavtra*, 15, April 1996, 1, 3.

——. 'Gennadii Zyuganov in his Own Words', *Transition*, vol. II, no. 11 (31 May 1996) 16–7.

——. 'Ya boyus' za Rossiyu', *Izbiratel'* (special edition of *SR*), 13 June 1996.

—— and Bondarenko, V. *Rossiya – strana slov* (ndp, 1996).

Index